A BRIT'S GU

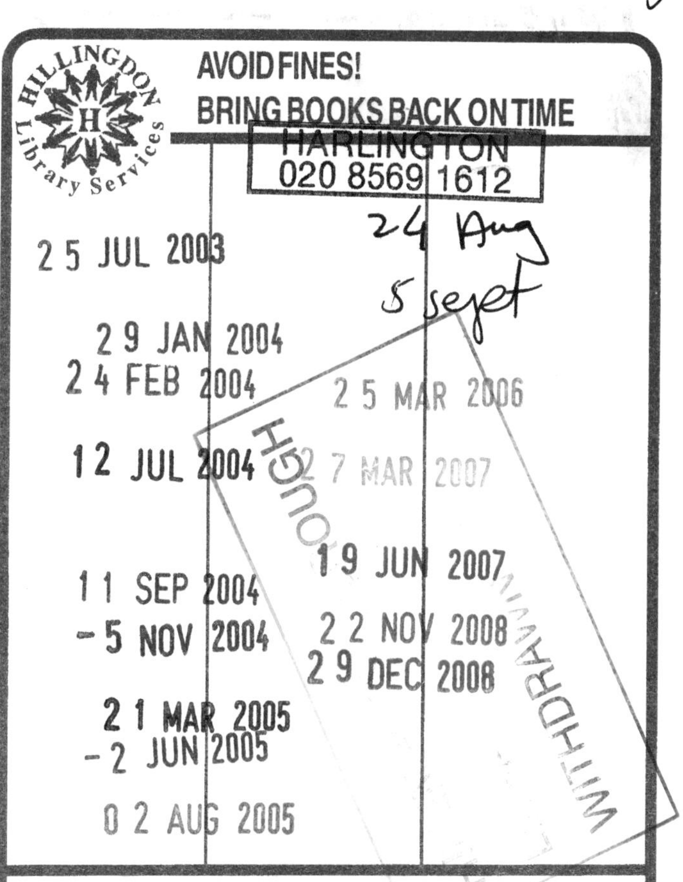

foulsham

LONDON • NEW YORK • TORONTO • SYDNEY

foulsham
The Publishing House, Bennetts Close, Cippenham,
Slough, Berkshire, SL1 5AP, England

Dedication

For Jennifer, who is just about ready to bite off a chunk of the Big Apple, and Loraine Heller, who enjoyed the best and worst of times all in the name of research!

ISBN 0-572-02823-7

Maps by PC Graphics (UK) Limited

Other books in this series:
A Brit's Guide to Las Vegas and the West 2002–3, Karen Marchbank, 0-572-02746-X
A Brit's Guide to Orlando and Walt Disney World 2003, Simon Veness, 0-572-02822-3
Choosing A Cruise, Simon Veness, 0-572-02728-9

Printed and bound in Great Britain by Creative Print and Design (Wales), Ebbw Vale

CONTENTS

Additional research by Amanda Statham

Acknowledgements

With grateful thanks for all their help to Clive Burrow, Audrey Bretillot and Rebecca Pisani at the New York Travel Advisory Bureau, Sarah Handy, Helen Povall and Christos Louvieris at NYC & Company Convention and Visitors' Bureau, Ian Rowe and Stacey Swiantek at iMar.com, the Insider's Marketplace, Tom Darro, Stan Rydelek and John Percy at Niagara Falls Convention and Visitors' Bureau and Markly Wilson and Deirdre Cumberbatch at the New York State Department of Economic Development.
My thanks also to the Lower East Side Tenement Museum, the Metropolitan Museum of Art, Ellis Island Immigration Museum, the Museum of Modern Art, the Museum of Jewish Heritage, the Whitney Museum of American Art, Intrepid Sea-Air-Space Museum, the Frick Collection, the Skyscraper Museum, the National Museum of the American Indian, the Children's Museum of Manhattan, the Empire State Building, the American Museum of Natural History, the New York Stock Exchange, the Brooklyn Museum of Art, NY Waterways, Harlem Spirituals, the Big Apple Greeters, David Watkins and Ponycabs, the Queens Jazz Trail, Gangland Tours, Big Onion walking tours, Rabbi Beryl Epstein and the Hassidic Discovery Center, former NYPD cop Gary Gorman, Gray-Line, Food Tours of Greenwich, Ryan Hawkins (known as jazz aficionado Ed Lockjaw), The Mark, Waldorf Astoria, Le Parker Meridien, The Wellington, The Doral, A Hospitality Company, Souperman, American Park at the Battery, Serafina Fabulous Pizza, The Boathouse, Picholine, Sylvia's Restaurant, The River Café, The Water Club, World Yacht Dining Cruise, Europa Grill, The 21 Club, Tavern on the Green, Russian Tea Room, Zoe's Restaurant and ONE c.p.s.
My thanks also to the following individuals who were a fount of great knowledge: Loraine Heller, Neal Smith, Russell Brightwell, Maria Pieri, the divine Kirsty Hislop, Annie Davies, Colin Macrae and Neil Wadey.

Introduction

Welcome to the 2003 edition of this guide book, which I hope will inspire you to want to visit the Big Apple again and again. Of course, given that it will reach the shelves of bookshops just over one year on from September 11 means that it would be impossible to write about the city without speaking of those terrible events. Like me, you can probably remember exactly where you were when you first heard the news about a plane flying into the World Trade Center. Like everyone else, you were probably completely overwhelmed by the scale of the tragedy and, like many people, were probably too distraught to contemplate visiting the city for some time.

In fact, many Brits were deeply traumatised by the events. For starters, so many of us have friends or acquaintances with connections to the city. All too many of us knew of someone who died in the Twin Towers. And unlike the New Yorkers, we haven't been going about our daily lives in the city since the atrocity, so in many ways our minds are still very focused on the actual events of September 11 rather than on what has followed.

Yet, as devastating as it all has been, New York can take many good things away from their subsequent experiences. The way everyone worked so hard to help each other. The sheer bravery and courage of so many thousands of people involved not just on day one but for many days afterwards to try to rescue any survivors. The unstinting, round-the-clock effort to sift through every piece of wreckage before it was cleared away in the hope of salvaging any reminders of those who died. The quiet dignity with which New Yorkers, Americans and many other nationals – including Brits – remembered their lost ones. The sheer pace at which Ground Zero was cleared. These are all the hallmarks of a city demonstrating its ability to come to terms with loss, remember it, but rise once again like a phoenix soaring from the ashes.

Ironically, the fledgling but fascinating Skyscraper Museum had mounted an exhibition in September 2001 to tell the story of how the Twin Towers had come into being. It turned out to be a fitting tribute of the World Trade Center's 30-year history and a timely reminder of one very important aspect of New York. The city has always been about regeneration, about removal of the old to make way for the new and, hopefully, the bigger and the better. In fact, in the 1960s, that is exactly what the Twin Towers were all about.

And, even as the city's workers carried out the sombre task of clearing the carnage, the city itself was already in the process of renewal, regeneration and growth. Quietly, with little fanfare or publicity, new hotels opened up all across the city, along with new restaurants, clubs, shops and businesses. Most fittingly of all, the Skyscraper Museum itself finally found a home just a few hundred metres from Ground Zero in the fabulous new Ritz Carlton Hotel in Battery Park. And the Ritz Carlton, with its amazing views of the Hudson River and Statue of Liberty, has become a new home to the Wall Street crowd. How fitting that they can sit in the beautiful new Rise bar on the hotel's 14th floor and sip their cocktails while looking at Madame Liberty herself

THE NEW YORK STATE OF MIND

I once saw a great sign on 5th Avenue around 58th Street, but I was on a bus at the time so I couldn't get a photo (believe me, I wanted to). It said: 'Don't even think about parking here.' Now that's the kind of thing you would think, possibly even say to yourself if you were in your car, but to make an official sign saying it? That, it seems, is the difference between us and the native New Yorker!

By this I don't mean the Algonquin Indians, but the modern-day residents, who are genuine born-and-bred New Yorkers rather than immigrants from around the globe or even other parts of America. They really are a breed unto themselves and I've learnt how you can spot them. In the first place they have a sort of totally cheesed-off-with-the-world don't-mess-with-me look. Secondly, they often speak incredibly quickly and it's as if they are eating their own words as they go along so it really is hard to understand them.

Scratch the surface though, and you just have your ordinary, everyday kind of person with the same kind of worries, fears and doubts as the rest of us. I've discovered two things work a treat. Firstly, smiling like mad and being genuinely polite. Secondly, the British accent. You can see them looking at you askance when you smile (I mean, smile? Who on earth does that in New York?), but sort of deciding that you're one of those British eccentrics they've heard about. It does the trick, though, because they'll more often than not respond in a helpful way.

And don't go thinking that all New Yorkers will tell you to f*** off if you ask for directions. Some will, but many are happy to help and I've even had people stop to help me work out where I'm going without any request on my part. This heady mix of rudeness and helpfulness is no better demonstrated than in the following anecdote from New York author Douglas Kennedy.

'On a crosstown bus I noticed two visitors from Japan having difficulty with the exact change for the fare,' he recounts. 'The driver, an overweight guy with a scowl, started giving them a hard time. "Like can't you read English or what?" he said loudly. "It says a buck-fifty. Surely they teach you how to count in Japan."

'The Japanese looked as if they wanted to commit hara-kiri on the spot until an elegantly dressed woman in her late sixties seated opposite the door came to their defence. Out of nowhere she turned to the driver and said: "Hey asshole, be polite." '

– a great reminder of what New York and America stand for.

I think we Brits need to take our cue from New Yorkers. For them, it's business as usual. The debates will continue for some time over the future of Ground Zero, but we need to keep it in perspective. The whole area is about the size of Trafalgar Square. Most of the hotels and shops surrounding it which were damaged have reopened and want people to return to the city. And the rest of New York is the same as it has ever been – loud, brash, bright and full of life. We can do our bit to support it by returning to enjoy all the many wonders the city has to offer.

Planning Your Holiday

One of New York's greatest charms is its cosmopolitan nature, its hugely diverse ethnic mix. In this city you will find any type of cuisine, often available at any time of the day or night. Where music's concerned, everything from jazz and R&B to techno and rap is out there any night of the week and the nightclubs are among the hippest and most happening of any in the world.

The drawback is that it may seem a bit overwhelming and it doesn't help that everyone gives the impression of being in the biggest hurry ever and far too busy to help. But beneath the ice-cool veneer of most New Yorkers you'll find people who will be willing to answer any question or plea for help you put to them. In this book, I hope to not only provide all the information you need about the sights, sounds and attractions, but to give an insight into what makes the city tick and how to really get the most out of it. The book is filled with tips and insider information, but I'm always open to hearing other people's views and am happy to receive suggestions at my email address: **karen_marchbank@hotmail.com.**

Once you have decided to go to New York, the next step is to work out what you want to do otherwise you could end up wasting a lot of valuable time. The city is so big and diverse and everyone's tastes are so different that each visit to New York is a unique experience. Are you a museum buff? Do you like to get off the beaten track? Want to see a great Broadway show and some of the great sights of the city? Your priorities will reflect not only your tastes, but whether it is your first, second or even third visit to the Big Apple and also the time you have available. Whatever the case, the key to making the most of your time is planning.

The thing I really try to stress is the importance of location, location, location. When you fly into New York, seeing all the skyscrapers from your lofty perch makes Manhattan look pretty small, but do not be fooled by this. It is a narrow island, but it's longer than it looks from high in the sky – 21km (13 miles) in fact – so don't be duped into believing it is easy to walk from Lower Manhattan to the Upper East Side. Nothing could be further from the truth.

It's also the case that the city's subway is nowhere near as fast as our much-maligned tube system in London, nor is it that good for getting from east to west or vice versa. That means using buses is often necessary and they, of course, like taxis, can get stuck in heavy traffic. So, when planning your activities for the day, it is best to stick to one particular area so that walking everywhere – which really is the best way to see the city – won't be so tiring.

If you really want to get an insight into how a New Yorker thinks, read the Metropolitan Diary in Monday's edition of the *New York Times*. It's full of stories of New York life supplied by the locals.

Most people tend to go for between two and seven days. For the former it's like dipping your toes in the water, for the latter it's a great big commitment to getting to know the city. Regardless of how many days you have, though, you can't fit everything in so you have to be selective.

I've tried to help you with your choices in as many ways as possible. For instance, I've put the top sights and museums in an order of importance so you can go straight to the ones you're most likely to want to see, and in each case I've specified the area they are in – again to help you plan your day. Most of the main Broadway shows are easy enough to plan for because they tend to be in the Theater District and the restaurant chapter gives an area-by-area guide which makes light work of planning for lunch and dinner.

I've also provided a complete outline of all the different transport systems in

New York and how to use them, plus a description of all the different neighbourhoods with itineraries so that you will be able to get the most out of them.

In each case I've arranged the different areas geographically from south to north rather than by an A-Z system because it just seems to make more sense to me. For instance, if you're looking for a restaurant, shop or hotel in one area, it's good to be able to see some alternatives in a nearby location without having to flick through pages and pages of text.

That means the Financial District – which takes in Battery Park, Battery Park City, Wall Street, the South Street Seaport and the Civic Center area – always comes first. It's followed by Chinatown/Little Italy, the Lower East Side, TriBeCa, SoHo, NoLiTa, Greenwich Village, West Village, East Village, Chelsea, Union Square, Gramercy Park, Madison Square, 34th Street and Herald Square, Murray Hill, the Theater District, Midtown, Midtown East, Midtown West, the Upper East Side, Upper West Side, Morningside Heights and Harlem.

I've put the hotels chapter towards the back of the book because I think choosing a hotel should be your final decision. If the sights, sounds, shops and museums you want to see are all in a particular area, then you should try to find a hotel or accommodation as close to it as possible. That way you can reduce the time and money you spend on travelling.

I've tried to include everything I believe the average Brit will be interested in seeing while they are in New York, but if you've come across a sight, museum, shop, gallery, coffee shop, club, hotel or restaurant not in this book, which you think is worth including, please feel free to contact me. My e-mail address is **karen_marchbank@hotmail.com.**

Finally, I'd just like to wish you a great trip to what is still one of the greatest cities in the world!

CHAPTER 1

All About New York

So what is New York all about? Due to the vast number of movies set in different periods of New York, many of the key people in its history, sights and areas are familiar to us Brits, though I suspect that, like me, you're a little hazy as to their whereabouts or true influence on the city.

Understanding a little of its history is a good way of understanding its modern-day psyche and to familiarise yourself with the different areas of New York and the buildings named after its great movers and shakers. Many of them were men and women of great vision and courage and their contributions to New York's rich and diverse culture, business and entertainment are all part of what makes the city so remarkable today.

A SHORT HISTORY OF NEW YORK

The great story that is New York's started in 1524 when Florentine Giovanni da Verrazano arrived on the island now known as Manhattan. It was a mixture of marshes, woodland, rivers and meadows and was home to the Algonquin and Iroquois tribes of Native Americans. No one settled on the island, though, until British explorer Henry Hudson arrived in 1609. Working for the Dutch West India Company, he discovered Indians who were happy to trade in furs, skins, birds and fruit. In 1613, a trading post was set up at Fort Nassau and by 1624 the Dutch West India Company was given the right to govern the area by the Dutch government.

Dutch settlers soon began to arrive; Manhattan was named New Amsterdam and governor Peter Minuit bought the island for $24 worth of trinkets and blankets. The Dutch, of course, thought they had a bargain. The irony is that they were trading with a tribe of Indians who were simply passing through the area! Peaceful relations between the Europeans and Native Americans were disturbed, however, by the settlers' insistence on taking over the land and a costly and bloody war ensued, lasting two and a half years. Finally Peter Stuyvesant was hired by the Dutch West India Company to restore peace.

Stuyvesant was an experienced colonialist and went about establishing a strong community with a proper infrastructure. One of the first things he did was to order the building of a defensive wall and ditch along what we know today as Wall Street. The new settlement prospered and even doubled in size, but Governor Stuyvesant was not well liked. He introduced new taxes, persecuted Jews and Quakers and even limited the amount of alcohol people could drink. Trouble followed, and the locals became less and less inclined to obey him. By the time four British warships sailed into the harbour in late 1664, he had no alternative but to surrender to Colonel Richard Nichols without a shot being fired. The colony was immediately renamed New York in honour of the Duke of York, brother to the English king, and thereafter remained mostly in the hands of the British until the end of the American Revolution.

A NEW COUNTRY FINDS ITS VOICE

By 1700, the population had reached 20,000, made up of immigrants from England, Holland, Germany, Ireland and Sweden. It was already the rich melting-pot of cultures and religions that it remains today. Over the next 74 years, the colony gradually began to establish itself and there was a growing belief among well-educated and powerful Americans – including Thomas Jefferson and Benjamin Franklin – that the government should be fair and democratic.

In 1764, following the Seven Years War between the British and French, the Brits passed a number of laws, including the Stamp Act, allowing them to raise taxes in the colony. In response, Americans from all over the country banded together and rescinded Britain's right to collect taxes from them. The Stamp Act was repealed but it seemed that the Brits hadn't learned their lesson. They introduced the Townshend Act, which imposed taxes on various imports and led to a bloody confrontation in 1770. In 1774, the Americans set up the Continental Congress, made up of representatives from each of the colonies. Later that year, those representatives urged all Americans to stop paying their taxes and just two years later the Declaration of Independence was drawn up, largely by Jefferson. During the War of Independence that inevitably followed, New York was considered strategically vital as it stood between the New England colonies and those in the south. In 1776, British commander Lord Howe sailed 500 ships into the harbour and occupied the city. George Washington's army was defeated and forced to leave. The peace process began in 1779 and led to a treaty in 1783. The Brits, who had remained in New York since the end of the war, left just before George Washington returned to claim victory.

New York then became the country's first capital and George Washington its first president, taking his oath of office in 1789. The city was capital for just one year, but business boomed. The New York Stock Exchange, established under a tree on Wall Street by Alexander Hamilton in 1792, positively buzzed with activity as new companies were set up, bought and sold. But as the city grew, it became clear

WHAT'S IN A NAME?

The Big Apple has become synonymous with New York City, but came into being during the 1920s when horse-racing writer John Fitzgerald was the first to popularise the term. On assignment in New Orleans for *The Morning Telegraph*, he overheard stablehands refer to New York City racing tracks as The Big Apple and decided to call his column on New York's racing scene 'Around the Big Apple'.

A decade later, jazz musicians adopted the term to refer to New York City. The favourite story of Big Onion tour guides is related to Small's Big Apple jazz club in Harlem. The story goes that when the musicians from the club went on tour around America they'd say to each other 'I'll see you in the Big Apple'.

But the term was still relatively unknown until it was adopted by the New York Convention & Visitors' Bureau in 1971, when they launched The Big Apple campaign. So there you have it – it's a marketing device invented by the city to lure in visitors and it certainly seems to work as more than 34 million business people and tourists arrive each year.

The name a lot of New Yorkers like to call the city is Gotham – taken from the Batman stories that are based in Gotham City and believed by many to be a thinly veiled reference to New York. The name Manhattan is derived from Mannahatta, the name given to the island by its first inhabitants, the Algonquin Indians.

that a proper infrastructure and sanitation system was needed, so the governors introduced a grid system throughout the entire island. North of 14th Street, it abandoned all the existing roads except for Broadway, which followed an old Indian trail, and set up wide avenues that ran south to north and streets that ran between the rivers. Everything, it seemed, was pushing the city north, from illness to prosperity: while the grid system was being put on paper, a series of epidemics drove residents from the old Downtown into what is now known as Greenwich Village.

THE RICH GET RICHER...

By 1818, reliable shipping services between New York and other American cities and Europe were well established and trade was booming. It was boosted further by the opening of the Erie Canal in 1825 which, together with the new railroads, opened trade routes to the Midwest. With so much spare cash to play with, businessmen started to build large summer estates and mansions along 5th Avenue up to Madison Square. At the same time, many charities and philanthropic institutions were set up and great libraries were built, as education was seen as being very important.

But the divide between rich and poor was getting wider. While water supplies, indoor plumbing and central heating were being installed in the 5th Avenue mansions, thousands of immigrant families – particularly from Ireland – had no choice but to live in the appalling tenement buildings that were being erected on the Lower East Side of Manhattan.

These people were forced to eke out a wretched existence in the old sweatshops by day and contend with the punitive living conditions of the tenements by night. Entire families were crammed into one or two rooms that had no windows, no hot water, no heat and, of course, no bathroom. Toilet facilities had to be shared with neighbours.

The impending Civil War over the question of slavery became a major issue for the poor of New York, who couldn't afford to buy their way out of conscription. Uppermost in their minds was the concern that freed slaves would be going after their jobs. The fear reached fever pitch and led to America's worst-ever riot, a four-day-long affair in which over 100 people died and thousands, mostly blacks, were injured. By 1865, however, the abolitionists won the war, finally freeing 4 million black people from the plight of slavery.

BOOM TIME FOR IMMIGRATION

At the same time, New York and Boston were being hit by great tidal waves of immigrants. In the 1840s and 1850s it was the Irish fleeing famine; in the 1860s it was the Germans fleeing persecution; and in the 1870s it was the Chinese, brought into America specifically to build the railroads. In the 1880s it was the turn of the Russians, along with 1.5 million Eastern European Jews. Over 8 million immigrants went through Castle Clinton in Battery Park between 1855 and 1890. Then the Ellis Island centre was built in 1892 and handled double that number. Between 1880 and 1910, 17 million immigrants passed through the city and, by 1900, the population had reached 3.4 million.

Of course, most of the new arrivals who chose to stay in New York ended up in the crowded tenements of the Lower East Side. Finally in 1879, after the terrible conditions were brought to light, the city passed new housing laws requiring landlords to increase water supplies and toilets, install fire escapes and build air shafts between buildings to let in air and light. The introduction of streetcars and elevated railways also helped to alleviate the transport problem.

THE GILDED AGE

Meanwhile, the wealthy were enjoying the Gilded Age, as Mark Twain dubbed it. Central Park opened in 1858 and more and more mansions were built on 5th

Avenue for the likes of the Whitneys, Vanderbilts and Astors. Row houses were also being built on the Upper West Side for wealthy European immigrants.

Henry Frick, who made his fortune in steel and the railroads, built a mansion (now a museum) on the east side of the park at 70th Street, just 10 blocks from the new Metropolitan Museum of Art. Luxury hotels such as the original Waldorf-Astoria and the Plaza opened, as did the original Metropolitan Opera House. The Statue of Liberty, St Patrick's Cathedral, the Brooklyn Bridge and Carnegie Hall were all built at this time.

Those were the days of the people whose names we associate with New York but don't necessarily know why – like Cornelius Vanderbilt, a shipping and railroad magnate; Andrew Carnegie, a steel and railroad baron; and John D Rockefeller, who made his millions in oil. The names of many of these millionaires live on in the gifts they gave back to the city: they provided concert halls, libraries, and art museums and donated entire collections to put in them. Carnegie built and donated Carnegie Hall to the city, Rockefeller was one of three major backers behind the opening of the Museum of Modern Art, and the Whitneys created a museum containing their own collection of modern American works of art.

At the same time, the structure of the city itself was undergoing a transformation. In 1904, the IRT subway opened 135km (84 miles) of track, which meant that people could move away from the polluted downtown areas, and by 1918 the New York City Transit System was complete. The turn of the century also saw the birth of another phenomenon, which was to become one of the city's most famous facets – the skyscraper. First to be built, in 1902, was the Flatiron Building, which was completed using the new technology for the mass production of cast iron. Frank Woolworth's Gothic structure followed in 1913. The beautiful Chrysler Building came in 1929 and the Empire State Building in 1931.

PROHIBITION ARRIVES

In the meantime, the Volstead Act of 1919 banned the sale of alcohol at the start of the Roaring Twenties. Fuelled by lively speakeasies, illegal booze, gangsters, the Charleston and jazz, this was the real heyday of famous venues like Harlem's Cotton Club and the Apollo Theater. After several glittering years, the fun and frolics came to an abrupt end with the collapse of the Wall Street stock market on October 29, 1929. It destroyed most small investors and led to huge unemployment and poverty right across the whole of America. Things only started to turn for the better after President

USEFUL WEBSITES

www.axisny.com Directory and reviews of restaurants and bars.
www.citysearchnyc.com Calendar of events happening in New York.
www.cityguideny.com The on-line site of the weekly *City Guide* which is provided to hotels.
www.clubnyc.com Complete list of what's cool, where and why.
www.downtown.com Directory of places to visit in Lower Manhattan.
www.halloween-nyc.com The official Halloween Parade site with history, how to get involved and information about the forthcoming event.
www.nycvisit.com The New York Convention and Visitors' Bureau's comprehensive listing includes suggested itineraries for where to stay and shop and what to do.
www.nytab.com The New York Travel Advisory Bureau's site helps in trip planning and gives information on major savings.
www.nytimes.com The on-line site for the *New York Times*.
www.villagevoice.com The on-line site of the *Village Voice*.

Franklin Roosevelt introduced the New Deal, employing people to build new roads, houses and parks.

In New York, Fiorella La Guardia was elected mayor and set up his austerity programme to enable the city to claw its way back to financial security. During his 12 years in office, La Guardia worked hard at fighting corruption and organised crime in the city, and introduced a massive public housing project.

These were also the days of a great literary and artistic scene in the city. Giants of the spoken and written word, including Dorothy Parker and George Kaufman, would meet at the famous Round Table of the Algonquin Hotel, where they were joined by stage and screen legends Tallulah Bankhead, Douglas Fairbanks and the Marx Brothers.

The Second World War was another watershed for New York, as people fled war-ravaged Europe and headed for the metropolis. Both during and after the war, huge new waves of immigrants arrived, fleeing first the Nazis and then the Communists. New York was as affected by McCarthy's hunt for 'reds' among the cultural and intellectual élite as the rest of the country, but it bounced back when a new building boom followed the election of President Truman, whose policies were aimed specifically at helping the poor.

The Port Authority Bus Terminal was finished in 1950, the mammoth United Nations Building was completed in 1953, and in 1959 work started on the huge Lincoln Center complex – built on the slums of the San Juan district that were the setting for *West Side Story*.

FROM BOOM TO BUST

By the 1950s, a new period of affluence had started for the middle classes of New York. The descendants of the earlier Irish, Italian and Jewish immigrants moved out to the new towns that were springing up outside Manhattan, leaving space for a whole new wave of immigrants from Puerto Rico and the southern states of America. It was also the decade of the Beat generation, epitomised by Jack Kerouac and Allen Ginsberg, which evolved into the hippie culture of the 1960s. This was when Greenwich Village became the centre of a new wave of artists extolling the virtues of equality for all. By the 1970s, however, this laissez-faire attitude, coupled with New York's position as a major gateway for illegal drug importation and the general demoralisation of the working classes and ethnic groups, led to an escalation in crime. Muggings and murder were rampant, and the city was brought to the brink of bankruptcy.

Chaos was only averted by the introduction of austerity measures, which unfortunately mostly affected the poor. But good news was just around the corner, as new mayor, Ed Koch, implemented major tax incentives to rejuvenate New York's business community. A boom followed, reflected in the erection of a series of mammoth new skyscrapers, including the World

BEAT IT

The Beat Movement was a partly social, partly literary phenomenon with three centres – Greenwich Village in New York, the North Beach district of San Francisco and Venice West in Los Angeles. Socially, the movement was all about rejecting middle-class values and commercialism and embracing poverty, individualism and release through jazz, sexual experience and drugs. The term 'beat' conveys both the American connotations of being worn-out and exhausted, but also suggests 'beatitude' or 'blessedness'. The chief spokesmen were Allen Ginsberg, Jack Kerouac, whose most famous novel is *On The Road*, Gregory Corso, William S Burroughs, Lawrence Ferlinghetti and Gary Snyder.

Trade Center and Trump Tower. The transformation was completed in the 1990s with Mayor Giuliani's clean-up operation. This was unpopular with the more liberal New Yorkers but there are many who believe it was his policies which turned New York into a city fit for the new millennium.

From the time of the earliest immigrants, New York has represented a gateway to a new life, a place of hope: the American dream offered a future filled with happiness and success. And nowadays New York still draws in people in their thousands. After all, as the song goes, 'If you can make it there, you'll make it anywhere'.

THE BEST TIMES TO GO

January to March and July and August are best for accommodation and good for flights. Just bear in mind that July and August are the hottest months, though it is not as bad as you might expect because all the shops and cabs have air-conditioning and you get blasts of lovely cool air from the shops as you pass.

In the run-up to Christmas it is very difficult to get accommodation in Manhattan, as it is in September and October when there are a lot of conventions. Surprisingly, the times around Thanksgiving and between Christmas and New Year are okay times to go because people tend to be at home with their families. April to June should be pleasantly cool (though it can be surprisingly warm) and is a favoured time to go.

In addition to the above advice, check the Festivals and Parades chapter (see page 176) to find out when there are major events happening in the city, as it tends to be a bit more crowded at these times.

CLIMATE

Month	Temp		Rainfall	
Jan	-3-3°C	(27–38°F)	8cm	(3in)
Feb	-3-5°C	(27–40°F)	8cm	(3in)
Mar	1–9°C	(34–49°F)	11cm	(4¼in)
Apr	7–16°C	(44–61°F)	10cm	(4in)
May	12–22°C	(53–72°F)	10cm	(4in)
June	17–27°C	(63–80°F)	8cm	(3in)
July	20–29°C	(68–85°F)	10cm	(4in)
Aug	19–29°C	(67–85°F)	10cm	(4in)
Sep	16–25°C	(60–77°F)	9cm	(3½in)
Oct	10–19°C	(50–66°F)	9cm	(3½in)
Nov	5–12°C	(41–54°F)	11cm	(4¼in)
Dec	-1-6°C	(31–42°F)	10cm	(4in)

WHAT TO WEAR

Layers are the key to comfortable clothes in New York, no matter what time of year you go. In summer the air-con in buildings can get pretty cold, while outside it is stiflingly hot. If you take a lightweight, rainproof jacket, you'll be covered for all eventualities, including the odd shower. In winter it is the other way round – warm buildings and cold streets – so it's best to have an overcoat of some sort, but nothing too heavy unless you're planning to be out of doors a lot. At any time of the year, the skyscrapers of the city act as a kind of wind tunnel and unless you're in the sun it can get nippy pretty quickly – another reason to make sure you have a cardigan or lightweight jacket in the summer. And in the winter, make sure you have a hat, scarf and gloves in your bag for times of emergency.

Don't worry if you spill wine all over your best outfit – most hotels have a valet service that can clean it for you overnight or there are plenty of dry cleaners throughout the city. Ask the hotel receptionist for directions to the nearest one.

DISABLED TRAVELLERS

According to the disabled people I've spoken to, New York is one of the easier destinations to tackle – and certainly puts Britain to shame. Most of the road corners, for instance, have kerbs that dip to the ground, making it a lot easier to wheel yourself about the city. Again, for the wheelchair-bound, the buses can be lowered to the same level as the pavement to allow easy access and, where possible, some of the subway stations have had elevators installed. To find out which stations are accessible to wheelchair passengers, phone 718-596 8585 any time 6am–9pm. For up-to-date information on the accessibility status of lifts and escalators, call 1-800 734 6772 24 hours a day.

One of my favourite New York tales comes from Colin Macrae, a disabled person who regularly travels all over the world with his wife Joan. They were in New York one cold Christmas and Colin was sitting in his wheelchair all by himself, huddled up against the biting wind, while his wife went off to sort out tickets for the Circle Line cruise. As he waited, Colin was approached by a tramp, who pressed a quarter into his hand saying: 'I don't have much, but you can have what I've got.' Then he rushed off before Colin could reply or give him his money back. Just goes to show, the most unexpected and heartwarming things can happen in this amazing city.

Anyway, to make your life as easy as possible, here are the main organisations that deal with different aspects of travel for the disabled.

RESOURCES FOR THE DISABLED

Note: TTY = Telecommunication devices for the deaf.

Hospital Audiences Inc: 220 West 42nd Street, 13th floor, New York, NY 10036. Tel 212-575 7660 (voice) or 212-575 7673 (TTY). Publishes a book, *Access for All* ($5), which gives comprehensive information on venue access, toilet facilities and water fountains for a whole range of cultural centres from theatres to museums and major sights.

In addition, it also has audio description services for people who are blind or visually impaired. Called **DESCRIBE,** this contains **Program Notes,** which describe all aspects of a show and staging in an audio cassette you can listen to before the performance. It also transmits a live **Audio Description**, during a pause in the dialogue, to audience members who have a small receiver. Reservations for both the tickets, which have to be bought either through HAI or the theatre, and receivers, which are provided free of charge, must be made through HAI. For more information call Describe on 212-575 7663.

New York Society for the Deaf: 817 Broadway at 12th Street. Tel 212-777 3900. Provides advice and information on facilities for the deaf.

Big Apple Greeter Access Coordinator: 1 Center Street, Room 2035, New York, NY 10007. Tel 212-669 2896 (voice) or 212-669 8273 (TTY). Will provide a free tour guide for anyone with a disability.

SIGN LANGUAGE INTERPRETED PERFORMANCES

The Theater Access Program: TAP is specifically for Broadway shows and is run by the Theater Development Fund. For more information phone 212-221 1103 (voice) or 212-719 4537 (TTY). Reservations for infrared headsets or neckloops for Broadway shows can be made by calling Sound Associates. Tel 212-582 7678.

Hands On: Provides sign language for Off-Broadway shows. For both voice and TTY phone 212-627 4898. Hands On also publishes a monthly calendar of events for the deaf community.

Lighthouse Incorporated: 111 East 59th Street. Tel 212-821 9200. Provides help and advice for blind people living in or visiting the city.

COMMUNICATION

PHONES

If you make any calls at all from your hotel you will pay a tremendous premium. To avoid this, you can either get a whole bucket of quarters to use a public payphone or get a BT International phone card before you leave home. A local call costs a minimum of 25 cents.

To call New York from abroad: Dial 001 and the prefix – for instance, the main prefix for Manhattan is 212 and the new one is 646 – then dial the seven-digit number.

To call abroad from New York: Dial 011 + country code + area code (dropping the first 0) + local number. The code for Britain is 44.

Useful numbers:
Operator: 0
Directory enquiries: 411 (free from payphones)
Long distance directory enquiries:
1 + area code + 555 1212
Free numbers directory:
1 + 800 + 555 + 1212 (no charge)

The American ringing tone is long and the engaged tone is very short and high-pitched, almost like a beep.

POST

To send a postcard costs 70 cents, to send a letter costs 80 cents for the first 25g (1oz). You can buy stamps in shops – the Duane Reade chain of chemists has machines, for instance – but there is a mark-up. If you don't want to pay over the odds for the convenience of these stamps, then go to one of the many post offices dotted all around the city. The main post office on 34th Street at 8th Avenue is a beautiful Beaux Arts building and incredibly large. If the queues are long, you can buy stamps from the vending machines. Once you've got your stamp, you need to post your card! Post boxes are square dark blue metal boxes about 1.2m (4ft) tall with a rounded top that has a pull-down handle. They have a sign saying US Mail and a striking big American eagle logo on the side and can be found on street corners.

If you're in Manhattan and you're dialling a 718, 646, 800 or any other area code, you need to dial 1 first.

THE INTERNET

easyEverything: 234 West 42nd Street between 7th and 8th Avenues. Tel 212-398 0724. Subway A, C, E, 1, 2, 3, 7, 9, S, B, D, F, Q to 42nd Street/Times Square. Open 24 hours, it has over 800 computers, plus scanners, and prices start at just $1.

Cybercafé: 273 Lafayette Street at Prince Street. Tel 212-334 5140. Subway 6 to Bleecker Street, 4, 5, 6 to Spring Street and N, R to Prince Street. Area: NoLiTa. It's open 9am–10pm and costs around $6 for half an hour.

VOCABULARY

It has often been said that the Brits and Americans are two races divided by a common language and when you make an unexpected faux pas you'll certainly learn how true this is. For instance, never, ever ask for a packet of fags as this is the American slang word for gays and a sense of humour is not their strong point! There are plenty of other differences, too, which may not necessarily cause offence, but which will cause confusion, so to help you on your way, here is a guide to American-speak.

General:

English	American
Air hostess	Flight attendant
Anti-clockwise	Counterclockwise
At weekends	On weekends
Autumn	Fall
Behind	In back of
Camp bed	Cot
Cinema	Movie theater
City/town centre	Downtown (not Lower Manhattan!)
Coach	Bus
Cot	Crib
Diary (appointments)	Calendar
Diary (records)	Journal
From... to...	Through
Lift	Elevator
Nappy	Diaper
Ordinary	Regular, normal
Paddling pool	Wading pool
Post, postbox	Mail, mailbox
Pram, pushchair	Stroller
Tap	Faucet
Toilet	Restroom (public) or bathroom (private)
Trunk call	Long-distance call

Money:

English	American
Bill	Check or tab
Banknote	Bill
Cheque	Check
25 cents	Quarter
10 cents	Dime
5 cents	Nickel
1 cent	Penny

There are no ground floors in America: what we call the ground floor, they call the first floor. It may seem a silly point, but it does cause confusion!

Eating and stuff:

One of the biggest disappointments I had on my first trip to America was to order my breakfast eggs 'sunny-side up', only to end up with what seemed like a half-cooked egg! The Americans don't flick fat over the top of the egg when frying it, but turn it over to cook on both sides. So for eggs cooked on both sides but soft, I have to order eggs 'over easy' and if you like yours well done, then ask for eggs 'over hard'.

There are plenty of other anomalies. Many standard American dishes come with a biscuit – which is a corn scone to us. Breakfast may also include grits, a porridge-like dish of ground, boiled corn, and hash browns, grated, fried potatoes. Foods and food terms that are specific to New York have been put in Chapter 7 Restaurants (see page 111). Here are some other differences:

English	American
Aubergine	Eggplant
Bill	Check or tab
Biscuit (savoury)	Cracker
Biscuit (sweet)	Cookie
Chick pea	Garbanzo bean
Chips	(French) fries
Choux bun	Cream puff
Clingfilm	Plastic wrap
Coriander	Cilantro
Cornflour	Cornstarch
Courgette	Zucchini
Crayfish	Crawfish
Crisps	Chips
Crystallised	Candied
Cutlery	Silverware or place-setting
Demerara sugar	Light-brown sugar
Desiccated coconut	Shredded coconut
Digestive biscuit	Graham cracker
Double cream	Heavy cream
Essence (eg vanilla)	Extract or flavoring
Filled baguette	Sub or hero
Fillet (of meat/fish)	Filet
Fizzy drink	Soda
Golden syrup	Corn syrup
Grated, fried potatoes	Hash browns
Grilled	Broiled
Icing sugar	Powdered/ confectioners' sugar
Jam	Jelly/conserve
Ketchup	Catsup

King prawn	Shrimp
Main course	Entrée
Malt liquor	Strong beer
Measure	Shot
Mince	Ground meat
Off-licence	Liquor store
Pastry case	Pie shell
Pips	Seeds (in fruit)
Plain/dark chocolate	Semi-sweet or unsweetened chocolate
Pumpkin	Squash
Scone	Biscuit
Shortcrust pastry	Pie dough
Single cream	Light cream
Soda water	Seltzer
Sorbet	Sherbet
Soya	Soy
Spirits	Liquor
Sponge finger biscuits	Lady fingers
Spring onion	Scallion
Starter	Appetiser
Stoned (cherries etc)	Pitted
Sultanas	Golden raisins
Sweet shop	Candy store
Take-away	To go
Toilet	Restroom (public) or bathroom (private)
Tomato purée	Tomato paste
Water biscuit	Cracker

New Yorkers may consider themselves broad-minded but, like any American, will be genuinely shocked if you ask where the toilet is. Ask for the restroom in a public place and the bathroom if you're in someone's house.

Shopping:

English	American
Braces	Suspenders
Bumbag	Fanny pack
Chemist	Drug store
Ground floor	First floor
Handbag	Purse
High street	Main street
Jumper	Sweater
Knickers	Panties
Muslin	Cheesecloth
Pants	Underpants
Queue	Line, line up
Suspenders	Garters
Till	Check-out
Tights	Pantyhose
Trainers	Sneakers
Trousers	Pants
Underpants	Shorts, underwear
Vest	Undershirt
Waistcoat	Vest
Zip	Zipper

Travelling around:

English	American
Aerial	Antenna
Articulated truck	Semi
Bonnet	Hood
Boot	Trunk
Caravan	House trailer
Car park	Parking lot
Car silencer	Muffler
Crossroads/junction	Intersection
Demister	Defogger
Dipswitch	Dimmer
Dual carriageway	Four-lane (or divided) highway
Flyover	Overpass
Give way	Yield
Jump leads	Jumper cables
Lorry	Truck
Manual transmission	Stickshift
Motorway	Highway, freeway, expressway
Pavement	Sidewalk
Request stop	Flag stop
Ring road	Beltway
Slip-road	Ramp
Subway	Pedestrian underpass
Turning	Turnoff
Underground	Subway
Walk	Hike
Wheel clamp	Denver boot
Windscreen	Windshield
Wing	Fender

NEW YORK TALK

Of course, in addition to the differences between American- and Brit-speak, the locals have a dialect and phraseology all of their own, influenced mainly by the Brooklyn accent, Mafia-speak and the fact that people often talk so quickly that words run into each other. Here are just a few that you may well come across.

All right already: Stop it, that's enough!
Big one: A $1,000 bill
Bloomies: Bloomingdales
Capeesh: Pronunciation of capisce, Italian for 'understand'
Cattle call: A casting call at a Broadway theatre
Dead soldier: Empty beer can or bottle
Do me a solid: Do me a favour
Don't jerk my chain: Don't fool with me
DPh: Damned fool, based on transposing PhD
Eighth Wonder of the World: The Brooklyn Bridge
Finger: Pickpockets (also mechanic, dip, cannon, goniff or moll buzzer)
Fuggedaboduid: No way
Guppies: Gay yuppies
JAPs: Jewish American princesses
Jocks: Sporty types, after their straps
Mazuma: Slang for money
Meet me between the lions: A favourite meeting place – the lion statues at the New York Public Library
Met: The Metropolitan Opera House or the Metropolitan Museum
No problem: You're welcome
Nudnik or nudge: A persistently dull and boring person
On account: Because
On line: Stand in a queue
Out in left field: Weird, unorthodox
Ozone: Very fresh, pure air
Shoot the works: Gamble or risk everything
Straphanger: Subway commuter
Suit: Businessman
Yard: Back garden

TOURIST INFORMATION

NYC & COMPANY CONVENTION & VISITORS' BUREAU

www.nycvisit.com

London: 33–34 Carnaby Street, London W1F 7DW. Tel 020 7437 8300 – line open 9.30am–5.30pm Monday to Friday.

New York City's official tourism agency, it has a walk-in visitors' information centre, which is open 10am–4pm Monday to Friday, and is filled with brochures on hotels, airlines, Broadway shows, shops, museums and sights. You can also discuss any queries you have with the information officers. Don't forget to pick up their NYC Guide, which has a good smattering of useful money-off coupons. The telephone line tends to be for quick questions and for telling people how to get a Visitors' Guide – send an A5 self-addressed envelope with a 72p stamp on it.

While you're at the NYC Center in New York, pick up a copy of the *City Guide* magazine. It not only has up-to-date listings on Broadway shows, but also has various money-off coupons that you may find useful.

New York: 810 7th Avenue at 53rd Street. Tel 212-484 1200. Fax 212-245 5943. Subway N, R to 49th Street, B, D, F, Q to 47th–50th Streets/Rockefeller Center. Area: Midtown.

A recently opened state-of-the-art visitors' information centre with touch-screen kiosks that provide up-to-date information on the city's attractions and events accompanied by a detailed map. There is also an ATM machine and a souvenir shop, plus an incredible range of brochures covering hotels, shops, museums, sights, tours and Broadway shows.

NEW YORK TRAVEL ADVISORY BUREAU

www.nytab.com

An independently run tourism agency, which is most famous for its own pocket guide to New York, the *NYPages*, and the NYCard, which gives discounts to hotel, museums and attractions – check the website for the latest update on all available discounts. Your free NYCard is on the back cover of this book, and full instructions on how to use it and some of the discounts are on pages 239–40. You can get a copy of *NYPages* with an additional card by sending £1.95 per visitor pack to: NYTAB, 11 Berkeley Street, London W1J 8DS. Or you can call 09060 40 50 60 from the UK. Calls cost £1.50 per minute, and will cost you about £4.50 in total, but *Brit's Guide* readers can get up to three visitor packs for no extra charge by saying: 'I'm a *Brit's Guide* reader'. Allow 28 days for delivery.

You must have plenty of change and singles ($1 bills) as you'll be tipping everyone for everything and you'll also need them for the buses.

BRITISH INFORMATION SERVICES

www.britainusa.com/consular/ny/ny.asp

845 3rd Avenue, NY, NY 10022. Tel 212-745 0277. Fax 212-745 0359. This is the information service of the British Embassy in Washington and acts as the political, press and public affairs office of the New York Consulate-General, which covers the states of New York, New Jersey, Connecticut and Pennsylvania.

CURRENCY

Americans use the dollar and the exchange rate is usually around $1.54, though we tourists are lucky if we get anything above $1.40. UK banks and bureaux de change charge a hefty commission and give poor rates of exchange. Thomsons only charge commission once, so if you change your money with them before leaving the UK and have money to change when you return you won't get charged commission again.

The Post Office here now offers commission-free money exchange.

A lot of people use travellers' cheques, but it is often a real palaver to cash them, especially at banks in New York. A lot simply won't take them, and if they do they'll need photo ID so you'll have to carry your passport around with you. Chase Manhattan Bank has more than 400 branches and doesn't charge a fee

TIPS ON TIPPING

You won't get a lunch, drink, ride or even taxi door being opened for you without a tip being involved in America and it can add quite a lot to your overall expenses when you're on holiday. It's something that doesn't come naturally to us Brits, but you need to get used to it quickly.

Waiters: General rule of thumb is 15 to 20 per cent. The best way to work it out is to double the sales tax, which will work out at 17 per cent, and add a little more if you are very impressed. Just remember, at a posh restaurant the tip alone can come to more than the price of a decent meal!

Taxi drivers: 15 per cent, and if you travel by private car or limousine they'll automatically add 20 per cent to the bill.

Hotel doormen: $1 for hailing a cab

Porters: $1 per bag

Maid service: $2 per day when you leave

Bartender: $1 a round

for exchanging currencies. Phone 212-935 9935 for branch details.

The alternative is to do as I do, exchange a reasonable amount of cash in one hit to use for tips, buses and in cafés, then use your credit card as much as possible (the exchange rate is generally reasonable). If you need extra cash, make sure you know your PIN number for your credit card and you'll be able to use any of the many ATMs (Automatic Teller Machine) around the city.

DISCOUNT DIVAS

NYC & Co: This company runs various money-off campaigns in association with the American Express Card that cover restaurants, hotels, theatres and sightseeing tours. The two main ones are Paint the Town Red, which runs from early January to the end of March, and Your Ticket to Summer, which runs from the beginning of June to the end of August. If you have an American Express Card, you can take advantage of great savings and extras at hotels such as the Waldorf-Astoria, the Carlton and Sheraton New York.

Each year the popular Summer Restaurant Week takes place during the last week in June when you can get three-course meals at more than 150 of the city's top restaurants for around $20 (excluding tip, tax and drinks). Many restaurants also continue serving their prix fixe lunches to the end of August. Establishments include Nobu, Gramercy Tavern, Union Square Café, La Caravelle and Montrachet. For further information check the website at **www.nycvisit.com** or phone either 1-800 NYC VISIT (toll-free within America) or 212-397 8222.

NYTAB: Your free NYCard is on the inside back cover of this book and will give you discounts to various museums, tours and hotels. Details can be found on page 20 in this chapter and at the back of the book on pages 239–40.

KIDS GO TOO

New York City is tremendous fun for children, and even has its very own **Children's Museum of Manhattan** in the Upper West Side (see page 103), not far from the dinosaur-packed **American Museum of Natural History** (see pages 96 and 206). Many other museums run programmes, tours and events for children (see page 109). **Central Park** is the perfect venue for much fun from skating to boating and biking plus its family-friendly attractions such as the **Carousel, Marionette Theater** and the **Central Park Wildlife Center** or zoo (see page 172).

Older children can get a chance to try out American sports at the **Chelsea Piers** (23rd Street and the **West Side Highway** in Chelsea, tel 212-336 6000). Visitors can get access to a swimming pool, baseball batting cages, basketball courts, an outdoor roller-skating rink, a golf driving range and rock climbing. In the meantime, parents can pamper themselves at the **Origins Spa**.

Then there are some great theme restaurants to choose from including the **Hard Rock Café, Planet Hollywood, Harley-Davidson Café** and **Mars 2112** (see pages 111–31). Finally, don't forget to take them to the world's most fantastic toy store, **FAO Schwarz** and the **Warner Brothers Studio Store** (see page 86).

If you need a babysitter, contact the **Baby Sitters' Guild** at 60 East 42nd Street, No 912, tel 212-682 0227, **www.babysittersguild.com** for licensed childcare.

CHAPTER 2

Getting Around New York

When most people talk about New York, they actually mean Manhattan, which is the long, thin sliver of an island in the middle of the four outer boroughs of Staten Island, Queens, the Bronx and Brooklyn.

You'll find diagrammatic maps, such as the one opposite, dotted through the book to help you focus on the basic geography of the area. Once you get the hang of roughly where everything is, you'll find it easier to use the subway and bus maps on the inside front and back covers, and the street maps in the centre pages.

ORIENTATION

Manhattan is 21km (13 miles) long and 3.2km (2 miles) wide for the most part and almost all of it above 14th Street is on the grid system that was introduced quite early on in New York's history. The main exception is Greenwich Village which, like Downtown, had already established its eccentric random arrangement of streets (like ours in the UK) and refused to get on the grid system. The other exception is Broadway, which follows an old Indian trail that runs largely north to south on the west side of the island, then cuts across to the East Side as it runs downtown.

Here are a few basic rules about the geography of Manhattan; it is useful to acquaint yourself with them as soon as possible, then you'll be able to walk around with confidence!

➡ The city is divided between East and West by 5th Avenue and all the street numbers begin there. This means that 2 West 57th Street is just a few steps to the west of 5th Avenue while 2 East 57th Street is just a few steps to the east of 5th Avenue.

➡ Most streets in Manhattan are one-way. With a few exceptions, traffic on even-numbered streets travels east and traffic on odd-numbered streets travels west. Traffic on major 'cross-town' streets – so-called because they are horizontal on the street maps of Manhattan – travels in both directions. From south to north, these include Canal, Houston (pronounced Howston), 14th, 23rd, 34th, 42nd, 57th, 72nd, 79th, 86th and 96th Streets.

To calculate the distance from one place to another, 20 north-south blocks or 10 east-west blocks approximately equal 1.6km (1 mile). This rule does not apply to the Financial District or Greenwich Village.

➡ When travelling north to south or vice versa, remember that traffic on York Avenue goes both ways, 1st Avenue goes south to north, 2nd Avenue goes south and 3rd goes north mostly, though there is a small two-way section. Lexington goes south, Park goes in both directions, Madison goes north and 5th Avenue goes south. Central Park West goes both ways, Columbus Avenue goes south, Amsterdam Avenue north, Broadway goes in both directions until Columbus Circle, after which it continues southbound only to the tip of Manhattan. West End Avenue and Riverside Drive go in both directions.

➡ Numbered avenue addresses increase from south to north.

➡ To New Yorkers, 'Downtown' does not mean the city centre, but means south, while 'Uptown' means north. You will need to get used to these terms if you are planning to use the subway – which is simpler to use than it looks at first!

6th Avenue was renamed Avenue of the Americas by the City, but is still actually referred to as 6th by the locals.

GETTING INTO THE CITY

FROM JOHN F KENNEDY INTERNATIONAL AIRPORT

JFK is in the borough of Queens and is the best place to enter or leave New York by air. It is 24km (15 miles) from Midtown Manhattan, a journey that will take you between 50 and 60 minutes. The cost of a yellow medallion taxi into town is a fixed rate of $35 (per taxi) as set by the New York Taxi and Limousine Commission. Bridge and tunnel tolls are extra (you can pay at the end of the journey) as is the 15 per cent tip. So think around $40.

There are various other ways to get into New York. An MTA bus and subway ride will each cost you $1.50 per person, private bus companies charge between $13 and $16 and the shuttle service costs $16. Private car services vary in price.

SuperShuttle: Tel 212-209 7000. A door-to-door shared limo-bus from the airport to your hotel operates 24 hours a day, 365 days a year. With your NYCard (see page 239) you'll get a $1 discount off the first person and every other person in your group (friends or family) will only be charged $9 – a great saving.

New York Airport Service: Tel 718-875 8200. Runs every 15–30 minutes to Manhattan and also operates a minivan service from drop-off points in Manhattan to many hotels.

New train service: By the beginning of 2003, the Port Authority should have opened a new train service linking JFK to Manhattan.

FROM NEWARK INTERNATIONAL AIRPORT

Hurrah! As of October 2002, getting into Manhattan from the airport became quicker and cheaper thanks to the opening of the $415million link to Newark International Airport. Follow the signs for the New Jersey Transit Train, which will take you to Penn Station in just 20 minutes for a fee of $11.15 one way. Alternatively, if you prefer the comfort and ease of a taxi, the journey will take a good 60 minutes. On the other hand, if you have a lot of luggage and are not staying particularly close to Penn Station, it may work out more time and cost effective simply to jump in a taxi.

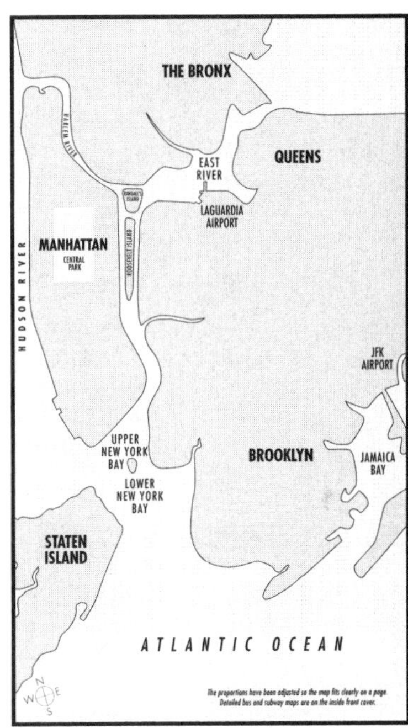

Areas of New York

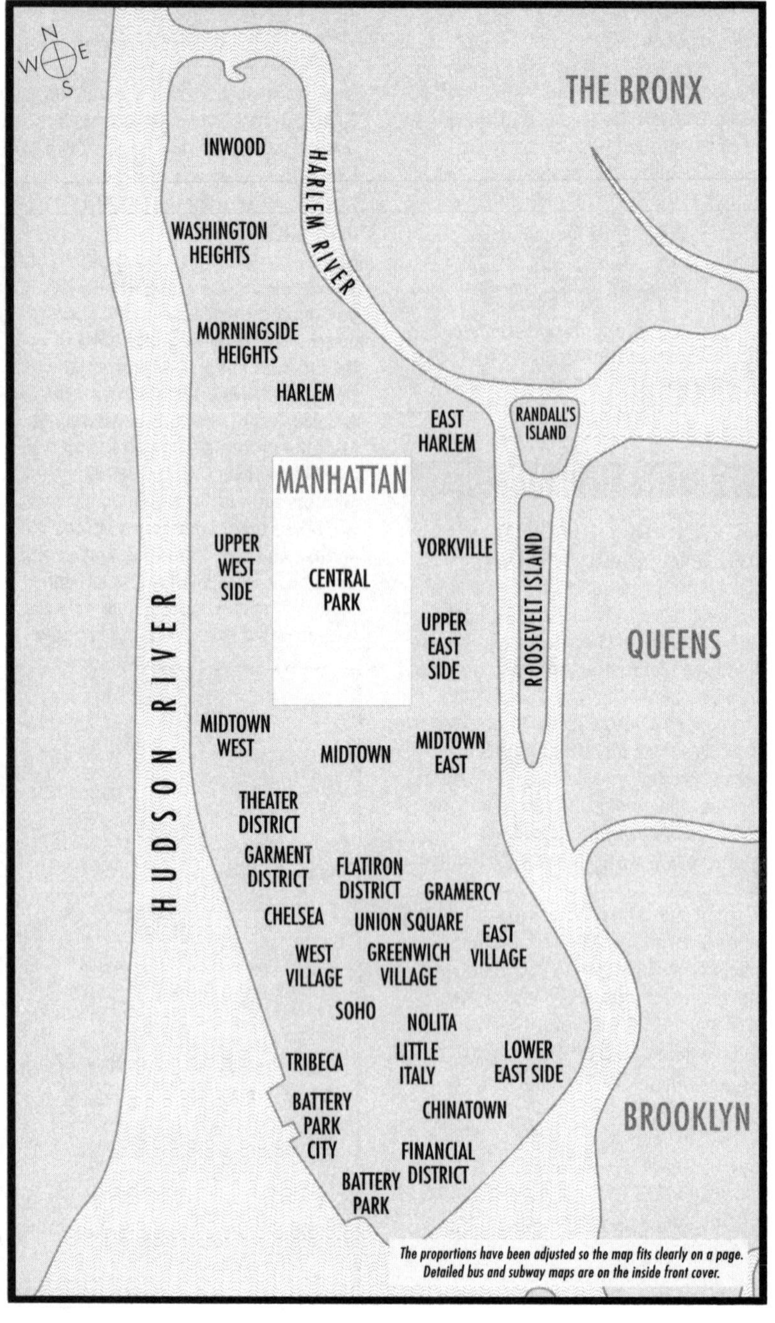

Areas of Manhattan

Set taxi fares start at $34 to West Manhattan and $38 to East Manhattan (as divided by 5th Avenue) plus bridge or tunnel toll and tip, so think around $50. Private bus companies charge between $11 and $15 and the shuttle service costs between $13.50 and $18.

SuperShuttle: As From John F Kennedy International Airport (see previous page).

The PATH: Tel 800-234 PATH. Rapid transit from Newark Penn Station (but you must take a taxi there from the airport) to stops in Lower and Midtown Manhattan. Operates 24 hours, fare $1.50.

Olympia Trails Airport Express Bus: Tel 212-964 6233. Operates between Newark and three Manhattan locations – Penn Station (34th Street and 8th Avenue), Port Authority Bus Terminal (42nd Street and 8th Avenue) and Grand Central (41st Street between Lexington and Park Avenues). Also hotel shuttle to all Midtown points between 30th and 65th Streets. Departs every 20 minutes, fare $11 (hotel shuttle $15).

GETTING AROUND BY TAXI

This is the preferred means of transport for many visitors to the city but, even though the fares are much cheaper than in London, the cost still mounts up pretty quickly. Fares start at $2 and increase 30 cents every 0.32km (1/5 mile), with a 50-cent surcharge at night, 8pm–6am. It's not just the cost of the ride you have to take into consideration, but the $1 tip to the hotel doorman and the 15 per cent tip to the driver. In the end it works out to be an expensive option if used too often.

In any case, you will need to have a good idea of where you are going and how to get there, as most of the cab drivers in New York are the latest immigrants to have arrived and have very little clue about how to get around the city. Fortunately, thanks to the grid system, it is relatively easy to educate yourself about where you are going and so you can give them directions!

➡ First off, never expect the driver to be the kind of chirpy, chatty Cockney character that you're used to in London. Most speak very little English and are not interested in making polite conversation, and many can be downright rude.

➡ Secondly, make sure you get on at the right place. If you are travelling uptown, but you're on a road heading downtown, walk a block east or west so you are heading in the right direction. It saves time and money, and if you don't, the taxi driver will know you're a tourist.

➡ Hailing a taxi is not necessarily as easy as it looks – you have to be aware of the lighting system on the top of the yellow medallion taxis. If the central light is on, it means the taxi driver is working and available. If all the lights are out, it means the driver is working but has a fare. If the outer two lights or all three lights are on, it means the taxi driver is off-duty – look carefully and you'll see the words.

➡ When you get to a toll, expect the taxi driver to turn around and demand the cash to pay for it, but you are quite within your rights to ask him to add it to your final fare.

➡ Beware of trying to get a cab at around 4pm. This is when most drivers change shifts so getting a taxi is well nigh impossible as they don't want to go anywhere but home! If you really need a taxi at this time be sure to call a car service company.

➡ Do not expect a taxi driver to change any bill larger than $20.

➡ In addition to the medallion on the roof, a legitimate taxi will have an automatic receipt machine mounted on the dashboard so that you can get an immediate record.

➡ If you find yourself below Canal Street after business hours or at the weekend, you may have difficulty finding a yellow cab. Your best bet is to phone one of the many companies listed under Taxicab Service in the Yellow Pages. Fares are slightly higher than metered cabs, but they are a safer option.

Don't assume your yellow cab driver will have the same level of knowledge about New York as black cab drivers do in London. Most are newcomers to the city, so always have the full address of the place where you are going.

CAR SERVICE COMPANIES

When you need to be certain you've got a taxi ride to the airport or some other destination, there are four main companies to phone, all of which provide a 24-hour service:

All City Taxis: Tel 1-718 402 2323.
Bell Radio Taxi: Tel 212-691 9191.
Sabra: Tel 212-777 7171.
Tel-Aviv: Tel 212-777 7777.

GETTING AROUND ON THE SUBWAY

The first time you take a look at a subway map of New York, you can be forgiven for thinking you need a degree in the whole system to get anywhere. The confusion is made worse by the fact that the signposts – both outside and inside the stations – are easily missed.

In addition, the Metropolitan Transportation Authority is undergoing a billion-dollar rejuvenation programme of many subway stops and have introduced new, clean trains on to the network, though as a New Yorker told me: 'We'll soon fix that. People just graffiti them up. It's disgusting but New York is a dirty city. If you don't have the dirt it doesn't feel right!' One of the things that happens on the subway is the train conductor will announce stops and interchanges. These, for the large part, are unintelligible, but the new trains have prerecorded announcements in a non-New York accent that can be understood! Here's a guide to some of the dos and don'ts to travelling around the subway that will hopefully make your life a lot easier.

➡ Don't look for obvious signs; instead look for either the very discreet 'M' signs in blue or the signature red and green glass globes – red means the entrance is not always open and green means it's staffed 24 hours a day.

➡ Before going down a subway entrance, check it is going in the right direction for you – many entrances take you to either 'Downtown' or 'Uptown' destinations, not both. It means that if you make the mistake of going in and swiping your ticket before you realise you're going in the wrong direction, you will have to swipe your card again to get in on the right side – so you'll end up paying double. The alternative is to travel in the wrong direction until you get to one of the larger subway stations (such as 42nd Street) and then change.

➡ If you're in one of the outer boroughs the same rules apply, but instead of looking for a Downtown or Uptown sign, look for one that says 'Manhattan'.

➡ Some trains are express – they stop only at selected stations. At some stations you have to go down two flights to get to the express trains, while at others you don't, and it is easy to get on an express train by mistake.

➡ There are conflicting opinions (hotly debated by the locals) as to whether it is worth waiting for an express. On the

Generally, if you're going downtown, use subway entrances on the west side of the road and if you're going uptown, use subway entrances on the east side. This way you should be heading in the right direction, but do always check before entering.

plus-side, they move quickly, but on the downside you could end up waiting ten minutes for one, so you won't have saved any time in the end.

➡ The same subway line (denoted by a specific colour, like red, blue, yellow or green) will have up to three or four different numbers or initials to identify it. For instance, the Red Line has trains with the numbers 1, 2, 3 and 9. Don't worry too much about the colours – they commemorate the different companies that started Manhattan's subway lines. The real trick is to find the station on any colour line that is closest to your destination, avenue and cross-street. In Manhattan, there isn't much difference between the train numbers apart from whether they are express or slow, but they will branch off in different directions once they reach the outer boroughs, so beware if you are travelling out of Manhattan.

➡ When examining a subway map, a number or letter in a diamond means rush-hour service, in a circle it denotes normal service and a square indicates a terminus, or the end of a line.

➡ Take care as some of the trains don't stop at all stops during off-peak periods. If the numbers against your destination on the subway map are written in a lighter tone, they are peak-time only.

➡ There are many different lines going to the same destinations, but they don't all exit at the same place. For example, if you arrive at Fulton Street on the New York subway and head for the exit you can come out at four completely different locations. The Red Line exits at Fulton and William Streets, the Brown Line exits at John and Nassau Streets, the Blue Line exits at Fulton and Nassau Streets and the Green Line exits at Broadway and John Street – all of which are quite a long way from each other.

➡ The locals consider that the subway is safe to travel up until around 11pm. After that time opinions vary, but when making up your mind do be aware that the subway service after 11pm is generally incredibly slow.

➡ The subway does have one very good point: because the island of Manhattan is largely made up of granite, they did not have to dig as deep as we have to in London to find the really strong foundation level. This means you generally only have to go down one flight of steps to find the line.

If you've been to New York before, it's worth bearing in mind there have been a few changes to the subway network – and all for the better – thanks to a $17 billion expansion and renovation programme. These are the new lines:

➡ The L line runs almost the full width of Manhattan along 14th Street from 8th Avenue in the west to 1st Avenue in the east on its way to Queens. Other stops on

TICKET TO RIDE

It's incredibly cheap to ride the subway and buses – a flat fare of just $1.50. And for that, if you use Metrocard, you can also transfer between subway and bus and from bus to bus for up to two hours from when you first board. Buying tickets has also got an awful lot easier thanks to the arrival of vending machines, which even take credit and debit cards and dispense all the different tickets.

You can buy tokens for single rides or there are different types of cards. These MetroCards can be bought at any subway station and other locations in pre-paid, sometimes discounted fares from $3 to $80. Seven-day ($17) and 30-day ($63) unlimited-ride MetroCards are also available. MTA has introduced $4 Fun Passes, which entitle you to unlimited rides on trains and buses for one whole day until 3am the following morning. Another MetroCard is the $15 card, which gives you 11 rides for the price of 10 and those rides can be taken at any time.

Manhattan include 6th Avenue, Union Square and 3rd Avenue.

➡ The new S line should not be confused with the shuttle between Times Square and Grand Central Station. It is another good east-west train linking West and East Villages in Greenwich and runs from West 4th Street to Grand Street.

➡ On Manhattan, the new V line largely runs in conjunction with the F line and includes new stops at 5th Avenue and 53rd Street and Lexington Avenue and 53rd Street.

My favourite MetroCard is the $15 pass. Up to four people can use it at one time and if you transfer to a bus you only have to swipe the ticket once and it will register for everyone. You can also top it up in small amounts, such as $5, which is really useful.

GETTING AROUND ON THE BUSES

Travelling by bus is always a little more nerve-wracking because you can never be sure whether you've arrived at your destination, but most people are pretty helpful if asked a direct question. I thought that taking to the buses would be more difficult than travelling by subway, but two of my friends put paid to that notion by going everywhere by bus on their first visit to New York. There are a few things that are helpful to know to avoid confusion or embarrassment.

➡ Often there are no route maps at the bus stops. However, as a general rule they run north to south, south to north, east to west or west to east.

➡ Get on the bus at the front and click in your MetroCard or subway token or feed in $1.50. Exact change is essential – and it must be all in coins as no dollar bills are accepted.

➡ Although there are bus exits at the back, you can also get off at the front!

➡ Requesting a stop may be a little confusing – there are no clearly marked red buttons to press; instead there are black strips that run the full length of the bus between the windows or at the back along the tops of the handles. Simply press one of these to request the next stop.

➡ If the bus says 'Limited Stopping' it means it only stops at major stops, such as the cross-town streets of 14, 23, 34, 42, 50, 57, 68, 72, 79 and 86.

WATER TAXI

A new addition to the transportation scene was the arrival in the summer of 2002 of the New York Water Taxi. The service started with stops between the Circle Line pier at West 42nd Street, Chelsea Piers at West 23rd Street, Battery Park City, South Street Seaport, Pier 11 at Wall Street and Fulton Landing in Brooklyn. In 2003 the service is expected to expand to include stops at the Intrepid Sea-Air-Space Museum, Greenwich Village and TriBeCa.

DRIVING IN NEW YORK

A word of advice: don't even think about it. Most of the streets will be jam-packed, while parking is extremely scarce and astronomically expensive – $8–10 an hour. You can park on the street, but watch out for what is known as alternate-side-of-the-street parking. This means you have to know which day of the week the cleaning truck comes by so you move the car over at the right time. Double-parking is common, so it is easy to get boxed in, and frustrated drivers simply get in their cars and honk the horn until the guilty owner moves their car. As one New Yorker told me: 'People do not know how to park here. New Yorkers are not good drivers and are the wildest parkers.'

If you plan to take a trip upstate, though, and wish to do so by car, then there are some dos and don'ts about car hire. Firstly **never** hire a car in Manhattan – unless you want to pay through the nose to the tune of around $90–120 a day. Take a ferry to the state of New Jersey and hire a car from there for $55–65 for a medium-sized car with unlimited mileage.

Secondly, don't even think about it in the summer or at weekends, because that's what most New Yorkers will be doing and you'll find hire cars thin on the ground. Hire cars are also snapped up in the autumn when New Yorkers like to go to the country to see the fall foliage.

Speed limits: Around town 30mph, on highways and freeways 50mph.

Private parking: There are many private parking facilities in the city, but they cost $25–40 per day.

Tow away: Illegally parked cars **will** be towed away and there's a $150 fine plus $15 per day to be paid. Collect your car from Pier 76, West 38th Street at 12th Avenue (Midtown West). Tel 212-971 0772. It's open 24 hours a day from Monday to Saturday.

FINDING A WC

I think it's worth raising this subject early as you'll probably be spending quite a lot of time walking around and you could easily get caught out. It is wise to know that public lavatories are thin on the ground in New York. In addition, subway loos – if they are actually open – are dangerous and unhygienic. I should also point out that it is considered impolite to use the word 'toilet' (*très* common, I'm afraid) – in America it is always referred to as the 'restroom'!

Okay, so you're in the middle of Greenwich Village, you're desperate, you don't want to pay through the nose for a beer so you can use the bar's facilities, so what do you do? I have it on good authority from those New Yorkers in the know that you should use the following:

Barnes & Noble: This is a newish chain of bookstores that offers restrooms because the company wants people to treat the stores as public meeting places. They tend to be hidden away at the back, so you'll have to ask the way and be prepared for a bit of a wait – sometimes the queues are quite long. The good thing is that Barnes & Noble are just about everywhere in New York now, though they have put a lot of independent booksellers out of business (see the Meg Ryan/Tom Hanks movie, *You've Got Mail*).

Department stores: They are hidden away, however, and you have to ask where they are (this is to deter street people from using them).

Government buildings: Try places like the United Nations, though you'll have to go through a security check.

Lincoln Center: There are ten 'stalls' open to the public, close to the entrance. No tips needed.

Hotels: The restrooms are usually on the ground floor or you can ask and will be told (amazing, huh?!).

McDonald's and **Burger Kings:** Unisex toilets that are usually clean and modern because they have been built to the McDonald spec rather than the typical New York building spec.

Public libraries: They all have public loos.

Restaurants: Some have signs saying 'For customers only', but if you ask authoritatively enough and look okay, they'll probably let you use them. The alternative is to stop for a cup of coffee and then you can use the restroom.

Statue of Liberty: In the gift shop.

CHAPTER 3

The New York Neighbourhoods

It's worth getting to know the neighbourhoods of Manhattan as each one has a distinct flavour and is filled with its own unique sights and sounds. From the historic Downtown area of the Financial District to the charming cobbled streets of Greenwich Village and the vibrancy of Times Square, each is well worth visiting in its own right.

Here's an outline of what you'll find in each neighbourhood, what makes them so special and how to make the most of your time there. In Chapter 14, Walking Tours of Manhattan, there is also a series of itineraries that will help you further to navigate the streets of New York.

DOWNTOWN

This is where the history of New York started and where some of the most important financial sites in the world were founded. The Downtown area covers the whole of the Financial District and the Civic Center, stretching from river to river and reaching as far north as the Brooklyn Bridge/Chambers Street.

Today, the winding, narrow streets of the true Downtown – a square mile area south of Chambers Street that stretches from City Hall to the Battery – are a dizzying juxtaposition of colonial-era buildings and towering temples of capitalism. In the beginning, they were the location of some of the most important events in American history. This is where the Bill of Rights was signed, where George Washington was inaugurated as the first president and where millions began their search for the American Dream.

THE WALL STREET SHUFFLE

The Dutch were the first to arrive and it was Peter Stuyvesant, New York's first governor, who ordered the building of a wooden wall at the northern edge of what was then New Amsterdam, to protect the colonialists from possible attacks from Indians and the British. The name stuck and today it is known as Wall Street. This aspect of New York's history is presented in an exhibition in the Ionic-looking Federal Hall National Memorial (26 Wall Street, tel 212-825 6888), built on the site of New York's original City Hall. Cross the road into Broad Street and you're at the neoclassical entrance to the New York Stock Exchange.

Other fascinating landmarks include the Federal Reserve Bank in Liberty Street at Maiden Lane, home to more gold than Fort Knox, and the neo-Gothic Trinity Church, where Alexander Hamilton, the country's first secretary of the treasury, was buried after losing a duel. There has been a church on this site since the end of the 17th century and for the first 50 years after Trinity was built, it was actually the tallest structure in New York!

Take yourself on a free two-hour, self-guided walking tour of The Street with Heritage Trails New York (212-908 4110).

Just off Wall Street at 25 Broadway is probably one of the poshest post office buildings in the world. Known as the old Cunard Building, it was once home to the booking offices of the steamship company in the days before aeroplanes took over the transportation needs of the masses from large liners, and the interior walls of the building are still lined with marble. There are other signs of its former use, too, with murals of ships and nautical mythology around the ceiling.

And it seems only fitting that the former headquarters of John D Rockefeller's Standard Oil Company at 28 Broadway should have become the home of one of New York's newest museums, the Museum of American Financial History.

BOWLING GREEN

Blink and you'll miss this oval of greenery at the end of Broadway. The way you know you're there is by the presence of the Greek revival-style US Customs House, which is now home to the Smithsonian National Museum of the American Indian and which has the world's largest collection devoted to North, Central and South American Indian cultures. Bowling Green was the sight of the infamous business deal between the Dutch colony of New Amsterdam and the Indians, who were conned into selling Manhattan for a bucket of trinkets.

In the 18th century, the tiny turfed area was used for the game of bowling by colonial Brits on a lease of 'one peppercorn per year'. The iron fence that encloses it now is the original and was built in 1771, though, ironically, the once-proud statue of King George III was melted into musket balls for use in the American Revolution.

If you need a coffee break, stop off at the New World Coffee shop at 1 Bowling Green opposite the American Indian museum.

BATTERY PARK AND CASTLE CLINTON

Thanks to hundreds of years of landfill, the whole Downtown area is quite different to how it once was. Years ago, State Street houses looked over Upper New York Bay and Water and Pearl Streets were named because they were at or near the water's edge. The excavation works required to build the deep foundations for the World Trade Center in the 1960s, destroyed by terrorists on September 11, 2001, created enough granite blocks of earth to form 23 acres of new land, which became home to Battery Park City and the World Financial Center.

In the Battery Park area, Castle Clinton originally stood on an island. Built in 1811 as one of several forts that defended New York harbour, it is now part of Manhattan, thanks to landfill. It has been an opera house, an aquarium and the original immigration sorting office, dealing with eight million immigrants before the opening of Ellis Island. It is now used as the ferry ticket office.

Battery Park is a beautiful spot for a picnic, or you can enjoy the fantastic views of the harbour and the Statue of Liberty by dining al fresco at the American Park at the Battery (see page 111).

BATTERY PARK CITY

West of Battery Park, you'll find a relatively new area of land known as Battery Park City, which is actually the area created by landfill. It's still pretty much a quiet district, though there has been plenty of development. This is home to two of New York's newest museums. The Museum of Jewish Heritage has been so successful, it has already undertaken steps to expand.

The ground floor of the plush new Ritz Carlton Hotel, in West Street, is the new home of the Skyscraper Museum, which tells the fascinating story of the creation of all those famous buildings. A bit further north is the World Financial Center, which has a full calendar of fairs and festivals. It's worth coming here for the Winter Garden, a huge, glass-ceilinged public plaza decorated by massive palm trees. From here you can see the posh private boats docked in North Cove.

For fantastic views of Dame Liberty and the harbour, treat yourself to a drink in the hip new bar, Rest, on the 14th floor of the Ritz Carlton Hotel in West Street.

EAST OF BATTERY PARK

If you really want to see what life was like in 18th-century Manhattan, then head for the Fraunces Tavern Block Historic District, which has 11 early 19th-century buildings that escaped the fire of 1835. The three-storey Georgian brick house that is home to the Fraunces Tavern Museum (on the corner of Pearl and Broad Streets) was built in 1904 and houses an exhibition on the site's history.

A little further north-east along Water Street to the Old Slip, you'll see the tiny First Precinct Police Station, which has been used for exterior shots for both *Kojak* and *The French Connection.* Fittingly, this is now the permanent home of the New York City Police Museum. Down on the water's edge of South Street is to be the new home of the Guggenheim's Downtown museum project. Plans for the balsawood and bendy-metal model to be turned into the real thing have been approved and it is expected that the new museum will attract more than three million visitors a year once it is opened.

Just off Water Street at 70 Pine Street is the incredibly beautiful art deco wedding cake-shaped American International Building. It has one of the most beautiful art deco lobbies in New York and visitors are welcome to come inside just for a look.

Don't miss the free outdoor concerts at the South Street Seaport Museum, held almost nightly throughout the summer.

A little further north at piers 16, 17 and 18, you find yourself in the heart of the South Street Seaport, which has a museum, a shopping and restaurant complex and the 150-year-old Fulton Fish Market, open 12pm–8am daily.

CITY HALL PARK AND THE CIVIC CENTER

City Hall Park is right opposite the entrance to Brooklyn Bridge and also the dividing point between the Financial District and Chinatown. From here you can stroll across the Brooklyn Bridge or visit the neo-Gothic Woolworth Building on Broadway at Barclay Street, which is likely to be your main reason for swinging by. If you do, check out the lobby's vaulted ceilings with its magnificent mosaics and mail boxes. When it was first built it was the tallest structure in New York and Woolworth paid cash for it!

Back in the 1930s, when Prosecutor Dewey decided to target organised crime, he made the Woolworth Building his base and during that time he locked up 15 prostitutes in the building for four months. In the end, he worked out that the prostitutes were controlled by Lucky Luciano and successfully prosecuted him for white slavery. 'Lucky' got 32 years in prison, but lived up to his name by serving just 10 before he was pardoned for his efforts on behalf of the American government during the Second World War. Just north of City Hall Park are the Police Plaza, US Courthouse, New York County Courthouse and Criminal Court Building.

It's useful to note that there is a new Lower Manhattan information kiosk in City Hall Park where you can find information on attractions and upcoming events plus maps and directions.

There is a farmer's market each Tuesday and Friday (April to December, 8am–6pm) in the City Hall Park where you can buy fresh fruits, vegetables and bread – a great way to create a picnic.

CHINATOWN AND FIVE POINTS

The sprawling mass that is Chinatown has spread its wings north into the remnants of Little Italy, east into the Lower East side and south in the Civic Center area. It is also home to the infamous Five Points area, once the most dangerous part of New York city.

Until recently only history books and tour guides referred to Five Points. The name is derived from the five streets that intersect next to Colombus Park. Originally called Orange, Mulberry, Anthony, Little Water and Cross Streets, they are now known as Bayard, Park, Worth, Mulberry and Baxter.

In the 1820s, a pond graced a lovely area where the rich had their country homes, but they started sub-letting to tanners, who polluted the lake. Attempts to get rid of the dreadful smells from the lake by building a canal down Canal Street failed, and in the end only the poorest came to live in the area, including freed slaves and immigrant blacks.

Irish immigrants arrived in the 1850s, then Italians and Eastern Europeans in the 1880s. Poverty was rife, and gangs flourished to such an extent that the streets were too unsafe for the police to patrol, and at least one person was killed each night. For almost 100 years, Five Points was considered the worst slum in the world and even shocked Charles Dickens. During that time the gangs were schools for criminals and politicians such as Johnny Torrio, Charles Lucky Luciano, Al Capone and Frankie Yale. Paul Kelly set up boxing gyms to teach them how to be gangsters, use guns and extort money. Amazingly, the gangs even produced flyers with their prices: $100 for the big job (murder), $50 for a slash on the face or $15 for an ear chewed off.

The appalling violence, corruption and history of this era has been brought to life by Martin Scorsese's movie *Gangs of New York*, starring Leonardo DiCaprio and Daniel Day Lewis. It truly gives an insight into the psyche of early American immigrants.

Fortunately, now it's a very different place. Many of the overcrowded tenements were pulled down at the turn of the 20th century to build a park. Since then, they've also built the Criminal Court Building nearby, retaining a contact with the violent past!

The original Chinese immigrants to New York in the 1850s huddled around Pell Street. Sadly, it was not long before the Tongs with their extortion rackets, illegal gambling and opium dens gave the area a new reputation for violence.

Have a game plan when visiting Chinatown – it's so crowded that it's easy to feel daunted by all the hustle and bustle. This section will help as will the Chinatown tour on pages 190–2.

As a result, the US Government passed the Exclusion Act in 1882, which banned Chinese from entering America.

That all changed in 1965 with the new Immigration Act and a new wave of Chinese immigrants arrived. Very quickly the women in particular were snapped up for poorly paid work in the garment industry, which gradually moved from its old Garment District above 34th Street into Chinatown. In more recent years, there have been more changes as a new wave of immigrants from the Fujian province of China have once again changed the face of the area. Now many of the well-off Cantonese have moved to Queens and the Mandarin-speaking Fujinese have the upper hand.

It's pointless arriving at Chinatown before 10am as only the local McDonald's will be open!

The best way to get to Chinatown by subway is to take the A, C, E, J, M, N, Q, R, W, Z, 6 to Canal Street. At 277 Canal Street at Broadway and up some rickety old stairs you will find Pearl River Mart, Chinatown's idea of a department store, stocking everything from crockery to Buddhas, pretty lacquered paper umbrellas, clothes, shoes and slippers.

Back on the street again and you could be forgiven for feeling a little overwhelmed by the licensed and unlicensed street traders of Chinatown, who sell anything from fake watches to jewellery. It's often impossible to walk on the pavements, but dangerous to step too far into the incredibly busy Canal Street, either.

Further down the road, you can get another real insight into the local lifestyle by visiting the Kam Man grocery store at 200 Canal Street. They offer a wide range from plucked ducks to squid. Not on your shopping list? Then here's something you can buy and eat while you walk around - a bag of Konja, which are filled with deliciously refreshing bite-sized pots of lychee jelly.

Mott Street is the main thoroughfare of Chinatown. Here, along with Canal, Pell, Bayard, Doyers and the Bowery, you'll find a host of restaurants to suit any appetite along with tea and rice shops. South towards Doyers Street you'll find the Church of the Transfiguration, which perfectly portrays the changing nature of the immigrant population here.

You'll have a hard time getting a taxi on Canal Street – they just don't make it into Chinatown that often. Head toward the Bowery and try to hail a taxi as it comes off the Manhattan Bridge, or use the subway stations at Canal and Broadway.

The oldest Catholic church building in New York, it was built in the early 19th century and Padre Felix Varela Morales, a Cuban priest who helped form the Ancient Hibernian Order, preached here. But between 1881 and 1943, no Chinese were allowed into it, apart from some wealthy merchants. It was first used by the Irish immigrants, then the Italians, but is now, finally, used by the Chinese and has services in Chinese.

May May restaurant at 35 Pell Street serves up fabulous dim sum. My favourite is the chicken and shrimp combo. *Dim sum,* incidentally, means the 'little delicacy that will lighten up your heart' – and it certainly does when it's good! Next door is the Chinese Gourmet Bakery and Vegetarian Food Center, from where you can buy enough ingredients to make your own picnic to eat sitting in the nearby Confucious Plaza.

Whether or not you choose to picnic, you should try to visit the beautiful Bowery Savings Bank on Bowery Street at Grand. When it was built in the 1890s, people liked to save locally and so the bankers tried to create the feeling that their building was a safe place for people to leave their money by making their banks stunningly beautiful inside. The neoclassical exterior is an incongruous sight here in Chinatown, but it's worth having a peek at.

LITTLE ITALY

Down Grand Street towards Mott and Mulberry Streets to Di Palo's marks the beginnings of what is left of Little Italy. Di Palo's at 210 Grand Street was founded 80 years ago and is still famous for its mozzarella, Italian sausages and salamis. It has its own cheese-ageing room and gets very, very crowded. A little further down is Ferrara's, the oldest and most popular pastry café in Little Italy.

Ferrara's in Grand Street near Mulberry is a perfect spot for a coffee and pastry break, while you'll find the restrooms on the first floor. You'll also get a real slice of the Italian lifestyle.

It has to be said that Little Italy is now little more than a tourist attraction, with the Italians having done a deal with the Chinese community to retain Mulberry Street between Hester and East Houston Streets. It's actually an area that was formerly home to Italians from the Naples area of Italy and, as such, it has taken St Gennaro, the patron saint of Naples, as its own saint. Every year in the third week of September, Italians flock from far and wide to celebrate the Feast of St Gennaro. Food carts line each side of Mulberry Street and there is much laughing, dancing and drinking until the early hours of the morning.

Little Italy's best feature is its wonderful restaurants with outdoor seating where you can watch the world go by while tucking into some great nosh. The restaurants have a reputation for being on the pricey side, but plenty have pasta and pizza specials for $8.95.

Little Italy is at its finest at the weekend in warm weather when the restaurants put their tables outdoors. Arrive early – around 12 noon – to get a seat outside, or late in the afternoon.

Just a little bit of gruesome history for you – Da Gennaro on the corner of Mulberry and Hester Streets was the original home of Umberto's Clam House (which is now further south on Mulberry). This was a favoured haunt of gangster Crazy Joey Gallo and where he was murdered in 1972 while celebrating his birthday.

Further north at 247 Mulberry between Spring and Kenmar Streets is the former home of the Ravenlight Club and Mafia headquarters for John Gotti. He was once known as the Teflon Don because no charges could be made to stick and this was where he made the policemen and judges on his payroll come to pay their respects.

The FBI were so determined to put him away they not only bugged the Ravenlight, but also all the parking meters around the streets, but still they got nowhere. Then Gotti's underboss, Sammy Gravano, became a supergrass. He had killed 19 people but got away with all those murders because he did a deal with the FBI that helped them put Gotti away.

LOWER EAST SIDE

One of the seedier parts of town, it has a fascinating history, but is now known for its trendy nightclubs and bargain shopping. The Lower East Side stretches from the East River ostensibly to Chrystie Street (though Chinatown is encroaching) and south from Canal Street to East Houston in the north, while Delancey is its main thoroughfare. The best way to get there by subway is on the J, M, Z or F trains to Delancey or Essex Streets.

In many respects the history of the Lower East Side is the history of America's immigration story which, in turn, has played a pivotal role in the country's history. At one time this was the most densely populated area in the world with 1,000 inhabitants crammed into a square mile, but more of that later. Almost from the word go, the Lower East Side was a settlement for new arrivals to New York because of its cheap housing and its proximity to where people disembarked. Once these immigrants had established themselves they moved on, leaving space for a new wave of arrivals. Street names such as Essex, Suffolk and Norfolk point to its first tenants. Since then it has been everything from a Kleine Deutschland to a Little Italy or Ireland.

While you're in the neighbourhood, don't miss Katz's Deli on East Houston Street – it's a real institution.

With each new wave of immigrants came friction between new and old arrivals, which often led to violence. The Protestant English were angry, for instance, when the Roman Catholic Irish built St Mary's on Grand Street in 1828 – and burnt it down. That led to the formation of the Ancient Order of Hibernians in 1830 – the organisation that started the St Patrick's Day parade. The Hibernians rebuilt the church and put walls around the outside. It is still in existence, but now runs a kosher soup service for local Jewish people.

SWEATSHOPS AND TENEMENTS

Other tenants of the early 1800s were relatively well-off Jews from Germany, who eventually moved further north. This was a pattern that was to be repeated again and again with each new wave of immigrants. But perhaps the saddest were the incredibly poor Jewish immigrants who started arriving from Eastern Europe in the 1860s and '70s. They were forced to eke out a miserly existence by day in sweatshops and had no choice but to live in tenement buildings at night. Whole families were crowded into 1.8m (6ft) square rooms with no heating, running water and often little light. Visit the Lower East Side Tenement Museum in Orchard Street for their full story.

The Lower East Side was once known as a mugger's paradise. It's no longer that bad, but you still need to be careful.

During this period Hester Street was the main thoroughfare and it was filled with shops and peddlers selling their wares – meat, fruit and vegetables. The peddlers did very well, though, as they paid no tax and had no overheads, such as rent. Often they made more than three times as much as teachers did. But the shopkeepers were unhappy with the unfair competiton and by the 1930s the city had banned peddlers and created the Essex Market.

A NEW DAWN

The main language in Hester Street between the 1880s and 1920s was Yiddish – a mixture of Hebrew, German and Slavic. The local newspaper, called *Forward*, was published in Yiddish and each edition sold 200,000 copies. Now the area is very quiet. There are many Jews left, but the new waves of immigrants include Puerto Ricans and Latins from the Dominican Republic.

If you want to see some real action you need to go to Delancey and the big shopping area around Orchard and Ludlow Streets. Here you'll find bargain basement products and cutting-edge designer fashions – many young designers have started in the Lower East Side before moving uptown. Orchard and Ludlow between Delancey and East Houston Streets are also the main drags for the new bars and clubs that have recently opened in the area. The best day to experience the Lower East Side is Sunday, when the market is open and the whole area is buzzing with people. A large chunk of it is still closed on Saturday to mark the Jewish Sabbath, but that is gradually changing due to the arrival of the Latinos.

An outstanding sight on Delancey is Ratner's Dairy Restaurant at 138 Delancey near Essex Street. It's not only a famous dairy restaurant, but also home to Lansky's Lounge, the chic nightspot that celebrates the place where mob boss Meyer Lansky used to hold court. The entrance is at 104 Norfolk Street. What's more, it's easier to get the whole Lower East Side experience now, since the opening of the Howard Johnson Express Inn on East Houston.

TRIBECA

This is where we start getting into the territory of New York pseudonyms. TriBeCa, like other pseudonyms such as SoHo, is a shortening of the area's location. In this case it means the triangle below Canal Street. It is bounded by Canal to the north, Murray to the south, West Broadway to the east and the Hudson River. To get here on the subway, use the 1 and 9 to Canal or Franklin Streets or the 1, 2, 3 and 9 to Chambers Street.

TriBeCa provides a good idea of what SoHo looked like 20 years ago. With the increasing pressure to find affordable housing, the empty warehouses of TriBeCa were ripe for the 'gentrification' process that has been happening all over New York including SoHo, the East Village and even the Lower East Side to a certain extent. And the area certainly has its fair share of pretty cast-iron buildings and quaint cobbled streets. Along Harrison Street is a row of well-preserved Federal-style townhouses and the area around White Street is particularly picturesque.

In the late 1970s, the former industrial buildings were targeted by estate agents for residential dwellings, but it was not really until the late 1980s that the area became a favourite with artists priced out of SoHo. Now TriBeCa is home to a variety of media and artistic businesses such as galleries, recording studios and graphic companies.

Its most famous film company, the TriBeCa Film Center at 375 Greenwich Street – which is part owned by Robert de Niro – has production offices and screening rooms and is used by visiting film makers. They, of course, frequent de Niro's extremely expensive TriBeCa Grill on the ground floor of the building. Visiting film makers have also been given a boost by the opening of the triangular-shaped TriBeCa Grand Hotel, which has its own private screening room.

Now the area is deemed quite hip – being home to Harvey Keitel and Naomi Campbell among others – it has attracted a lot of upper middle-class families, while restaurants and nightclubs are frequented by residents from the nearby Battery Park City. It is also home to the new TriBeCa Film Festival, which showcases independent movies during the second week of May.

SOHO

SoHo means south of Houston, pronounced 'How-ston'. It is bounded by Lafayette Street at its eastern border, 6th Avenue to the west and Canal Street to the south. The best subways are C, E to Spring Street and N, R to Prince Street.

If you're looking for a delicious latte and snack in SoHo, try the aptly named Space Untitled in Green Street between Houston and Prince Streets.

The main drag is on West Broadway and the whole area is reminiscent of Hampstead Village in London. Okay, so there are no hills and the roads are wider, but it has the same boutiquey, picturesque, design-conscious element.

It's hard to imagine the totally trendy and oh-so-expensive SoHo as a slum, yet just over 30 years ago this was the case. Despite the arrival of cutting-edge artists in the 1940s, who'd spotted the great potential of the massive loft spaces once used by manufacturers and wholesalers, the whole area was run-down and shabby.

Then, in the 1960s, those same artists were forced to fight for their very homes when the city decided to pull down all the buildings because they were only supposed to be used for light industry and definitely NOT for living in. The artists successfully argued that the architecture of the cast-iron buildings was too valuable to be destroyed and the whole area was declared an historic district.

In the 1970s, art galleries first started moving into the area and the art boom of the 1980s truly transformed it. Then in 1992 the Guggenheim opened its downtown site on Broadway at Prince Street. These events coincided with a kind of bubble-bursting feeling for the more cutting-edge artists, especially those who could no longer afford SoHo's sky-rocketing rents. Many have now moved on to Chelsea and TriBeCa. SoHo is now a wealthy residential neighbourhood occupied by anyone rich enough to afford the large loft spaces that are prevalent.

TASTES GOOD TO ME

SoHo is home to a complete first in New York City – a shop that can sell both wine and food. Vintage New York at 482 Broome Street at Wooster Street (212-226 9463) is owned by a vineyard from New York State, which means it can open on Sundays and sell proper alcoholic wine and food together – both of which are otherwise illegal in New York. The true secret to this little gem is that you can get five 1 oz tastes of different wines for just $5, which actually works out to be one of the cheapest glasses of wine going in Manhattan! All the wines, incidentally, are from vineyards in the State of New York. Best time to visit Vintage is during the week when there are stools to sit on at the tasting bar.

There are two cracking restaurants just off the beaten track in MacDougal Street – San Souci and Restaurant Provence – where you'll get a delicious meal for about half the price of the average SoHo restaurant.

All the same, you'll find plenty of art galleries, museums and one-off boutique shops to keep you happy, although you'll need plenty of dosh for the latter. Then, of course, there are the plethora of chic restaurants, cafés and bars. Those in the know, however, head for the more reasonably priced cafés and bars along Elizabeth and Prince Streets.

Great museums in the area include the MoMA's New Museum of Contemporary Art, the Alternative Museum and the Museum for African Art. And no day in SoHo would be complete without a drink at the SoHo Grand Hotel, where you'll learn the meaning of 'design-conscious'!

NOLITA

North of Little Italy and east of SoHo, mainly along Crosby and Lafayette Streets between Kenmare and East Houston, is a new area of town now known as NoLiTa. It's pretty edgy but up-and-coming and filling up with funky coffee shops, bars, restaurants and shops.

GREENWICH VILLAGE

This is one of the prettiest areas of New York and although the radical free-thinkers have gone, its quaint cobbled and tree-lined streets, shops and Federal and Greek-style buildings are well worth a visit. Greenwich Village proper is bounded in the north by 14th Street, in the south by Houston, in the east by Broadway and in the West by 7th, where it becomes the West Village, which stretches west to the Hudson River.

When the Dutch first arrived in Manhattan, 'the Village' as it is known in New York, was mostly woodland, but was turned into a tobacco plantation by the Dutch West India Company. Then in the early 1800s people started fleeing from a series of cholera and yellow fever epidemics in the unhygienic Downtown.

When the wealthy moved on to their 5th Avenue mansions at the end of the 19th century, though, rents came down and a whole new breed of artists, radicals and intellectual rebels moved in, creating a kind of Parisian Left Bank feel to the neighbourhood. Over the years it has been home to such literary lions as Mark Twain, Edgar Allen Poe, Dylan Thomas, Eugene O'Neill and Jack Kerouac.

Now the writers and artists have largely been forced out by the soaring rents – a tiny two-bed apartment costs at least $2,500 a month – and in their place have come upper middle-class Americans for whom making money is the abiding principle. Yet there is still the sense of a community spirit, many restaurants cater mostly to locals rather than tourists and the Village is home to great, long-running Off-Broadway shows such as *The Blue Man Group's Tubes* and *Hedwig and the Angry Inch*.

WASHINGTON SQUARE PARK

If you take the A, B, C, F, S or V subway to West 4th Street and Washington Square, you'll find yourself in the heart of what many people consider to be the Village – and in one of the very few genuine squares in Manhattan! The first thing you'll notice is the Stanford White-designed marble square Triumphal Arch at the bottom of 5th Avenue, built in 1892 to commemorate George Washington's inauguration as the first US president.

The next thing you'll probably notice is how dingy it all looks and I suspect you may be even a little concerned about the 'grungy' nature of many of the people there, but this area is considered 'alternative' rather than dodgy. It's full of locals skating, playing chess and just hanging out, plus students from the nearby New York University. It used to be a place where a lot of people took drugs, but that problem is largely in the past.

A little-known fact is that the park was once used by City officials to

GREAT TOURS OF THE VILLAGE

If eating's your bag, then you'll love iMar's Foods of New York tour of Greenwich and West Village, which not only shows you the sights, food shops, restaurants and architectural secrets of the area, but will also give you a chance to taste the foods that are unique to this corner of New York. Another great tour, also run by iMar, is the Literary Pub Crawl, which takes you to watering holes once frequented by the literary giants who lived in the Village. See the tours section of Chapter 4 for details. And finally, of course, don't miss the Village itinerary given in Chapter 13, Walking Tours of Manhattan.

conduct public hangings until they were moved to Sing Sing penitentiary. Apart from the arch and the people, the other main point of interest in the park is the Dog Run. A uniquely New York phenomenon, the idea is that instead of taking your dog for a walk along the roads, you bring them to dog runs where they can literally run around off the lead. It's rather like a parent taking their child to the swings – hilarious and has to be seen to be believed!

Tomoe Sushi, on Thompson Street, looks pretty grotty from the outside but has incredible queues – and not without reason. You can get the best sushi in New York here and for about a tenth of the price it would cost you at Nobu.

North from the park on 6th Avenue between Waverly Place and 9th Street are Bigelow's Pharmacy, the oldest traditional chemist in America, and Balducci's, the Village's most famous food emporium. Across the street is the beautiful Jefferson Market Courthouse, which is now used as a library, and just off 10th Street is one of the most famous rows of mews houses in the Village – Patchin Place, which has been home not only to many a writer, including e e cummings and John Reed, but also to Marlon Brando.

BLEECKER STREET

Effectively the main drag of the Village, this is one of the best places to be in New York, filled as it is with sidewalk cafés, shops, restaurants and clubs. The corner of Cornelia and Bleecker Streets gives you access to some of the best food shops and restaurants you could frequent while in Manhattan. At 259 Bleecker is Zito's old-fashioned Italian bread shop, which still uses the ovens that were built here in the 1860s and were once used by the whole community. They are particularly famous for focaccia with different toppings, such as onions and olive oil and rosemary, and their prosciutto bread is unique to them.

Next door is Murray's cheese shop with more than 350 cheeses from around the world. Nothing is pre-cut and they have great names such as Wabash Cannonball, Crocodile Tears, Mutton Buttons and Cardinal Sin, a British cows'-milk cheese. They also have 15 different types of olives and sell chorizos, pâtés and breads. Opposite at 260 Bleecker is Faico's, a landmark shop that has been here since 1900 (positively ancient by New York standards!). They are famous for their range of sausages, which are made every single morning and sold not only to local residents but to many of the local restaurants. They also sell home-cooked ready-made meals and offer a huge deli selection.

Around the corner is Cornelia Street, home to four of the best restaurants in the Village. The Cornelia Street Café is also a jazz club (just $5 to get in for the whole evening), while Home Restaurant specialises in American comfort food with a gourmet twist, Le Gigot is a traditional country French restaurant and Little Havana is a great Cuban restaurant.

On Bleecker Street are two incredible bakery shops with their own seating areas. Bruno's Pasticceria is run by popular chef Biagio. He does an amazing range of tarts and mousses for $2 to $3 with names like Kiss Cream, Wildberries, Green Apple and Apricot. The café itself has a lot of atmosphere and old world charm. Next door is Rocco, run by Rocco, who used to be a head pastry chef at Bruno's until 1972 when he opened his own place here. An Italian cheesecake filled with ricotta cheese is just over $4 for an entire cake. The interior is much more modern, with steel-framed chairs, mirrors and more seats than Bruno's.

WEST VILLAGE

The West Village is on the other side of 7th Avenue, an amazingly pretty collection of cobbled streets with picturesque homes and lined with trees. These are among some of the oldest remaining houses in New York – many being built in the 1820s, others in the 1850s – and quite a few have the one thing that is so rare in Manhattan – a back garden, albeit tiny.

TAKE IT EASY IN THE SPEAKEASY

On the corner of Bedford Street, number 86 is one of the most famous former speakeasies in New York. Known as Chumley's, you won't see its name advertised anywhere outside, but there is a back entrance on Barrow Street that will take you directly into the bar. The front entrance merely has the old grille, used for checking out potential customers during Prohibition, and the number 86.

On the small stretch of Barrow Street heading to Bedford Street is the wonderful Ithaka Tavern, a Greek restaurant with the most amazing conservatory area that has murals designed to transport you to Greece. Famous for its large portions, it's usually pretty empty at lunchtimes as most of the locals are at work.

In the old days a dumb waiter took two people at a time to the gambling den upstairs, and the best table in the house was right by the entrance to the cellar, where people would hide if there was a raid. Now Chumley's does fish and chips and shepherd's pie-type food and usually has a roaring fireplace in the winter, while the walls are still lined with all the book jackets donated by many of the writers who once frequented it.

At the corner of Grove Street is the oldest wooden house in the West Village. Built in 1822, it's the most exclusive cottage in the area and costs $6,000 a month to rent, but you do have your own little garden – bargain! All around Grove Street the houses are covered in vines, which blossom in May and have grown in the area for 150 years.

A MATTER OF RIGHTS

Christopher Street, the main drag of the West Village, is the heart of the gay community and a shopping paradise for antique lovers. Sheridan Square, one of the Village's busiest junctions, has been the scene of two major riots. First were the New York Draft Riots of 1863, sparked off by the requirement to join the army for the Civil War. The rich could buy their way out, but the poor had no choice and were fearful they would lose their jobs to the newly freed black slaves.

The second riot is the more famous one in 1969 and is known as the Stonewall Riot. This was sparked by the police raiding the Stonewall gay bar and arresting its occupants – an event which frequently occurred at the many gay watering holes in the area. This time the community decided to fight back and over the period of three nights, the gay community held its ground in the Stonewall as it was surrounded by police. It was the crucial first step made by gay people in standing up for their rights.

Christopher Street is still filled with bars, restaurants and bookstores that are used by gays – though not exclusively – but many members of the gay community have moved on to Chelsea.

THE MEATPACKING DISTRICT

The Meatpacking District is to be found in the north-western corner of the West Village, south of West 14th Street around West and Washington Streets near Gansevoort Street. Cattle are not actually slaughtered in this area, but large carcasses of beef are cut up in wholesale markets and distributed throughout the city.

However, many of the old warehouses are no longer in use and the lofts are being used as nightclubs. One of the trendiest is Hogs and Heifers, which is frequented by a mix of motorcycle groups and celebrities. Many women leave their bras on the ceiling as a memento. It's definitely an 'edgy' area and is also a hangout for transvestite prostitutes.

EAST VILLAGE

Forget the picturesque cobbled streets of Greenwich and the West Village, once you cross the Bowery (otherwise known as Skid Row) and head up to St Mark's Place you are in the heart of the East Village and an area more reminiscent of the Lower East Side than a village. No matter where you are in New York, it's easy to spot an East Villager – they have long hair and more metal in their face than a jewellery shop window display. You also know when you've entered the area by the tattoo shops and boutiques selling punk and leather outfits.

Where Greenwich Village has become upper middle-class, the East Village retains its roots as a Bohemian enclave of free thinkers and non-conformists, though the tramps are gradually being replaced by a more genteel set attracted by newly built apartment blocks and the reasonable, though rising, rents.

This was once the home of Beat Generation writer Allen Ginsberg (on East 7th Street) and was frequented by Jack Kerouac and other radical thinkers of the 1950s. Amazingly, one of the area's oldest clubs, CBGB on the Bowery, is still going strong. The punk rock club is famous for hosting Blondie, the Ramones, Talking Heads and the Police.

Now, though, the area is most well known for its second-hand shops, which can be found in great quantities along 7th Street and 2nd and 3rd Avenues. There's a tiny Little India on 6th Street, where you'll find a row of curry houses, but the most famous eating outlets are Stingy Lulu's and Yaffa Café, both on St Mark's Place heading towards Tompkins Square Park. And that's about as far as you'll want to go. The formerly dangerous area of Alphabet City (Avenues A, B, C and D) has been much cleaned up, but the muggers and drug pushers still frequent the area beyond B later in the evening.

CHELSEA

This neighbourhood is only likely to be on your must-visit list if you like art galleries, want to go clubbing or you're gay. However, it's actually worth a visit if you want to see an up-and-coming area in the process of 'gentrification'. Once the enclave of slaughterhouses and the working classes, its mixture of sought-after brownstone townhouses and warehouses made it a perfect target for artists priced out of SoHo, and although it's still rough around the edges, many of the quaint streets and buildings have been restored.

In the mood for some star-spotting? Try The Park on 10th Avenue, the latest hotspot for real and aspiring film execs.

It is bounded by 6th Avenue in the east, the Hudson River in the west, 16th Street in the south and 29th Street in the north. If you get off the A, C, E line at 14th Street and walk north on 8th Avenue, you'll see the main drag with its restaurants, shops, bars and gyms. Along the way you'll notice an abundance of Chippendale-type male bodies – the neighbourhood's gay boys, who love to flaunt their pecs in the local nightclubs.

At the corner of 19th, you'll spot the Joyce Theater, famous for dance and its fancy art deco building. Just a little

BAG YOURSELF A BAGEL

The best places for bagels are:
Yonah Schimmel's: 137 East Houston Street between Forsyth and Eldridge Streets in the Lower East Side, near to Katz's Deli.
Bagels on the Square: 7 Carmine Street between Bleecker Street and 6th Avenue in Greenwich Village on the SoHo side.
Bagel Buffet: 406 6th Avenue between West 8th and 9th Streets in the Village on the Washington Square side.
Bagelry: 1324 Lexington Avenue between East 88th and 89th Streets on the Upper West Side.
Columbia Hot Bagels: 2836 Broadway between West 110th and 111th Streets in the Columbia University/Morningside Heights area.

further north and you're not only in the Chelsea Historic District – the blocks around 9th and 10th Avenues at 20th, 21st and 22nd Streets – but at the heart of the new gallery community in the 20s between 10th and 12th Avenues.

First port of call should be the Dia Center for the Arts, a four-storey, 3,700 sq m (40,000sq ft) warehouse, which opened in 1987, and which still plays a pivotal role in the art world. Other great galleries nearby include No 535, DCA Gallery, Max Protetch Gallery, 303 Gallery and the D'Amelio Terras Gallery. Two blocks north on 24th Street is the 1,950 sq m (21,000sq ft) Gagosian Gallery and the Andrea Rosen Gallery. For those who may be interested, Annie Leibovitz's studio is on 26th.

CHELSEA HOTEL

One of the most infamous of all of New York's hotels, the red-brick Chelsea Hotel is not only still going strong but also in the midst of a great revival. Before Sex Pistols frontman Sid Vicious moved in with his girlfriend Nancy Spungen and allegedly killed her back in the 1970s, famous inhabitants included Mark Twain, Dylan Thomas, William S Burroughs, Arthur Miller and Arthur C Clarke.

Built in 1883 and named an historic landmark in 1966, its lobby walls are covered with plaques commemorating venerated guests and their artworks, while the Spanish El Quijote restaurant is famous for its lobster specials. Downstairs in the basement is Brit girl Serena Bass's Moroccan den, Serena's. Maybe it's thanks to her star-studded family tree, which includes Kate and Minnie Driver, but Serena's has become a new icon for New York, attracting stars such as Leonardo DiCaprio and Brazilian supermodel Giselle.

UNION SQUARE

Take the L, N, Q, R, W, 4, 5, 6 to Union Square at 14th Street. This area was once pretty run down and overrun with drug pushers and muggers, but now it's one of the trendiest neighbourhoods in New York. The stretch of Park Avenue South between 14th and 23rd Streets is filled with some truly hip eateries and is known as Restaurant Row.

The new West Court hotel on Park Avenue South at 16th Street is home to one of the hippest new bars in New York – Union Square's answer to The Royalton.

Along here you'll find Tammany Hall, the most corrupt City Hall in New York's history. It was home to Jimmy Walker, ostensibly a popular mayor, but a man who had been elected by the gangsters in the 1920s, which is effectively how organised crime was born in America. The gangsters were impossible to prosecute because they knew all the judges, cops and politicians in New York and virtually lived at Tammany Hall. In the end, Jimmy even had showers installed. Eventually, in the face of mounting financial problems in the city, Jimmy Walker was forced to resign and his successor, Guardia (pronounced Gwar-dia), decided to go after the gangs.

In the middle of Union Square is Luna Park, a great casual place for a bite to eat in the summer, with outdoor seating. Picnics are also getting very popular and it's easy to buy plenty of fresh fruit and food at the Farmers' Market held every Monday, Wednesday, Friday and Saturday. It sells fruit and veg, breads and pastries, cheese, eggs and meats from New York State farmers.

Further north on Broadway to Madison Square Park, you'll find Theodore Roosevelt's birthplace at 28 East 20th Street. It's not the original building, but it does house some great memorabilia from the former president's life. It's open 9am–5pm, Wednesday to Sunday and costs $2 to go in. Just around the corner is the wonderful, triangular Flatiron Building, at the end of what was once known as Ladies Mile, the city's most fashionable shopping district along Broadway and 6th Avenue from Union Square.

GRAMERCY PARK

To the east of the Flatiron Building on East 20th and 21st at Irving Place is one of the prettiest squares in New York City. The park itself was once a swamp but has now been beautifully laid out, though you won't be able to stroll around inside as it's only open to residents of the surrounding square or guests of the Gramercy Park Hotel.

The most famous building in the neighbourhood is The Players at 16 Gramercy Park, a private club created for actors and theatrical types by actor Edwin Booth when Gramercy Park was the centre of the theatre scene. Booth was the greatest actor in America in the 1870s and 1880s and opened the Gothic Revival-style house as a club in 1888 so that actors and literary types could meet in private to interact. One tragic event sadly overshadowed the end of Booth's life – his brother John Wilkes Booth killed Abraham Lincoln.

MADISON SQUARE GARDEN

It's a weird but true fact that the ugly Madison Square Garden building is to be found miles away above Penn Station on 33rd Street. The reality is that there have been four Madison Square Gardens and only the first two were, in fact, built at Madison Square Garden. Now the former site of the old venue has been used for Cass Gilbert's New York Life Building, which was erected in 1928, and which now overshadows what is known as The Little Church Around the Corner just off 5th Avenue at 29th Street. Its real name is the Episcopal Church of the Transfiguration and its stained glass windows remember famous actors such as Edwin Booth, who frequented the church at a time when being an actor or actress was not considered an honourable profession.

34TH STREET

You'll have two major reasons for coming to this part of New York – the divine Empire State Building and the shopping. Macy's is here, as well as a range of chains and most importantly a lot of retail outlets for the nearby Garment District. This area, it has to be said, was once pretty seedy, but thanks to the efforts of the 34th Street Business Improvement District Partnership, it has been transformed.

Now the streets are constantly maintained, clean and lined with pretty flower tubs and green benches. The BID has even installed some smart green telephones with a semi enclosure to block out some of the street noise. The kiosk at Herald Square is in matching green as is the city's one and only automatic pay toilet right next door. It's pretty swanky and, most importantly, it's **clean!** The size of the average New York bedroom, you've enough room to swing a cat if you feel like it and 25 cents gets you 20 minutes inside.

There are free historic walking tours of 34th Street given by an architect every Thursday starting from the Empire State Building at 12.20pm.

If you plan to do the Empire State, make it your first port of call before the crowds and queues build up. Take the B, D, F, N, Q, R, V, W to 34th Street and walk one block east to 5th Avenue where you'll find the beautiful art deco entrance. Once you've had your fill of the views, come back down to earth and take a cheap coffee break at the little-known Graduate Center at 365 5th Avenue on the corner of 34th Street – it's diagonally opposite the Empire State.

Here you can get ordinary and flavoured filtered coffee or a luscious latte and even a croissant and sit in relative piece at any time of the day before 4pm, which is when the graduates start arriving en masse. The building used to be the home of a department store, which is why there are ribbons and ties sculpted into the exterior columns. Now it is used as a research centre for students and there are free concerts. Anyone can sign up to use a computer for up to two hours for free.

HERALD SQUARE

Head west again to Herald Square, which is named after the now defunct newspaper, and which is home to the famous Macy's, the world's largest retail outlet. Its top-sellers among its Brit clients are the extremely well-priced Levis and beauty products, while the seventh floor is dedicated to childrens' goods and it even has a McDonald's – the only department store in town to make such a proud boast.

For the grown-ups there is the wonderful Cucina & Co in the basement. A combination of buffet foods to eat in and take away, a grill restaurant and a coffee shop, it also has a sandwich station, pasta station and take-out meals at incredible prices. Bearing in mind the average New Yorker spends $10 for a sandwich-style lunch and drink, Cucina's $3.99 lunches are amazing, as are their $7.95 meal specials.

But don't expect it to look cheap, this is a wonderful space filled with fabulously fresh food in an indoor-market setting, famous for its lobsters (two dozen go each day), whole salmon displays (they get through six a day) and caviar. It is now one of the largest retail sales points for caviar in New York and they ship it all over the world.

SHOPPERS' PARADISE

Between 5th and 8th Avenue, 34th Street is a shopper's paradise, but one of the highlights is the new Sephora beauty emporium – one of many that have sprung up all over the city. With its sparkling floor-to-ceiling windows and stylish displays, this is a pristine shrine to beauty products and fragrances (see page 92 for more details).

Fancy a free makeover? They're available during the week at Sephora on 34th Street between 6th and 7th Avenues. Phone 212-629 9135 for an appointment.

Other great shops in the area include Old Navy, the high-value end of the

Banana Republic chain, Kids R Us, Daffy's and its amazingly cheap designer selection – HMV, H&M and Kmart.

PENN STATION

One block south on 33rd Street and 7th Avenue is the entrance to Penn Street Station. Before you enter you'll see a Lindy's pastry shop, one of two that are famous for their New York cheesecakes (the other is in Times Square), but they're rather overpriced.

There's a free tour of Penn Station on the fourth Monday of each month starting from the 34th Street Partnership Information Kiosk at 12.30pm.

As you enter Penn Station, you'll see a handy Duane Reade (think Boots) on the left. Walk down to the round area that sits under the Madison Square Garden building and on your left you'll see the information booth for the 34th Street Partnership. All around are coffee shops, bakeries and a sit-down restaurant called Kabooz. None of them is a patch on Cucina & Co or the Graduate Center, but if you're in a rush you may have no choice. The restrooms are even worse. Sure, they have running water, but it just happens to be all over the floor. They're dirty, too, and pretty crowded. A good alternative is to head for the Hotel Pennsylvania on 7th Avenue opposite Penn Station, where you'll find clean WCs situated on the ground floor.

The main taxi ranks for Penn Station are on 7th Avenue opposite the Pennsylvania Hotel and on 8th Avenue opposite the majestic Beaux Arts General Post Office building, but unless you have a lot of heavy luggage with you, it's best to walk a block north as the queues can get quite long.

GARMENT DISTRICT

From 34th Street to 42nd Street between 6th and 8th Avenues, you'll find the Garment District of New York. Having shrunk a little in the past – a lot of work disappeared overseas or moved downtown to the cheap labour available in Chinatown – the area is once again up-and-coming as designers are now choosing to have their clothes manufactured in New York. If you wander around this area – and you may well if you're in search of sample sales – you'll notice all the racks of clothes being pushed around the streets. The reason for this is that no one manufacturer makes an entire piece of clothing. They are shunted from company to company, with all the different bits being sewn on at different places!

MURRAY HILL

It's a testimony to man's desire to tame his environment that the majority of Manhattan is flat. This is as a result of the zoning plans created in the early 19th century, when the streets and avenues were laid out north of Downtown, except for the Village. At the same time, the city flattened the majority of Manhattan except for what is now Morningside Heights and Harlem, as nobody believed anyone would live up there! The only other area that was not flattened is Murray Hill, a largely residential neighbourhood, which lies between 5th and 3rd Avenues and 32nd and 40th Streets.

The most famous resident of the area was the multi-millionaire JP Morgan. His son lived in a brownstone on the corner of 37th Street and Madison Avenue, which is now the headquarters of the Lutheran Church. JP Morgan lived in a house next door until he had it knocked down to make way for an expansion of his library. Now known as the Pierpoint Morgan Library, it has a unique collection of manuscripts, paintings, prints and furniture, which the financier collected on his trips to Europe.

MIDTOWN

Technically Midtown starts at 34th Street, but for the purposes of this area guide, I'm starting at the more realistic 42nd Street. From this point on, between 5th Avenue and Broadway are some of the most beautiful and famous shops, hotels and buildings in the world. 5th Avenue, itself, of course is known for its shopping and is home to marvellous institutions such as Saks, Bergdorf Goodman, Tiffany's (my favourite jewellers), Trump Tower and the children's paradise of FAO Schwarz.

Weird but true, there are no coffee shops or coffee carts on 5th Avenue. If you want a drink, your best bet is to try one of the side streets leading off to 6th Avenue for a coffee shop.

Fabulous hotels in the area include the media-den of the Royalton, the famous Algonquin and the chi-chi Plaza Hotel with its views of Central Park. Opposite St Patrick's Cathedral on 5th Avenue is the main entrance into the Rockefeller Center complex of 19 statuesque buildings with the famous ice-skating rink in the middle of its central plaza. There's so much to do here, from browsing in the shops, to checking out the architecture or visiting the beautifully restored art deco Radio City Music Hall. Further north on 57th Street are two wonderful New York institutions, Carnegie Hall and Warner Le Roy's magnificently OTT Russian Tea Rooms, whose seven storeys include a two-storey ballroom and house, a revolving aquarium and a model of the Kremlin.

MIDTOWN EAST

Running east of 5th Avenue to the East River, this area also has its fair share of New York landmarks. No visit to the city would be complete without a visit to the magnificent, marble-filled Grand Central Station at 42nd Street, which has been restored to its former glory. It may be overshadowed by the MetLife Building from the outside, but nothing can take away from its gorgeous interior. The ceiling, incidentally, has been painted to show the sky as seen by God above.

The area along East 45th Street between Vanderbilt and Lexington Avenues is packed with food carts selling everything from steak sandwiches to baked potatoes.

To the east is the stunning Chrysler Building, which many argue is even more beautiful than the Empire State Building, and down by the river is the monolithic United Nations building. Of course no visit to Park Avenue would be complete without a visit to the Waldorf-Astoria, which has a choice of cocktail bars – though the lobby bar is probably best for people-watching.

MIDTOWN WEST

TIMES SQUARE AND THE THEATER DISTRICT

If you arrive at Times Square by day there will be no neon signs to dazzle you, so the first thing you'll notice is the lack of a square. Like Greeley and Herald Squares, Times Square is no more than a junction where Broadway crosses 7th Avenue. The whole Theater District area starts on the boundary with the Garment District at 41st Street, goes north to 53rd Street and is bounded by 6th and 8th

Avenues. The best way to get there is to take the 1, 2, 3, 7, N, Q, R, S, W to Times Square/42nd Street.

It came into being at the end of the 19th century – previously the theatre district had been in the Union Square area and then Chelsea – when Oscar Hammerstein I (father of the great lyricist) built his opulent Olympia Theater on Broadway between 44th and 45th Streets. Until then, it had been an unfashionable area housing the city's stables and blacksmiths and was known as Long Acre Square.

In 1904, when the *New York Times* set up shop in what is now 1 Times Square, the area was renamed in its honour (it's since moved its offices to around the corner). That same year a massive fireworks display on New Year's Eve became the precursor to the now famous annual countdown watched by millions of people. The surrounding Theater District, home to the Ziegfeld Follies at the New Amsterdam Theater, Minsky's and Gypsy Rose Lee, blossomed in the 1920s. In fact, so many theatres burst on to the scene that even though many were converted into cinemas in the 1940s, during a clean-up of the burlesque shows by Mayor La Guardia, there are still 30 theatres in the area.

BAD TIMES COME

Sadly, by the 1960s, Times Square had lost its shine and the economic problems of the 1970s and 1980s compounded the situation. If you've ever seen de Niro's movie *Taxi Driver*, you'll have some idea of the level of drugs, prostitution and seedy strip joints that crowded the area. Crime rose dramatically and until fairly recently it was a very unsafe area.

Things started to change in the early 1990s and were helped by the establishment of the Times Square Business Improvement District, which worked hard to clean things up and pay for security guards, and the discovery of an ages-old law that prevents sex shops from operating within a certain distance of schools or churches. Since then crime in the area has dropped by 60 per cent and many New Yorkers complain of its relative cleanliness. The arrival of the Disney company, which spent millions renovating the New Amsterdam Theater to put on *The Lion King*, was the last nail in the coffin as far as many were concerned.

In all honesty, I really don't feel these dirt purists should fret too much. To my mind, there is still definitely an edgy vibe to the neighbourhood, while the stream of traffic that puffs its way through each minute, and the grunginess of many visitors stops Times Square from being what some people think of as a squeaky-clean environment and I'm not the only one to think so.

Broadway isn't called The Great White Way for nothing. It's at its magnificent best around Times Square, of course, but the most wonderful way to see it is from a few blocks north when you really can appreciate the glittering beauty of all those neon signs.

All the same, it's safe enough for the most part and has plenty to offer everyone. New hotels have sprung up and corporate companies have moved into the neighbourhood including media giants Viacom, MTV, VH-1 studios, ABC TV's *Good Morning America*, Condé Nast Publications and Reuters news service.

There's the huge new ESPN Zone, a 3,900sq m (42,000sq ft) sports dining and entertainment complex, Nasdaq Marketplace Site with its sign – the largest video screen in the world – and Madame Tussaud's. In between are the Virgin Megastore, the Coco Chanel-style beauty emporium of Sephora, the Warner Bros Studio Store and the World

Wrestling Federation entertainment and dining complex, which includes a restaurant and hot new nightclub. Oh, and, of course, there are the 30 theatres and nearly 50 cinema screens to entertain the masses.

HELL'S KITCHEN/CLINTON

Running up the west side of Midtown from 34th Street to 57th from around 8th Avenue to the river is an area known as Hell's Kitchen. It started life in the latter part of the 19th century when a lot of poor Irish immigrants arrived and it became something of a ghetto. They were later joined by blacks, Italians and Latinos and inevitably gangs were formed. The big employers were the docks (see Marlon Brando's *On the Waterfront* for an insight into the lifestyle – it's set in Brooklyn but is equally true of all the dock areas), but when container ships came into play many lost their jobs. Other local industries included slaughterhouses and glue and soap factories.

If you have an evening out on the *World* Yacht, you'll find yourself walking through Hell's Kitchen/Clinton in search of a taxi. The best thing to do is to adopt the New York Walk, (i.e. walk quickly and confidently) and head east to 7th or 6th Avenues where it's easiest to pick up a cab.

A lot of the gangs were put out of business by the police in 1910, but it remained a scary area until fairly recently. It was renamed Clinton in 1959 to hide its violent past – which is long before Bill came on the scene, so there's no link to the former president. Now a lot of people in the area work in the Theater District and it's gradually moving up in the world. 9th and 10th Avenues are full of restaurants, the *Intrepid* Sea-Air-Space Museum is on the river and, on the whole, the area is pretty safe until around 11pm.

UPPER EAST SIDE

One of the most conservative areas of New York, the Upper East Side stretches from Central Park South to 98th Street and is centered on 5th, Madison, Park and Lexington Avenues. It came into being after Central Park was finally completed in 1876 and the rich and famous of the Gilded Era – the Whitneys, Carnegies, Fricks, Vanderbilts and Astors – decided to build their mansions alongside. It was a time when neo-classicism was the favourite architectural design, but many of the houses left standing are not the originals as the grandiose properties were built and rebuilt in an ever more opulent style or replaced with apartment blocks.

Jim's Shoeshine on East 59th Street between Madison and Park Avenues is a real institution that has existed since the 1930s.

Two things have always remained the same, though. The neighbourhood is known as the Silk Stocking District because of the vast family fortunes represented in the area, and the grand old apartment houses are known as 'white glove' buildings because of the uniforms of the doormen. The buildings are more than ever in demand. For instance, Jackie Onassis' former 14-room apartment at 1040 5th Avenue near East 86th Street recently sold for a whopping $9 million. Just so you know, the mansion on the corner of East 86th was one of nine mansions once owned by the Vanderbilts. Now nearby residents include Michael J Fox and Bette Midler.

If you're serious about your designer clothes, then you'll be visiting the area to see the designer stores lining Madison Avenue. If you're clever you won't buy, just store up the information about the latest designs for when you go rummaging through the designer selections at Daffy's or the sample sales (see Shopping on page 82).

This area is also full of museums and what a staggering array you have to choose from. They range from the world's largest and, arguably, most magnificent – the Metropolitan Museum of Art – to the bijou jewel of the Frick Collection, housed in the magnate's former mansion. Near to the Frick is the joyous Whitney Museum, with its emphasis on contemporary art.

Further north are the marvellous Guggenheim, with its amazingly beautiful exterior, the Cooper-Hewitt Museum, the Jewish Museum and the International Center of Photography. Finally, up in the beginnings of East Harlem, populated by Latin Americans, are the Museum of the City of New York and the Museo del Barrio.

YORKVILLE

Between Lexington Avenue and the East River from East 77th to 96th Streets is the working- to middle-class enclave of Yorkville, which has an interesting mix of cultures, singles and families. It was originally populated by German-Hungarians, who moved northwards from their first stopping point in the East Village's Thompkins Square with the arrival of Italian and Slavic immigrants. Now, though, you'd be hard-pressed to find the few remnants of German culture, as most left the neighbourhood during the Second World War to avoid anti-German feelings.

Fancy the idea of a picnic by the river? Then stop off at the Vinegar Factory in 91st Street where you'll find an extensive selection of cheeses, meats, breads and salads, and head for the nearby Carl Schurz Park.

The most famous resident in the area is the mayor, who lives in the official residence at Gracie Mansion overlooking the East River and Carl Schurz Park at East 89th Street. Tours are available on Wednesday though you need to book in advance (tel 212-570 4751).

UPPER WEST SIDE

Central Park divides the Upper East and West Sides not only geographically, but in terms of attitude, too. If the East Side is upper crust, conservative old money, then the West Side is more artistic, counting among its famous residents Woody Allen, who even plays jazz once a week at his local bar. It's a vibrant neighbourhood filled with bars, restaurants, shops, museums and, of course, the culture of the Lincoln Center.

One of my favourite spots in the area is the Saloon Grill on Broadway at West 64th Street, which has great views of the Lincoln Center. Find a shady spot outside to sit and have lunch or use it for a mid-morning or mid-afternoon break. It's very good value for money.

It all starts around Columbus Circle on West 59th Street – a nightmare for any pedestrians – which is marked by Donald Trump's International Hotel with its showy Unisphere, a replica of the one at the 1964 World's Fair held in Queens. As you navigate the traffic lights to cross the roads, you can ponder on the fact that this is where Jo Colombo, the boss of one of the five Mafia families of New

WHICH MET'S THE MET?

Traditionally the Metropolitan Opera House, with its crystal chandeliers and red-carpeted staircases, has been known as the Met. Increasingly, though, the Metropolitan Museum of Art is being referred to by the same moniker, which is leading to a certain amount of confusion. It probably depends which establishment you stumble across first. My greatest love is for the museum so to me that will always be the Met!

York, was shot, and that beneath the tarmac is one of the biggest police precincts in New York – home to 38,000 of NYPD's finest.

Up Broadway and left down West 63rd Street past the Empire Hotel – home to the Iridium, one of the finest jazz clubs in New York – you'll find the Lincoln Center. Once the whole area was filled with the slums that housed poor Puerto Ricans (the setting for the 1961 movie *West Side Story)* until Robert Moses proposed the building of various cultural centres that include the Metropolitan Opera House, the New York State Theater and Avery Fisher Hall. To see more, join one of the popular backstage tours (see page 136) or enjoy the free lunchtime music supplied by jazz and folk bands during the summer.

BUILT TO LAST

One of the things the Upper West Side is known for is its beautiful buildings including the Beaux Arts Ansonia Hotel on Broadway between 73rd and 74th Streets, which has been called home by Babe Ruth and Igor Stravinsky in its time. Starting on the southern tip of Central Park West, which runs all the way up Central Park, is the art deco stunner at No 55, which was used as the setting for *Ghostbusters*.

On 67th Street near Central Park West is the Hotel des Artistes which, as the name suggests, was built for artistic types, who have used it as their residence since it opened in 1918. Over the years it has been home to Noel Coward and Isadora Duncan. Back on Central Park West between 71st and 72nd Streets is the yellow façade of the art deco Majestik apartment house, which was built in 1930.

Across the way is the famous Dakota Building, which was the first apartment block ever to be built on the Upper West Side in 1884, and was named after the distant territory to indicate its remoteness from anything else on the West Side. Of course, since then it has had a long line of famous inhabitants including Leonard Bernstein, Judy Garland and Boris Karloff. Its most famous resident of all, John Lennon, was gunned down outside the building by a crazed fan in 1980. His wife Yoko Ono still lives in the building – she owns several apartments – and donated the money to build the Strawberry Fields memorial to her former husband in Central Park, just across the road.

Once you cross West 59th Street going north, 8th, 9th, 10th and 11th Avenues become Central Park West, Columbus, Amsterdam and West End Avenues respectively.

A couple of blocks north between 73rd and 74th is the neo-Renaissance style Langham, which was built in 1905, and between 74th and 75th is the San Remo, which was built in 1930, where Rita Hayworth died of Alzheimer's in 1987. Another block north, on the corner of 75th, is the French Second Empire-style building of the Kenilworth. Between them, these grand apartment blocks have housed more celebrities than any other part of town, including Lauren Bacall, Dustin Hoffman and Steve Martin.

MUSEUM MANIA

On Central Park West at 77th Street is the New York Historical Society, which was formed in 1804 and was the only art museum in the city until the opening of the Metropolitan Museum of Art in 1872. It was founded to chronicle New York's history but is still home to the world's largest collection of Tiffany stained-glass shades and lamps and two million manuscripts, including letters sent by George Washington during the War of Independence.

Just a few blocks from these museums is Zabar's on Broadway at West 80th Street, the famous food emporium seen in *Friends*. It's jam-packed with fresh meats, cheeses and fruits – in fact, everything you need to create a picnic.

Next door is the real big boy of museums – the American Museum of Natural History, which was the brainchild of scientist Albert Smith Bickmore. It first opened at the New York Arsenal in Central Park in 1869, but by 1874 had moved to these bigger premises. Architect Calvert Vaux, who was also responsible for the Met Museum and largely responsible for Central Park, created the bulk of the building, which has since had a Romanesque-style frontage added to it on its 77th Street side and a Beaux Arts-style frontage added on to the Central Park West side.

This is one of my favourite museums in all of New York. It's cram-packed with well-laid-out exhibitions that really bring the world of science, scientific discovery and expeditions to life, while the Rose Center and Big Bang Theater attract major crowds to see the 13-billion-year history of the universe. The Upper West Side's Museum Half Mile also includes the Children's Museum of Manhattan on 83rd Street between Broadway and Amsterdam Avenue where interactive exhibits keep the wee ones happy.

At the top end of the Upper West Side, West 106th Street is now known as Duke Ellington Broadway. This is where the great musician lived, premiered many of his songs and was buried. Over 10,000 people came to his funeral and there is a memorial to him on 5th Avenue at West 110th by Central Park's Harlem Meer.

MORNINGSIDE HEIGHTS

Further north the terrain gets hilly as you reach Morningside Heights, home to the Cathedral of St John the Divine and Columbia University, one of the most exclusive universities in America where a year's tuition will set you back around $35,000. Even so, it has 20,000 students of whom 4,000 are undergraduates. This is a beautiful area, which is bounded by 8th Avenue to the east and West 125th Street to the north.

A great pit-stop in the Columbia University area is Tom's Restaurant on Broadway at 112th Street. If you recognise the diner's exterior, that's because it was used in *Seinfeld*.

HARLEM

Harlem is a huge area that covers a substantial part of the northern reaches of Manhattan above Central Park, though it has various subsections. What we refer to when we use the name Harlem is actually the African-American area, which stretches from 8th Avenue in the west to 5th Avenue in the east and goes north to the East River. The area from East 96th Street east of 5th Avenue

Many avenues and streets in Harlem have two names that reflect both historical and more modern influences. For instance, Lenox Avenue is known as Malcolm X Boulevard and 7th Avenue is known as Adam Clayton Powell Junior Boulevard – both named after major African-American activists.

going up to the East River is Spanish Harlem, known as El Barrio and populated largely by Puerto Ricans.

Named after the Dutch town of Haarlem, Harlem received its first Dutch settlers in the mid-19th century when the area was used as farmland and as an escape from the dust and traffic of Midtown. Better-off immigrant families started moving here following the arrival of the railroad link and the building of attractive brownstone townhouses. Then property speculators, eager to take advantage of the new subway heading for Harlem, started building good-quality homes for the upper middle classes in the early 1900s. But they'd got a little ahead of themselves. A couple of mini depressions and Harlem's distance from Midtown Manhattan put the dampers on hopes of a major middle-class movement into the area.

The African-American estate agents spotted a golden opportunity, bought up a whole batch of empty homes cheaply and started renting them out to blacks eager to escape the gang warfare of the West 40s and 50s in Hell's Kitchen and Clinton. This was the beginning of Harlem as the capital of the black world and when African-Americans started migrating from America's Southern states, they headed straight here.

And it's no wonder really. Brits are frequently shocked to discover that the blacks may have been freed from slavery by the end of the 19th century, but there was still segregation until the 1960s. Black people were not allowed to sit on the same benches as whites, they had to drink at different water fountains and in church they were forced to wait until after the whites for Communion. When great black musicians such as Duke Ellington and Louis Armstrong went on tour, they had to stay at black-only hotels and eat at black-only restaurants.

Back in Harlem, at least, there was some semblance of belonging and thanks to the influx of political activists, professionals and artists to the area following the opening of the subway lines between 1904 and 1906, many African-American organisations had sprung up by the early 20s. They included the National Urban League, which helped people who were moving into the area to get training for jobs, and the White Rose Mission, which helped African-American female migrants coming to New York from the South. They were followed by the political Universal Negro Improvement Association and the Union Brotherhood of Sleeping Porters, whose leader Phillip Randolph was at one time considered to be the most dangerous black in America by the government.

Instead of heading for the somewhat touristy Sylvia's Restaurant on 125th, try the M&G Soul Food Diner at West 125th at Morningside Avenue for a truly traditional Southern meal to the background sounds of great soul singers.

THE GLORY DAYS OF HARLEM

The 1920s and 1930s were a great time for the neighbourhood, filled as it was with poets, writers, artists, actors and political activists. The combination of prohibition and great jazz musicians, including Count Basie, Duke Ellington and Cab Calloway, made famous nightspots such as the Cotton Club attractive to the upper middle classes who came in their droves to enjoy Harlem's speakeasies.

If you really want to experience the life and times of Harlem, pick up a copy of *Harlem's Culture: Guide to Great Events*, available at cultural institutions such as the Schomburg Center.

But all this was hardly doing anything for the lot of the average African-American who lived in the area. The speakeasies were strictly for whites only and even WC Handy, who co-wrote a song with Duke Ellington, was not allowed into the Cotton Club to hear it being played for the first time. Then there was the matter of the racism on 125th Street – Harlem's epicentre which runs from Frederick Douglas Boulevard to Malcolm X Boulevard. The white-owned shops and hotels here, which were used by the African-Americans, were staffed by whites and it was impossible for blacks to get anything but the most menial jobs.

In 1934 Adam Clayton Powell Junior, preacher at the Abyssinian Baptist Church, organised a boycott of these businesses, entitled Don't Buy Where You Can't Work. The campaign was successful and the shops started hiring blacks. Now along 125th Street, you can still see the remnants of the great businesses of those times.

You can start your modern-day experience of Harlem with a tour round the famous Apollo Theater on 125th Street, which was the focal point for African-American entertainment between the 1930s and 1970s. Known for its legendary Amateur Night, which is still going strong and now broadcast on TV, it has launched the careers of Ella Fitzgerald, Marvin Gaye, James Brown and even The Jackson Five.

At the corner of 7th Avenue stands the former Theresa Hotel, now an office block, but which was once considered to be the Waldorf of Harlem. Back in the days of segregation Josephine Baker stayed in the penthouse with its vaulted ceiling and views of both rivers. Malcolm X's Unity organisation was based here in the 1950s and 1960s and in a show of support for African-Americans, Fidel Castro moved his entire entourage to the Theresa when he came to New York in 1960 for a United Nations conference.

A little further down the street is Blumsteins, once the largest department store in Harlem. With its dilapidated frontage and peeling paintwork, it's hard to imagine this as the Macy's of the area, but indeed it was.

Manna's Restaurant on Lenox Avenue at 134th Street has a tremendous selection of fresh foods and drinks and is incredibly well priced.

Another major epicentre for Harlem is up on 135th to 137th Streets between Powell Boulevard and Malcolm X Boulevard. You can either walk from 125th Street or take the 2, 3 subway to 135th Street station. Once there you'll find yourself right outside the Schomburg Center, which chronicles the history of black people in North America, South America and the Caribbean. Opposite is the Harlem Hospital Center where Martin Luther King was operated on after being shot. It was the first hospital in New York to be integrated rather than segregated.

A couple of blocks north and you'll find the famous Abyssinian Baptist

Church at 132 West 138th Street. It was originally founded in 1808, and as the blacks moved from the Lower East Side to Greenwich Village, then up to the West 50s and 60s before finally finding a home in Harlem, the church moved with them. This church was built in 1923 and, with Adam Clayton Powell Junior as its preacher for many years before he became a senator, it was a centre of political activity, particularly in the 1920s.

If you want to experience a gospel choir in action, THE place to go is the Abyssinian Church on 138th Street, but you'll need to arrive early because it gets packed. Another great place is the Second Canaan Baptist on 110th and Lenox Avenue.

One block west on 138th and 139th Streets between Powell and Frederick Douglas Boulevards are the four rows of Stanford White houses built in 1891 and known as Striver's Row because this is where the middle and upper classes strove to live. The houses were filled by doctors, lawyers, nurses from Harlem Hospital, jazz musicians and politicians such as Malcolm X. Boxer Harry Wills, known as the Brown Panther, lived here. He was paid $50,000 **not** to fight Jack Dempsey when the mayor banned the fight because he thought a black boxer fighting a white man would lead to riots.

It is interesting to note that the alleys at the back of these buildings were originally created for parking horses and carriages. Houses were usually built back to back so the alleys are a rarity, but a boon for the current occupants who find the space extremely useful to park their BMWs. Nowadays you can still see the old signs that say 'Walk your horses' or 'Park your carriages'.

If you're concerned about wandering the streets of Harlem by yourself, try either a Big Onion Walking tour or a Harlem Spirituals bus tour.

DECLINE AND FALL

Sadly, the good times didn't last long and, from the 1940s to the 1960s, Harlem declined into an urban no-man's-land as a result of a lack of government support and racial conflict. The once-fine apartment blocks grew shabbier as landlords were either too unscrupulous or unable to afford to maintain them on the cheap rental income.

Eventually City Hall and certain businesses started investing in the area. In 1976 the city began reclaiming properties abandoned by landlords who couldn't afford to pay their taxes. You can still buy one of these blocks for $1 if you have the $2 million needed to renovate them. Fortunately, a lot already have been refurbished and with the influx of banks and even Starbucks, a small but important step towards 'gentrification' is taking place.

For some time the brownstones of Hamilton Heights and other neighbourhoods have been targeted by those trying to escape the substantial rents required to live elsewhere in Manhattan. There have been other significant developments, too. Former president Bill Clinton has his offices on 125th Street between Lenox and 5th Avenues (it's the one with the huge Gap advert down the side). He's always been a favourite with African-Americans because he did a lot for racial equality and was invited to move his offices to Harlem from Carnegie Hall. Former baseball star Magic Johnson has also been doing much to encourage a sense of pride in the community.

RENAISSANCE

Now many people are predicting a renaissance for Harlem and suggest house prices could sky-rocket within the next two to five years, though it's unlikely that would help the really poor people of Harlem. Other good things are happening, though. Old nightspots once frequented exclusively by the African-Americans have been bought up and are being earmarked for renovation, including the Renaissance Ballroom, which was once a neighbourhood institution. Everyone would watch the Harlem Rennies basketball team in action early in the evening, and then clean up to hit the nightclub to swing to the music of great musicians. It was shut in the 1940s, but is now owned by the Abyssinian Church who are hoping to renovate it.

Another major venue was Small's Big Apple jazz club. Its sister establishment, Small's Paradise, was a restaurant in the 1930s and 1940s. It was so popular and the dance floor so small that it was said people had to dance on a dime here. It enjoyed a revival from the 1960s and was where Professor du Bois, who once ran the National Association for Advancement of Coloured People, held a birthday party in the 1980s. It closed in the same decade, but is now owned by the Abyssinian and there's a chance it may reopen as a tourist centre.

HAMILTON HEIGHTS

This neighbourhood is up on the high ground north of Morningside Heights and is effectively the middle-class enclave of Harlem. It takes its name from Alexander Hamilton, the first secretary of the treasury to the newly formed United States of America. He lived here from 1802 until he was killed in a duel in 1804.

The area is now the home of City College, one of the senior colleges in the New York university system. It was founded in the 19th century to educate the children of the working classes and immigrants and used to be known as the poor man's Columbia. It used to be free, but now it charges $3,000 per term, though that is still a lot cheaper than private universities, which charge around $25,000 per year.

Further north on West 145th Street off Amsterdam is the area known as Sugar Hill, which was made famous in the Duke Ellington song *Take the A Train to Sugar Hill.* Now a conservation area, it is filled with beautiful brownstone townhouses, and was dubbed Sugar Hill because life here was considered to be so sweet.

Go to Chapter 13 on page 181 to find detailed walking tours around Manhattan.

CHAPTER 4

Seeing the Sights

The major sights are often the number one priority – especially for first-time visitor – so to try to make your life a little easier I have indicated the location of each of the following sights. I suggest you read Chapter 3 so you get a good feel for each of the neighbourhoods and that way you can make the most of your time by planning your days in specific areas of the city. For instance, if you plan to see the Empire State Building, bear in mind it is close to the Morgan Library and deep in the heart of the 34th Street shopping district.

Sadly, but completely appropriately, many sights and buildings have tightened security arrangements following the tragic events of September 11. For this reason you should allow extra time when planning your schedules.

The sights mentioned have been listed according to their popularity. I have not included in this chapter the many museums and galleries or shopping 'Meccas' that are also worth visiting. It is best to read the other chapters dealing with these, too, before deciding what you want to do for a day. Finally, make sure you read the section entitled Orientation (see page 22), to help you make sense of those New York streets! Once you get your head tuned into the grid system, it will all become second nature.

THE BIG ONES

EMPIRE STATE BUILDING
34th Street

✉ 350 5th Avenue at 34th Street
☎ 212-736 3100
www.esbnyc.com
🚗 Subway B, D, F, Q, N, R, W to 34th Street
🕒 9.30am–midnight, last lifts go up at 11.15pm
$ Entrance $9 adults, $7 over 60s, $4 5–11s, under fives free. No credit cards

It is hard to believe that the Empire State, which was for almost 40 years the world's tallest building, was nearly not built at all. Just weeks after its building contract was signed in 1929, the Wall Street Crash brought the financial world to its knees. Fortunately, the project went ahead and was even completed 45 days ahead of schedule, rising to 443m (1,454ft) tall in 1931. The lobby interior features art seco design incorporating rare marble imported from Italy, France, Belgium and Germany. A six-year-long renovation was recently completed at a cost of $67 million – $26 million more than the whole original building cost!

Fancy a drink when you're in the Empire State area? To avoid the pricey snack bars in the Empire State, get back down to ground level and visit the Starbucks next door.

There are two observation decks, one on the 86th floor and another on the 102nd floor. Sadly, they recently decided to close the higher deck. Your best bet is to arrive as early in the morning as possible (it opens at 9.30am) to avoid long waits. Weekends, of course, get really crowded. Once you reach the 86th floor you can enjoy some fabulous views of Manhattan and the outer boroughs and really get your bearings.

You buy your tickets on the concourse level below the main lobby, but don't have to use them on the same day. The building now also has two virtual reality rides that simulate a flight around the skyscrapers and bridges of New York. The New York SkyRide is found on the second floor and is open seven days a week 10am–10pm. Entrance $13.50 adults, $10.50 4–12s.

GROUND ZERO

Financial District

✉ West Street between Liberty and Vesey Streets

☎ Call NYC&Co for an update on 212-484 1200 or NYTAB at **www.nytab.com**

🚗 Subway 1,2 to Chambers Street

As the situation at Ground Zero changes monthly, even weekly at times, it is advisable to contact the tourist information offices above to find out where and when you can view the site.

STATUE OF LIBERTY AND ELLIS ISLAND IMMIGRATION MUSEUM

Battery Park

☎ 212-269 5755 **www.statueoflibertyferry.com**

🚗 Statue of Liberty and Ellis Island Ferry, which leaves every 20 minutes from Gangway 5 in Battery Park Subway 4, 5 to Bowling Green

🕘 8.30am–5.30pm

$ $10 adults, $8 seniors, $4 for 4–12s, under threes free. No credit cards

The Statue of Liberty is one of the biggest attractions in New York and well worth seeing along with the Ellis Island Museum, as the latter will give an excellent insight into the immigration story of America – and the psyche of the average American. There is one ferry which takes you first to the Statue of Liberty and then on to Ellis Island. To get your tickets you need to go to Castle Clinton, the low, circular brownstone building in Battery Park. It is open 9am–3.30pm, which coincides with the last boat departure. New security measures will add up to an hour in waiting time and backpacks and other luggage are no longer allowed on the ferries.

Combination tickets giving entry to both the Empire State Observatory and the SkyRide cost $17 for adults and just $10 for children.

The ferry stops off at the Statue of Liberty first and the best time to get your photos of the green lady is while you are still on the boat. At the moment there is no access to the interior of the statue and it seems it may stay closed for some time to come.

Don't spoil your day of sightseeing by missing the boat. The last Statue of Liberty and Ellis Island Museum boat leaves at 3.30pm and the museum closes at 5.30pm. Only the first ferry of the day gives you access to the crown of the statue.

Once you've looked at the exterior and taken your photos you may be hungry or in need of a WC break, but if you can, I'd advise you to wait until you get to Ellis Island. The Statue of Liberty café is extremely small and there are simply not enough loos. There is space to eat outside, but not very much. At Ellis Island you'll find plenty of WCs on all the different levels, a large café and a huge

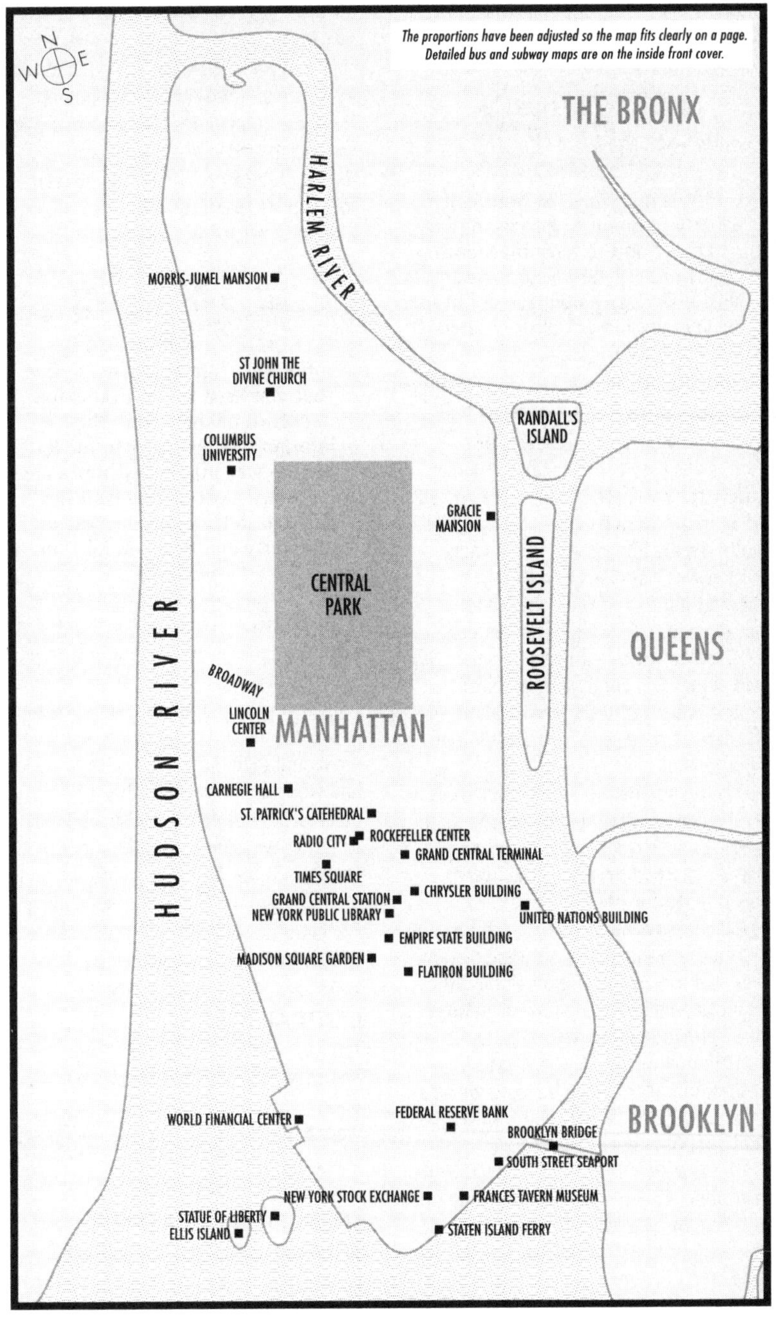
The proportions have been adjusted so the map fits clearly on a page.
Detailed bus and subway maps are on the inside front cover.
N
W
E
S
THE BRONX
HARLEM RIVER
MORRIS-JUMEL MANSION
ST JOHN THE DIVINE CHURCH
RANDALL'S ISLAND
COLUMBUS UNIVERSITY
GRACIE MANSION
CENTRAL PARK
ROOSEVELT ISLAND
QUEENS
HUDSON RIVER
BROADWAY
LINCOLN CENTER
MANHATTAN
CARNEGIE HALL
ST. PATRICK'S CATEHEDRAL
RADIO CITY
ROCKEFELLER CENTER
GRAND CENTRAL TERMINAL
TIMES SQUARE
GRAND CENTRAL STATION
CHRYSLER BUILDING
NEW YORK PUBLIC LIBRARY
UNITED NATIONS BUILDING
EMPIRE STATE BUILDING
MADISON SQUARE GARDEN
FLATIRON BUILDING
WORLD FINANCIAL CENTER
FEDERAL RESERVE BANK
BROOKLYN BRIDGE
BROOKLYN
SOUTH STREET SEAPORT
NEW YORK STOCK EXCHANGE
FRANCES TAVERN MUSEUM
STATUE OF LIBERTY
ELLIS ISLAND
STATEN ISLAND FERRY

Major sights in Manhattan

amount of outdoor seating which looks right out over the Statue of Liberty and the skyscrapers of Lower Manhattan.

When leaving the Statue of Liberty to go on to Ellis Island DO NOT get on the ferry that takes you to New Jersey. That is on the left. It IS clearly signposted, but it is very easy to get disorientated!

The Ellis Island Immigration Museum is the most visited museum in New York, particularly beloved by crowds of Americans who come to take a look at where their immigrant ancestors arrived. In use from 1892 to 1954, it 'processed' up to 10,000 immigrants a day. Each person was examined and then interviewed to find out if they could speak English. A luckless two per cent were turned away - mostly because they had simple but contagious medical conditions that led the immigration authorities to believe they wouldn't be able to work.

Visitors follow the immigrants' route as they entered the main baggage room and went up to the Registry and then the Staircase of Separation. Poignant exhibits include photos, video clips, jewellery, clothing, baggage and the stark dormitories. The Immigrant Wall of Fame lists half a million names, including the grandfathers of Presidents Washington and Kennedy, whose descendants contributed to the $150-million restoration of the main building with its copper roof and railway station-like glass and wrought-iron entrance.

This is a great museum and well worth allocating a good portion of your day to. All the films and the guided tour are free. The Ranger Tours last 45 minutes and leave at 11am, 2pm, 3pm and 4pm. At 2pm there is a re-enactment of a board of inquiry, which decides an immigrant's fate. The movie, *Island of Hope, Island of Tears* runs in Theater 1 at 30 minutes past the hour every hour 9.30am–3.30pm and lasts 45 minutes. It also runs on the hour in Theater 2, 10am–4pm. There is also a play, *Embracing Freedom, The Immigrant Journey to America,* which can be seen at 10.30am, 11.15am, 12.15pm, 1.15pm, 2.45pm and 3.30pm.

The tour, film and play are free but you need to get tickets for each of them from the information desk (just to the left on your way in). Busiest times are obviously just after a boat has arrived, so try to be the first off the ferry and head straight for the desk.

The museum is very well laid out, has lots of benches everywhere and is so big it never feels too crowded. If you're on a tight schedule and don't have much time to see the museum, turn right when you arrive and take the lift to the third floor and work your way down. It's the quickest way of doing it. Also, you may like to know there is an ATM in the corridor on the way to the café, which is on your right as you enter the building. The café is a little pricey but you can bring your own picnic and sit outside and enjoy the fabulous views.

CENTRAL PARK

Think of New York and Central Park immediately springs to mind. It's the playground of New Yorkers and a wonderful place to spend time during your stay. For a complete description of the park and all its facilities, see page 172.

TIMES SQUARE AND THE THEATRE DISTRICT

Another iconic area of New York and a must-see place. Full details of what to see and do are given on pages 132–48

ROCKEFELLER CENTER

Midtown

✉ Midtown at 5th Avenue
West 48th to West 50th Streets
between 5th and 6th Avenues

☎ 212-632 3975

🚗 Subway B, D, F, V to 47th–50th Streets/Rockefeller Center

Built in the art deco style in the 1930s, the Center was named after the New York benefactor whose fortune paid for its construction. As well as Radio City Music Hall (see below), it houses opulent office space, restaurants, bars, shopping on several levels and even gardens. To help you find your way round the 19 buildings that make up the Center, collect a map at the lobby of the main building (30 Rockefeller Center). At Christmas time, the central plaza is turned into an ice rink and a massive Christmas tree with 8km (5 miles) of fairy lights draws huge crowds. And for those of you who like to get your Metropolitan Museum shop 'fix' while in New York, you don't need to schlep all the way to the Upper East Side, as there is a branch of the shop just off the main Rockefeller Center Plaza by the ice rink.

RADIO CITY MUSIC HALL

Midtown at 6th Avenue

✉ 50th Street and 6th Avenue

☎ 212-247 4777
www.radiocity.com

🚗 Subway B, D, F, V to 47th–50th Streets/Rockefeller Center

🕒 Tours Mon to Sat 10am–5pm, Sun 11am–5pm

$ Entrance $12 adults, $6 children

While you're at the Rockefeller Center, you won't want to miss out on this fabulous building, which has been fully restored to its original art deco movie palace greatness and is utterly beautiful. This is where great films such as *Gone With The Wind* were given their premieres and it has the largest screen in America. Make a point of visiting the loos – they have a different theme on each floor, from palm trees to Chinese and floral. There are even cigar-theme loos for the boys. On the tour you are shown around the whole building and then introduced to a Rockette.

To see the Radio City Music Hall, you have to buy your ticket in the morning to see what time your tour is, but it is well worth planning your day around this.

NBC TOURS

Rockefeller Center/Midtown

✉ Lobby level of 30 Rockefeller Plaza

☎ 212-664 7174

🚗 Subway B, D, F, V to 47th–50th Streets/Rockefeller Center

🕒 Mon to Sat 9.30am–4.30pm

$ Entrance $8.25

Another 'sight' at the Rockefeller Center; this gives a brief, not very detailed look behind the scenes at NBC.

MADAME TUSSAUD'S

Times Square

✉ 234 West 42nd Street

☎ 212-512 9600
www.madame-tussauds.com

🚗 Subway A, C, E, 1, 2, 3, 7, N, Q, R, S, W to Times Square/42nd Street

🕒 Daily 10am–8pm. Last tickets sold at 6pm

$ Entrance $19.95 adults, $17.95 for 60 and over, $15.95 children 4–12

Madame Tussaud's has been spreading its wings around the globe and has recently opened attractions in Las Vegas, Hong Kong, and this one in New York. If wax models (albeit extremely well done) are your thing, then it is worth visiting this new sight in the heart of New York's Times Square as the celebs reflect personalities synonymous with the city, such as Woody Allen, Leonard Bernstein, Jacqueline Kennedy Onassis, John D Rockefeller, Yoko Ono, Donald Trump, Andy Warhol and former mayor Rudolph Giuliani.

I can't stress enough how important it is always to carry water around with you whether you are sightseeing or shopping. No matter what the weather, it is incredibly easy to get dehydrated.

NASDAQ MARKETSITE

Times Square

✉ 4 Times Square between 43rd Street and Broadway
☎ 877-627 3271
🚗 Subway 1, 2, 3, 7, N, Q, R, S, W to 42nd Street/Times Square
⏲ Mon to Thurs 9am–8pm, Fri 9am–10pm, Sat 10am–10pm, Sun 10am–8pm
$ Entrance $7. $2 discount with your NYCard

This wall of light soars seven storeys above Broadway. Guided tours inside give you a chance to see the robot-controlled television studios used by all the major networks to report market news. Upstairs you can watch a film about Nasdaq, the world's first electronic stock market, and test your investing savvy while playing an interactive computer.

BRONX ZOO

A wonderful zoo, which combines conservation and ecological awareness with Disney-style rides and a children's zoo. Further details are given on page 219.

NEW YORK BOTANICAL GARDEN

Home to the Bronx River Gorge, it not only gives a fascinating insight into the geological history of New York, but also has acres and acres of beautiful gardens. Further details are given on page 218.

HISTORIC RICHMOND TOWN AND ST MARK'S PLACE, STATEN ISLAND

The two top historical sights on Staten Island, both give a unique insight into the New York of yesteryear. Further details are given on page 223.

TICKET TO RIDE

The CityPass is an excellent way to avoid long queues and save money if you visit at least three of the following: the American Museum of Natural History, the Empire State Building, the *Intrepid* Sea-Air-Space Museum, the Guggenheim Museum and the Museum of Modern Art. Additions include the Whitney Museum of American Art and Circle Line harbour tour either for a day cruise around the Statue of Liberty or a city lights cocktail cruise of the Manhattan skyline. You can buy a CityPass from any participating attraction for $38 (normal value $85) for adults and $31 for 12–17s. For more information call 707-256 0490 or look at the website **www.citypass.com**.

SOUTH STREET SEAPORT

Financial District

✉ Water Street to the East River between John Street and Peck Slip
☎ 212-732 7678
🚗 Subway A, C, J, M, Z, 1, 2, 4, 5 to Fulton St–Broadway Nassau

You don't have to pay to enter the museum to get a feeling of the maritime history of the city – the ships are all around you. The Seaport is a rare New York approximation of a typical American shopping mall and is full of dining options. You can even eat outside, overlooking the Brooklyn Bridge. It's also worth noting that the area is both home to the South Street Seaport Museum (see page 110) and the 150-year-old Fulton Fish Market, which brings the entire area to (somewhat smelly!) life from midnight to 8am. From April to October tours are available at 6am on the first and third Thursdays of the month, though you must reserve your $10 tickets in advance. Tel 212-748 8590.

STATEN ISLAND FERRY

Battery Park

✉ Ferry Terminal, Battery Park

☎ 718-815 2628

🚗 Subway 5 to Bowling Green; N, R to Whitehall Street

$ No charge

Probably the best sightseeing bargain in the world, it passes close to the Statue of Liberty and gives dramatic views of Downtown. Runs 24 hours a day.

BUILDINGS OF NOTE

BROOKLYN BRIDGE

This Gothic creation was considered one of the modern engineering feats of the world when it was completed in 1883 after 16 long years of construction, and at the time was both the world's largest suspension bridge and the first to be built of steel.

For a completely different 'insider' view of the modern-day history of Brooklyn Bridge, try Gary Gorman's Brooklyn Bridge tour. A former member of the NYPD, he relates fascinating stories of talking down would-be suicide victims (see page 73).

The original engineer, John A Roebling, died even before the project began and his son, who took over, had to oversee the building from his Brooklyn apartment after being struck down by the bends. In all, 20 people died during the construction of the bridge. Take the A or C train to High Street station and stroll back on the walkway – a great way to see some incredible views of the downtown skyscrapers.

CHRYSLER BUILDING

Midtown

✉ 405 Lexington Avenue at 42nd Street

🚗 Subway S, 4, 5, 6, 7 to Grand Central/42nd Street

Opened in 1930, this was William van Alen's homage to the motor car. At the foot of the art deco skyscraper are brickwork cars with enlarged chrome hubcaps and radiator caps. Inside, see its marble and chrome lobby and inlaid-wood elevators. Its needle-like spire is illuminated at night and the building vies with the Empire State for the prettiest-of-them-all crown.

Just across the way from the Federal Reserve Bank is probably the poshest McDonald's in the world at 160 Broadway. It has doormen, a chandelier and a grand piano upstairs.

FEDERAL RESERVE BANK

Financial District

✉ 33 Liberty Street between William and Nassau Streets

☎ 212-720 6130

🚗 Subway 4, 5 to Wall Street

Yes, this really is the place where billions of dollars' worth of gold bars are stashed (as stolen by Jeremy Irons in *Die Hard 3*) on behalf of half the countries of the world and where they print money. Security, as you can imagine, is tight, but you can still do a free one-hour tour, providing you phone at least seven days in advance. Your name will be placed on a computer list, but the minimum age is 16. Passport or picture identification is essential.

FLATIRON BUILDING
Flatiron District

✉ 175 5th Avenue between 22nd and 23rd Streets

🚗 Subway F, V, N, R, 6 to 23rd Street

The Renaissance palazzo building was the first-ever skyscraper when it was completed in 1902 and is held up by a steel skeleton.

GRACIE MANSION
Yorkville

✉ Carl Schurz Park, 88th Street at East End Avenue

☎ 212-570 4751

🚗 Subway 4, 5, 6 to 86th Street

Now the official residence of the mayor, you must phone ahead to make an appointment to see it and it's only open on Wednesdays, March to November. The tour takes you through the mayor's living room, a guest suite and smaller bedrooms. The best part, though, is the view down the river.

GRAND CENTRAL STATION
Midtown

✉ East 42nd Street between Lexington and Vanderbilt Avenues

🚗 Subway S, 4, 5, 6, 7 to Grand Central/42nd Street

Even if you're not going anywhere by train, this huge, vaulted station, which was opened in 1913, is well worth a visit. A $196-million, two-year renovation programme was recently completed and the ceiling once again twinkles with the stars and astrological symbols of the night skies, and to the chandeliers, marble balusters and clerestory windows of the main concourse. It now also houses a Mediterranean restaurant, Michael Jordan's Steakhouse and a cocktail lounge modelled on a Florentine palazzo. The lower level dining concourse offers meals to take away, while shopping outlets include Banana Republic, Godiva chocolates and Kenneth Cole. Complete your trip to this elegant edifice by tucking in at the Oyster Bar.

If you go to Grand Central Station on a Wednesday at 12.30pm, you can go on a free tour sponsored by the Municipal Arts Society. Tel 212-935 3960.

MADISON SQUARE GARDEN'S ALL ACCESS TOUR
34th Street

✉ 4 Pennsylvania Plaza

☎ 212-465 6741
www.thegarden.com

🚗 Subway A, C, E, 1, 2, 3 to 34th Street/Penn Station

$ Entrance $15 adults, $12 children 12 and under

This is the round building that sits right on top of Penn Station and the entrance is on 7th Avenue between 32nd and 33rd Streets. It occupies the site of the original Pennsylvania Station, an architectural masterpiece that was even more beautiful than Grand Central Station, but which was razed in the 1960s. (One good thing came out of its destruction, though, the creation of the Landmarks Preservation Commission, which has helped to protect many buildings and areas in New York from developers.)

If you plan to see the Empire State Building, do the New York Skyride and take in Madison Square Garden's All Access Tour, buy a combination discount ticket for $28 adults, $21 for 5-12s, from either the New York Skyride or Madison Square Garden box offices. You'll save $4.50 and $3.50 respectively.

Madison Square Garden's arena is 10 storeys tall, covers 3.24 hectares (8 acres) and is famous for its circular ceiling, which is suspended by 48 bridge-like

Above: New York Hilton

Right: The steps of the New York Public Library

Below: Ellis Island Immigration Museum

Above: Statue of Liberty

Above right: Empire State Building and the Chrysler Building

Right: Rockefeller Center

Top: East River skyline
Above: Times Square
Right: Broadway

Above: Brooklyn Bridge

Below: New York Botanical Garden

FANTASTIC FUN FOR FREE

You don't have to pay for everything in New York and while summer is generally the best time for free concerts and plays – particularly in Central Park – there are good freebies to be bagged at other venues all year round. Here are a few:

Museum of American Folk Art: Enjoy folk paintings, furniture, pottery, quilts and other decorative arts from the 18th century to the present. Entrance free Tues to Sun until 7.30pm. Tel 212-595 9533, or visit **www.folkartmuse.org.**

Cooper-Hewitt National Museum of Design: (see page 104) Historical and contemporary designs can be viewed for free on Tuesday evenings 5–9pm. Tel 212-849 8400 or see their website at **www.si.edu/ndm.**

Take a guided tour with a Big Apple Greeter: Get a feel for New York as a real New Yorker sees it (see page 77).

World Financial Center's Winter Garden: (see page 67) Enjoy concerts and dance performances under huge palm trees at this stunning, glass-enclosed shopping and business complex on Lower Manhattan's waterfront. Special summer events are held out of doors. Tel 212-945 0505, or visit **www.worldfinancialcenter.com.**

New York Mercantile Exchange: Watch millions of dollars-worth of commodities change hands. Monday to Friday trading at the Comex Division is 8.30am–2.30pm, trading at the Nymex Division is 9.30am–9.30pm. North End Avenue, World Financial Center, NY, NY10282-1101. Tel 212-299 2499 or visit **www.nymax.com**.

See a taping of a TV show: By calling in advance, you can attend free tapings of popular TV shows like *Late Night with David Letterman* (tel 212-975 5853) and *The Montel Williams Show* (tel 212-830 0364).

Rockefeller Center: (see page 61) Explore a famous art deco masterpiece on a free, self-guided tour of this majestic building. Pick up maps in the main lobby at 30 Rockefeller Center where you can also enjoy the summer gardens or view the spectacular Christmas tree during the holiday season. Tel 212-698 2950.

Union Square Green Market: Taste farm-fresh produce, home-made breads, cheeses, cider and more; some vendors offer free samples. Tel 212-477 9220.

6th Avenue Antiques Market: Browse for bargains at the famous market between 24th and 27th Streets (free admission weekends only). Other outdoor markets include the famous fleas at Columbus Avenue and West 76th Street (Sundays only) and the weekend market on Houston Street between Sullivan and Thompson.

New York Philharmonic, City Opera, Shakespeare in the Park: Revel in the best classical music, jazz, drama, opera and dance that New York has to offer at free warm-weather performances in the city parks by these and many more. Tel 212-360 3444.

Cathedral of St John the Divine: See the world's largest Gothic cathedral, near Columbia University in Harlem and explore its Biblical garden and children's sculpture garden. Tel 212-316 7540, or visit **www.stjohndivine.org.**

New York Public Library: (see page 66) Explore thought-provoking exhibitions at this breathtaking Beaux Arts library. Tel 212-592 7000. Time your visit well and you could then enjoy free concerts, outdoor movies and other special events in the adjacent Bryant Park. Tel 212-983 4142.

Battery Park Promenade: (see page 183) Catch the breeze and enjoy stunning views of New York Harbour and the Statue of Liberty. In nearby Hudson River Park, the Battery Park City Authority presents a Sounds at Sunset summer series of poetry readings, cabaret and classical music. Tel 212-416 5394.

cables. Every year it hosts 500 events from concerts to boxing, wrestling, basketball and hockey, bringing in five million people. Its most famous residents are the New York Knickerbockers (known as the Knicks), basketball team, the New York Rangers ice hockey team and the New York Liberty women's pro basketball team.

Below the arena are the theatre, exhibition centre, box office and two club restaurants. Incidentally, this is actually the fourth Madison Square Garden building. The first two were built at Madison Square on the site of the current New York Life Building, the third was built on 8th Avenue between 49th and 50th Streets, a site now home to the Worldwide Plaza, and this building opened in 1968 with a gala featuring Bob Hope and Bing Crosby.

During the course of the one-hour tour, you will hear about its history, see the inner workings, gain access to the locker rooms of both the Knicks and the Rangers and the Walk of Fame.

MERCHANT'S HOUSE MUSEUM

East Village

- ✉ 29 East 4th Street
- ☎ 212-777 1089
  www.marchantshouse.com
- 🚗 Subway 6 to Astor Place
- 🕘 Thurs to Mon 1pm–5pm
- $ Entrance $5 adults, $3 students and children

Built in 1832, this was home to prosperous merchant Seabury Tredwell and his family for nearly 100 years.

MORRIS JUMEL MANSION

Harlem

- ✉ Roger Morris Park, 65 Jumel Terrace at 160th Street
- ☎ 212-923 8008
- 🚗 Subway B, C to 163rd Street
- 🕘 Wed to Sun 10am–4pm
- $ Entrance $3 adults, $2 children. Two-for-one admittance with your NYCard

Built by British colonel Roger Morris in 1765, this is the oldest house in Manhattan. It was confiscated by George Washington in 1776 and briefly used as his war headquarters until the Brits kicked him out of New York. Charles Dickens visited it, and if you want to see a really historical sight so should you!

NEW YORK PUBLIC LIBRARY

Midtown

- ✉ 5th Avenue between 40th and 42nd Streets
- ☎ 212-592 7000
- 🚗 Subway B, D, F, V, S, 4, 5, 6, 7 to 42nd Street

Opened in 1911, this is one of the best examples of the city's Beaux Arts architecture. Inside you'll find more than 8.5 million volumes guarded by the twin marble lions of Patience and Fortitude.

The steps up to the New York public library are a sun trap during the day and a great place for a sandwich or drink stop.

NEW YORK STOCK EXCHANGE

Financial District

- ✉ 20 Broad Street at Wall Street
- ☎ 212-656 3000
- 🚗 Subway 4, 5 to Wall Street; J, M, Z to Broad Street
- $ Entrance free, but you need tickets, which are handed out from 9am, so go early

Amazing fact: the stock exchange was founded by 24 brokers meeting beneath a tree; now more than 1,300 members crowd on to the building's trading floor. It's still an interesting place to visit. At the time of going to press, the stock exchange was closed to the public, though this may change, so call to check.

TRUMP TOWER

Midtown

- ✉ 5th Avenue between 56th and 57th Streets
- 🚗 Subway F, N, R, Q, W to 57th Street

Donald Trump's monument to opulence includes an extravagant pink marbled atrium with waterfalls and plenty of upmarket shops. This is not to be confused with Trump International Hotel and Tower at Columbus Circle.

UNITED NATIONS BUILDING
Midtown

- ✉ 1st Avenue and 46th Street
- ☎ 212-963 4440 for tour reservations
- 🚗 Subway 6 to 51st Street; Grand Central/42nd Street
- 🕐 Jan to March 9am–5pm
- $ $7.50 adults, $6 seniors, $5 students and children

Tours of the General Assembly, the Economic and Social Council and other areas every half hour. Despite its fame, this is not the most exciting tour in the world! No children under 5.

WOOLWORTH BUILDING
Civic Center/Financial District

- ✉ 233 Broadway at Park Place
- 🚗 Subway 1, 2 to Park Place; N, R to City Hall

There is no official tour of the city's second skyscraper, which was built in 1913 at a cost of $13.5 million, but it's worth taking a sneak look inside the lobby. Incidentally, one-time shop assistant FW Woolworth's building was derided as a 'cathedral of commerce' when it opened, but the millionaire took this as a compliment. Just to prove a point, he can be seen counting his money in the carved ceilings.

The Winter Garden is not just a pretty place to enjoy a drink or two – it also has a series of free concerts and fairs.

WINTER GARDEN AT THE WORLD FINANCIAL CENTER
Battery Park City

- ✉ 250 Vesey Street at West Street
- ☎ 212-945 0505
- 🚗 Subway N, R to Cortlandt Street

The World Financial Center is actually the main focal point for Battery Park City, a strip of land running down the west side of Lower Manhattan from Chambers Street to South Park. It was created by landfill from the digging work required to build the foundations for the World Trade Center. Now the World Financial Center has its own complex of four office towers, but is most famous for the beautiful glass-roofed Winter Garden that looks out right over the pretty boats moored in North Cove. Filled with fabulous palm trees, it is also home to upscale shops including Anne Taylor, Urban Athletics and Gap Kids.

Come also for Sunday brunch or drinks at the Hudson River Club, which has fabulous views over the harbour. It's pricey, though. Drinks are from $10.

RELIGIOUS BUILDINGS

CATHEDRAL OF ST JOHN THE DIVINE
Morningside Heights

- ✉ 1047 Amsterdam Avenue at 112th Street
- ☎ 212-316 7540 **www.stjohndivine.org**
- 🚗 Subway 1 to 110th Street
- 🕐 Mon to Sat 7am–6pm, Sun 7am–8pm. Public tours run from Tues to Sat at 11am and on Sun at 1pm
- $ Entrance free but tours cost $3

The world's largest Gothic cathedral also has one of the world's largest rose windows with 10,000 pieces of glass.

For some of the best views in Manhattan outside of the Empire State Building, go on a Vertical Tour at the Cathedral of St John the Divine. A nice little bonus is that you'll know your money goes to help people in the community.

Even more amazing are the main bronze doors, which weigh 3,000 tonnes each and are only opened for an official visit by the bishop. It is an Episcopal church built in 1892 and has 4.9 hectares (12 acres) of land, which includes its school and accommodation for the clergy. A lot of people will tell you that the church, according to its original plans, is still not complete. The reality is rebuilding never will be finished because the church prefers to channel its funds into helping the poor and needy. Still, it's not as if they are ever going to run out of space. It has a capacity to seat 3,000 people, but because it holds so many art and performing art events, they have chairs rather than pews.

The more adventurous may want to tackle the Vertical Tours, which run on the first and third Saturdays of each month at noon and 2pm. You climb 38m (124ft) up spiral stone staircases to the top of the cathedral for spectacular views. Cost is $10, phone 212-932 7347 to reserve your place!

One of the highlights of the cathedral's calendar is the Feast of Assisi when real animals including an elephant and a llama are taken up to the altar to be blessed by the cathedral clergy. Inspired by St Francis of Assisi, whose life exemplified living in harmony with the natural world, the feast usually takes place on the first Sunday in October.

You can see both St John the Divine and Riverside Church in our Morningside Heights Mini Tour in Chapter 14 Walking Tours of Manhattan (see page 214).

At the back of the cathedral, behind the main altar, are seven different chapels, which represent different countries in Europe. These are used for weddings, christenings and the services (at least two a day). The shop is also at the back on the left-hand side and money raised from it is put towards the church's housing and other ministries. There are plenty of WCs at the back of the shop along with drinks machines.

RIVERSIDE CHURCH

Morningside Heights

✉ Riverside Drive between 120th and 122nd Streets

🚗 Subway 1, B, C to 116th Street

Famous for having the world's largest tuned bell and its Carillon concerts on Sundays at 12.30pm and 3pm. You can also go for the great views of Upper Manhattan and the Hudson River. Nearby is the Theological Seminary at West 120th and Broadway. Woody Allen likes to use this façade in many of his movies.

ST PATRICK'S CATHEDRAL

Midtown

✉ 5th Avenue and 50th Street

🚗 Subway 6 to 51st Street and E, V to 5th Avenue/53rd Street

The seat of New York's Catholic Archdiocese, it took 21 years to build, but the impressive design and gorgeous stained glass windows were definitely worth the wait.

The steps leading up to St Patrick's form a perfect picnic spot for a lunch or snack stop.

TOURS

Time is a precious commodity when visiting New York, so you want to make sure any tour you take pays for itself both financially and in terms of time. Your choice of tours will depend on whether it is your first, second or third visit to the city. For instance, newcomers need to get their bearings and two ways of doing this are to take a boat tour, which goes in a semi-circle around Manhattan from Midtown on one side to

Midtown on the other, and a bus tour, such as Gray Line's Manhattan Essential New York tour is known as the New York 101 (101 being slang for a first-year university course) because it covers so much of the city in one day. An alternative is the New York Visions tour, which takes a lot less time, is cheaper and is generally more fact-filled. Bus tours are also useful when you want to visit an area such as Harlem or the Bronx, but are unsure of your personal safety, in which case the Harlem Spirituals/New York Visions tours are your best bet. Then there are helicopter tours, which will certainly give you breathtaking views, but won't show you the full ins and outs of each area.

If you take a tour of New York, you are likely to hear the word 'stoop'. This is taken from a Dutch word by original settlers and refers to the steps up to a townhouse, such as a brownstone – another New York term, this time for much sought-after townhouses specifically made out of brown stone.

The reality is that the best way to see New York, get to know the city and find those interesting nooks and crannies is on foot, which possibly explains why the Big Onion walking tours are so popular – or it could be that they are just so darned good – and why so many people take advantage of the Big Apple Greeters, who can show you any area or sight you wish to visit. Taking a selection of these sorts of tours is definitely good for first and second timers, and given the broad selection of Big Onion tours available, there'll probably be a tour to interest you each time you go back. There are also bike tours, cemetery tours and a reasonable selection of food tours.

Then there's a new organisation called iMar, that co-ordinates unique insights into aspects of New York life through one of its inhabitants.

The following categories of tour have been put in alphabetical order for ease of use. Within each category I have started with what I consider to be the most important or useful tours.

It is appropriate to tip your tour guide around 15 per cent of the cost of the ticket, but don't feel obliged if you've not been over-impressed by them.

AIR TOURS

LIBERTY HELICOPTER TOURS

Chelsea

✉ VIP Heliport, West 30th Street and 12th Avenue

☎ 212-967 6464

🚗 Subway A, C, E to 34th Street/Penn Station

Simple bird's-eye-view tours of Manhattan cost $48 Mon to Thurs and $52 Fri to Sun. The most expensive tour, with views of all five boroughs and Ellis Island, costs $155 Mon to Thurs and $180 Fri to Sun.

BIKE TOURS

CENTRAL PARK BICYCLE TOURS AND RENTALS

Colombus Circle

✉ 59th Street and Broadway

☎ 212-541 8759

🚗 Subway A, B, C, D, 1, 2 to Columbus Circle/59th Street

$ $35 adults, $20 children (includes bike rental)

A two-hour bike tour of Central Park from April to November that includes stops at Shakespeare Garden, Strawberry Fields, Belevedere Castle and other sights, plus bike rentals.

CANAL STREET BICYCLE SHOP

Chinatown

✉ 6th Avenue at Canal Street
☎ 212-334 8000
🚗 Subway A, C, E to Canal Street

Rent your bike and head off to the Financial District, which is almost deserted on a Sunday.

Once you have your bike don't feel you have to cycle everywhere. You're allowed to take bikes on the subway so you can save your energy for the parks.

METRO BICYCLE

Upper West Side

✉ 231 West 96th Street
☎ 212-766 9222
🚗 Subway 1, 2, 3, A, C, B, D to 96th Street

If you want to check out the Upper West Side or the northern reaches of Central Park, this is the place to rent your bike.

PONYCABS

SoHo

✉ 517 Broome Street at Thompson Street
☎ 212-254 8844
🚗 Subway C, E to Spring Street, N, R to Prince Street
$ $15 for 30 minutes, $30 for 1 hour. Discount with your NYCard

Technically not bicycles, but three-man tricycles (one 'driver' to pedal and two passengers!). So amazing looking that even seen-it-all-before New Yorkers stop to stare. That may be a little off-putting for some, but I found it an excellent way to see SoHo without breaking into a sweat or breaking the bank! My Ponycab was powered by actor and teacher David Watkins, who was a mine of information about New York. Don't forget to tip – 'drivers' earn their money! In good weather only. You can either reserve in advance and arrange a meeting point or turn up at the hub.

BOAT TOURS

CIRCLE LINE

West Midtown

✉ Pier 83, West 42nd Street
☎ 212-563 3200
🚗 Subway A, C, E to 42nd Street

Tickets available for full island, semi-circle or sunset/harbour lights cruise. Prices start from $14 adults, $7 children 12 and under. In addition, you can take a three-hour Latin DJ dance cruise, a full-day cruise to Bear Mountain ($33 adults, $30 for 12 and under), a Seaport Liberty cruise and a Seaport live music cruise. $3 off all cruises with your NYCard.

The harbour cruises are very informative and give a great insight into Manhattan and beyond, but it can sometimes be hard to hear when you're on the upper deck. If you want to hear everything, it's probably best to stay inside.

NY WATERWAY

Financial District

✉ Pier 17 at South Street Seaport
☎ 800-533 3779
🚗 Subway J, M, Z, 1, 2, 4, 5 to Fulton Street

Harbour cruise prices start at $10 adults, $5 children and go up to $17 adults, $8 children. Discount of 15 per cent off all cruises with your NYCard.

Offers a wide variety of special sightseeing options all the year round, including New York Harbor cruises and evening cruises with on-board entertainment. Also available in the summer are day-trip cruises to Sandy Hook Beach and, for baseball fans, cruise packages that include a round-trip sail on the *Yankee Clipper* or *Mets Express*, tickets, souvenirs and the ubiquitous hot dog.

THE BEAST
Financial District

✉ Pier 16, South Street Seaport
☎ 212-563 3200
🚗 Subway J, M, Z, 1, 2, 4, 5 to Fulton Street
✉ Also Pier 83 West 42nd Street, West of Theater District
🚗 Subway A, C, E to 42nd Street
🕒 May to Oct, daily 10am to 7pm
$ Tickets $15 adults, $10 children. $3 discount with your NYCard

Take a spin on a thrilling speedboat ride for a quick and memorable tour of Lower Manhattan and see the sights fly by as you reach an incredible speed of 40mph. *The Beast* stops by the Statue of Liberty for photos. Boats leave on the hour.

BATEAUX NEW YORK
Chelsea

✉ Pier 61 at Chelsea Piers
☎ 212-352 2022
🚗 Subway C, E to 23rd Street
$ Brunch ticket $45, dinner $105–120, tax included

Indulge in a dinner (7pm–10pm daily) or brunch (noon–2pm weekends) cruise around Lower Manhattan.

WORLD YACHT DINNER CRUISES
Theater District

✉ Pier 81 at West 41st Street and Hudson
☎ 212-630 8100
🚗 Bus number 42 along 42nd Street
$ Tickets from $43.71 (Sunday brunch) to $70.47 dinner Sun to Thurs, $83.46 Fri and Sat. 10 per cent off with your NYCard

With menus created by a selection of New York's best chefs, linen table cloths, live music, a dance floor and world-class videos, this is an upmarket experience you are sure to enjoy. The cruise lasts three hours and also provides spectacular views of the harbour. Note that the dress code is smart and that jackets are required, so make sure you allow yourself time to get on your glad rags.

BUS TOURS

HARLEM SPIRITUALS/ NEW YORK VISIONS
Midtown

✉ 690 8th Avenue between West 43rd and West 44th Streets
☎ 212-391 0900
🚗 Subway A, C, E to 42nd Street

One of the most reputable tour companies in New York, the guides are highly qualified, great founts of knowledge and very friendly, while the buses are modern and comfortable with the all-important air conditioning.

The company started out purely as the Harlem Spirituals, one of the first to provide entertaining and genuine insights into what was a much-maligned area, and has done so well it has expanded to include the New York Visions, which provide tours of the rest of Manhattan as well as the Bronx and Brooklyn.

The Harlem Spirituals branch runs the gospel tours, which include combined walking (though not too far!) and riding tours of Harlem on Sunday when you attend a church service, hear a gospel choir and have brunch at a soul food restaurant, and weekday gospel tours with lunch. Heritage and jazz tours include a combined walking and riding tour through Harlem's historical sites, soul food and jazz lunches and a night at the Apollo.

From the moment the bus departs its Midtown starting point, the guide will be telling you a great deal about the sites and architecture all the way up the Upper West Side to Harlem. The tours also include Morningside Heights, the famous Sugar Hill Historic District, views of the Cathedral of St John the Divine, Striver's Row and the main drag of black Harlem - 125th Street between Lenox Avenue and Frederick Douglas Boulevard. Tickets cost $33–85 for adults, $23–50 for children, depending on the tour you choose. You can also obtain a discount with your NYCard.

The New York Visions branch runs a variety of other in-depth tours around the city, beginning with their New York, New York tour, which starts at 9.30am Monday to Saturday and finishes at 1.30pm – a respectable amount of time in which the tour covers all the major areas of New York from Morningside Heights, Upper West Side, 5th Avenue, the Rockefeller Center, Times Square, Greenwich Village, SoHo, Chinatown and the Financial District. You can either continue on to the Statue of Liberty and the Ellis Island Immigration Museum, stop off at the South Street Seaport for a spot of shopping or an exciting boat ride on *The Beast*, or return to Midtown in the coach. Tickets cost $35–43 for adults and $25–30 for children, depending on whether or not you choose to go to the Statue of Liberty. There is also a selection of combined Bronx and Brooklyn tours starting at $35 for adults and $23 for children.

If you plan to do the Statue of Liberty and Ellis Island Museum another day, why not end your New York Visions tour in Chinatown/Little Italy and take your pick of the many excellent cheap restaurants for a spot of lunch?

GRAY LINE

West Midtown

✉ 8th Avenue at 42nd Street
☎ 212-397 2600
www.graylinenewyork.com
🚗 Subway A, C, E to 42nd Street
$ Tours $26–75

The oldest sightseeing bus company in New York, it has much to offer the visitor, although the average tour guide gives very little information in comparison with the New York Visions tours. Still, if you don't want to be overwhelmed by information on your first visit to New York, then try the Essential New York tour ($69 adults, $48 children). A double-decker bus tour with 40 hop-on, hop-off steps, it comes with a choice of one-hour harbour cruises or ferry with close-up views of the Statue of Liberty and Ellis Island, a ticket to the Empire State Building and a one-day fun pass to New York's subway and bus systems.

Gray Line also offers other 'Loops', which run around Downtown, Midtown, Uptown and Brooklyn. You can do as few or as many as you like and the buses run all day 8.30am–5pm, so you can spend as long as you like in each area, giving you plenty of flexibility.

SEX AND THE CITY

Upper East Side

✉ Bus outside the Plaza Hotel in 5th Avenue at 59th Street
☎ 212-334 0492
www.nytix.com
🕒 Sat 2.30pm and 11am some Sundays
🚗 Subway 4, 5, 6, N, R, W to 59th Street/Lexington Avenue
$ $25

If you can't get enough of Carrie and co, then here's a chance to check out the stomping grounds of the girls from *Sex and the City*. During the three-hour bus tour, you'll visit D&G in SoHo, where Carrie shops for shoes, and the New York Sports Club where Miranda works out, and bars like Tao where Carrie, Samantha, Charlotte and Miranda do their flirting. Most importantly of all, you'll get some behind-the-scenes scoops on the show and the actors.

92ND STREET Y

Upper East Side

✉ 1395 Lexington Avenue

☎ 212-996 1100
www.92ndsty.org

🚗 Subway 4, 5, 6 to 86th Street

$ Prices vary

A Jewish organisation that caters to all aspects of Jewish life, it also runs a wide selection of tours covering every aspect of city life. They'll create a customised tour for you if you prefer.

CEMETERY TOURS

✉ PO Box 750841, New York, NY 11375

☎ 718-760 4000

$ Prices vary according to size of group

Okay, so technically this is not a bus tour as your mode of transportation will be a hearse, but it still has wheels and travels on roads... As the title indicates, you'll get a fully detailed tour of New York's cemeteries, visiting gravesites of well-known VIPs, celebrities, politicians and sports stars. Er, enjoy!

INSIDER TOURS

iMAR, THE INSIDER'S MARKETPLACE

☎ 212-334 2211 ext 101
www.iMar.com

One of the most exciting organisations in New York, this company runs tours with a difference – they are unique experiences of residents of New York who can impart great insider advice on everything from shopping to a debriefing from one of the FBI officers involved in bringing down Teflon Don John Gotti. In addition, they also offer some great services, such as saving you a good spot for you to enjoy the free Shakespeare in the Park series or even a spot to see the free Monday night films that are shown throughout the summer in Bryant Park (just look for the iMar balloon).

They have tours of a children's puppet theatre, a pub crawl of Hemingway's old haunts in the Village, insider tours of Brooklyn and the chance to attend a private pre-release screening of a Hollywood moviewith a top American movie critic.

All the tours and services are displayed on their website and can be booked either via the internet or over the phone.

Gangland Tours: Tel 718-349 6567 or 212-334 2211 ext 101. **www.ganglandtours.com.** Cost $85 each (minimum of two people).

Pace yourself. There's no point trying to pack so much into your day that you arrive back at your hotel exhausted with your head ringing. Less can often be more!

Take advantage of the fact that it's easy to get a table at a restaurant in the Village between 6 and 7pm to eat first, as this tour kicks off at 8.30pm and lasts about an hour and a half. Your 1.8m (6ft) guide Paul Zukowski greets you, in his three-piece pinstripe and spatz shoes, just outside Greenwich's famous Village Vanguard in Bleecker Street, where you pick up your white stretch limo. While you tour round the Village and the Lower East Side, he'll regale you with details of the gangsters who lived and worked on the streets of New York – and died on them. Despite the sometimes grim subject matter, I found it absolutely fascinating.

VIP tour of NYPD sites: Tel 212-334 2211 ext 101. **www.iMar.com.** Cost $30 each (minimum of four people).

Born in Brooklyn, your guide Gary Gorman is a former cop who shares a lifetime of knowledge and experience on the organisation and workings of the NYPD on this three-hour tour by car. You'll be shown all the major sights from the Mounted Unit HQ to the 9th Precinct (used in *Kojak* and *NYPD Blue*) and more. A charming and hugely knowledgeable guide, Gary makes this a brilliant way to spend an afternoon.

Foods of New York: Tel 212-334 5070, 212-334 2211 ext 101. **www.foodtours@aol.com.** Open Tues to Sat 11am–2pm. Cost $30 per person.
A great-value tour, considering the amount of food you eat along the way, with a friendly atmosphere as they only take a maximum of 16. Just some of the stores in the Village and SoHo you'll stop at to sample their wares are Zito's old-fashioned bread shop, Murray's famous cheese shop, and Faicco's world-famous pork shop, and you'll end up at Vintage New York on Broome Street, where you get the chance to taste five wines from New York State. And, as well as all you'll learn about the food of New York, especially of the Italian community, you'll gain hints about architecture and properties in the Village, and visit a real speakeasy.

In the unlikely event you still feel peckish after the food tour, head back to Fish at 280 Bleecker Street where you can get six oysters and a glass of wine or beer for an unbelievable $8.

Mystical World of Hassidic Jews: Hassidic Discovery Welcome Center, 305 Kingston Avenue, Brooklyn. Tel 718-953 5244, 1-800 838 TOUR or 212-334 2211 ext 101. **www.jewishtours.com.** Subway 3 to Kingston Avenue. Open Sun 10am–1pm for individuals or Sun to Thurs for groups of 10 or more. $36 per person.
The Lubavitcher Jewish community in Crown Heights, Brooklyn, is focused on sharing what they have with the outside world, hence this unique opportunity to get an insight into a Hassidic community. Guided by Rabbi Beryl Epstein – a man with a charming manner and great sense of humour – you'll hear about the history of the Hassidic Jews; visit the synagogue to learn about some of the Jewish customs and traditions; watch a scribe working on a Torah scroll; and see the Rebbe's library, a Matzoh bakery and a Hassidic art gallery. A real insight into a fascinating culture.

It's easy getting to the Hassidic Discovery Welcome Center by the 3 train (the red line), but allow about an hour from Midtown. The subway exit is right by the synagogue and you simply walk a few yards up Kingston Avenue to two brown doors just by a book shop. There is no dress code, but it would be inappropriate for women to turn up in a sleeveless top.

The Kingston Avenue subway stop for the Hassidic tour is just one away from Eastern Parkway, the subway stop for the Brooklyn Museum of Art and the Botanical Gardens – both great places to visit on a Sunday afternoon.

Jazz Nights and Sounds: Tel 212-334 2211 ext 101. **www.iMar.com.** Cost $25 per person.
With a collection of jazz records that would be the envy of any much-older collector and ranging from blues jazz to hard bop, Ryan Hawkins' forte is discussing all your musical likes and dislikes so he can build up a personal jazz collection for you. The following day, he'll send you a top 10 he's sure you'll like, and give you free updates so you can come back for more. He can also take you to a second-hand store, and tell you

ON THE LOOKOUT FOR SEX IN THE CITY?

Hey, we can't guarantee you'll get the fabulous lifestyle of Carrie and co, but we can tell you the *Sex and the City* hotspots.

Shopping

Patricia Field Boutique (see page 89)

Patricia Field is the designer who creates all of the fabulous fashion for the TV series, so anyone who emulates Carrie's style has to pay a visit. You can stock up on the cool bags and jewellery that the cast wear, in particular the Mia and Lizzie diamond horseshoe necklaces Carrie sported in the last series.

Tracey Feith (see page 89)

Sarah Jessica Parker wore one of Feith's red and blue silk creations in the last series and the shop sold out of the style in days.

Manolo Blahnik (see page 90)

No true *Sex and the City* experience would be complete without wearing a pair of towering Manolo heels. Check out the SJP ankle-strap stiletto named after the show's star.

Bars

Monkey Bar: 60 East 54th Street between Madison and Park Avenues. Tel 212-838 2600. Subway E, V to 5th Avenue. Area: Midtown.

The venue Mr Big and Carrie chose to discuss how to stay 'just friends' after their affair. It's very upmarket – think dark wood and a resident pianist – plus it has original murals of frolicking monkeys dating back to the 1930s (hence the name).

Tortilla Flats: 767 Washington Street at West 12th Street. Tel 212-243 1053. Subway 1, 9 Christopher Street. Area: West Village.

The ice-breaking date between Carrie and Aidan, accompanied by Miranda and Steve, was filmed at this Mexican party spot. Margaritas are the fashionable tipple.

Restaurants

Park View At The Boathouse (see page 126)

The episode where Mr Big and Carrie fell into the boating lake was shot in Manhattan's oasis of calm, Central Park. The Boathouse is often cited as one of the most romantic places in town by those in the know. You can have dinner, rent a boat or act like the locals, and sip a drink while the sun goes down over the skyscrapers.

Eleven Madison (see page 119)

One of New York's hottest eateries, this is where Mr Big chose to tell Carrie he was getting married to Natasha (the stick with no soul) over dinner. Carrie had one too many Cosmopolitans, the girl's favourite cocktail, and fell down the stairs as she walked out.

Nightclubs

Tunnel (see page 152)

Recreate the episode where Carrie and the girls decided they didn't want to stay in on a Saturday night and headed off to a gay club. Tunnel is wall-to-wall muscle, sweaty bare torsos and waving glow sticks to a background of hard house and banging techno.

Tours (see page 72)

all about the jazz-club scene in the Village, Harlem, Queens and Brooklyn. If you like, he'll organise a night out with you, though you'll have to pay your own entrance fees.

For more advice on choosing a jazz venue, see page 147.

WALKING TOURS

BIG ONION WALKING TOURS

✉ PO Box, 20561, Cherokee Station, New York, NY 10021-0070
☎ 212-439 1090
www.bigonion.com
🕘 Sat and Sun 1pm. Always call after 10.30am on the morning of your tour to verify schedule as it will change if the weather is bad
$ $12 adults, $10 students and over 60s

Amazingly informative ethnic, architectural and historic walking tours, which you can just turn up to. The company was set up by Seth Kamil, a doctoral candidate in American Urban & Ethnic History at Columbia University, in 1991 and all the guides hold advanced degrees in American history from Columbia or other New York Universities. These are not for the faint-hearted as you'll be on your feet for a full two hours, but they are informative and gem packed. Tours include the East Village, Central Park, Gay New York, Financial District, Gramercy Park and Union Square, Greenwich Village, Historic Lower Manhattan, Historic TriBeCa, The Jewish Lower East Side, Presidential New York, Revolutionary New York, Roosevelt Island, SoHo and NoLiTa and the Upper East Side. 'Big Onion' was the nickname given to New York in the 19th century by non-New Yorkers who believed it smelled because of the immigrants' heavily spiced cooking!

Some Big Onion tours can get a little crowded. If so, make sure you stand as close to the guide as possible to hear their pearls of wisdom and you'll still get good value for money.

Big Onion's Multi-ethnic Eating Tour: Meet on the corner of Essex and Delancey Streets. Subway J, M, Z to Essex Street, F to Delancey Street.

This is one of the more popular tours, which covers the Lower East Side, Chinatown and Little Italy, and anywhere between 60 and 100 people can turn up outside the Olympic Restaurant to be divided between two guides. Maybe it's because of the food, for which you pay no premium, and which includes delicious spicy tofu, Mozzarella and Italian sausage, chicken and shrimp and vegetarian dim sum, plus other food favourites of the locals – all eaten outdoors in the streets. But it is a good way to get an insight into areas you may not be entirely happy about wandering around on your own.

But even without the food, it gives a fascinating insight into the history of the area and what modern-day life is like. You'll see the immigrant school attended by both Walter Matthau and Tony Curtis, discover how 1,000 people used to live in just one square mile, find out about the old street peddlers and why they were banned by the city and see the new Garment District. And one of the things that is most striking about the area is the way new waves of immigrants take over the shops and buildings. What was once a very high-density Jewish area is now populated by Puerto Rican immigrants. And before the Jews and Chinese were the English, Irish and Italians.

You'll end the tour deep in the heart of Chinatown outside a vegetarian food

GREETINGS FROM THE BIG APPLE

It's certainly a novel idea and it's also a winner – the Big Apple Greeters are ready to take you on a personalised and entirely customised tour of any part of New York any day of the week and it costs absolutely nothing. The idea is simple: New Yorkers who are proud of their neighbourhoods and have a little spare time will spend between two and four hours with you. They will take you round any area you like and help you do just what you want to do, be it shopping, sightseeing or eating and drinking, rain or shine. This is an excellent way to orientate yourself in Manhattan or any part of the city that takes your fancy and is particularly good for the lone traveller in need of a little confidence boost. All you need to do is make your request at least 10 working days in advance (the more the better) and confirmation will be awaiting you upon your arrival at your hotel. The service is entirely free and no Big Apple Greeters worth their salt will take a tip, but I found that it was no problem to get them to agree to letting me pay for a spot of brunch or lunch. And they're well worth it.
Tel 212-669 8159, fax 212-669 3685
E-mail bigapple@tiac.net
Website **www.bigapplegreeter.org**

centre and the Chinese Gourmet Bakery. It may be good to stop for a drink before you head off to the nearest subway stops at Canal Street. You have the A, C, E, J, M, N, Q, R, W, 6 lines to take you just about anywhere in Manhattan.

Big Onion's Historic Harlem Tour: Meet at the Schomburg Center at 135th Street and Lenox Avenue. Subway 2, 3 to 135th Street.

A brilliant way to get to know a major chunk of Harlem, its history, politics and

If you need to visit the loo before you start this tour, head for the McDonald's diagonally opposite the meeting point.

modern-day life through the eyes of a history graduate.

You'll hear about Martin Luther King and other African- American activists, local literary salons and gospel churches. You'll learn about the old neighbourhood joints of the Renny and Savoy, how the Apollo and Cotton Clubs were only open to rich white folk looking for an 'authentic black' experience, the campaign to allow black people to work in the shops they bought their food and clothes from, Striver's Row, the architecture and the old black pressure groups, two of whose buildings are now home to beauty parlours!

For a cheap and delicious meal before the Harlem tour head for Manna's Restaurant on Lenox Avenue at 134th Street. After the tour you'll find yourself outside the Apollo. Just a few metres east is a clean McDonald's with TVs on one wall (and a loo on the opposite side).

Along the way you'll hear about the African-American women who would go to the bus stations looking for black women arriving from the south. They would bring them up to the White Rose Mission where they would be protected from unscrupulous men while they found a job, and how the Savoy nightclub was closed down by police because of the inter-racial mingling.

SAVOR THE APPLE

✉ PO Box 914, Ansonia Station, New York, NY 10023
☎ 212-877 2903
$ Prices vary

Marlayna gives her personal tours of different parts of the city, but is particularly knowledgeable about Greenwich Village, the East Village and Harlem, where she has many contacts.

TALK-A-WALK

✉ 30 Waterside Plaza, NY 10010
☎ 212-686 0356
Fax 212-689 3538
$ $9.95

Walking tour guides on cassettes – they're excellent. It's best to order them before you leave home and they'll post them to you. There is a choice of four, each looking at the history and the architecture of historic Downtown.

KRAMER'S REALITY TOUR PULSE THEATER
West Midtown

✉ 432 West 42nd Street between 9th and 10th Avenues
☎ 212-268 5525
🚗 Subway A, C, E to 42nd Street/Penn Station
🕘 Sat and Sun at noon
$ $37.50

The real Kramer behind the *Seinfeld* character, Kramer has come out of the woodwork and invented his own three-hour tour based on all the *Seinfeld* spots in the city. Kenny Kramer will answer questions, share backstage gossip and the real-life incidents behind the show.

SAVORY SOJOURNS
Chelsea

✉ 144 West 13th Street
☎ 212-691 7314
www.savorysojourns.com
$ $85–250

For a unique insight into the fine foods and culinary skills of some of New York's finest restaurants, look no further than Savory Sojourns. They promise to give you an insider's guide to New York's best culinary and cultural destinations followed by a great slap-up meal. Areas covered include Upper East Side, Chinatown, Little Italy, Greenwich Village, Flatiron and Chelsea Market.

ALLIANCE FOR DOWNTOWN NEW YORK
Financial District

✉ Tours start at the steps of the Smithsonian Institution Museum of the American Indian, 1 Bowling Green
☎ 212-606 4064
www.downtownny.com
🚗 Subway 4, 5 to Bowling Green
🕘 Thurs and Sat at noon

Free walking tour for individuals and groups exploring the 'birthplace' of New York, including the Customs House, Trinity Church, Wall Street and the Stock Exchange, among others.

JOYCE GOLD HISTORY TOURS OF NEW YORK
Chelsea

✉ 141 West 17th Street
☎ 212-242 5762
www.nyctours.com
🕘 Start at 1pm for 2–3 hours
$ $12

Specialists in unusual, in-depth weekend forays into many of the city's distinctive neighbourhoods. Fascinating tours include the East Village, culture and counter-culture, Downtown graveyards and Greenwich Village highlights.

MUNICIPAL ART SOCIETY
Midtown

✉ 457 Madison Avenue between East 50th and East 51st Streets
☎ 212-935 3960 and 212-439 1049
www.mas.org
🚗 Subway 6 to 51st Street

Walking tours taking in both historical and architectural sights. Well-run, informative and very enjoyable. Telephone or visit their website.

CHAPTER 5

Shopping

Well, it's one of the main reasons Brits cite for visiting New York and it definitely lives up to its reputation. You can get a taste of fantastic American service at the fabulous and famous department stores, and shop until you drop for cheaper CDs, clothes, shoes and cameras. Although New York City does have real American malls like the one at the South Street Seaport, it is better known for its many boutiques.

The distinct atmosphere of each New York neighbourhood is reflected in the type of shopping available there. The upper section of 5th Avenue in the Midtown area is where you will find all the top department stores and other posh shops. Even posher – exclusive, actually – is Madison Avenue, which is home to American and European designers including Prada, Valentino and Versace.

The Villages are excellent for boutique shops that tend to open late but stay open late, too. In Greenwich Village you'll find jazz records, rare books and vintage clothing and the West Village's tree-lined streets are full of fine and funky boutiques and popular restaurants that cater to a young, trendy crowd. On the major shopping streets of Bleecker, Broadway and 8th, you'll find everything from antiques to fashion and T-shirt emporiums. There are plenty of up-and-coming designers and second-hand shops in the East Village. Try 9th Street for clothes and 7th for young designers.

The Flatiron District around 5th Avenue from 14th to 23rd Streets is filled with wonderful old buildings that are brimming with one-of-a-kind shops and designer boutiques. SoHo is filled with boutiques selling avant-garde fashion and art, plus restaurants and art galleries, all housed in handsome cast-iron 1850s' buildings. West Broadway is the main drag, but other important streets include Spring, Prince, Green, Mercer and Wooster. High-profile recent openings include Prada and Earl Jean.

New Yorkers in the know head to Aaron's in Brooklyn at 627 5th Avenue (tel 718-768 5400 or visit www.aarons.com) where you can buy in-season women's designer fashions at up to 33 per cent discounts.

In TriBeCa you will find trendsetting boutiques such as the fantastic new Issey Miyake flagship store, art galleries and restaurants in an area that combines loft living with commercial activity.

Last but not least is the Lower East Side, which is to bargains what Madison Avenue is to high-class acts. Many of the boutiques offer fashion by young designers, some of whom go on to open outlets in the posher areas, and famous-name gear at huge discounts. This whole area reflects the immigrant roots of New York and stands out as a bargain hunter's paradise particularly when the market is open on Sundays. Orchard Street from Houston to Delancey Street is famous for leather goods, luggage, designer clothes, belts, shoes and fabrics. Ludlow Street is famous for trendy bars, and boutiques filled with clothes by up-and-coming designers.

TAXES AND ALLOWANCE

US taxes: You will have to add local taxes on to the cost of your purchases – this can add anything from 7 to 9 per cent, depending on where you are buying. (New York sales tax is 8.25 per cent, though it has now been dropped on clothes and shoes costing under $110).

UK allowances: Your UK duty-free allowance is just £145 and, given the wealth of shopping opportunities, you're likely to exceed this, but don't be tempted to change receipts to show a lesser value as, if you are rumbled, the goods will be confiscated and you'll face a massive fine. In any case, the prices for some goods in America are so cheap that, even once you've paid the duty and VAT on top, they will still work out cheaper than buying the same item in Britain. Duty can range from 3.5 to 19 per cent depending on the item: for example, computers are charged at 3.5 per cent, golf clubs at 4 per cent, cameras at 5.4 per cent and mountain bikes at a massive 15.8 per cent. You pay this on goods above £145 and then VAT of 17.5 per cent on top of that.

Duty free: Buy your booze from US liquor stores – they're better value than the airports – but remember your allowance is 1 litre of spirits and two bottles of wine.

TOP TIPS FOR SHOPPING

There are some useful tips to follow when shopping in the Big Apple to save yourself time and money:

➡ If you're on a really tight schedule, call ahead and book appointments with the **personal shoppers** of major stores. They're very helpful and their service is absolutely free. Bargain! Call Macy's on 212-695 4400 and Bloomingdale's on 212-705 2000.

➡ Alternatively, you can arrange to go on a shopping tour of everything from Saks Fifth Avenue to discount-hunting at Century 21. Joy Weiner of **Shopping Tours of New York** plans customised shopping tours for groups of one to 15 or more by taxi, limo or minivan. Call 212-873 6791 for more information. Another personal shopping service is provided by **Intrepid New Yorker**, tel 212-534 5071.

The voltage system is different in America so any plug-in electrical goods will not work properly in the UK without an adaptor.

➡ You have a right to a **full refund** on goods you return within 20 days with a valid receipt unless the shop has signs saying otherwise. Always check, though, especially if the item is in a sale.

➡ Call in advance for **opening hours.** Smaller shops downtown – in SoHo, the Villages, Financial District and Lower East Side – tend not to open until noon or 1pm, but are often open as late as 8pm. Many are also closed on Mondays.

➡ You can **put items on hold** for a day or two until you make a decision – and if you're still thinking about it the next day you should buy it or you'll be kicking yourself on the flight home.

➡ You can **avoid sales tax** if you arrange to have your purchases shipped outside of New York State – a facility that is available at larger stores and those that are more tourist orientated.

➡ **Watch out for** 'Sale' signs on the Midtown section of 5th Avenue in the 30s and 40s. Here most of the shop windows are filled with signs that say 'Great Sales!', 'Going Out Of Business!' – yet they have been around for years and are still going strong. Most of what is on sale can be bought cheaper elsewhere and with a guarantee.

DEPARTMENT STORES

New York has big-name department stores that are as much a sight as a shop. If you want to experience more than one, give yourself plenty of time for browsing in each, carry a bottle of water with you to stop yourself getting dehydrated and take plenty of tea or coffee breaks. Most of the following are in the Midtown area either in or near 5th Avenue. Standard opening times are Monday to Friday 10am–8pm, Saturday 10am–7pm and Sunday noon–6pm.

5TH AVENUE

Bergdorf Goodman: 754 5th Avenue at 57th Street. Tel 212-753 7300. Subway N, R, W to 5th Avenue/59th Street; F to 57th Street.
An air of understated elegance pervades every department – not surprising, given that it has been around for generations of New Yorkers. It is not only still going strong, but positively booming and has even opened a Bergdorf Goodman Men on the opposite side of the street.

The only major department store NOT to open on a Sunday is Bergdorf Goodman, but it's still well worth a visit.

Lord and Taylor: 424 5th Avenue at 39th Street. Tel 212-391 3344, **www.maycompany.com**. Subway B, D, F, V to 42nd Street; 7 to Fifth Avenue.
Good service but at much cheaper prices. The store is famous for its animated window displays at Christmas time.

Saks Fifth Avenue: 611 5th Avenue at 50th Street. Tel 212-753 4000, **www.saksfifthavenue.com**. Subway E, V to 5th Avenue/53rd Street.
Not only is this one of the finest shopping institutions in New York, it also has fabulous views of the Rockefeller Center and is right next door to the beautiful St Patrick's Cathedral. Saks is a classic and has all the big names. There is a fabulous beauty area on the ground floor where you can get a personal consultation and a makeover.

Takashimaya: 693 5th Avenue between 54th and 55th Streets. Tel 212-350 0100. Subway N, R to 5th Avenue; 4, 5, 6 to 59th Street.
Hugely expensive, but filled with truly gorgeous things laid out in a six-storey townhouse building.

An elegant spot for tea is to be found in The Tea Box, a café in the basement of Takashimaya. It has a superb range of teas and a great selection of teapots to buy.

Tiffany & Co: 727 5th Avenue at 57th Street. Tel 212-755 8000 Website **www.tiffany.com**. Subway N, R to 5th Avenue/59th Street.
Audrey Hepburn's shop in *Breakfast at Tiffany's*, it surpasses all expectations. One of the few stores that still has lift attendants, who are very happy to explain exactly where everything is. Drool over the golden counters downstairs before taking the lift up to the first floor ('elevator to second' in American-speak) where the more moderately priced silver wing may be able to tempt you to part with wads of cash. And why not? It's well worth it for the exquisite wrapping of each purchase and the divine blue Tiffany drawstring bags!

MIDTOWN – 34TH STREET

Macy's: Herald Square at West 34th Street, 6th Avenue and Broadway. Tel 212-695 4400, **www.macys.com**. Subway B, D, F, N, Q, R, V, W to 34th Street.
This is a beast of a gigantic store, filling as it does an entire city block, so you can be forgiven for getting yourself lost. If you enter from the Herald Square side,

you'll find the Visitors' Centre on the mezzanine level up to your left. Here you can pick up your free Macy's tote bag or rucksack with any purchase over $35, on production of a special voucher – try the leaflet rack at your hotel. Along the way you'll pass the delightful Metropolitan Museum Shop. A favourite area with Brits is the jeans department and, of course, the beauty counters that throng the ground floor. If you're with children, head for the seventh floor where they'll find all their needs catered to, along with the only McDonald's inside a department store in New York. Don't miss the coffee shops, restaurant and food store run by Cucina & Co in the basement (see page 93).

Macy's is the venue for a Thanksgiving Day Parade, Fourth of July Fireworks and a Spring Flower Week in April.

UPPER EAST SIDE

Barneys: 660 Madison Avenue at 61st Street. Tel 212-826 8900, **www.barneys.com**. Subway N, R, W to 5th Avenue; 4, 5, 6 to Lexington Avenue. Open until 8pm every night.
A truly up-to-the-minute fashion outlet, this store is filled with all the top designers and a good selection of newer ones. There isn't really a Brit equivalent, the nearest thing is Harvey Nichols, but it doesn't come close. It has eight floors of fashion and there's everything from big name designers to more obscure, but very hip, small labels. There is a branch

If you plan to be in New York in August or March, get on down to the Barneys Warehouse Sale – call ahead for locations or check the website.

called Coop on 18th Street in Chelsea, and there's a branch at the World Financial Center downtown, but this is the $100-million megastore. Miss it and miss out!

Bloomingdale's: 1000 3rd Avenue at 59th Street. Tel 212-355 5900, **www.bloomingdales.com**. Subway 4, 5, 6 to 59th Street; N, R to Lexington Avenue. After Saks, this is probably the most famous of all 5th Avenue's department stores. You can't go wrong with anything you buy from here. A truly glitzy shop filled with all the right designers. Don't miss out on your free gift with any purchases, however small, with your NYCard.

DISCOUNT STORES

Century 21: 22 Cortlandt Street at Broadway. Tel 212-227 9092. Subway 1, 2, 4, 5, A, C to Fulton Street/Broadway Nassau. Area: Financial District.
Excellent discounts on everything from adult and children's clothing to goods for the home. Arrive early to avoid the lunchtime rush.

Daffy's: 111 5th Avenue at 18th Street. Tel 212-529 4477. Subway L, N, R, 4, 5, 6 to 14th Street/Union Square. Area: Union Square.
333 Madison Avenue at 44th Street. Tel 212-557 4422. Subway S, 4, 5, 6, 7 to 42nd Street/Grand Central. Area: Midtown East.
1311 Broadway at West 34th Street. Tel 212-736 4477. Subway B, D, F, N, Q, R to 34th Street. Area: 34th Street.
135 East 57th Street between Lexington and Park Avenues. Tel 212-376 4477. Subway 4, 5, 6 59th Street; N, R Lexington Avenue. Area: Midtown East.
You'll find an amazing range of designer stock from all over the world at all four outlets, and if you're prepared to hunt through the rails you may find some real bargains.

Filene's Basement: 620 6th Avenue at 18th Street. Tel: 212-620 3100. Subway F,

HOW TO FIND A REAL BARGAIN

Goods at normal prices in New York are cheaper than here in Britain, but it is possible to find whatever you are looking for at even better prices.

➡ Consult **Insider Shopping,** a phone- and internet-based service designed to help you zero in on bargain opportunities. Either dial 212-55-SALES or go to the website at **www.inshop.com** to find out about sales and promotional events at exclusive Manhattan retailers such as Bloomingdale's and Barneys.

➡ If shopping bargains are your main reason for visiting New York, then bear in mind that the **major sales** are held in **March and August.** The winter sales seem to start earlier and earlier and may even begin before Christmas.

➡ Check out the **Sales and Bargains** section of *New York* magazine, the ads in the *New York Times* and the Check Out section of *Time Out.*

➡ Get a copy of **S&B Report** from 108 East 38th Street, Suite 2000, NY, NY 10016.

➡ Bear in mind that many of the **vintage clothing** outlets are excellent for barely worn designer clothes and some even specialise in never-worn-before sample sales.

➡ Look out for the **designer shopping tour** of the Lower East Side on the Insider's Marketplace website at **www.imar.com.**

➡ Head for the premium **shopping bargain outlet of Woodbury Common,** just an hour out of New York in the Central Valley, tel: 845-928 4000. It has discounts of between 25 and 65 per cent at a huge number of factory outlets for designers and department stores such as Ann Taylor, Banana Republic, Barneys, Betsey Johnson, Burberry, Calvin Klein, Christian Dior, Donna Karan, Gap, Giorgio Armani, Gucci, Nike, Saks, and Versace. Do you want me to go on? You can easily reach Woodbury on a Gray Line tour bus to the area (see page 72).

V to 14th Street. Area: Union Square.
Part of the Boston-based bargain-basement chain. In addition to this store it also has an outlet on Broadway at West 79th Street in the Upper West Side.

Loehmann's: 101 7th Avenue between 16th and 17th Streets. Tel 212-352 0856, **www.loehmanns.com**. Subway 1 to 18th Street. Area: Union Square.
A five-storey building filled with bargains for men and women. Head straight to the top floor for designer labels such as Donna Karan, Calvin Klein and Versace. The other floors feature accessories, bags, clothing and shoes all at great prices.

ANTIQUES AND FLEA MARKETS

In balmy weather, nothing beats strolling through the treasure trove of antiques, collectables and one-off pieces at any of New York's outdoor markets or in some of the unusual individual shops.

SOHO

The SoHo Antiques Fair: Broadway and Grand Street.
Antiques and collectibles all the year round.

CHELSEA

The Annex Antiques Fair & Flea Market: 26th Street and 6th Avenue. Tel 212-243 5343.
Browsers come year-round to pick through several parking lots full of vintage clothing, furniture, pottery, glassware, jewellery and art. Get there early for the best finds. Weekends only.

Chelsea Antiques Building: 110 West 25th Street. Tel 212-929 0909.
This 12-storey building houses 90 galleries of antiques and collectables with merchandise ranging from Japanese textiles to vintage phonographs and radios.

The Garage: 112 West 25th Street. Tel 212-647 0707.

The Garage is exactly that – a two-storey parking garage that transforms into another bustling venue at the weekend.

The Showplace: 40 West 25th Street. Tel 212-633 6010.

Like an indoor extension of the outdoor market (which is open on weekends only), with a small café downstairs.

UPPER EAST and UPPER WEST SIDES

Green Flea Indoor/Outdoor Market: Saturdays on West 84th Street between Columbus and Amsterdam Avenues, 10am–5.30pm and on Sundays at Columbus Avenue between 76th and 77th Streets, 10am–5.30pm. Tel 212-721 0900.

Antiques, collectibles, bric-a-brac, handmade pottery and discount clothing.

WEST VILLAGE

Susan Parrish Antiques: 390 Bleecker Street between Perry and West 11th Streets. Tel 212-645 5020.

American quilts from the 1800s to 1940.

EAST VILLAGE

Irreplaceable Artefacts: 216 East 125th Street between 2nd and 3rd Avenues. Tel 212-777 2900.

Great for actual architectural bits and bobs.

MADISON SQUARE

Old Print Shop: 150 Lexington Avenue between East 29th and East 30th Streets. Tel 212-683 3950.

This is the place for Americana up to the 1950s.

MIDTOWN EAST

Lillian Nassau: 220 East 57th Street between 2nd and 3rd Avenues. Tel 212-759 6062.

The place for art nouveau lamps and glassware, especially original Tiffanys.

Manhattan Arts & Antiques Center: 1050 2nd Avenue between East 55th and East 56th Streets. Tel 212-355 4400.

BOOKS

Books are big business in New York and book readings are also a popular form of entertainment. If you want to get a real slice of the New York lifestyle, there are a number of places that specialise in readings. Regular spots include: The Drawing Center (35 Wooster Street between Grand and Broome Streets, tel 212-219 2166) has readings related to their exhibitions; The Poetry Project at St Mark's Church (131 East 10th Street, tel 212-674 0910) has three evening readings a week, Mondays and Wednesdays at 8pm, and Fridays at 10.30pm; The 92nd Street Y (1395 Lexington Avenue, tel 212-229 2744) also has a great series of lectures and readings, as does The Dia Center for the Arts (548 West 22nd Street, tel 212-989 5912). Also check out Barnes & Noble (see opposite) for more.

FINANCIAL DISTRICT

Borders Books & Music: 461 Park Avenue at 57th Street. Tel 212-980 6785. Subway N, R to Lexington Avenue; 4, 5, 6 to 59th Street. Area: Midtown East.

Excellent outlets for books, CDs, videos and more obscure books, too.

GREENWICH VILLAGE

Shakespeare & Co: 716 Broadway at Washington Place. Tel 212-529 1330. Subway N, R to 8th Street; 6 to Astor Place.

This is an excellent bookstore. Unlike many a Barnes & Noble, where the staff sometimes don't appear to recognise joined-up writing, all the assistants here are graduates and will be genuinely helpful.

NOLITA

Tower Books: 383 Lafayette Street at 4th Street. Tel 212-228 5100. Subway B, D, F, Q to Broadway/Lafayette; 6 to Bleecker Street.

Contemporary fiction and a huge magazine section.

WEST VILLAGE

Three Lives Bookstore: 154 West 10th Street off 7th Avenue. Tel 212-741 2069.
A delightful shop with a charming ambience, known for attentive staff with encyclopedic knowledge.

EAST VILLAGE

St Mark's Bookshop: 31 3rd Avenue on the corner of 9th Street. Tel 212-260 7853. Subway 6 to Astor Place. Area: East Village.
An excellent bookstore with a broad range of books. The bulletin board in the front gives details of local literary events.

UNION SQUARE

Barnes & Noble: 105 5th Avenue at 18th Street. Tel 212-807 0099, **www.bn.com**. Subway L, N, R, 4, 5, 6 to 14th Street/Union Square.
This is the original store of one of the largest chains of bookstores in America and, as well as a massive selection of books, it also has CDs and videos. Barnes & Noble are responsible for putting many independent bookstores out of business, but are well worth a visit. Many have coffee shops and seating areas for you to look through books before buying. You'll see them everywhere.

Strand Book Store: 828 Broadway at 12th Street. Tel 212-473 1489, **www.strandbooks.com**. Subway L, N, R, 4, 5, 6 to 14th Street/Union Square.
The whole area used to be famous for antiquarian booksellers, but the Strand is the only one left. This store has over two million second-hand and new books on any subject you'd care to name – all at around half the published price.

MIDTOWN EAST

Urban Center Books: 457 Madison Avenue, between East 50th and East 51st Streets. Tel 212-935 3595. Subway 6 to 51st Street or E, F to 5th Avenue.
Housed in the pretty Villard Houses, this bookstore is a treasure trove for anyone interested in architecture and buildings.

CAMERAS AND ELECTRONICS

Have a clear idea of what you're looking for before buying – pick up a copy of Tuesday's *New York Times* to check out prices in the science section first. Of course, you can always find electrical items at really cheap prices in the Chinatown stretch of Canal Street, but you won't get a guarantee!

US video tapes are not compatible with British machines unless they have the PAL mark.

FINANCIAL DISTRICT

J&R Music World: 33 Park Row at Center Street. Tel 212-732 8600, **www.jandr.com**. Subway N, R to City Hall; J, M, Z, 6 to Chambers Street.
Check out the weekly ads in the *New York Post* and *Village Voice* to get an idea of what's on offer. Also sells jazz, Latin and pop music.

GREENWICH VILLAGE

The Wiz: 726 Broadway between Washington and Waverly Places. Tel 212-677 4111, **www.thewiz.com**. Subway N, R to 8th Street; 6 to Astor Place.
The last word in bargain-basement buys. Phone ahead for other locations.

MADISON SQUARE

Fotografica: 112 West 20th Street between 5th and 6th Avenues. Tel 212-929 6080. Subway F, V to 23rd Street.
A vast stock of used camera equipment at trade prices. Owner Ed Wassel will be happy to order anything not in stock.

GARMENT DISTRICT

B&H Photo & Video: 420 9th Avenue between West 33rd and West 34th Streets. Tel 212-444 6600, **www.bhphotovideo.com**. Subway A, C, E to 34th Street/Penn Station.

This store stocks every conceivable piece of electronic imaging, audio, video and photo equipment you've ever heard of. A shop for the professionals.

Willoughby's: 136 West 32nd Street between 6th and 7th Avenues. Tel 212-564 1600, **www.willoughbys.com**. Subway B, D, F, Q, N, R, V, W, 1, 2, 3 to 34th Street. Area: Garment District. Reputedly the world's largest collection of cameras and all things audio, but the service isn't brilliant so make sure you know what you want before you go.

CHILDREN

All these stores are to be found in the Midtown section of 5th Avenue.

FAO Schwarz: 767 5th Avenue at 58th Street. Tel 212-644 9400, **www.fao.com**. Subway N, R to 5th Avenue. Area: Upper East Side.

If you stay at the new Ritz Carlton Hotel in Battery Park City, you'll be entitled to a 10 per cent discount at FAO Schwarz.

The most famous children's store in the whole wide world, it's not only huge, but is also an entertainment centre in its own right with giant, oversized displays that take your breath away and every conceivable toy your child could want.

The Disney Store: 711 5th Avenue at 55th Street. Tel 212-702 0702, **www.disney.com**. Subway E, F at 5th Avenue. Area: Upper East Side.
Also at 218 West 42nd Street. Tel 212-302 0595. Subway 1, 2, 3, 9, N, R to Times Square/42nd Street. Area: Theater District.
If it comes with a pair of ears, then you'll find it here!

Toys R Us: 1514 Broadway at 44th Street. Tel 212-225 8392, **www.toysrus.com**. Subway N, Q, R, S, W, 1, 2, 3, 7 to Times Square.
Move over FAO Schwarz, it's time to make room for the amazing new toy emporium in the heart of the rejuvenated Times Square district. The three-storey, glass-enclosed building is home to an 18m (60ft) Ferris wheel, a giant roaring dinosaur and a life-size Barbie townhouse.

Warner Brothers Studio Store: 1 Times Square. Tel 212-840 4040. Subway N, R, 1, 2, 3, 7 to Times Square.
The last word in items that feature Bugs Bunny, Daffy Duck, Tweety and Sylvester. There are four floors with clothes for adults as well as children, toys and original cartoon drawings (cels).

FASHION

You can get everything from top designers to up-and-coming newcomers. The main shopping areas for fashion are the Upper East Side (for posh), SoHo (for designer), the East Village and Lower East Side (for cheap designer). Call ahead for opening times as many shops do not open until late – but they stay open late.

TRIBECA

TriBeCa Issey Miyake: 119 Hudson Street at North Moore Street. Tel 212-226 0100. Subway 1, 2 to Franklin Street. The new Prada store got the old Guggenheim Museum space in SoHo, Issey Miyake got Frank Gehry, the architect of the amazing Guggenheim Museum in Bilbao. Now serious shoppers mingle with art buffs who come to see the titanium tornado that swirls through this two-storey, 279sq m (3,000sq ft) boutique, plus art by Gehry's son Alejandro. Fortunately, the purpose of the shop (sorry, but that's what it is!) has not been forgotten and the entire Issey collection is here including the Pleats Please, Haat, A/POC and fragrance lines. What's more, the staff are actually helpful. A truly wonderful experience – especially if you can afford $1,600 for a shirt. Otherwise wait for the sales!

LOWER EAST SIDE

Nova USA: 100 Stanton Street at Ludlow Street. Tel 212-228 6844. Subway J, M, Z, F to Delancey Street.
Great for basic but brilliant sportswear, Cameron Diaz and Helena Christensen are just two of the many women who stock up on these casually cool bits of kit when they're in Manhattan.

For info on sample sales in the Lower East Side area, go to www.lowereastsideny.com

SOHO

agnès b: 103 Green Street between Spring and Prince Streets. Tel 212-925 4649. Subway N, R to Prince Street.
Superb designs for women – simple but stunning.

Anna Sui: 113 Greene Street between Prince and Spring Streets. Tel 212-941 8406. Subway N, R to Prince Street.
Get the glamour-with-a-hint-of-grunge look with Anna's dresses, skirts, blouses, platform boots and scarves. The small collection for men includes trousers, shirts and jackets from the outrageously loud to the positively restrained.

Avirex: 652 Broadway between Bleeker and Bond Streets. Tel 212-925 5456.
Great for flight and varsity jackets.

Banana Republic: 552 Broadway between Spring and Prince Streets. Tel 212-925 0308. Subway N, R to Prince Street.
A classy and reputable chain, famous for classic clothing in feel-good fabrics such as cashmere, suede, velvet and soft cotton. Best buys are in the frequent sales.

Betsey Johnson: 138 Wooster Street between Houston and Prince Streets. Tel 212-995 5048. Subway C, E to Spring Street; N, R to Prince Street.
A wonderful combination of party and working clothes.

Canal Jeans: 504 Broadway between Spring and Broome Streets. Tel 212-226 1130. Subway N, R to Prince Street.
An excellent place to find jeans and casual co-ordinates at great prices – how about $40 for some Ralph Laurens and $20 for a parka? Also vintage clothes and accessories. Some of the best bargains to be found in New York.

A great place for a pit stop is at the Universal News and Café Corp at 484 Broadway between Broome and Grand Streets, where you'll not only be able to find a snack, but also check out their magazine range of 7,000 titles!

Catherine Malandrino's: 468 Broome Street at Greene Street. Tel 212-925 6765. Subway 6 to Spring Street.
The designer's own sexy French knitwear in block colours stand alongside more tailored knitted skirts and jackets.

Club Monaco: 520 Broadway at Spring Street. Tel 212-941 1511. Subway 6 to Spring Street.
Once a Canadian company offering high fashion at high street prices, Ralph Lauren loved it so much he bought it.

D&G: 434 West Broadway between Prince and Spring Streets. Tel 212-965 8000. Subway N, R to Prince Street. .
Shop for jeans, suits, bags and dresses to a background of (loud) pop music. *Sex and the City*'s Carrie's favourite shop!

Earl Jeans: 160 Mercer Street between Houston and Prince Streets. Tel 212-226 8709. Subway N, R to Prince Street, 6 to Spring Street.
Self-taught California designer Suzanne Costas has not only created jeans that actually fit women, but made them sexy too. Her ultra-low-slung jeans have been the definitive favourites of stars like Cameron Diaz and Kate Moss for some

time and now visitors to New York can get their hands on them too.

Hotel Venus: 382 West Broadway between Spring and Broome Streets. Tel 212-966 4066. Subway C, E to Spring Street.
One of Patricia Field's outlets. Her trend-setting club and streetwear is so outrageous it attracts a large following among the drag-queen and stripper crowd. But don't let that put you off if you fancy a corset, fake fur coat, bodysuit or bikini that's completely OTT. Patricia, by the way, is now known for dressing Sarah Jessica Parker of *Sex and the City*.

J Crew: 99 Prince Street between Mercer and Greene Streets. Tel 212-966 2739. Subway N, R to Prince Street.
American-style men's and women's clothes plus shoes and accessories.

Keiko: 62 Green Street between Spring and Broome Streets. Tel 212-226 6051. Subway N, R to Prince Street.
Designer swimwear for all tastes – and you may recognise the odd super-model here, too.

Marc Jacobs: 163 Mercer Street between Houston and Prince Streets. Tel 212-343 1490. Subway N, R to Prince Street.
Minimalist and luxury garments displayed in a renovated garage.

Phat Farm: 129 Prince Street between West Broadway and Wooster Street. Tel 212-533 7428. Subway C, E to Spring Street.
If you're into hip-hop baggies, you'll find everything you need here.

Prada: 575 Broadway at Prince Street. Tel 212-334 8888. Subway N, R to Prince Street.
Art is the byword of this incredible new $40 million flagship store for Prada. Once the Guggenheim's SoHo museum, the two-level space has now been designed by architect Rem Koolhaas and includes a zebrawood 'wave' in the entry hall and shoe display steps which can be converted into auditorium seating. Other neat design elements include dressing rooms behind a wall that switches from translucent to transparent (be warned!) and clothes suspended from the ceiling in metal cages. And therein lies one of the main drawbacks of the store from a punter's point of view. Prada's entire collection is to be found here, yet all the empty areas make people feel as if there isn't that much to buy. On top of that, the store has taken being 'cool' so seriously that the staff are positively frosty. Deal with them by either telling yourself that you earn a lot more than they do, or as one woman put it: 'You can have fun by asking the sales people for things from the storage rooms and keep them running!'

Steven Alan: 60 Wooster Street between Spring and Broome Streets. Tel 212-334 6354. Subway 6 to Spring Street.
A small but perfectly formed boutique filled to the rafters with up-and-coming designers such as Kayatone Adeli's cute disco top and Daryl K's hipster trousers.

Stüssy Store: 140 Wooster Street between West Houston and Prince Streets. Tel 212-995 8787. Subway N, R to Prince Street.
Everything you could want if you're after a West Coast look.

NOLITA

Calypso St Barths: 280 Mott Street between East Houston and Prince Street. Tel 212-965 0990. Subway 6 to Spring Street.
A French boutique with a Caribbean influence, this shop is filled with designs from Christiane Celle. There's a riot of sexy silk slip dresses, tie-dye tops and cute beaded cardigans.

Le Sportsac: 176 Spring Street between West Broadway and Thompson Streets. Tel 212-625 2626. Subway C, E to Spring Street.
Beloved of Japanese trendoids and US out-of-towners, not to mention Brit hipsters, Le Sportsac offers great nylon

bags in every style, size, colour and pattern and they're reasonably priced, too. Worth a visit as the range isn't available in the UK.

X-Large: 267 Lafayette Street at Prince Street. Tel 212-334 4480. Subway N, R to Prince Street.
Get your urban street clobber here. Sized for boys, but good for girls, too.

Tracey Feith: 209 Mulberry Street between Spring and Kenmare Streets. Tel 212-334 3097. Subway 6 to Spring Street.
Tucked away in the hip NoLiTa, here you can get a dress made to order if you've $550 to burn. Just remember, Sarah Jessica Parker wore one of Feith's red and blue silk creations in *Sex and the City* and the shop sold out of the style in days.

GREENWICH VILLAGE

Dollhouse: 400 Lafayette Street at 4th Street. Tel 212-539 1800. Subway N, R to Prince Street.
As the name suggests, it's all very much for young girls or the young at heart. Nicole Murray specialises in gear for the body-conscious, and prices are excellent.

A sales tax of 8.25 per cent always used to be added on to all label prices. Now New York City has abolished the sales tax on all clothing and footwear under $110.

Patricia Field: 10 East 8th Street between 5th Avenue and University Place. Tel 212-254 1699. Subway A, C, E, F, V, S to West 4th Street.
Once only famous for her outrageous club clobber, Patricia is the designer who creates all the fashion for the girls in *Sex and the City.* So if you want to emulate Carrie, Mia or Lizzie, then come here to stock up on cool bags and jewellery worn by the cast.

Untitled: 26 West 8th Street between 5th and 6th Avenues. Tel 212-505 9725. Subway A, C, E, F, V, S to West 4th Street.
Contemporary clothing and accessories from exclusive New York designers as well as the likes of Vivienne Westwood.

Urban Outfitters: 628 Broadway between Houston and Bleecker Streets. Tel 212-475 0009. Subway F, V, S to Broadway/Lafayette Street; 6 to Bleecker Street.
The last word in trendy, inexpensive clothes. Also has vintage urban wear. There's one in London now so it's not as special as it used to be, but still worth a visit for its mix of hip clothes, accessories, toys and other what-nots.

WEST VILLAGE

Lulu Guinness: 394 Bleecker Street between 11th and Perry Streets. Tel 212-367 2120. Subway A, C, E to 14th Street, L to 8th Avenue; 1, 2 to Christopher Street.
Our own home-grown Brit girl Lulu, who started out in Notting Hill, West London, has arrived in the Big Apple. Her vintage-inspired accessories include embroidered and appliquéd bags and purses. If you think you can get it all in the UK, think again – Lulu's produced some fab bags just for New Yorkers.

EAST VILLAGE

Mark Montano: 434 East 9th Street between 1st Avenue and Avenue A. Tel 212-505 0325. Subway 6 to Astor Place.
Drew Barrymore, Johnny Depp and Kate Moss are all fans of the funky designer who uses bright, often vintage fabrics to create designs with style.

Religious Sex: 7 St Mark's Place between 2nd and 3rd Avenues. Tel 212-477 9037. Subway 6 to Astor Place.
If you're feeling outrageous (sequinned thong, anybody?) you'll find the clothes you want here.

Trash and Vaudeville: 4 St Mark's Place between 2nd and 3rd Avenues. Tel 212-982 3590. Subway 6 to Astor Place.
You'll get the East Village look in no time

CLOTHES SIZES

Clothes sizes for men and women are one size smaller in America, so a dress size 10 in the US is a size 12 in the UK, a jacket size 42 is a UK 44. But it's the opposite with shoes – an American size 10 is our size 9.

if you step into this punk/grunge paradise. Here you'll find outrageous rubber dresses and shirts, black leather outfits and plenty of studded gear and footwear to match.

CHELSEA

Co-op Store: 236 West 18th Street between 7th and 8th Avenues. Tel 212-716 8816. Subway 1, 2 to 18th Street.
One of the best stores in New York.

After you've been to the Co-op, pop to the Cafeteria at 119 7th Avenue at West 17th Street. It's where you go to see and be seen!

MIDTOWN

Gianni Versace: 647 5th Avenue between 51st and 52nd Streets. Tel 212-317 0224. Subway E, V to 5th Avenue/ 53rd Street.
A beautiful shop, housed in the former Vanderbilt mansion, selling beautiful clothes for the rich and famous.

Gucci: 685 5th Avenue at 54th Street. Tel 212-826 2600. Subway E, V to 5th Avenue/53rd Street.
So you may not be able to afford anything on display, but it's essential to know what 'look' you are trying to achieve when you browse through the copy-cat shops downtown.

Jimmy Choo: 645 Fifth Avenue at 51st Street. Tel 212-593 0800. Subway E, V to 5th Avenue/53rd Street.
Originally part of Jimmy's upscale ready-to-wear 'chain' of stores – think London, Paris, Los Angeles and New York – the designer has sold up most of his shares and gone back to his couture clients. Now the thongs, slingbacks and skinny high-heeled shoes are designed by his daughter Sanda Choi, but still remain the favourites of celebs like Madonna and Sarah Jessica Parker. A pair of women's shoes will set you back $400–600. Men's loafers, sneakers and thongs start at just $250.

Levis: 3 East 57th Street between 5th and Madison Avenues. Tel 212-838 2125. Subway N, R, W to 5th Avenue/59th Street.
If you've ever had trouble getting a pair of jeans that fit you perfectly, you can get yourself measured and your jeans custom-cut and sent to you.

Liz Claiborne: 650 5th Avenue at East 52nd Street. Tel 212-956 6505. Subway 6 to 51st Street; E, F to Lexington Avenue.
Career and sportswear with style for women.

Manolo Blahnik: 31 West 54th Street between 5th and 6th Avenues. Tel 212-582 3007. Subway E, V to 5th Avenue/53rd Street.
Anyone serious about their shoe collection wouldn't miss this mecca for celebs. In fact, Manolo has even designed the SJP – an ankle-strapped stiletto named after Sarah Jessica Parker.

UPPER EAST SIDE

Billy Martin's Western Wear: 220 East 60th Street. Tel 212-861 3100. Subway 6 to 68th Street.
Everything for the posh cowboy.

Calvin Klein: 654 Madison Avenue at 60th Street. Tel 212-292 9000. Subway N, R to Lexington Avenue; 4, 5, 6 to 59th Street.
CK's leading outlet seems to have enjoyed as much attention from the designers as the clothes themselves!

Diesel: 770 Lexington Avenue at 60th Street. Tel 212-308 0055. Subway N, R to Lexington Avenue; 4, 5, 6 to 59th Street.
A massive store in which you'll find

everything from denim to vinyl clothing, shoes and accessories.

D&G: 825 Madison Avenue between 68th and 69th Streets. Tel 212-249 4100. Subway 6 to 68th Street.
Shop for jeans, suits, bags and dresses to a background of (loud) pop music.

Emporio Armani: 601 Madison Avenue between 57th and 58th Streets. Tel 212-317 0800. Subway N, R to 59th Street.
Armani's line for younger people.

Giorgio Armani: 760 Madison Avenue at 65th Street. Tel 212-988 9191. Subway 6 to 68th Street.
A huge boutique, which sells all three of Armani's lines. Come here to find well-tailored classics.

Lingerie & Company: 1217 3rd Avenue at 70th Street. Tel 212-737 7700. Subway 6 to 68th Street.
A user-friendly shop for gorgeous undies.

Prada: 841 Madison Avenue at 70th Street. Tel 212-327 4200. Subway 6 to 68th Street.
Check out the season's look before you head for the bargain basement stores.

Ralph Lauren: 867 Madison Avenue at East 72nd Street. Tel 212-606 2100. Subway 6 to 68th Street.
Worth a visit just to see the store – it's in an old Rhinelander mansion and is decorated with everything from Oriental rugs to riding whips, leather chairs and English paintings. The clothes are excellent quality too.

VINTAGE FASHION

LOWER EAST SIDE

Cherry: 185 Orchard Street between Houston and Stanton Streets. Tel 212-358 7131. Subway F, V to 2nd Avenue.
A cool vintage shop, which stocks all manner of goodies and shoes dating back as far as the 1940s.

SOHO

Transfer International: 594 Broadway, Suite 1002, between Prince and Houston Streets. Tel 212-941 5472, **www.transferintl.com**. Subway N, R to Prince Street.
Specialises in Gucci, Prada, Chanel and Hermès – one of the best places to buy post-worn designer clothes and accessories. They also carry agnès b and Betsey Johnson.

The Americans still work in feet and inches – good news for older Brits.

NOLITA

Screaming Mimi: 382 Lafayette Street between 4th and Great Jones Streets. Tel 212-677 6464. Subway N, R to NYU 8th Street.
Everything from polyester dresses to denim shirts and tropical prints from the 1960s. There is also jewellery, sunglasses and other accessories, plus a home department upstairs.

GREENWICH VILLAGE

Stella Dallas: 218 Thompson Street between Bleecker and West 3rd Street. Tel 212-674 0447. Subway A, C, E, F, V, S to West 4th Street.
An amazing vintage shop full of girly chiffon and other items.

EAST VILLAGE

Tokyo Joe: 334 East 11th Street between 1st and 2nd Avenues. Tel 212-473 0724. Subway 6 to Astor Place.
The pre-worn designer offerings are advertised on a blackboard outside.

Tokio: 7 East 7th Street between 1st and 2nd Avenues. Tel 212-353 8443. Subway 6 to Astor Place; N, R to 8th Street.
Plenty of vintage and downtown designer gear.

CHELSEA

Out Of Our Closet: 136 West 18th Street between 6th and 7th Avenues. Tel 212-633 6965. Subway 1, 2 to 18th Street.

Used designer fashions in excellent condition at a fraction of the price.

UNION SQUARE

Cheap Jack's: 841 Broadway between 13th and 14th Streets. Tel 212-777 9564. Subway L, N, Q, R, 4, 5, 6 to Union Square/14th Street.
A massive outlet, it has a huge selection but is definitely on the pricey side.

UPPER EAST SIDE

Gentlemen's Resale: 322 East 81st Street between 1st and 2nd Avenues. Tel 212-734 2739. Subway 6 to 77th Street.
Top-notch designer suits at a fraction of the original price.

BROOKLYN

Domsey's Warehouse: 496 Wythe Avenue at South 9th Street. Tel 718-384 6000. Subway J, M, Z to Marcie Avenue Station.
Well worth the trip for an excellent selection.

BEAUTY

SOHO

Sephora: 555 Broadway between Prince and Spring Streets. Tel 212-625 1309. Subway 6 to Spring Street.
One of the new Sephora beauty emporiums – there are other outlets in 34th Street, Times Square and Midtown. Phone for details of one near you. The one thing that you can guarantee to be cheaper here than in the UK is the American-brand beauty products. They have everything from Hard Candy to Philosophy, Benefit and Nars. The shops may seem overwhelming at first with their rows and rows of scents, lipsticks, nail polishes and cosmetics, but the staff are very friendly and will even talk you through many of the brands. You can make an appointment for a tour (212-629 9135) or ask for a free makeover.

Shu Uemura Beauty Boutique: 121 Greene Street between Prince and Houston Streets. Tel 212-979 5500. Subway N, R to Prince Street.
A pioneer in relaxed beauty shopping.

FOOD

LOWER EAST SIDE

Russ & Daughters: 179 East Houston Street between Allen and Orchard Streets. Tel 212-475 4880. Subway F to 2nd Avenue.
Along with Katz's Deli, this is one of the most famous outlets in the Lower East Side. Established in 1914 it sells every possible kind of fish, caviar, pickled vegetables and bagels.

LITTLE ITALY

Di Palo's: 206 Grand Street at Mott Street. Tel: 212-226 1033. Subway J, M, N, Q, R, W, Z, 6 to Canal Street.
One of the last remaining Italian speciality food stores in Little Italy, it was founded 80 years ago and is particularly famous for its mozzarella and Italian sausages and salami. It even has its own ageing room for cheeses.

GREENWICH VILLAGE

Aphrodisia: 264 Bleecker Street between 6th and 7th Avenues. Tel 212-989 6440. Subway A, C, E, F, V, S to West 4th Street.
Famous for its huge selection of bulk herbs, spices, teas and pot-pourris.

Balducci's: 424 6th Avenue at West 9th Street. Tel 212-673 2600. Subway A, C, E, F, V, S to West 4th Street.
One of the most famous gourmet food emporiums in New York. You can find everything from fresh vegetables and fruit to edible flowers and hung game.

Faicco's Sausage Store: 260 Bleecker Street between 6th and 7th Avenues. Tel 212-243 1974. Subway A, C, E, F, V, S to West 4th Street.
A landmark Italian speciality food shop established in 1900, it is famous for its own sausages that are made daily (and sold to many of the neighbouring restaurants), its home-made mozzarella cheese, again made daily, plus rice balls made with three cheeses and rolled in breadcrumbs. Other specialities include prosciutto balls, potato croquettes, fried ravioli and stuffed breads.

JEWELLERY

Want a true sparkler? Then look no further than the 47th Street Diamond District where the little gems are traded, cut and set. More than 2,600 independent businesses are to be found in a single block between 5th Avenue and the Avenue of the Americas (6th Avenue). Many have booths in jewellery exchanges such as the World's Jewelry Exchange at 50 West 47th Street (tel 212-997 0111). Clustered near the Diamond District are a prestigious group of internationally renowned jewellers including **H Stern** (645 5th Avenue, tel 212-688 0300) and **Martinique Jewellers** (1555 Broadway between 46th and 47th Streets, tel 212-869 5765). Other jewellers of note include **Wempe** (700 5th Avenue at 55th Street, tel 212-397 9000) and **Tourneau** (500 Madison Avenue at 52nd Street, tel 212-758 6098), which are both famous for fine watches. **Fortunoff** (681 5th Avenue at 54th Street, tel 212-758 6660) offers discounts on a large variety of jewellery items, including engagement rings, pearls, brand-name watches and gold bracelets and necklaces. **Robert Lee Morris** (400 West Broadway, tel 212-431 9405) in SoHo is one of only two or three American jewellery designers with an international reputation.

If you'd like a taste of the foods sold in some of the shops in the Village, try out the Foods of New York tour, which also introduces you to great restaurants in the area (see page 74).

Murray's Cheese Shop: 257 Bleecker Street between 6th and 7th Avenues. Tel 212-243 3289. Subway A, C, E, F, V, S to West 4th Street.
The owner travels all over the world to bring back a fascinating selection of more than 350 cheeses with amazing names such as Wabash Cannonball, Crocodile Tears, Mutton Buttons and Cardinal Sin, a British cow's-milk cheese. They also sell olives, chorizos, pâtés and breads.

Pasticceria Bruno: 245 Bleecker Street between 6th and 7th Avenues. Tel 212-242 6031. Subway A, C, E, F, V, S to West 4th Street.
An Italian-French bakery run by one of the top 10 pastry chefs in New York. It does miniature and large fruit tarts, mousses, cookies, sorbets, ice-cream cakes and home-made chocolates, and you can sit down to try any of them with a nice cup of tea or coffee.

Rocco's: 243 Bleecker Street between 6th and 7th Avenues. Tel 212-242 6031. Subway A, C, E, F, V, S to West 4th Street. Famous for its fresh cannollis (an Italian pastry filled with cream), it sells large and small sizes of everything from Italian cheesecakes to chocolate, hazelnut and lemon cakes. You can eat in, too, with a cup of delicious coffee.

Zito's: 259 Bleecker Street between 6th and 7th Avenues. Tel 212-929 6139. Subway A, C, E, F, V, S to West 4th Street. Just about the oldest bread shop in New York, its ovens date back to the end of the 19th century and it is now famous for its old-world-style Italian breads. The focaccias come with many different toppings from onions and olive oil to rosemary. Their prosciutto bread is exclusive to them.

34TH STREET

Cucina & Co: The basement of Macy's, 151 West 34th Street, 6th Avenue and Broadway. Tel 212-868 2388. Subway B, D, F, N, Q, R, V, W to 34th Street.
One of the most fabulous grocer's markets in New York, now famous for its supplies of lobster and caviar.

UPPER EAST SIDE/YORKVILLE

The Vinegar Factory: 431 East 91st Street between York and 1st Avenues. Tel 212-987 0885. Subway 4, 5, 6 to 86th Street.
One of the most famous markets in the city. Here you'll find stacks of cheeses, meats, breads, salads and cakes – in fact, everything you need to create your own perfect picnic.

UPPER WEST SIDE

Zabar's: 2245 Broadway at 80th Street. Tel 212-787 2000. Subway 1, 2 to 79th Street.
Just about the most famous food store in New York and also considered to be one of the finest. It has a tremendous range of cheeses, fresh fruit and veg, meats, fish and even bagels. In fact it's so famous it's even featured in *Friends.*

DRINK

LOWER EAST SIDE

Schapiro's Winery: 124 Rivington Street between Essex and Norfolk Streets. Subway J, M, Z, F to Essex/Delancey Street.
The Schapiro family have been running this winery since 1899 and it's decorated with the old casks and bottles. It's the city's only kosher wine and spirits warehouse and sweet wine is made on the premises. There is a free tour at 2pm on Sundays. From Monday to Thursday there are hourly tastings 11am–5pm and on Fridays before 3pm.

SOHO

Vintage New York: 482 Broome Street at Wooster Street. Tel 212-226 9463. Subway 6 to Spring Street.
SoHo is home to a complete first in New York City – a shop that can sell both wine and food. And the reason why is because it is owned by a vineyard from New York State, which means it can open on Sundays and sell alcoholic wine and food together – both of which are otherwise illegal in New York. All the wines are from New York State vineyards and you can get five tastes for just $5.

You can only buy wine and spirits from liquor stores and to make your life even more difficult, the liquor stores do not sell mixers or even beer!

EAST VILLAGE

Astor Wines & Spirits: 12 Astor Place at Lafayette Street. Tel 212-674 7500. Subway 6 to Astor Place.
Has a wide range of wines and spirits.

UNION SQUARE

Union Square Wine and Spirits: 33 Union Square West between 16th and 17th Streets. Tel 212-675 8100. Subway 4, 5, 6, L, N, Q, R, W to Union Square.
A great selection, good prices and the staff know their wines.

MIDTOWN EAST

Park Avenue Liquor Shop: 292 Madison Avenue between 40th and 41st Streets. Tel 212-685 2442. Subway 4, 5, 6, 7 to Grand Central/42nd Street.
Specialises in Californian wines and European bottles. Discounts with bulk purchases.

Don't be fooled by the bottles of wine you may see in certain shops in New York. They are either non-alcoholic or low alcohol as it is illegal for food stores to sell wine. Beer, however, can be sold in food shops.

Schumer's Wine & Liquor: 59 East 54th Street between Park and Madison Avenues. Tel 212-355 0940. Subway E, F to Lexington Avenue, 6 to 51st Street.
With a great range of American and European wines, they also stock a good range of spirits and champagne.

UPPER EAST SIDE/YORKVILLE

Sherry-Lehmann: 679 Madison Avenue between 61st and 62nd Streets. Tel 212-838 7500. Subway 4, 5, 6 to 59th Street. The most famous wine shop in New York. A huge selection and well situated for that Central Park picnic.

Best Cellars: 1291 Lexington Avenue between 86th and 87th Streets. Tel 212-426 4200. Subway 4, 5, 6 to 86th Street. One of the best value stores in the city for fine wines under $10.

MUSIC

GREENWICH VILLAGE

Tower Records: 692 Broadway at 4th Street. Tel 212-505 1500 **www.towerrecords.com**. Subway N, R to 8th Street.
An excellent range of CDs and tapes. Around the block from the Village shop on Lafayette Street is the knockdown Tower Clearance shop.

THEATER DISTRICT

Virgin Megastore: 1540 Broadway between 45th and 46th Streets. Tel 212-921 1020, **www.virgin.com**. Subway N, Q, R, S, W, 1, 2, 3, 7 to 42nd Street/Times Square.
A huge emporium with everything from CDs to tapes and vinyl.

UPPER WEST SIDE

Tower Records: 1961 Broadway at 66th Street. Tel 212-799 2500. Subway 1, 9 to 66th Street/Lincoln Center.
The Lincoln Center branch also has an excellent range of CDs and tapes.

SPECIALITY AND GIFT SHOPS

WEST VILLAGE

Flight 001: 96 Greenwich Avenue between Jane and 12th Streets. Tel 212-691 1001. Subway 1, 2, 3, 9 to 14th Street.
A travel accessories shop that looks like a sleek 1960s' airport lounge, it stocks fabulously cool carry-on items such as digital cameras, spray-on vitamins and WAP-activated global travel guides. It also has a range of very practical but funky luggage.

MXYPLYZYK: 125 Greenwich Avenue at 13th Street. Tel 212-989 4300. Subway 1, 2, 3, 9 to 14th Street.
Kitschy-cool gifts and what-nots including Devil Ducks (with horns – glow-in-the-dark or plain red) and tractor-seat stools for when you're tired of serious shopping.

Tea and Sympathy: 108-110 Greenwich Avenue between 12th and 13th Streets. Tel 212-807 8329. Subway 1, 2, 3, 9 to 14th Street.
Filled with all things the Brit abroad loves, this is a combination of a shop and café offering sausage rolls, fish and chips and 'proper' tea. Liz Hurley orders food for her fashion shoots, David Bowie had his 50th birthday bash here and Kate Moss and Rupert Everett are regulars.

GREENWICH VILLAGE

Village Comics: 214 Sullivan Street between West 3rd and Bleecker Streets. Tel 212-777 2770. Subway C, E to West 4th Street.
If comics are the name of the game for you, then there's a good chance you'll find a back issue of what you're looking for. It also has a mail order service.

CHELSEA

IS: 136 West 17th Street between 6th and 7th Avenues. Tel 212-620 0300. Subway A, C, E, 1, 9 to 14th Street.
A designer stationery store with a distinctly hip edge, it has classy personalised notepaper in fluorescent colours and citrus-coloured notebooks in funky 1960s-style graphics.

SMOKER'S CORNER

Amazingly, the best shop to buy your ciggies from is a chain of chemists called Duane Reade – the New York equivalent of our Boots!

CHAPTER 6

Museums

The museums and other cultural institutions of New York are a major reason why people visit the city, and I for one couldn't wait to check out the Metropolitan or discover the delights of the Museum of Modern Art. There's a huge range to see, though, and on your first visit you want to be sure that you won't feel that you've wasted your time. For this reason, I've given you my Top 10 and I'd be pretty darn surprised if anyone hated any of them.

MUSEUMS

METROPOLITAN MUSEUM OF ART

Upper East Side

✉ 5th Avenue at 82nd Street

☎ 212-535 7710 or 212-879 5500
www.metmuseum.org

🚗 Subway 4, 5, 6 to 86th Street

🕐 Sun and Tues to Thurs 9.30am–5.30pm, Fri and Sat 9.30am–9pm

$ Suggested price $10 adults, $5 students, under 12s free with an adult

With 5,000 years of art spread over 139,500sq m (1.5 million sq ft), it's impossible to see everything and you won't absorb much if you attempt it. On my first visit, I thought it would be good to see something American as I was in that country, and was delighted by the Tiffanys in the American Wing. It also has American arts and crafts and neo-classical sculptures in the garden court. The two real 'musts' for the first visit are the Temple of Dendur, which was built by Egypt to thank the American people after America helped rescue monuments threatened by the Aswan Dam, and the Egyptian art exhibits. Other 'greats' include the recently updated Greek and Roman displays, the Japanese and Chinese exhibits and the medieval art. Free hour-long tours leave from the front hall at 10.15am and 11.15am and 1.15pm, 2.15pm and 3.15pm. Also included in the admission price is admission on the same day to The Cloisters (see page 104).

AMERICAN MUSEUM OF NATURAL HISTORY

Upper West Side

✉ Central Park West at 79th Street

☎ 212-769 5000
www.amnh.org

🚗 Subway B, C to 81st Street

🕐 Sun to Thurs 10am–5.45pm, Fri and Sat 10am–8.45pm

$ Suggested price: $10 adults, $6 under 13s. Combined entrance and ticket to the Space Show (call 212-769 5200 for recorded information) $19 adults, $11.50 for under 13s

Like the Metropolitan, this is an epic of a museum, best seen in parts rather than attempting the whole. The new Rose Center for Earth and Space is like a spectacular museum within a museum and incorporates the newly revamped Hayden Planetarium as its centrepiece. This is the place to come to learn about both the inner workings of Earth and the outer reaches of the universe. Top of the must-see exhibits is the Space Theater, which is billed as the most technologically advanced in the world and shows incredibly realistic views of outer space. The Big Bang Theater gives a dramatic recreation of the first minutes

Above: New York subway
Right: Grand Central Terminal
Below right: New York Stock Exchange
Below: UN Building

Left: Chinatown

Below: New York traffic

Bottom: Winter Garden

Bottom left: Little Italy

Above: Hansom cab ride
Left: Greenwich Village
Below: South Street Seaport
Below left: Midtown 57th Street

Three views of Central Park from the air (above), at a summer concert (right) and dining at the Central Park boathouse (below)

Bottom: Bryant Park

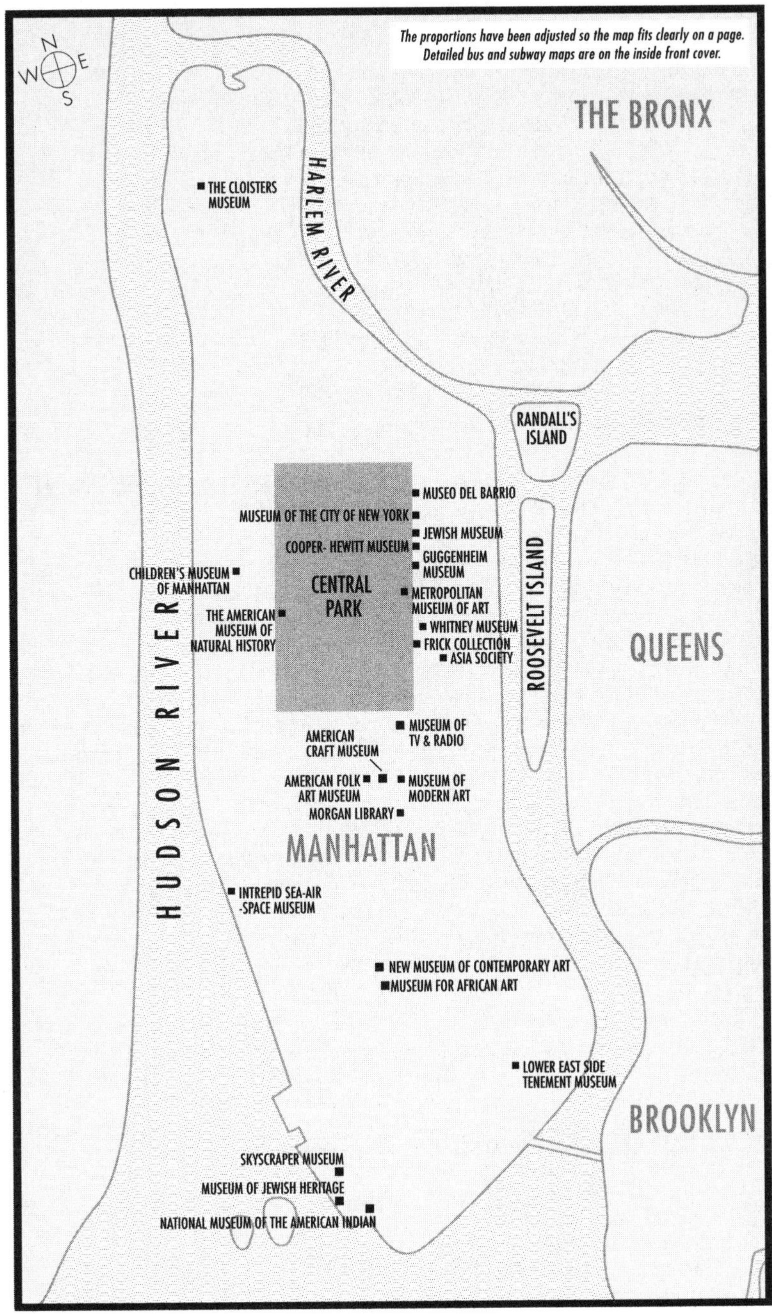

Museums in Manhattan

TOP 10 MUSEUMS

It's useful to make a list of the museums you most particularly want to see. As you get to know New York, you'll form your own opinions, but, in the meantime, here are my favourites. They cover a broad spectrum, from the history of New York to art and the world's amazing natural history, and should keep you out of mischief!

- Metropolitan Museum of Art (see page 96)
- American Museum of Natural History (see page 96)
- Ellis Island Immigration Museum (see page 58)
- Lower East Side Tenement Museum (see page 98)
- Museum of Modern Art (MoMA) (see page 99)
- Museum of Jewish Heritage (see page 100)
- *Intrepid* Sea-Air-Space Museum (see page 100)
- Frick Collection (see page 101)
- Solomon R Guggenheim Museum (see page 101)
- Skyscraper Museum (see page 101)

of the origins of the universe and is found inside an 26.5m- (87ft-) wide sphere that appears to float in a glass-walled ceiling. Try to leave time for other magnificent exhibits such as the amazing dinosaur collection, the Native American section and the seven continents. It is worth noting that there is much fun to be had, too – as you trace the roots of evolution you can travel back in time by using the many interactive computer exhibits. Other highlights include the Imax theatre, which shows exciting nature programmes, and the amazing collection of gems – worth a staggering $50 million – including the famous Star of India blue sapphire.

ELLIS ISLAND IMMIGRATION MUSEUM

Battery Park

This is featured in the major sights to visit while you are in New York. See pages 58–60.

Before you take one of the walking tours at the Lower East Side Tenement Museum, it is worth watching the slide show and film.

LOWER EAST SIDE TENEMENT MUSEUM

Lower East Side

✉ 90 Orchard Street at Broome Street
☎ 212-431 0233
www.tenement.org
🚗 Subway F to Delancey Street; B, D, Q to Grand Street; J, M, Z to Essex Street
🕘 Sun to Thurs 9am–6pm, Fri 9am–4pm
$ $9 adults, $7 students for one hour; $8 adults, $6 students for 45-minute tours. 25 per cent discount with your NYCard.

After they had gone through Ellis Island, what happened to many of those millions of immigrants? They ended up in tenements on the Lower East Side of New York and now there is a museum that tells their poignant stories.

The museum consists of several tenement houses – essentially America's first public housing, predating almost every housing law in the US. These houses contain several apartments, faithfully restored down to the last detail, complete with furniture and clothes. It's a must-see for an understanding not only of this neighbourhood, which continues to function as a launching pad for fresh generations of artists and retailers, but also of the American success story. It's also very popular with children, as they're allowed to try on the clothes.

THE INSIDE STORY

If you're in a rush, try a one-hour tour. From January to March and July to September, the Insider's Hour gives you a quick peek around the most diverse art collections, wondrous gardens, fascinating animal collections, backstage magic, historical exhibitions and interactive exhibits. Participating institutions include the Metropolitan Museum of Art (see page 96), Lower East Side Tenement Museum (see page 98), *Intrepid* Sea-Air-Space Museum (see page 100), American Museum of Natural History (see page 96), Bronx Zoo (see page 219), Museum of Modern Art (see page 99), Museum of Jewish Heritage (see page 100) and National Museum of the American Indian (see page 107).

For information and a complete list of participating institutions, send a stamped, self-addressed envelope to Insider's Hour, NYC & Co, 810 7th Avenue, 3rd Floor, New York, NY 10019. Details of times are available at the NYC & Co website at **www.nycvisit.com** or CitySearch at **www.newyork.citysearch.com.**

MUSEUM OF MODERN ART

Midtown

- ✉ 11 West 53rd Street between 5th and 6th Avenues
- ☎ 212-708 9400 **www.moma.org**
- 🚘 Subway E, V to 5th Avenue
- 🕘 Sat to Tues and Thurs 10.30am–5.45pm, Fri 10.30am–8.15pm. Also open Fridays 4.30pm–8.15pm, pay what you wish
- $ Entrance $12 adults, $8.50 students, free for under 16s if with an adult

Founded in 1929 by three private citizens, including Abby Rockefeller, this was the first museum to devote its entire collection to the modern movement. Since then it has retained its pioneering sense of the new, and was the first museum to see architecture, design, photography and film as art forms. The museum's collection, which started with a gift of eight prints and one drawing, dates from the 1880s to the present day and now encompasses more than 100,000 works.

Make the most of a trip to see the MoMA QNS by using the courtesy weekend shuttle service, the Queens Artlink, which also takes you to the Isamu Oguchi Garden Museum, Socrates Sculpture Park and the American Museum of the Moving Image. Call 212-708 9750 for details.

Many of the icons of modern and contemporary art are here including Van Gogh's *The Starry Night*, Monet's *Water Lilies*, Picasso's *Les Demoiselles* and Andy Warhol's *Gold Marilyn Monroe*. The collection includes paintings, sculptures, drawings, photographs, films, film stills and videos. Films are screened daily in the two cinemas (cost included in the museum entrance price, though you need to get a special ticket to reserve your place). Free gallery talks are given at 1pm and 3pm every day except Wednesday and on Fridays at 6pm and 7pm for $4 you can take a personalised audio self-guided tour.

Note: Now undergoing a $650 million expansion, MoMA exhibits are being mounted in a temporary space (MoMA QNS) at 45-20 33rd Street at Queens Boulevard in Long Island City. Take the 7 train to 33rd Street and the museum is a few hundred metres down the road. The museum will maintain a full exhibition schedule including a Picasso and Matisse exhibition in 2003.

MUSEUM OF JEWISH HERITAGE: A LIVING MEMORIAL TO THE HOLOCAUST

Battery Park City

✉ 18 First Place at Battery Place, Battery Park City

☎ 212-509 6130 or to order tickets by phone 212-945 0039
www.mjhnyc.org

🚗 Subway N, R to Rector Street or 4, 5 to Bowling Green

🕘 Sun to Wed 9am–5pm, Thurs 9am–8pm, Fri and eve of Jewish holidays 9am–3pm in winter, 5pm in summer. Saturdays and Jewish holidays closed

$ Entrance $7 adults, $5 students, under 6s free. Two for one admission with your NYCard

Joy, tradition, tragedy and unspeakable horror are the powerful themes of this museum, which tells the moving story of 20th-century Jewish life from the perspective of those who lived it. Created as a living memorial to the Holocaust, it puts the tragedy into the larger context of modern Jewish history and includes 24 original films that feature testimonies from Steven Spielberg's Survivors of the Shoah Visual History Foundation, as well as the museum's own video archive.

Make the most of your visit to the Museum of Jewish Heritage by renting an audio guide, narrated by Meryl Streep and Itzhak Perlman, cost $5.

Before entering the museum, take a look at the six-sided shape of the tiered roof, a symbolic reminder of the six million who died in the Holocaust and of the Star of David. Anyone who has ever been to one of the former concentration camps in Europe will be aware of the stark reality of the Holocaust, but this museum does offer some relief in the form of the story of survival and what the Jewish people have achieved since those grim days. In fact, the museum has done so well it is in the process of expanding its exhibition and meeting space. Due to be completed in autumn 2003, the expansion includes a cinema/ lecture hall, memorial garden, family history center, library and café.

INTREPID SEA-AIR-SPACE MUSEUM

Clinton

✉ USS *Intrepid*, Pier 86, 46th Street at the Hudson River

☎ 212-245 2533
www.intrepidmuseum.org

🚗 Subway A, C, E to 42nd Street

🕘 Open from the last Monday in May to the first Monday in September Mon to Fri 10am–5pm, Sat, Sun and holidays 10am–7pm

$ Entrance $10 adults, $5 under 12s. $2 off with your NYCard

A thoroughly enjoyable museum, which appeals to all ages and sexes. All the staff are very friendly and there are former members of the crew around the ship who are happy to give an insight into its history and life on board. *Intrepid* was one of 24 Second World War US aircraft carriers and despite incidents of serious damage to these ships, none of them was ever sunk during the war. *Intrepid*'s worst moment came on November 25, 1944 when two Kamikaze pilots hit the ship five minutes apart, killing 69 men and seriously injuring 85 others. The second plane exploded on the hangar deck and the ship burned for about six hours, but *Intrepid* made it back to America for repairs and returned to the

The only way to see the submarine at *Intrepid* is on a tour and long queues build up very quickly, so get there early and see it before anything else.

war. Stories of life on board the ship are told by veterans at film screenings throughout the ship and there are also plenty of hands-on exhibits to keep children happy. One of the best exhibits is the F-18 navy jet flight simulator, which costs an extra $5, but is great fun.

FRICK COLLECTION

Upper East Side

✉ 1 East 70th Street at 5th Avenue

☎ 212-288 0700, **www.frick.org**

🚗 Subway 6 to 68th Street

🕐 Tues to Thurs and Sat 10am–6pm, Fri 10am–8.45pm, Sun 1–6pm

$ Entrance $10 adults, $5 students and seniors 62+; children under 10 not admitted and under 16s must be with an adult

When it opened to the public in 1935, the limestone mansion that was built for coal and steel industrialist Henry Frick quickly became a popular attraction in New York. The Frick now offers an intimate look into what was once a grand home in the last days of America's Gilded Age. Its artwork and objects from the 14th to the 19th centuries, such as fine French furniture, bronzes, Chinese porcelains and Limoges enamels, are arranged as if the Fricks still lived here. The walls are lined with Holbeins, Vermeers, Rembrandts, Turners, Gainsboroughs and Van Dycks.

This is the closest that the Americans will come to creating the atmosphere of an English stately home, and the serenity of this bijou museum is lovely. Get a preview by looking at the virtual reality tour on the Frick's website.

Now you can really soak up the ambiance with a glass of wine from the bar in the Garden Court when the museum stays open late on Friday evenings.

SOLOMON R GUGGENHEIM MUSEUM

Upper East Side

✉ 1071 5th Avenue at 89th Street

☎ 212-423 3500
www.guggenheim.org

🚗 Subway 4, 5, 6 to 86th Street

🕐 Sun to Wed 9am–6pm, Fri and Sat 9am–8pm

$ Entrance $12 adults, $8 students and senior citizens, under 12s free. Fri 6–8pm pay what you wish. $2 off with your NYCard

The main Guggenheim Museum in New York is probably best known for its beautiful building, which was designed by Frank Lloyd Wright and is now one of the youngest buildings in the city to be designated a New York City landmark. It houses one of the world's largest collections of Kandinksy, as well as works by Chagall, Klee, Picasso, Cézanne, Degas, Gauguin and Manet. It also has Peggy Guggenheim's entire collection of cubist, surrealist and abstract expressionist art.

Check out the Guggenheim's sculpture gallery for some of the best views of Central Park.

SKYSCRAPER MUSEUM

Battery Park

✉ The Ritz Carlton Hotel, 2 West Street between Battery Place and West End.

☎ 212-968 1961
Website **www.skyscraper.org**

🚗 Subway 4, 5 to Bowling Green

$ Entrance to the museum when it has an exhibition is generally free, though it is suggested that you give a donation of $2

Located in New York City, the world's first and greatest vertical metropolis, the museum celebrates the city's rich architectural heritage and looks at what historical forces and which individuals shaped the different skylines of its history. Through exhibitions, programmes and publications, the museum offers a fascinating insight into how individual buildings were created, complete with detailed information about how the contractors bid for the work, what was involved and how the building work was executed, all with comprehensive photographic illustrations.

Since 1997, the museum has presented exhibitions in temporary spaces – two vacant banking halls on Wall Street in the heart of New York's historic Financial District – including Downtown New York, Building The Empire State and Big Buildings. The exhibitions are surprisingly moving as they manage to convey the very real human sacrifices and energy put into creating these incredible buildings. Most moving of all was its recent homage to the Twin Towers, which marked the entire 30-year history of the World Trade Center.

THE A-Z OF OTHER MUSEUMS IN NEW YORK

THE ALTERNATIVE MUSEUM
SoHo

✉ 594 Broadway between Prince and Houston Streets

☎ 212-966 4444 or 787-861 1206
www.alternativemuseum.org

Be prepared to prove you're a student if you want to make the most of discounted admissions to museums.

A small series of galleries focusing on contemporary art and culture that has shown ground-breaking work by Andres Serrano and David Hammonds, among many others.

AMERICAN CRAFT MUSEUM
Midtown

✉ 40 West 53rd Street between 5th and 6th Avenues

☎ 212-956 3535
www.americancraftmuseum.org

🚗 Subway E, V to 5th Avenue

🕘 Tues to Sun 10am–6pm, Thurs 10am–8pm

$ Entrance $8 adults, $5 students and seniors, under 12s free

Just across the way from the MoMA (see page 97), this is an easy museum to fit in – especially as the MoMA doesn't open until mid-morning. It has everything from wood and metal to clay, glass and fibre. In addition to the permanent collections, there are temporary shows too.

AMERICAN FOLK ART MUSEUM
Midtown

✉ 45 West 53rd Street between 5th and 6th Avenues

☎ 212-265 1040
www.folkartmuseum.org

🚗 Subway E, V to 5th Avenue

🕘 Tues to Sun 10am–6pm, except Fri 10am–8pm

$ Entrance $9 adults, $5 students and seniors, under 12s and members free

The first entirely new museum building in New York since 1966, the $18 million structure was designed by award-winning architects Tod Williams and Billy Tsien. From a punter's point of view, this new museum provides an excellent opportunity to get to grips with American folk art. And for Brits who'd like an insight into the American psyche, a visit here should be closely followed by one to the neighbouring American Craft Museum.

AMERICAN MUSEUM OF THE MOVING IMAGE
Queens

It's only a short trip to Queens and worth a visit here if you are into films. See page 221.

ASIA SOCIETY

Midtown East

✉ 25 Park Avenue at 70th Street

☎ 212-288 6400
www.asiasociety.com

🚗 Subway 4, 5, 6 to 59th Street

🕐 Tues to Sun 11am–6pm, Fri 11am–9pm

$ Entrance $7 adults, $5 students and senior citizens, members and under 16s free

Founded in 1956 by John D Rockefeller III with his collection of Asian art, the society aims to build an awareness of the 30 Pan-Asian countries, which include Japan, New Zealand, Australia and the Pacific Islands. To this end it runs films, lectures and seminars in conjunction with its exhibitions and even has a regular schedule of Asian musicians who play at the museum.

BROOKLYN MUSEUM OF ART

One of the largest museums in the world, it is easy to reach in Brooklyn if you have the time to plan it into your schedule. See page 217.

BROOKLYN CHILDREN'S MUSEUM

New York's first children's museum, it has a great programme of events and workshops and is particularly worth the trip if you are on a family holiday. See page 218.

CHILDREN'S MUSEUM OF ART

Little Italy

✉ 182 Lafayette Street between Broome and Grand Streets

☎ 212-274 0986

🚗 Subway N, R to Prince Street, B, D, F, Q to Broadway-Lafayette Street, 6 to Spring Street.

$ Entrance $5

Under sevens can have an artistic ball here with art computers, an art playground and a giant chalkboard. There are also regular performing arts workshops.

CHILDREN'S MUSEUM OF MANHATTAN

Upper West Side

✉ 212 West 83rd Street between Broadway and Amsterdam Avenue

☎ 212-721 1234

🚗 Subway 1, 9 to 86th Street

🕐 Wed to Sun (and public school holidays) 10am–5pm

$ Entrance $6 adults and children, $3 seniors, infants under 1 are free

The CMOM is entirely dedicated to children under the age of 10 – and their families. This is a fabulous place and almost worth a visit even if you don't have kids! Its mission statement is to inspire children and their families to learn about themselves and our culturally diverse world through a unique environment of interactive exhibits and programmes.

After you've checked out CMOM, cross the street for a light snack and drinks at Café Lalo, which serves up great cakes and featured in the Meg Ryan and Tom Hanks movie *You've Got Mail.*

And they certainly achieve it with their inspiring exhibits, such as the zany and fun-filled Body Odyssey, which shows children just what they're made of. Youngsters aged five and over can rush through the blood tunnel, hold their noses and slime around in the digestive tract, or take deep breaths and wind their way down the windpipe. On the way, they will learn about where burps come from, what makes a cut stop bleeding and where shed skin goes.

Other exhibits include WordPlay for tots aged six months to four years. The Time Warner Media Center helps children aged six and above to get behind the scenes of a professionally equipped TV studio and produce their own show, and the CMOM Theater takes children into a magical world of dance, music, theatre and puppetry.

THE CLOISTERS

Washington Heights

- ✉ Fort Tyron Park, Fort Washington Avenue at Margaret Corbin Plaza, Washington Heights
- ☎ 212-923 3700
- 🚗 Subway A to 190th Street
- 🕘 March to Oct Tues to Sun 9.30am–5.15pm, Nov to Feb Tues to Sun 9.30am–4.45pm
- $ Suggested donation $10 adults (includes free same-day admission to the Metropolitan Museum of Art – see page 96), $5 students, under 12s free if with an adult

Rockefeller cash allowed the Metropolitan Museum to buy this beautifully red-tiled Romanesque building 70 years ago. Now it is used purely to display examples of medieval art and architecture, including five cloisters – hence the name – from ruined French monasteries dating from the 12th to the 15th centuries. It is stunning to look at and houses some really exciting exhibits.

It's a long way north to The Cloisters. If you want to make the most of your time in the vicinity, combine a visit with a walking tour of Harlem or follow one of the walking tours in Chapter 14.

COOPER-HEWITT NATIONAL DESIGN MUSEUM

Upper East Side

- ✉ 2 East 91st Street at 5th Avenue
- ☎ 212-849 8400
- 🚗 Subway 4, 5, 6 to 86th Street
- 🕘 Sun noon–5pm, Tues 10am–9pm, Wed to Sat 10am–5pm
- $ Entrance $5 adults, $3 students and seniors. Free on Tues 5pm–9pm

The only American museum devoted entirely to historical and contemporary design, the Cooper-Hewitt covers everything from applied arts and industrial design to drawings, prints, textiles and wall-coverings. Take time to look at the exterior of the building itself, which was designed in a Georgian style for tycoon Andrew Carnegie.

EL MUSEO DEL BARRIO

Spanish Harlem

- ✉ 1230 5th Avenue at 104th Street
- ☎ 212-831 7272
  www.elmuseo.org
- 🚗 Subway 6 to 103rd Street
- 🕘 Wed to Sun 11am–5pm
- $ Suggested donation $5 adults, $3 students and seniors, under 12s free with an adult

Opened in 1969 by a group of Puerto Rican parents, teachers and artists, it houses 8,000 objects of Caribbean and Latin American art from pre-Colombian times to date. Exhibits include musical instruments, miniature houses, dolls and masks.

FRAUNCES TAVERN MUSEUM

Financial District

- ✉ 54 Pearl Street at Broad Street, first and second floors
- ☎ 212-425 1778
- 🚗 Subway 4, 5 to Bowling Green; 1, 2 to Wall Street; N, R, to Whitehall
- 🕘 Tues, Wed, Fri 10am–5pm, Thurs 10am–7pm, Sat 11am–5pm
- $ Entrance $3 adults, $2 children and seniors, under 6 and members free

Don't miss the cosy restaurant at the Fraunces Tavern Museum – it serves lovely food in a stately tourist environment.

When New York was (briefly) capital of America, the Fraunces Tavern housed the Departments of Foreign Affairs, Treasury and War and was where George Washington delivered his famous farewell speech to his officers. Now, nestled among the skyscrapers of the Financial District, this 18th-century Georgian building, along with four adjacent 19th-century buildings, houses a fine museum dedicated to the study of early American history and culture. Although well preserved, an awful lot of restoration work has been done to keep its 1783 façade.

ISAMU NOGUCHI GARDEN MUSEUM

The Japanese sculptor's art can be seen at this museum in Queens. See page 222.

JULIA DE BURGOS LATINO CULTURAL CENTER AND TALLER BORICUA GALLERY

Spanish Harlem

- ✉ 1680 Lexington Avenue at 106th Street
- ☎ 212-831 4333
- ⌚ Tues to Sun noon–6pm except Thurs 1–7pm

Another excellent location to see works by Latino artists. Around the museum, watch out for pavement artwork by James de la Vega, a young local artist.

JEWISH MUSEUM

Upper East Side

- ✉ 1109 5th Avenue at 92nd Street
- ☎ 212-423 3200 **www.thejewishmuseum.org**
- 🚗 Subway 4, 5, 6 to 96th Street
- ⌚ Sun 10am–5.45pm, Mon to Wed 11am–5.45pm, Thurs 11am–8pm, Fri 11am–3pm
- $ Entrance $8 adults, $5.50 students and seniors. Free admission on Tuesdays from 5–9pm

Impressive annual exhibitions. The core exhibit is called The Jewish Journey and sets out how the Jewish people have survived through the centuries and explores the essence of Jewish identity. Many of the objects were actually rescued from European synagogues before the Second World War.

MORGAN LIBRARY

Midtown East

The bijou Morgan Library will be closed until the end of 2004.

- ✉ 29 East 36th Street between Madison and Park Avenues
- ☎ 212-685 0008 **www.morganlibrary.org**
- 🚗 Subway 6 to 33rd Street
- ⌚ Tues to Thurs 10.30am–5pm, Fri 10.30am–8pm, Sat 10.30am–6pm, Sun noon–6pm
- $ Entrance $7 adults, $5 students, under 12s free with an adult. Free entry and 10 per cent discount in the shop with your NYCard

A gem of a museum, housed in an Italianate building that was once Pierpoint Morgan's library. The collection contains medieval and Renaissance manuscripts; drawings and prints from the 14th century onwards, including works by Degas, Blake, Pollock and Rubens; ancient Middle Eastern seals and tablets; and music manuscripts including original handwritten works by Beethoven, Bach, Brahms and Schubert. The shop, incidentally, has some great upmarket souvenirs and some lovely child-friendly games.

MOUNT VERNON HOTEL MUSEUM AND GARDEN

Upper East Side

- ✉ 421 East 61st Street between 1st and York Avenues
- ☎ 212-838 6878
- 🚗 Subway 4, 5, 6 to 59th Street
- ⌚ Tues to Sun 11am–4pm. Closed in August and some holidays
- $ Entrance $4 adults, $3 students and seniors, under 12s free

An amazing structure that dates back to the Colonial era, this was once the coach house of the daughter of America's second president, John Adams. An early 18th-century building, it has been lovingly restored by the Colonial Dames of America who will sometimes be on hand to talk about the furnishings and park at the back.

MUSEUM FOR AFRICAN ART

SoHo

✉ 593 Broadway between Houston and Prince Streets

☎ 212-966 1313
www.africanart.org

🚗 Subway B, D, F, Q to Broadway/Lafayette Street; N, R to Prince Street; 6 to Bleecker Street

🕐 Tues to Fri 10.30am–5.30pm, Sat and Sun noon–6pm

$ Entrance $5 adults, $2.50 students and children; Sundays free

When the museum moved to its new headquarters in SoHo, acclaimed designer Maya Lin, creator of the National Vietnam Veterans' Memorial in Washington, completely redesigned the interior to create a wonderfully serene setting. Exhibitions change approximately every six months.

MUSEUM OF AMERICAN FINANCIAL HISTORY

Financial District

✉ 28 Broadway at Bowling Green Park

☎ 212-908 4110
www.financialhistory.org

🚗 Subway 5 to Bowling Green, N, R to Rector Street

$ Suggested donation $2

Housed appropriately enough in the former headquarters of John D Rockefeller's Standard Oil, this new museum traces the growth of the world's largest financial superpower. It is the largest public museum archive of financial documents in the world.

MUSEUM OF CHINESE IN THE AMERICAS

Chinatown

✉ First floor, 70 Mulberry Street on the corner of Bayard Street

☎ 212-619 4785

🚗 Subway N, R, 6 to Canal Street

🕐 Tue to Sat noon–5pm

$ Entrance $3 adults, $1 over 12s and seniors, free for under 12s

A fascinating little museum tucked away on the first floor of the community centre. It has photographs, personal belongings and talks to reveal the history of Chinese immigrants to both North and South America.

MUSEUM OF TELEVISION AND RADIO

Midtown

✉ 25 West 52nd Street between 5th and 6th Avenues

☎ 212-621 6600
www.mtr.org

🚗 Subway E, F to 5th Avenue; B, D, F, Q to 47th–50th Streets/Rockefeller Center

🕐 Tues, Wed, Sat and Sun noon–6pm, Thurs noon–8pm, Fri noon– 9pm

$ Entrance $6 adults, $4 students and seniors, $3 under 13s

In addition to the exhibits, the museum also has a daily programme of screenings in two cinemas and two presentation rooms. Pick up a copy of the daily schedule in the lobby on your way in. You can also make an appointment with the library to check out the museum's collection of over 100,000 radio and TV programmes before accessing them on the custom-designed database.

MUSEUM OF THE CITY OF NEW YORK

Spanish Harlem

✉ 1220 5th Avenue at 103rd Street

☎ 212-534 1672
www.mcny.org

🚗 Subway 6 to 103rd Street

🕐 Sun noon–5pm, Wed to Sat 10am–5pm

$ Suggested donation $12 families, $7 adults, $4 children, students and seniors. Two-for-one admission with your NYCard

The entire breadth of New York's history and the people who played parts in its development are celebrated at this fascinating museum. Prints, photographs, paintings and sculptures and even clothing and decorative household objects are used to tell the story of New York. It is particularly noted for its Broadway memorabilia.

The Museum of the City of New York is very relaxed about defining your family. Groups can buy a family ticket at the Museum of the City of New York even if they are not related.

NATIONAL MUSEUM OF THE AMERICAN INDIAN

Bowling Green/Financial District

✉ George Gustave Heye Center, US Custom House, 1 Bowling Green between State and Whitehall Streets

☎ 212-514 3700

🚗 Subway 1, 9 to South Ferry; N, R to Whitehall Street

🕐 Daily 10am–5pm except Thurs 10am–8pm

$ Entrance free

The first museum dedicated entirely to Native American history, art, performing art and culture. The collection includes fabulous leather clothing, intricately beaded head-dresses, sashes, hats and shoes, explaining the white man's influence on Indian culture as well as their own centuries-old traditions. Despite the size and grandness of the beautiful building, it only has 500 pieces on display and thus seems quite small. However, it is very well laid out and the explanations of each piece have usually been given by Native Americans.

NEUE GALERIE MUSEUM FOR GERMAN AND AUSTRIAN ART

Upper East Side

✉ 1048 Fifth Avenue at 86th Street

☎ 212-628 6200
www.neuegalerie.org

🚗 Subway 4, 5, 6 to 86th Street

🕐 Fri 11am–9pm, Sat to Mon 11am–6pm

$ Entrance $10 adults, $7 students and seniors. Under 12s not permitted, under 16s only with an adult

Opened in November 2001, this was founded by the late German Expressionist art dealer Serge Sabarsky and chairman of the MoMA board Ronald S Lauder. It does exactly what it says on the tin by exhibiting fine and decorative arts of Germany and Austria from the first half of the 20th century. A real bonus is the building itself – a wonderful Louis XIII-style, Beaux Art landmark.

While you're on the Museum Mile, take a pit stop at the fabulous Sabarsky Café in the Neue Galerie, which is open every day except Wednesday.

NEW MUSEUM OF CONTEMPORARY ART

SoHo

✉ 583 Broadway between Houston and Prince Streets

☎ 212-219 1222
www.newmuseum.org

🚗 Subway F, S to Broadway/Lafayette Street; N, R to Prince Street; 6 to Bleecker Street and Prince Street

🕐 Tues to Sun noon–6pm, Thurs noon–8pm

$ Entrance $6 adults, $3 students, under 18s free. $3 Thursdays 6–8pm

When they say 'contemporary', they really mean it. All the works exhibited are by living artists, often looking at social issues through modern media and machinery. The area downstairs at the museum is open free to the public and contains the bookstore, a spacious reading room and an exhibition space for interactive projects, installations and performances.

NEW YORK CITY POLICE MUSEUM

Bowling Green/Financial District

✉ 100 Old Slip at South Street
☎ 212-480 3100
www.nycpolicemuseum.org
🚗 Subway 4, 5 to Bowling Green
🕘 Mon to Sun 10am–5pm
$ Suggested donation $5

Having opened in January 2000, this is one of the very latest attractions in the Downtown area and it's a little corker. It is now permanently housed in the former 1st precinct building – the oldest cop shop in New York. Highlights include the Mounted Unit – one of the oldest and most prestigious within the NYPD – and the K-9 dog unit. In addition to the police memorabilia – a line-up of guns, uniforms and badges – there's even the Tommy gun with its original violin case that was used to kill mobster Frankie Yale. Plus, you can have a go at playing detective yourself in the interactive crime scene area.

THE NEW YORK CITY TRANSIT MUSEUM

Brooklyn Heights

A great little museum that is particularly popular with children. See page 216.

THE NEW YORK HALL OF SCIENCE

Queens

A great science museum with demos. See page 220.

NEW YORK HISTORICAL SOCIETY

Upper West Side

✉ 2 West 77th Street at Central Park West
☎ 212-873 3400
www.nyhistory.org
🚗 Subway B, C to 81st Street
🕘 Tues to Sat 10am–5pm in winter, Tues to Fri 10am–5pm in summer
$ Entrance $5 adults, $3 children and seniors

When this jewel was formed in 1804 it was the only art museum in the city until the opening of the Metropolitan Museum of Art in 1872. The Historical Society was founded to chronicle New York's history and is home to the world's largest collection of Tiffany stained-glass shades and lamps, two million manuscripts, including letters sent by George Washington during the War of Independence, and a lock of the former president's hair.

SCHOMBURG CENTER FOR RESEARCH IN BLACK CULTURE

Harlem

✉ 515 Malcolm X Boulevard at 135th Street
☎ 212-491 2200
www.schomburgcenter.org
🚗 Subway 2, 3 to 135th Street
🕘 Mon to Wed noon–8pm, Thurs to Sat 10am–6pm
$ Entrance free. Tours by appointment

If you want to see the Schomburg Center at its best, phone or check out the website in advance to find out about film screenings and jazz concerts.

Established in 1926 by Arthur Schomburg, it has more than five million items including books, photographs, manuscripts, art works, films, videos and sound recordings that document the historical and cultural development of black people in the United States, the Caribbean, the Americas, Africa, Europe and Asia. The research unit is open to anyone, while there are exhibitions on art dating back to the 17th century that include masks, paintings and sculptures. Incidentally, the corner of Malcolm X Boulevard, where the Schomburg sits, was once home to Harlem's version of Speaker's Corner where people used to come and talk about their political beliefs and organisations.

MUSEUMS FOR CHILDREN

In addition to the child-specific Children's Museum of the Arts, Children's Museum of Manhattan and Brooklyn Children's Museum, it's good to note what is available for youngsters at the mainstream museums.

American Museum of Natural History: (see page 96) Excellent exhibits for children. The Hall of Planet Earth, a spectacular, state-of-the-art addition to the museum, explains how the earth evolved, why there are oceans, continents and mountains, and all about earthquakes and storms.

Bronx Zoo: (see page 219) The Children's Zoo gives kids the chance to learn about wildlife by crawling through a prairie dog tunnel, climbing a spider's web and getting close to domestic animals. They'll also really love the new Congo Gorilla Forest.

Brooklyn Museum of Art: (see page 217) Offers a drop-in programme called Arty Facts for 4- to 7-year-olds, in which they learn about different works of art between 11am and 2pm on Saturdays.

Jewish Museum: (see page 105) Offers a new children's exhibit called Pickles and Pomegranates: Jewish Homes Near and Far, in which youngsters can play house in a replica of a Lower East Side tenement and a home in Persia.

Lower East Side Tenement Museum: (see page 98) Similar themes of struggle and triumph among America's first urban pioneers spring to life, with a hands-on tour of the 1916 Confino Family Apartment that lets children try on period clothing and operate an authentic Victrola, a hand-cranked gramophone.

Metropolitan Museum of Art: (see page 96) Self-guided children's tours called Art Hunts with special themes. In addition, it has special tours for groups of children aged 6–12 and their families in which they are taken to a specific part of the museum and encouraged to hunt for items to do with the theme of the day and then draw them. Beyond that, two must-see exhibits that always wow children are the awesome Egyptian Temple of Dendur and the medieval armour collection.

Museum of Modern Art: (see page 99) Here you can pick up a guidebook from the gift shop for children aged 5–12 and go on an Art Safari. This helps them to explore eight artworks featuring animals and encourages them to look, question and talk about what they see. The museum also has special family tours on Saturdays 10–10.45am (before the museum opens to the public) after which a film series is screened at noon.

New York Botanical Garden: (see page 218) The Everett Children's Adventure Garden has 40 hands-on plant discovery activities throughout 5 hectares (12 acres) of gardens.

Solomon R Guggenheim Museum: (see page 101) Occasional tours on Sundays between 2pm and 4pm when children aged 5–10 can see special exhibitions and afterwards take part in an art workshop.

Staten Island's Children's Museum: 1000 Richmond Terrace, Staten Island 718-735 4400. Science and nature are the order of the day here – children will love exhibits like Bugs and Other Insects, where they get to crawl through a human-sized anthill, and Pigtails and Hardhats, where they'll learn the basics of home construction through the classic story of *The Three Little Pigs.*

Whitney Museum: (see page 110) Free Look Out! tours for children at 1pm on Saturdays with a teenage guide who will tell the youngsters about the artists and their work. From October to May, they also run workshops in which children get to discover the inside world of an artist, but you must book the $6 tickets in advance.

SOUTH STREET SEAPORT MUSEUM

Fulton Street/Financial District

✉ 207–211 Water Street at Beekman Street

☎ 212-748 8600
www.southstseaport.org

🚗 Subway A, C to Broadway/Nassau Street, 2, 3, 4, 5 to Fulton Street

🕐 April 1 to Sept daily 10am–6pm, Thurs 10am–8pm, Oct to Mar Wed to Mon 10am–5pm

$ Entrance $6 adults, $5 seniors, $4 students, $3 children including all tours, films, galleries and museum-owned ships

A sprawling mass of buildings house galleries, 19th-century buildings, a visitors' centre and a selection of ships, all of which give an insight into life in the olden days of New York. The museum is also the venue for a series of free outdoor summer concerts held almost nightly.

STUDIO MUSEUM IN HARLEM

Harlem

✉ 144 West 125th Street between 7th and Lenox Avenues

☎ 212-864 4500

🚗 Subway A, B, C, D and 2, 3, 4, 5, 6 to 125th Street

🕐 Mon to Fri 10am–6pm

$ Entrance $5 adults, $3 students and seniors, $1 children

Works of art by African-American, African and Caribbean artists.

WHITNEY MUSEUM OF AMERICAN ART

Upper East Side

✉ 945 Madison Avenue at 75th Street

☎ 212-570 3676
www.whitney.org

🚗 Subway 6 to 77th Street

🕐 Tues to Thurs, Sat and Sun 11am–6pm, Fri 1–9pm

$ Entrance $10 adults, $8 students, under 12s free. First Friday of every month 6–9pm pay what you wish

The Whitney may be housed in one of the most ghastly looking buildings in the world – a grey, granite series of cubes designed by Marcel Breuer – but it has a world-class collection of 20th-century art. And yet it all came about almost by accident. Gertrude Vanderbilt Whitney offered her entire collection to the Metropolitan but was turned down, so she decided to set up her own museum. In 1931 the Whitney was founded with a core group of 700 art objects.

Subsequently, the museum's holdings have been greatly enriched by other purchases and the gifts of other major collectors. It now has a permanent collection of 12,000 works including paintings, sculptures, drawings, prints, photographs and multimedia installations and is still growing. As well as the wide range of artists in its collection, the Whitney has huge bodies of works by artists including Alexander Calder, Edward Hopper, Georgia O'Keefe, Gaston Lachaise and Agnes Martin.

Although the Midtown branch (below) is known for exhibitions of works by contemporary artists, the main museum still likes to mount cutting-edge exhibitions. To make the most of your visit, you can take an audio tour.

The shop in the basement, next to the restaurant, is filled with funky and colourful gifts. There's some great stuff for kids including soap crayons that will wash off baths and tiles and colourful blocks of soap that can be moulded into sculptures.

WHITNEY MUSEUM OF AMERICAN ART AT PHILIP MORRIS

Midtown

✉ 120 Park Avenue at 42nd Street

☎ 212-878 2550

🚗 Subway S, 4, 5, 6, 7 to 42nd Street/Grand Central

🕐 Mon to Fri 11am–6pm, Thurs 11am–7.30pm. The Sculpture Court is open Mon to Sat 7.30am–9.30pm, Sun 11am–7pm

$ Entrance free

The midtown branch of the Whitney is devoted to exhibitions of individual contemporary artists.

CHAPTER 7

Restaurants

New Yorkers take their restaurants very seriously – not surprising, given that many New York apartments have tiny kitchens if they have one at all.

Of course, like everything American, big is best and in the case of restaurants big doesn't necessarily refer to size, but to the reputation of the chefs, many of whom have become celebrities in their own right. And in many cases getting into their establishments is a hard task. If your heart is set on a meal at a landmark New York restaurant, you will need to book weeks ahead. At other restaurants in the speciality category you will still have to book ahead – especially if you want to eat out at the weekend.

The number of restaurants in New York precludes me from giving all but a 'best of the best' kind of listing here. I have gone for the well known, the excellent and the trendy and added a few neighbourhood joints for good measure.

$	Under $30 per head
$$	Under $60 per head
$$$	$60 and up!

LANDMARK RESTAURANTS

Aureole: French, Upper East Side, $$$
Four Seasons: Continental, Midtown East, $$$
La Caravelle: French, Midtown, $$$
Le Cirque 2000: French, Midtown East, $$$
Oyster Bar: Fish, Grand Central Station, $$
Russian Tea Room: Russian, Midtown, $$
21 Club: American, Midtown, $-$$$

BATTERY PARK AND BATTERY PARK CITY

AMERICAN PARK AT THE BATTERY $$$

✉ Battery Park opposite 17 State Street
☎ 212-809 5508
🚗 Subway 4, 5 to Bowling Green; N, R, to Whitehall

A superb American restaurant in an elegant, glass building that shows off the spectacular views of the Hudson and East Rivers and the Statue of Liberty. In good weather you can eat outside on the terrace. Sumptuous American dishes include sautéed day-boat sea scallops, whole roasted black sea bass and free-range stuffed chicken breast.

GIGINO AT WAGNER PARK $

✉ 20 Battery Place at Hudson River
☎ 212-528 2228
🚗 Subway 5 to Bowling Green; 1, 9 to South Ferry

Great little café/diner near the Museum of Jewish Heritage in the Battery Park area. Good for a coffee and sarnie pit stop.

HUDSON RIVER CLUB $$$

✉ 4 World Financial Center, 250 Vesey Street at West Street
☎ 212-786 1500
🚗 Subway N, R, 1, 2 to Cortlandt Street

Specialising in American cuisine from the Hudson Valley, the delicious food is

Sometimes the only way to get into a very popular restaurant is to go very early or very late in the evening.

matched by the spectacular views of the North Cove Harbour and the Statue of Liberty. If you don't want to splash out on an expensive meal, at least treat yourself to a $10 drink at the bar. Sunday brunch is a real favourite with the Wall Streeters who live in the area, so if you'd like to join them, book in advance.

2 WEST **$$-$$$**

✉ 2 West Street between Battery Place and West End

☎ 212-344 0800

🚗 Subway 4, 5 to Bowling Green

The lobby-level restaurant of the Ritz Carlton has fabulous views of the Hudson River and Statue of Liberty, plus outdoor seating for al fresco dining in the warmer months. The menu offers American classics plus global fusions including chicken *pot au feu* and soba noodles with seafood stir-fry. The lunch menu also offers quick and easy Bento Boxes with Italian and Spanish themes.

FINANCIAL DISTRICT AND SOUTH STREET SEAPORT

KOODO SUSHI **$$**

✉ 129 Front Street on the lower level of Seaport Suites Hotel between Pine and Wall Streets

☎ 212-425 2890

🚗 Subway 1, 2, 4, 5 to Wall Street

This place doesn't look like much, but it's brand new and has one of the best sushi chefs in town. The fish is impeccable, but the chef really shines in his daily specials - take hostess Michelle's advice on this.

MARKJOSEPH STEAKHOUSE **$$**

✉ 261 Water Street between Peck Slip and Dover Street

☎ 212-277 0020

🚗 Subway: 1, 2, 4, 5, A, C, J, M, Z to Fulton Street/Broadway Nassau

A recent opening, this restaurant has already made its mark as one of the best steak houses in the city. The porterhouse is so tender some people have said it 'could be eaten through a straw'. Team it with the delicious hash browns. Wearing a jacket is advisable.

QUARTINO **$$**

✉ 21 Peck Slip at Water Street

☎ 212-349 4433

🚗 Subway 1, 2, 4, 5, A, C, J, M, Z to Fulton Street/Broadway Nassau

Northern Italian fare in a **very** charming, high-ceilinged, wooden-tabled space. The small menu includes delicious and well-priced thin-crust pizzas and just one or two daily specials. Again, like MarkJoseph's, it's just a stone's throw from the main tourist drag of Fulton Street, but is remarkably unexplored by anyone but locals.

TRIBECA

HARRISON **$$**

✉ 355 Greenwich Street at Harrison Street

☎ 212-274 9310

🚗 Subway 1, 2 to Franklin Street

Created by the owners of the hip Red Cat in Chelsea, this restaurant serves up delicious Continental cuisine in an elegant setting.

LE ZINC **$**

✉ 139 Duane Street between West Broadway and Church Street

☎ 212-513 0001

🚗 Subway A, C, 1, 2 to Chambers Street

A casual, well-priced bistro. Here you'll get French food infused with Asian and Hungarian. Delicious stuff.

MONTRACHET **$$$**

✉ 239 West Broadway between Walker and White Streets

☎ 212-219 2777

🚗 Subway 1, 2 to Franklin Street

One of the best French bistros in the city and well known for excellent service.

NOBU **$$$**

✉ 105 Hudson Street at Franklin Street

☎ 212-219 0500

🚗 Subway 1, 9 to Hudson Street

A wonderful Japanese restaurant serving excellent cuisine mostly to celebrities. If

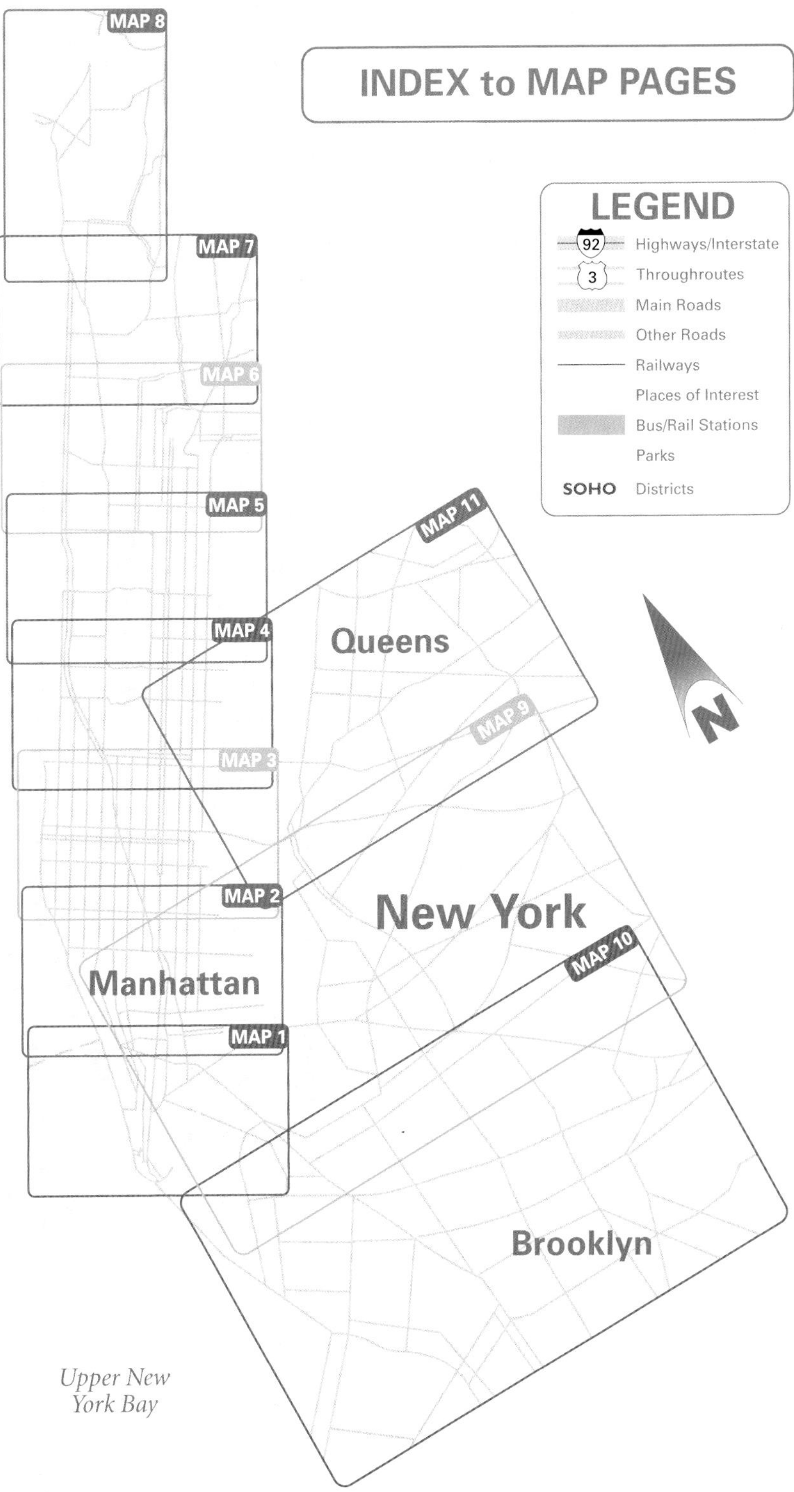
INDEX to MAP PAGES
LEGEND
Highways/Interstate
Throughroutes
Main Roads
Other Roads
Railways
Places of Interest
Bus/Rail Stations
Parks
SOHO Districts
MAP 8
MAP 7
MAP 6
MAP 5
MAP 4
MAP 3
MAP 2
MAP 1
MAP 11
MAP 9
MAP 10
Queens
New York
Manhattan
Brooklyn
Upper New York Bay
N

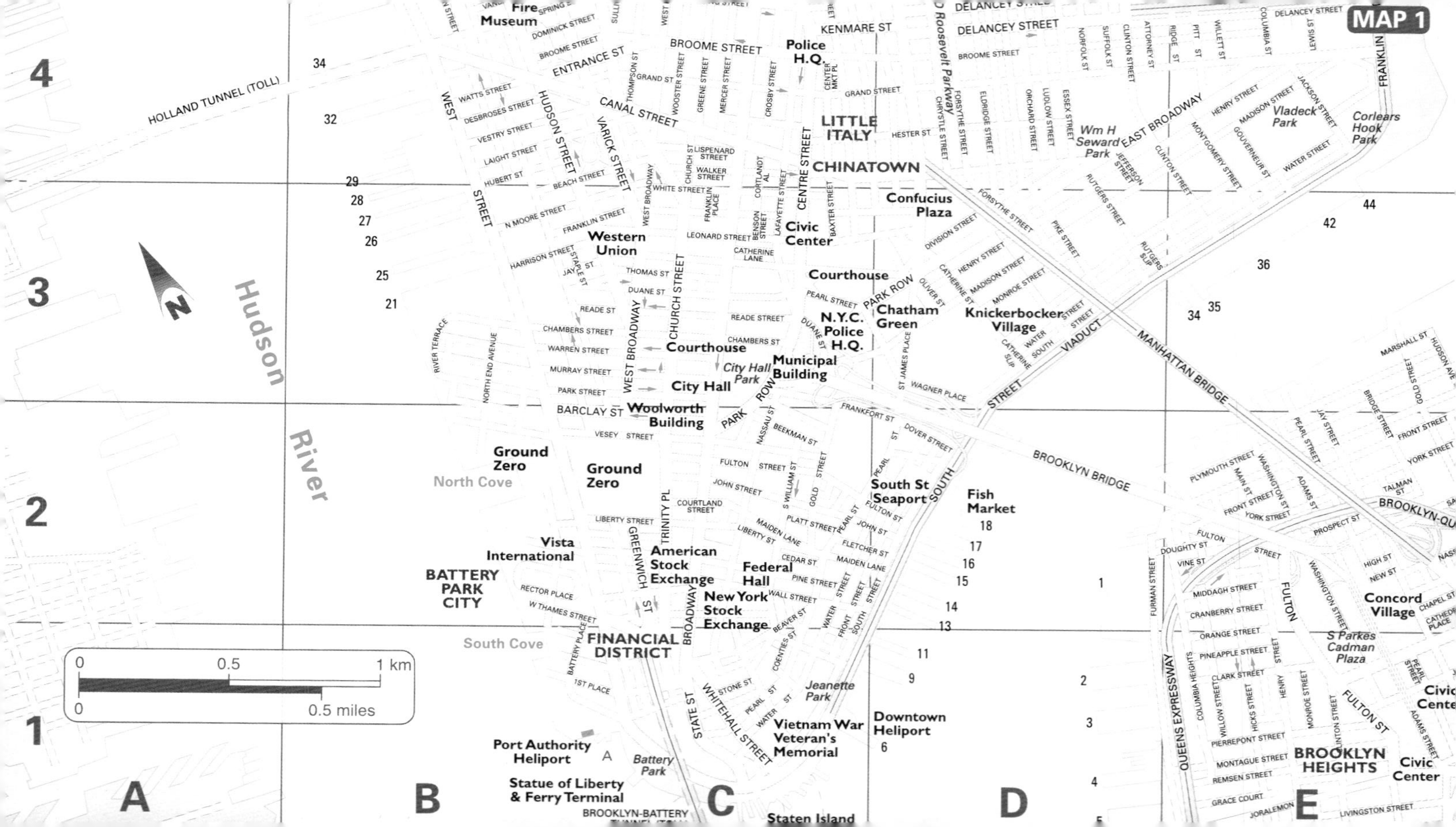

MAP 1
Hudson River
HOLLAND TUNNEL (TOLL)
North Cove
South Cove
BATTERY PARK CITY
FINANCIAL DISTRICT
Vista International
Ground Zero
Ground Zero
Woolworth Building
City Hall
City Hall Park
Courthouse
Municipal Building
Western Union
American Stock Exchange
New York Stock Exchange
Federal Hall
N.Y.C. Police H.Q.
Chatham Green
Courthouse
Civic Center
Confucius Plaza
CHINATOWN
LITTLE ITALY
Police H.Q.
Fire Museum
Knickerbocker Village
South St Seaport
Fish Market
Downtown Heliport
Vietnam War Veteran's Memorial
Jeanette Park
Battery Park
Port Authority Heliport
Statue of Liberty & Ferry Terminal
Staten Island
BROOKLYN-BATTERY
Wm H Seward Park
Vladeck Park
Corlears Hook Park
Concord Village
S Parkes Cadman Plaza
BROOKLYN HEIGHTS
Civic Center
BROOKLYN BRIDGE
MANHATTAN BRIDGE
QUEENS EXPRESSWAY
SOUTH STREET VIADUCT
WEST STREET
BROADWAY
WEST BROADWAY
CHURCH STREET
CENTRE STREET
CANAL STREET
HUDSON STREET
VARICK STREET
PARK ROW
EAST BROADWAY
DELANCEY STREET
FRANKLIN
FULTON
FURMAN STREET
0 0.5 1 km
0 0.5 miles
A B C D E
1 2 3 4

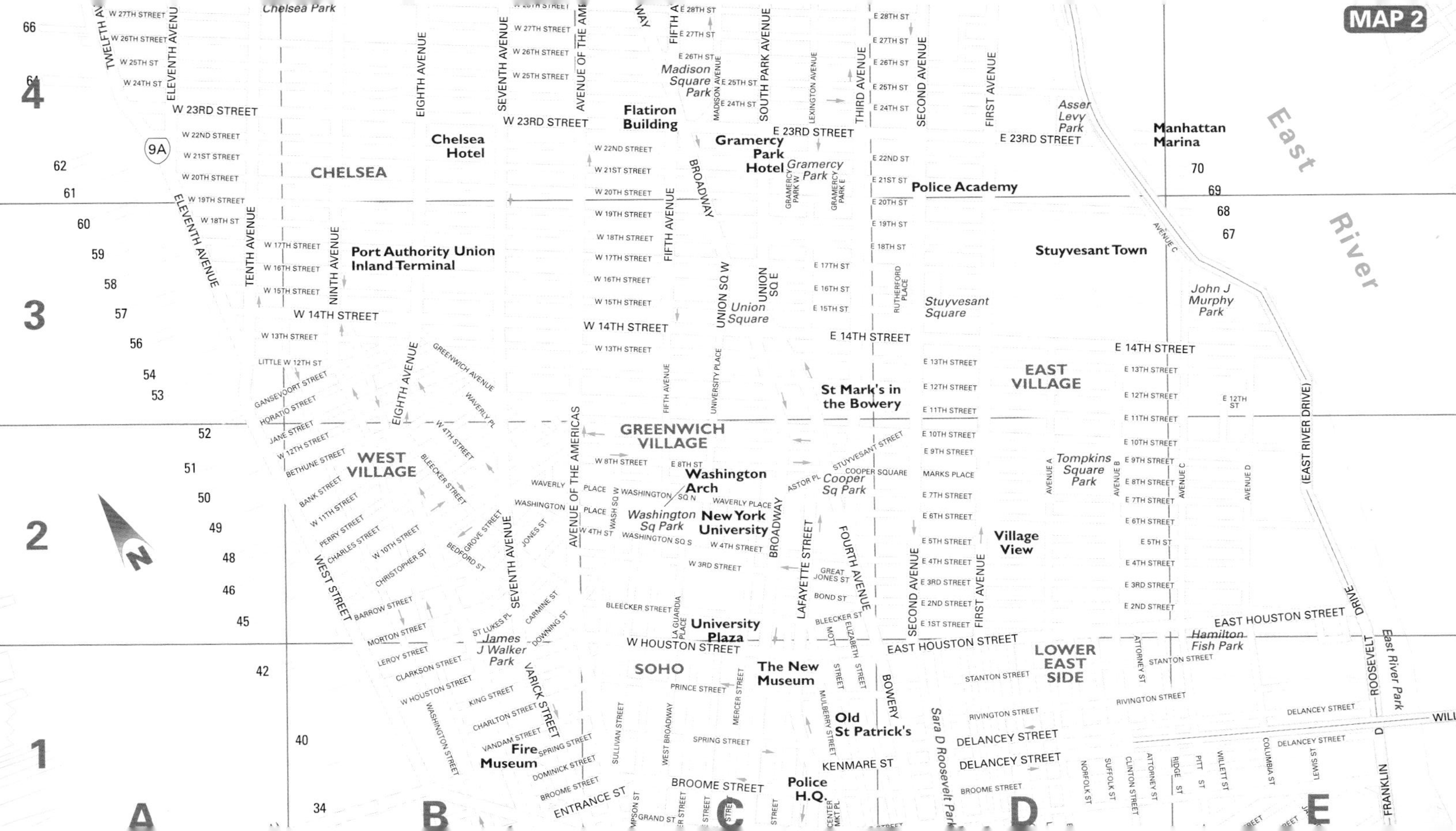

MAP 2
1
2
3
4
A
B
C
D
E
N
CHELSEA
WEST VILLAGE
GREENWICH VILLAGE
EAST VILLAGE
SOHO
LOWER EAST SIDE
Chelsea Park
Chelsea Hotel
Port Authority Union Inland Terminal
Flatiron Building
Madison Square Park
Gramercy Park Hotel
Gramercy Park
Police Academy
Manhattan Marina
Asser Levy Park
Stuyvesant Town
Stuyvesant Square
John J Murphy Park
Union Square
St Mark's in the Bowery
Washington Arch
Washington Sq Park
New York University
Cooper Sq Park
Village View
Tompkins Square Park
University Plaza
The New Museum
James J Walker Park
Fire Museum
Old St Patrick's
Police H.Q.
Sara D Roosevelt Park
Hamilton Fish Park
East River Park
East River
TWELFTH AVENUE
ELEVENTH AVENUE
TENTH AVENUE
NINTH AVENUE
EIGHTH AVENUE
SEVENTH AVENUE
AVENUE OF THE AMERICAS
FIFTH AVENUE
BROADWAY
MADISON AVENUE
SOUTH PARK AVENUE
LEXINGTON AVENUE
THIRD AVENUE
SECOND AVENUE
FIRST AVENUE
AVENUE A
AVENUE B
AVENUE C
AVENUE D
(EAST RIVER DRIVE)
W 23RD STREET
E 23RD STREET
W 14TH STREET
E 14TH STREET
W HOUSTON STREET
EAST HOUSTON STREET
WEST STREET
BLEECKER STREET
LAFAYETTE STREET
FOURTH AVENUE
BOWERY
DELANCEY STREET
KENMARE ST
BROOME STREET
ROOSEVELT DRIVE
FRANKLIN D
9A

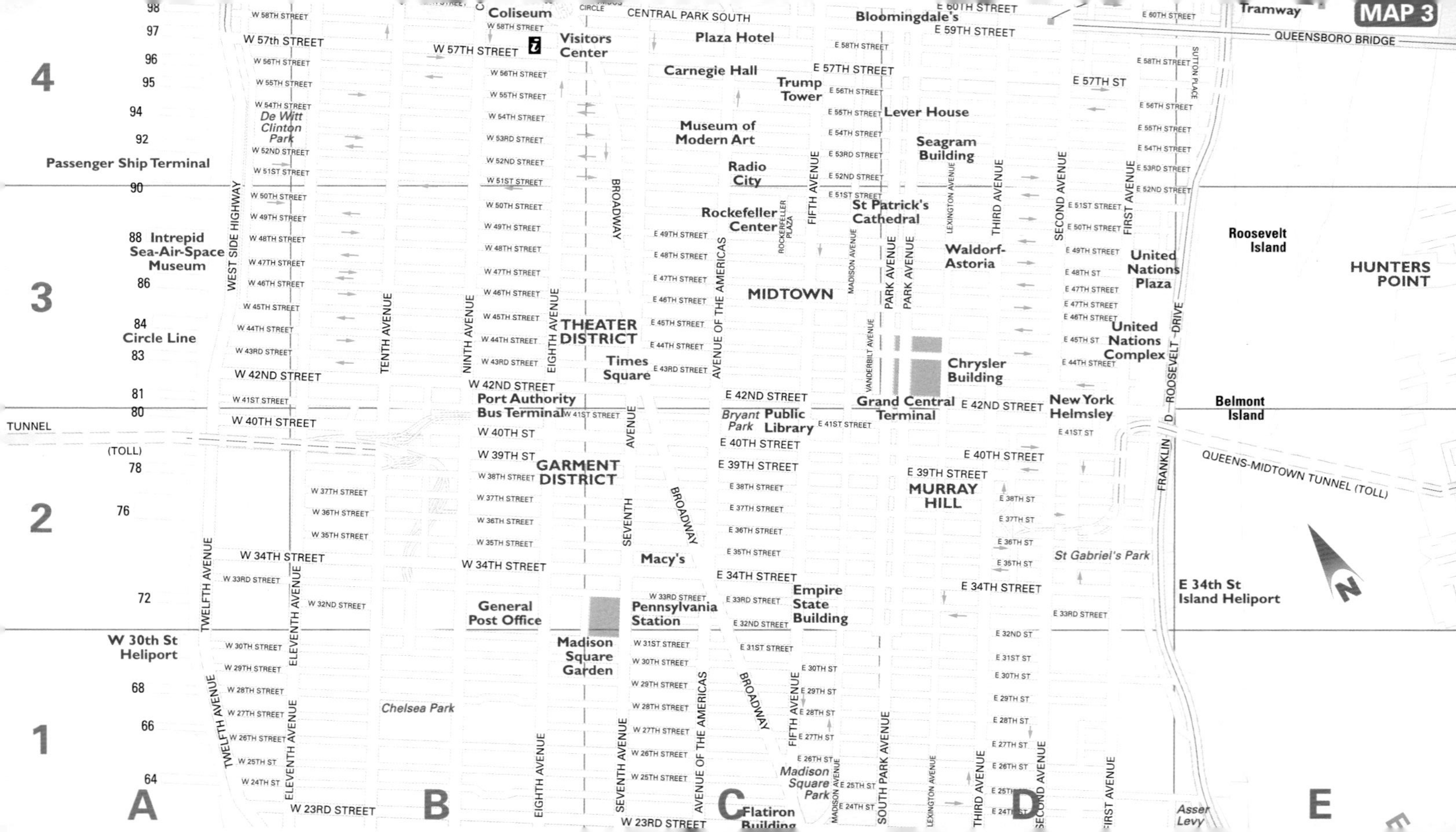

MAP 3
Passenger Ship Terminal
Intrepid Sea-Air-Space Museum
Circle Line
W 30th St Heliport
De Witt Clinton Park
Chelsea Park
Coliseum
Visitors Center
Plaza Hotel
Carnegie Hall
Trump Tower
Bloomingdale's
Lever House
Museum of Modern Art
Seagram Building
Radio City
Rockefeller Center
ROCKEFELLER PLAZA
St Patrick's Cathedral
Waldorf-Astoria
MIDTOWN
THEATER DISTRICT
Times Square
Port Authority Bus Terminal
GARMENT DISTRICT
Bryant Park
Public Library
Grand Central Terminal
Chrysler Building
New York Helmsley
United Nations Plaza
United Nations Complex
MURRAY HILL
Macy's
General Post Office
Madison Square Garden
Pennsylvania Station
Empire State Building
Madison Square Park
Flatiron Building
St Gabriel's Park
E 34th St Island Heliport
Roosevelt Island
Belmont Island
HUNTERS POINT
Asser Levy
Tramway
QUEENSBORO BRIDGE
QUEENS-MIDTOWN TUNNEL (TOLL)
TUNNEL (TOLL)
FRANKLIN D ROOSEVELT DRIVE
WEST SIDE HIGHWAY
TWELFTH AVENUE
ELEVENTH AVENUE
TENTH AVENUE
NINTH AVENUE
EIGHTH AVENUE
BROADWAY
SEVENTH AVENUE
AVENUE OF THE AMERICAS
FIFTH AVENUE
MADISON AVENUE
VANDERBILT AVENUE
PARK AVENUE
SOUTH PARK AVENUE
LEXINGTON AVENUE
THIRD AVENUE
SECOND AVENUE
FIRST AVENUE
SUTTON PLACE
CENTRAL PARK SOUTH
W 57th STREET
W 42ND STREET
W 34TH STREET
W 23RD STREET
E 59TH STREET
E 57TH STREET
E 42ND STREET
E 34TH STREET
N
A B C D E
1 2 3 4

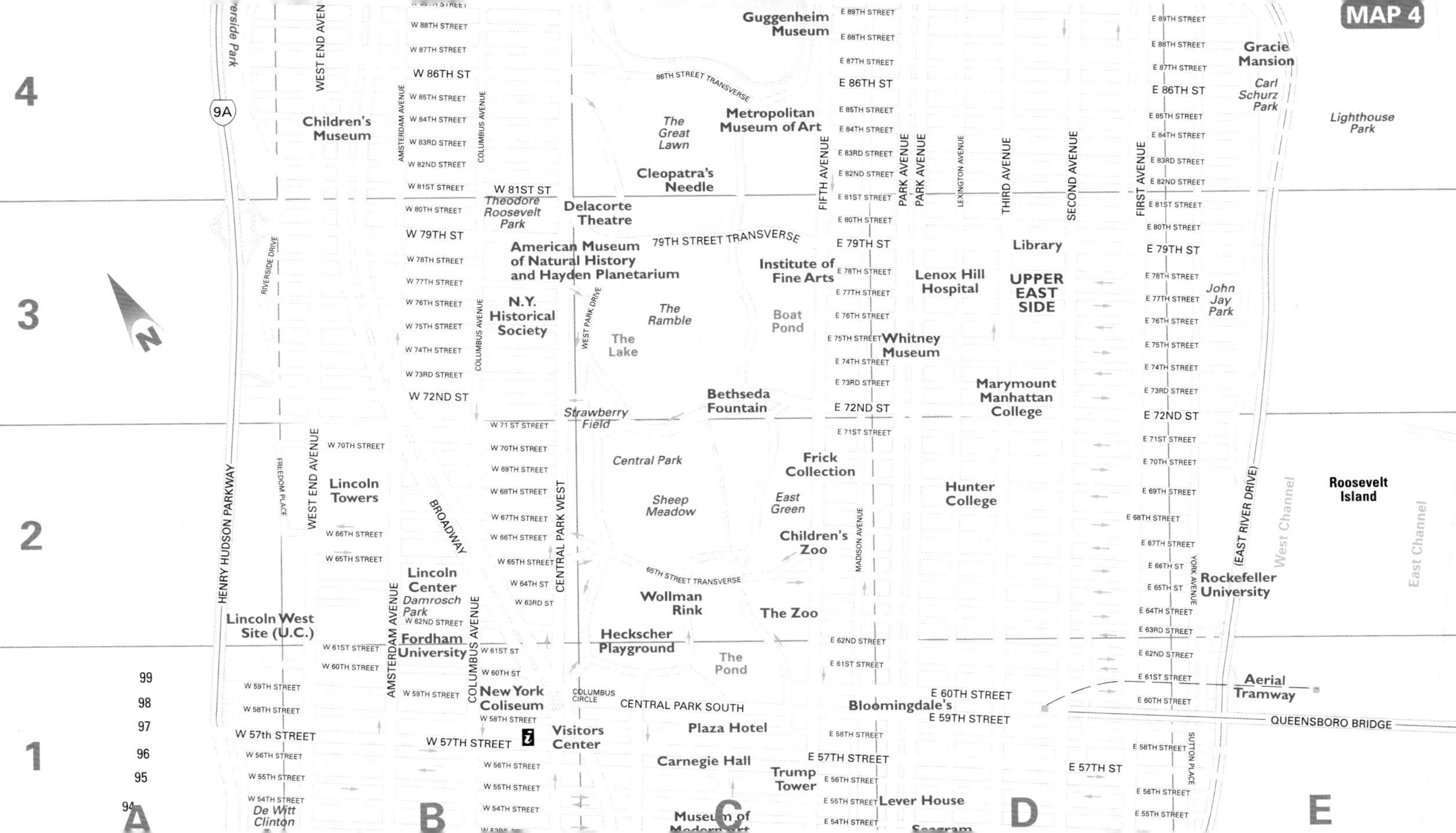

MAP 4
4
3
2
1
A
B
C
D
E
N
9A
99
98
97
96
95
94
HENRY HUDSON PARKWAY
RIVERSIDE DRIVE
FREEDOM PLACE
WEST END AVENUE
AMSTERDAM AVENUE
BROADWAY
COLUMBUS AVENUE
CENTRAL PARK WEST
WEST PARK DRIVE
CENTRAL PARK SOUTH
86TH STREET TRANSVERSE
79TH STREET TRANSVERSE
65TH STREET TRANSVERSE
FIFTH AVENUE
MADISON AVENUE
PARK AVENUE
LEXINGTON AVENUE
THIRD AVENUE
SECOND AVENUE
FIRST AVENUE
YORK AVENUE
SUTTON PLACE
(EAST RIVER DRIVE)
QUEENSBORO BRIDGE
W 86TH ST
W 81ST ST
W 79TH ST
W 72ND ST
W 57th STREET
W 57TH STREET
E 86TH ST
E 79TH ST
E 72ND ST
E 60TH STREET
E 59TH STREET
E 57TH STREET
E 57TH ST
Guggenheim Museum
Children's Museum
Metropolitan Museum of Art
The Great Lawn
Cleopatra's Needle
Theodore Roosevelt Park
Delacorte Theatre
American Museum of Natural History and Hayden Planetarium
N.Y. Historical Society
The Ramble
The Lake
Boat Pond
Institute of Fine Arts
Lenox Hill Hospital
Library
UPPER EAST SIDE
Whitney Museum
Marymount Manhattan College
Bethesda Fountain
Strawberry Field
Central Park
Sheep Meadow
Lincoln Towers
Frick Collection
East Green
Hunter College
Children's Zoo
Lincoln Center
Damrosch Park
Wollman Rink
The Zoo
Heckscher Playground
The Pond
Fordham University
Lincoln West Site (U.C.)
New York Coliseum
Columbus Circle
Visitors Center
Plaza Hotel
Bloomingdale's
Carnegie Hall
Trump Tower
Lever House
De Witt Clinton
Gracie Mansion
Carl Schurz Park
Lighthouse Park
John Jay Park
Rockefeller University
Aerial Tramway
Roosevelt Island
West Channel
East Channel

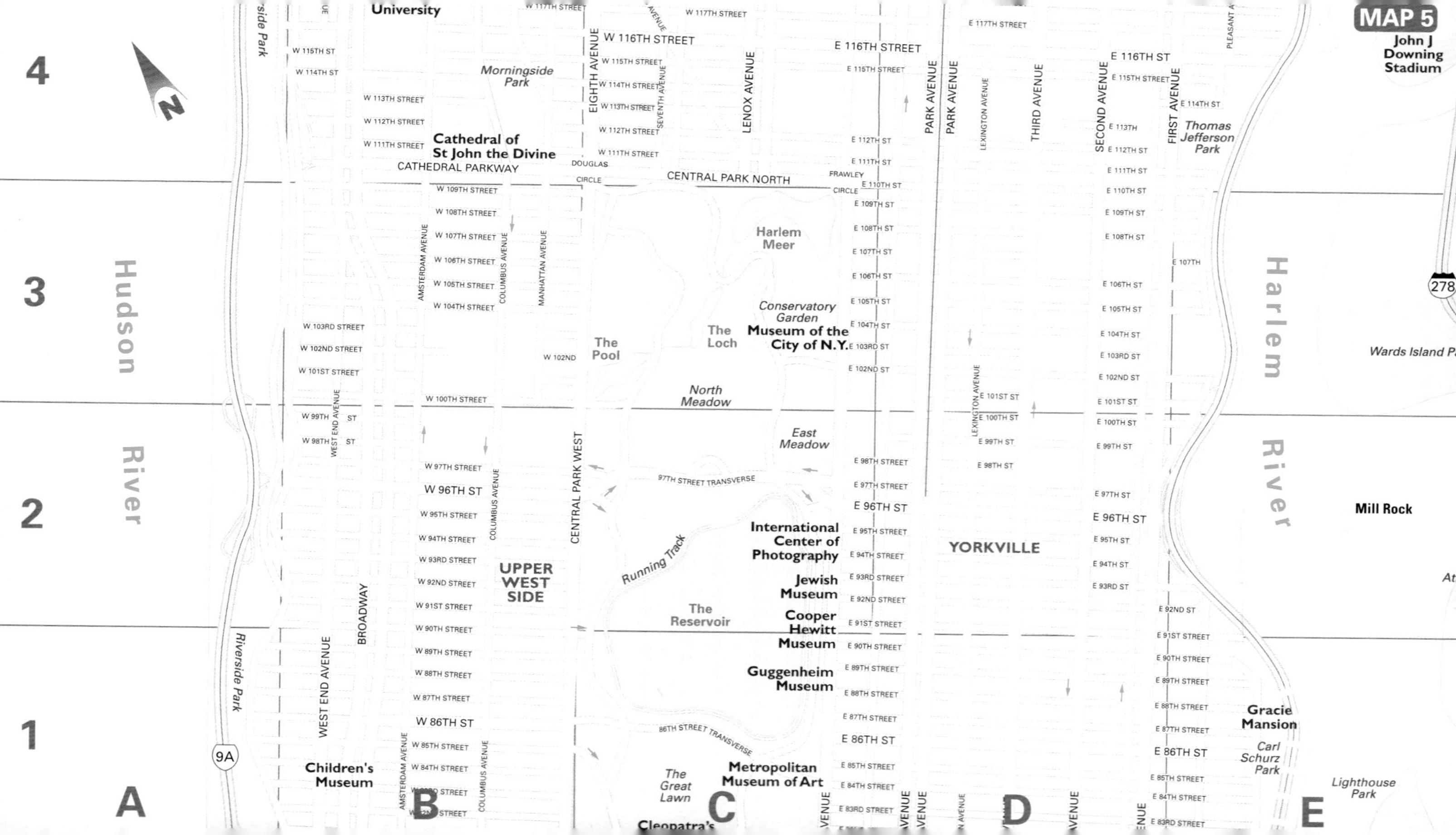

MAP 5
John J Downing Stadium
University
Morningside Park
Cathedral of St John the Divine
CATHEDRAL PARKWAY
DOUGLAS CIRCLE
CENTRAL PARK NORTH
FRAWLEY CIRCLE
W 116TH STREET
E 116TH STREET
EIGHTH AVENUE
SEVENTH AVENUE
LENOX AVENUE
PARK AVENUE
LEXINGTON AVENUE
THIRD AVENUE
SECOND AVENUE
FIRST AVENUE
Thomas Jefferson Park
Harlem Meer
Conservatory Garden
Museum of the City of N.Y.
The Loch
The Pool
North Meadow
East Meadow
97TH STREET TRANSVERSE
Running Track
The Reservoir
86TH STREET TRANSVERSE
The Great Lawn
Cleopatra's
International Center of Photography
Jewish Museum
Cooper Hewitt Museum
Guggenheim Museum
Metropolitan Museum of Art
YORKVILLE
UPPER WEST SIDE
CENTRAL PARK WEST
AMSTERDAM AVENUE
COLUMBUS AVENUE
MANHATTAN AVENUE
WEST END AVENUE
BROADWAY
W 96TH ST
W 86TH ST
E 96TH ST
E 86TH ST
Riverside Park
Children's Museum
Hudson River
Harlem River
Wards Island Pa
Mill Rock
Gracie Mansion
Carl Schurz Park
Lighthouse Park
9A
278
1
2
3
4
A
B
C
D
E

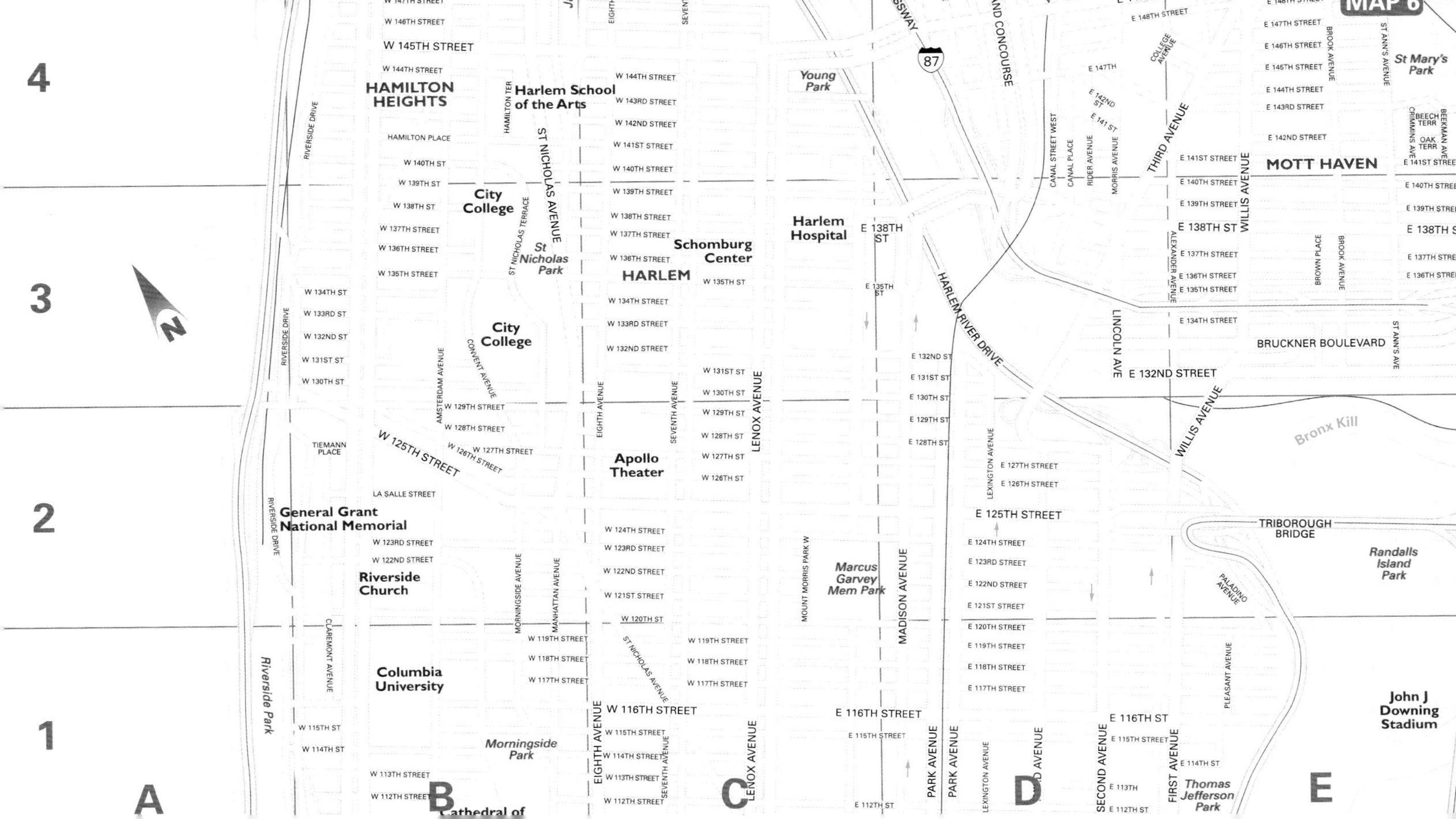
MAP 6
HAMILTON HEIGHTS
Harlem School of the Arts
City College
St Nicholas Park
Schomburg Center
HARLEM
Harlem Hospital
Young Park
MOTT HAVEN
St Mary's Park
General Grant National Memorial
Riverside Church
Apollo Theater
Columbia University
Morningside Park
Riverside Park
Marcus Garvey Mem Park
Randalls Island Park
John J Downing Stadium
Thomas Jefferson Park
Bronx Kill
TRIBOROUGH BRIDGE
W 125TH STREET
W 145TH STREET
W 116TH STREET
E 116TH STREET
E 125TH STREET
E 132ND STREET
E 138TH ST
RIVERSIDE DRIVE
ST NICHOLAS AVENUE
AMSTERDAM AVENUE
EIGHTH AVENUE
SEVENTH AVENUE
LENOX AVENUE
MADISON AVENUE
PARK AVENUE
LEXINGTON AVENUE
SECOND AVENUE
FIRST AVENUE
THIRD AVENUE
WILLIS AVENUE
HARLEM RIVER DRIVE
BRUCKNER BOULEVARD
LINCOLN AVE
87

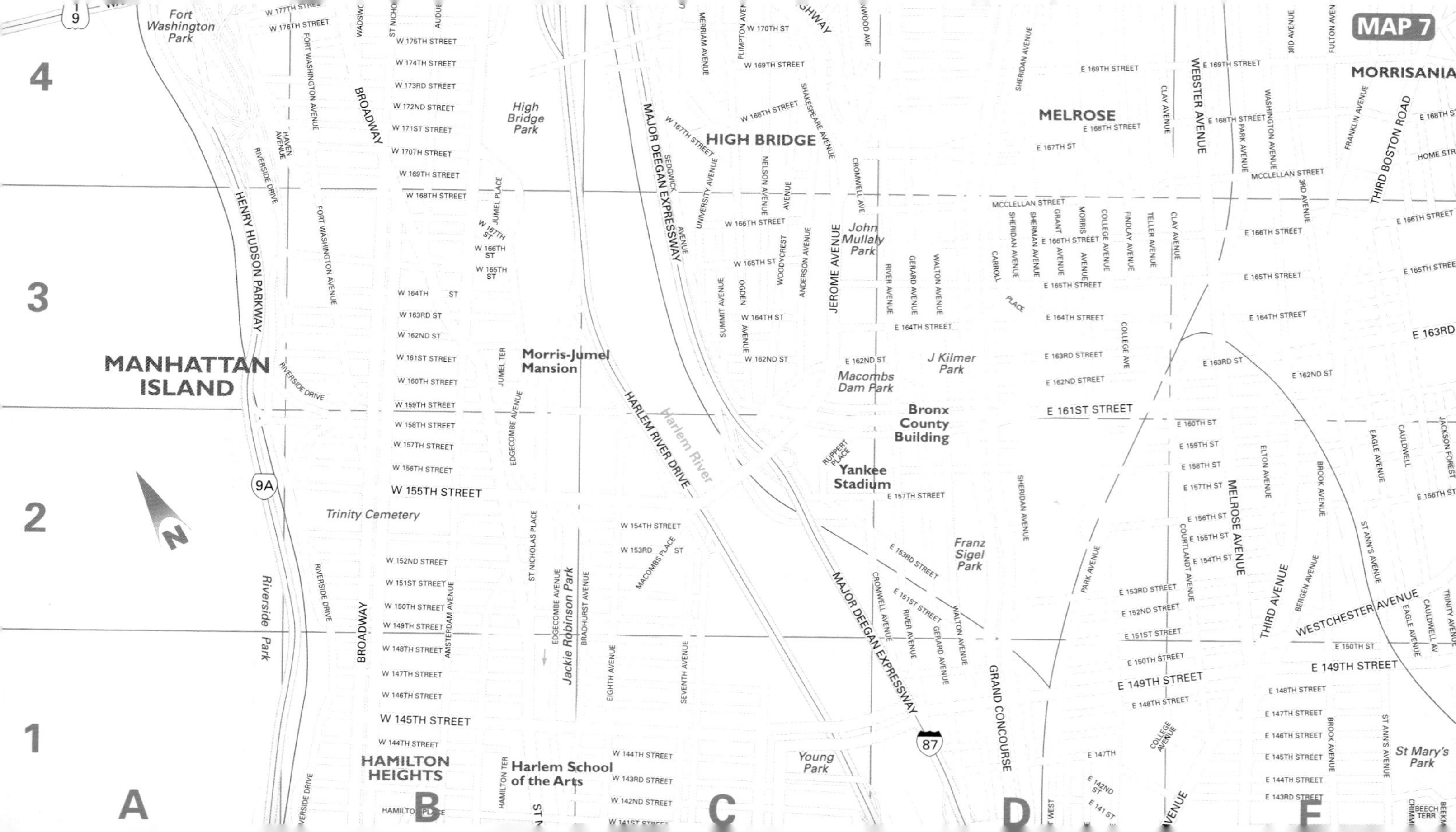

MAP 7
A
B
C
D
E
1
2
3
4
MANHATTAN ISLAND
HENRY HUDSON PARKWAY
9A
9
Riverside Park
Fort Washington Park
RIVERSIDE DRIVE
HAVEN AVENUE
FORT WASHINGTON AVENUE
BROADWAY
Trinity Cemetery
W 155TH STREET
W 145TH STREET
HAMILTON HEIGHTS
AMSTERDAM AVENUE
HAMILTON TER
High Bridge Park
JUMEL PLACE
JUMEL TER
Morris-Jumel Mansion
EDGECOMBE AVENUE
ST NICHOLAS PLACE
Jackie Robinson Park
BRADHURST AVENUE
EIGHTH AVENUE
SEVENTH AVENUE
MACOMBS PLACE
Harlem School of the Arts
HARLEM RIVER DRIVE
Harlem River
MAJOR DEGAN EXPRESSWAY
SEDGWICK AVENUE
UNIVERSITY AVENUE
HIGH BRIDGE
SUMMIT AVENUE
OGDEN AVENUE
NELSON AVENUE
WOODYCREST AVENUE
ANDERSON AVENUE
SHAKESPEARE AVENUE
MERRIAM AVENUE
PLIMPTON AVENUE
JEROME AVENUE
CROMWELL AVE
John Mullaly Park
Macombs Dam Park
RUPPERT PLACE
Yankee Stadium
Bronx County Building
J Kilmer Park
RIVER AVENUE
GERARD AVENUE
WALTON AVENUE
Franz Sigel Park
87
Young Park
GRAND CONCOURSE
SHERIDAN AVENUE
SHERMAN AVENUE
GRANT AVENUE
MORRIS AVENUE
CARROLL PLACE
MCCLELLAN STREET
E 161ST STREET
MELROSE
PARK AVENUE
COLLEGE AVENUE
FINDLAY AVENUE
TELLER AVENUE
CLAY AVENUE
WEBSTER AVENUE
E 149TH STREET
COURTLANDT AVENUE
MELROSE AVENUE
ELTON AVENUE
THIRD AVENUE
BERGEN AVENUE
BROOK AVENUE
WESTCHESTER AVENUE
ST ANN'S AVENUE
EAGLE AVENUE
CAULDWELL AV
TRINITY AVENUE
JACKSON FOREST
St Mary's Park
WASHINGTON AVENUE
3RD AVENUE
FULTON AVENUE
FRANKLIN AVENUE
THIRD BOSTON ROAD
HOME STREET
MORRISANIA

MAP 8
KINGSBRIDGE HEIGHTS
W 230TH ST
W 230TH ST
W 227TH
INDEPENDENCE AVENUE
HENRY HUDSON PARKWAY
ARLINGTON AVENUE
NETHERLAND
STREET
IRWIN AVENUE
KAPPOCK STREET
KNOLL CRESCENT
JOHNSON AVENUE
TERRACE VIEW AVENUE
ADRIAN AVENUE
VAN CORLEAR PLACE
FT CHARLES PLACE
MARBLE HILL
BROADWAY
SEDGWICK AVENUE
W 197TH STREET
WEBB AVENUE
CLAFLIN
STRONG STREET
5
PALISADE
AVENUE
LEYDEN
STREET
W 225TH ST
W 195TH STREET
Kingsbrid
Armo
HENRY HUDSON BRIDGE
EAMES PL
Spuyten Duyvil Creek
W 193RD
KINGSBRIDGE ROAD
THE BRONX
Baker Field
W 220TH ST
W 219TH ST
MAJOR DEEGAN EXPRESSWAY
192ND STRE
W 218TH STREET
9A
9
PARK TER W
PARK TER E
W 216TH STREET
W 215TH STREET
W 215TH STREET
UNIVERSITY AVENUE
AQUEDUCT WEST
W 190TH STR
Inwood Hill Park
Isham Park
W 213TH ST
W 212TH ST
ISHAM
DEVOE TERR
Devoe Park
FATHER ZEISER PARK
WEST FORDHAM RO
GRAND AVE
4
W 211TH ST
10TH AVENUE
STREET
87
W 184TH STRE
PAYSON AVENUE
SEAMAN AVENUE
COOPER STREET
W 207TH STREET
VERMILYEA AVENUE
AVENUE
W 204TH STREET
SHERMAN AVENUE
POST
PLACE
LORING PLACE NORTH
ANDREWS AVENUE NORTH
NORTH STREE
EVELYN PLACE
W 207TH STREET
W 206TH STREET
W 183RD
HAMPDEN
W 183RD STRE
BUCHANAN PLA
AQUEDUCT AVENUE EAST
STAFF ST
W 205TH STREET
9TH STREET
W 182ND STRE
RIVERSIDE DRIVE
ACADEMY STREET
W 204TH ST
HALL OF FAME TERRACE
CLINTON PLA
AVENUE
W 203RD ST
SEDGWICK
W 181ST STR
AMSTERDAM AVENUE
The Cloisters
DYCKMAN
W 202ND STREET
Hall of Fame
W 201ST ST
THAYER STREET
W 180TH STREET
DAVIDSON AVENUE
ARDEN STREET
STREET
Bronx Comm College
3
SICKLES
Harlem River
W 179TH STREET
WASHINGTON HEIGHTS
ELLWOOD
NAGLE
ST
Fort Tryon Park
LORING PL
HENNESSY PLACE
OSBORNE PLACE
STREET
LORING PL N
WEST BURNSIDE AVENUE
GRAND AVENUE
HENRY HUDSON PARKWAY
BOGARDUS PLACE
HILLSIDE AV
TREMONT AVE
BROADWAY
CEDAR AVENUE
BILLINGSLEY
PHELAN TERRACE
LORING PLACE S
ANDREWS AVENUE S
HARRISON AVENUE
FAIRVIEW AVENUE
W 193RD ST
High Bridge Park
W 177TH ST
W 192ND STREET
W TREMONT AVENUE
PALISADE PLACE
JEROME AVENUE
W 191ST STREET
MONTGOMERY AVE
MORRIS HEIGHTS
WADSWORTH TERRACE
W 190TH STREET
AMSTERDAM AVENUE
POPHAM
N
BENNETT AVENUE
OVERLOOK TERRACE
WADSWORTH AVENUE
W 189TH STREET
ST NICHOLAS AVE
AUDUBON AVENUE
W 175TH STREET
GRAND AVENUE
DAVIDSON AVENUE
W 188TH STREET
LAUREL HILL TERRACE
2
CHITTENDEN AV
W 187TH STREET
HARLEM RIVER DRIVE
MAJOR DEEGAN EXPRESSWAY
FORT WASHINGTON AVENUE
W 186TH STREET
W 174TH ST
FEATHERBED LANE
Yeshiva University
W 185TH STREET
PINEHURST AVENUE
W 184TH STREET
CABRINI BOULEVARD
W 183RD STREET
COL R MAGAN PL
GABLE
W 182ND STREET
W 81ST STREET
MACOMBS ROAD
W 180TH STREET
W 172ND STREET
Washington Bridge Bus Terminal
W 179TH STREET
EDW L GRANT HIGHWAY
JESUP AVENUE
WASHINGTON BRIDGE
W 178TH
WADSWORTH AVENUE
ST NICHOLAS AVENUE
AUDUBON AVENUE
UNDERCLIFF
1 9
W 177TH STREET
Fort Washington Park
W 176TH STREET
FORT WASHINGTON AVENUE
MERRIAM AVENUE
PLIMPTON AVENUE
W 170TH ST
INWOOD AVE
W 175TH STREET
1
W 174TH STREET
W 169TH STREET
W 173RD STREET
BROADWAY
W 172ND STREET
High Bridge Park
W 168TH STREET
SHAKESPEARE AVENUE
W 171ST STREET
W 167TH STREET
HIGH BRIDGE
HAVEN AVENUE
W 170TH STREET
MAJOR DEEGAN EX
SEDGWICK
A
RIVERSIDE DRIVE
W 169TH STREET
B
C
NELSON AVEN
CROMWELL AVE
W 168TH STREET

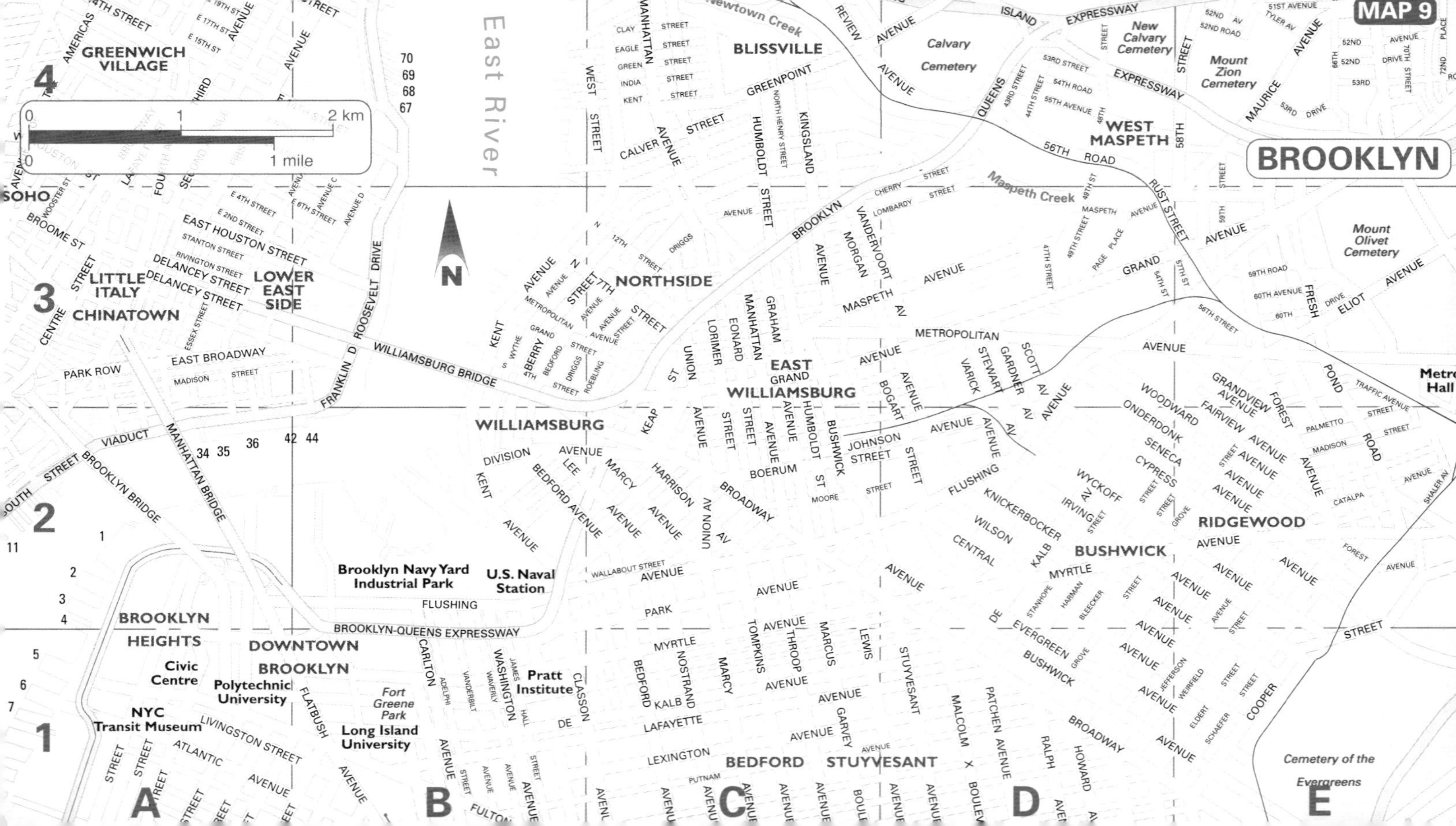
MAP 9
BROOKLYN
East River
GREENWICH VILLAGE
SOHO
LITTLE ITALY
CHINATOWN
LOWER EAST SIDE
WILLIAMSBURG
NORTHSIDE
BLISSVILLE
EAST WILLIAMSBURG
WEST MASPETH
BUSHWICK
RIDGEWOOD
BEDFORD STUYVESANT
BROOKLYN HEIGHTS
DOWNTOWN BROOKLYN
Civic Centre
Polytechnic University
NYC Transit Museum
Long Island University
Fort Greene Park
Pratt Institute
Brooklyn Navy Yard Industrial Park
U.S. Naval Station
Calvary Cemetery
New Calvary Cemetery
Mount Zion Cemetery
Mount Olivet Cemetery
Cemetery of the Evergreens
Newtown Creek
Maspeth Creek
BROOKLYN BRIDGE
MANHATTAN BRIDGE
WILLIAMSBURG BRIDGE
FRANKLIN D ROOSEVELT DRIVE
BROOKLYN-QUEENS EXPRESSWAY
Metro Hall
0 1 2 km
0 1 mile
N
1
2
3
4
A
B
C
D
E

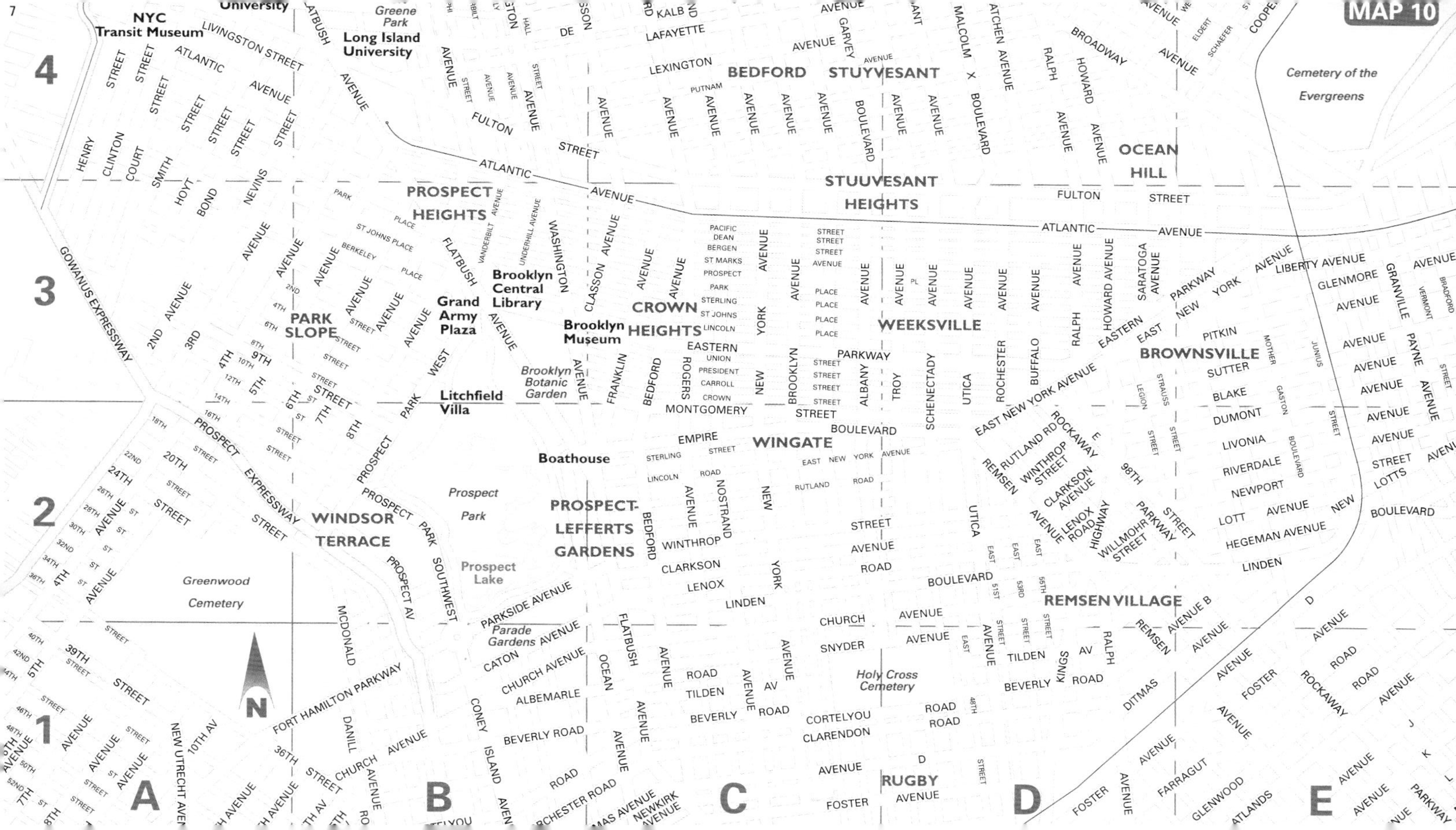
MAP 10
7
1
2
3
4
A
B
C
D
E
N
NYC Transit Museum
Long Island University
Greene Park
Cemetery of the Evergreens
BEDFORD STUYVESANT
OCEAN HILL
STUYVESANT HEIGHTS
PROSPECT HEIGHTS
CROWN HEIGHTS
WEEKSVILLE
BROWNSVILLE
PARK SLOPE
Grand Army Plaza
Brooklyn Central Library
Brooklyn Museum
Brooklyn Botanic Garden
Litchfield Villa
Boathouse
WINGATE
WINDSOR TERRACE
Prospect Park
Prospect Lake
PROSPECT-LEFFERTS GARDENS
Parade Gardens
Greenwood Cemetery
Holy Cross Cemetery
REMSEN VILLAGE
RUGBY
GOWANUS EXPRESSWAY
PROSPECT EXPRESSWAY
FORT HAMILTON PARKWAY
ATLANTIC AVENUE
FLATBUSH AVENUE
EASTERN PARKWAY
LINDEN BOULEVARD

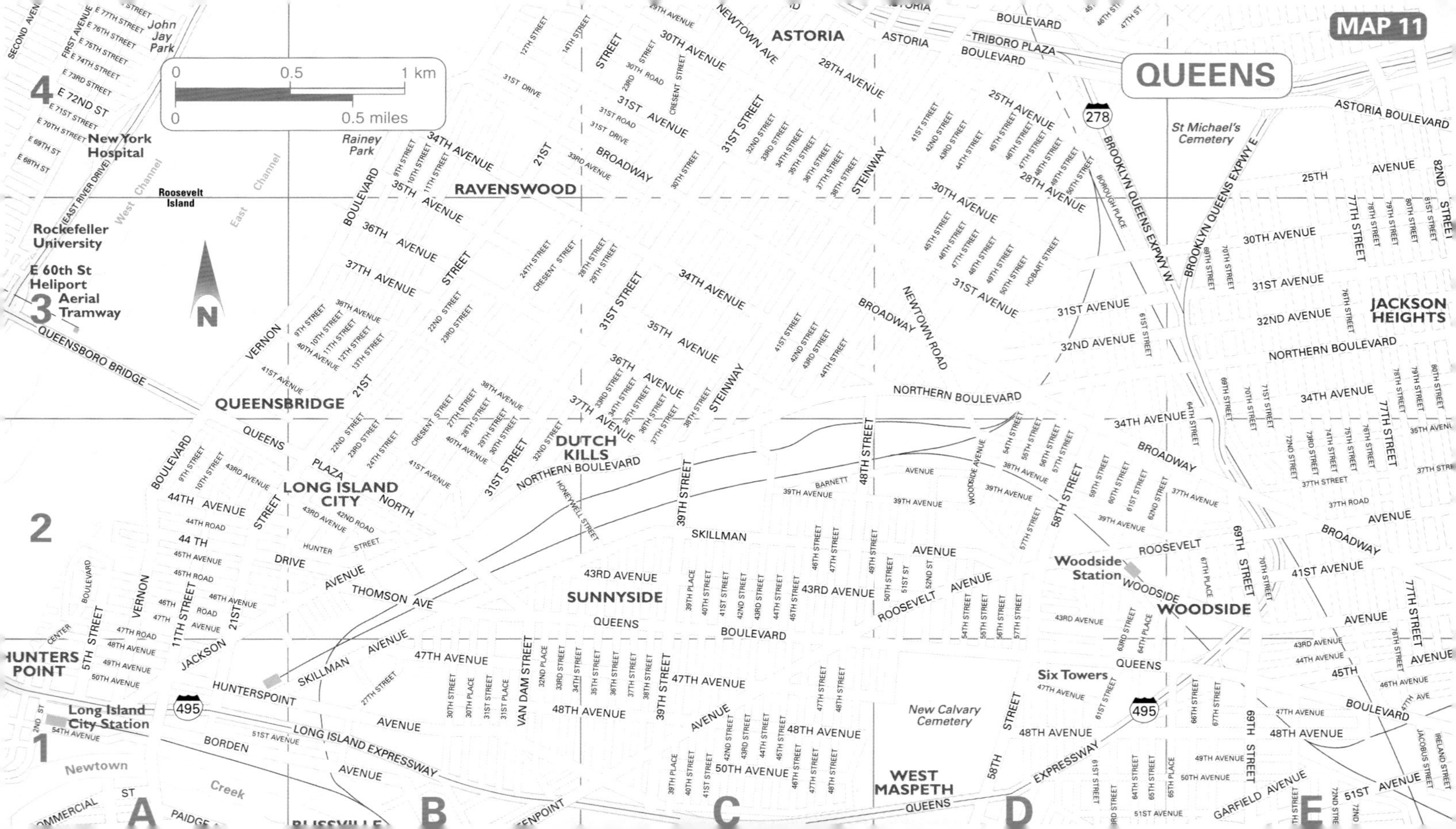

MAP 11
QUEENS
HUNTERS POINT
Long Island City Station
Newtown Creek
LONG ISLAND CITY
QUEENSBRIDGE
QUEENSBORO BRIDGE
Roosevelt Island
West Channel
East Channel
Rainey Park
Rockefeller University
E 60th St Heliport
Aerial Tramway
New York Hospital
John Jay Park
RAVENSWOOD
ASTORIA
DUTCH KILLS
SUNNYSIDE
WEST MASPETH
New Calvary Cemetery
Six Towers
Woodside Station
WOODSIDE
JACKSON HEIGHTS
St Michael's Cemetery
LONG ISLAND EXPRESSWAY
BROOKLYN QUEENS EXPWY W
BROOKLYN QUEENS EXPWY E
TRIBORO PLAZA
ASTORIA BOULEVARD
NORTHERN BOULEVARD
QUEENS BOULEVARD
495
278
0
0.5
1 km
0.5 miles
N
1
2
3
4
A
B
C
D
E

Manhattan Street Index

Single bold number refers to map number
Alpha numerics refer to those within specified map

Queens Street Index

Brooklyn Street Index

RESTAURANTS WITH GARDENS

Aureole: French, Upper East Side, $$$
Barbetta: Northern Italian, Midtown West, $$$
Bottino: Italian, Chelsea, $$
Restaurant Provence: French, SoHo, $$
Tavern on the Green: American gourmet, Central Park West, $$$

you can get in you'll enjoy the décor and dining. Your best bet is to book weeks ahead to get a chance of a table, or go at lunchtime.

NOBU, NEXT DOOR $$

Next to the celebrity haunt is an outlet for mere mortals who can sample some of the food everyone is raving about. Still very much worth a visit.

ODEON $$

✉ 145 West Broadway between Duane and Thomas Streets
☎ 212-233 0507
🚗 Subway 1, 9 to Chambers Street

A *très* hip hangout that still attracts celebrities for its cool atmosphere and American-French cuisine. You'll need to book ahead.

TRIBECA GRILL $$

✉ 375 Greenwich Street at Franklin Street
☎ 212-941 3900
🚗 Subway 1, 9 to Franklin Street

Robert de Niro and Drew Nierporent's popular new American restaurant. The $20 prix fixe lunch attracts major crowds so be warned!

CHINATOWN

JOE'S SHANGHAI $

✉ 9 Pell St between Bowery and Mott Street
☎ 212-233 8888
🚗 Subway J, M, N, R, Z, 6 to Canal Street

A Chinese restaurant known for the most fabulous soup dumplings in New York.

LITTLE ITALY

FERRARA PASTRIES & CAFÉ $

✉ 195 Grand Street between Mulberry and Mott Streets
☎ 212-226 6150
🚗 Subway S to Grand Street

Mulberry Street and the intersection with Grand Street is all that remains of Little Italy, yet it's still a vibrant area with plenty of pavement tables outside the classic pizzerias and trattorias. If you just want a snack and a sugar attack, then pop into the oldest remaining pastry joint in the area. It serves up delicious drinks and cakes and makes a great pit stop if you're just wandering around the area.

LOWER EAST SIDE

aKa $

✉ 49 Clinton Street between Rivington and Stanton Streets
☎ 212-979 6096
🚗 Subway F to Lower East Side/ 2nd Avenue

Once a dress shop, this small but perfectly formed café turns out inventive and tasty dishes from its shoebox-sized kitchen. Try the open-faced lamb tongue sandwich with almond butter and redcurrant jelly for just $8. No single dish costs more than $13 and you can even get a 10 per cent discount with your NYCard.

ALIAS $

✉ 76 Clinton Street at Rivington Street
☎ 212-505 5011
🚗 Subway F to Lower East Side/ 2nd Avenue

Just down the street from aKa, this place is a touch more 'evening'. It has lower lighting, tablecloths and a small but serious wine list, but remains funky with laid-back clients and staff. Chef Scott Ehrlich turns out some pretty big tastes from his mini kitchen but at far less than Midtown pricing – 10 per cent NYCard discount.

KATZ'S DELICATESSEN $

✉ 205 East Houston Street at Ludlow Street

☎ 212-254 2246

🚗 Subway F to 2nd Avenue

A real institution, this deli has been here since 1888. The sandwiches may sound pricey at around $9, but I defy you to finish one. Luckily, there are plenty of brown paper bags around to take your leftovers away with you as everybody else does. Stick to the sandwiches though – the soups are a bit disappointing. You get a ticket on the way in, order your food at the counter and get your ticket filled out, then you pay as you leave.

If the canteen-style seating seems familiar to you, it's because that orgasm scene with Meg Ryan and Billy Crystal in *When Harry Met Sally* was filmed here!

SOHO

BALTHAZAR $$

✉ 80 Spring Street between Broadway and Crosby Streets

☎ 212-965 1414

🚗 Subway N, R to Prince Street

A classy French brasserie serving up good food to a trendy crowd.

BLUE RIBBON $$

✉ 97 Sullivan Street between Prince and Spring Streets

☎ 212-274 0404

🚗 Subway C, East to Spring Street

This place gets packed at any time of the day or night so don't try it if you are on a tight schedule, but the eclectic and seafood dishes are worth the wait.

CANTEEN $$

✉ 142 Mercer Street at Prince Street

☎ 212-431 7676

🚗 Subway N, R to Prince Street

A super-stylish space that attracts a trendy crowd but is not at all snooty. The American-Asian food isn't cheap but it is delicious.

FANNELLI CAFÉ $

✉ 94 Prince Street at Mercer Street

☎ 212-226 9412

Contemporary crowds pack an old saloon-style bar and dining room serving American food. It does an excellent selection of sandwiches for lunch.

LUCKY STRIKE $$

✉ 59 Grand Street between West Broadway and Wooster Street

☎ 212-941 0479

Restaurateur Keith McNally's hot spot has become a watering hole for models, celebrities and club kids as well as SoHo's art crowd. The menu is French, chocolate and Lucky martini.

MERCER KITCHEN $$

✉ Mercer Hotel, 99 Prince Street at Mercer Street

☎ 212-966 5454

Jean-Georges Vongerichten (he of Jean Georges fame) oversees the eclectic French-inspired cuisine that is served to a trendy crowd in a chic environment.

RESTAURANT PROVENCE $$

✉ 38 MacDougal Street at Prince Street

☎ 212-475 7500

One of the hidden gems of SoHo, this is a beautifully rustic restaurant with a fountain in the garden. The food is country-style French cooking and the most expensive main course is $25. Try the prix fixe brunch for $19.50 or make a reservation for about 6.30pm to get a table in the garden.

RESTAURANTS WITH VIEWS

2 West: American Fusion, Battery Park City, $–$$$
American Park at the Battery: American, Battery Park, $$$
Jean Georges: French, Midtown West, $$$
Park View At The Boathouse: American, Central Park, $$–$$$
River Café: American, Brooklyn, $$$
World Yacht River Cruise: American, Midtown West, $$

THOM $$

✉ 60 Thompson Street between Spring and Broome Streets

☎ 212-431 0400

🚗 Subway C, E to Spring Street

Based in the newest SoHo hotel, this is a fashionable restaurant in its own right and serves up delicious American cuisine at reasonable prices.

VERUKA $$

✉ 525 Broome Street between Thompson Street and 6th Avenue

☎ 212-625 1717

Upbeat late-night joint serving an international menu. You don't have to eat here, you can just hang out in the lounge. Look out for Johnny Depp.

ZOE $$

✉ 90 Prince Street between Broadway and Mercer Street

☎ 212-966 6722

Fabulous Californian-style American food in a beautiful environment. Dishes include pan-seared skate with pistachio-scallion couscous, stuffed aubergine and lemon-caper emulsion or rotisserie Long Island duck breast with mushroom and goats' cheese turnover, ginger-maple Brussel sprouts and juniper sauce. The amazing range of breads include everything from soda to focaccia and come with butter that includes sesame seeds, poppy seeds, salt and pepper and garlic, plus their own spread made with white beans

There are many more restaurants for the Villages and Chelsea in Chapter 8, plus many of the bars referred to in Chapter 9 serve meals, too.

NOLITA

FIVE POINTS $

✉ 31 Great Jones Street between Lafayette Street and Bowery

☎ 212-253 5700

🚗 Subway B, V, S to Broadway/Lafayette; 6 to Bleecker Street

Named after the once infamous gangland area of Five Points, this is actually a popular neighbourhood restaurant with a friendly bar, so don't worry. Try out the Maine scallop with oxtail sauce or the beef 'n' reef pasta bowl.

INDOCHINE $$

✉ 430 Lafayette Street between Astor Place and 4th Street

☎ 212-505 5111

🚗 Subway 6 to Astor Place

A bit of a celebrity haunt, this serves delicious Vietnamese-French fusion food in tiny portions.

GREENWICH VILLAGE

BABBO $

✉ 110 Waverly Place between MacDougal and 6th Avenues

☎ 212-777 0303

🚗 Subway A, B, C, D, E, F, Q to Washington Square

A recent Italian newcomer that is already famous for its 'tasting' menu (a little bit of everything).

CORNELIA STREET CAFÉ $$

✉ 29 Cornelia Street between Bleecker and West 4th Streets

☎ 212-989 9319

A fabulous neighbourhood restaurant which serves lunch and dinner seven days a week. Specials include home-made seafood cakes, herb-crusted salmon, lobster ravioli and Thai bouillabaisse. It's also famous for its jazz club in the basement, which begins at 9pm and costs just $5 for the whole evening.

GOTHAM BAR AND GRILL **$$$**

✉ 12 East 12th Street between 5th Avenue and University Place

☎ 212-620 4020

🚗 Subway L, N, R, 4, 5, 6 to Union Square/14th Street

Always highly rated by Zagat, the excellent American cuisine is served up in a superb environment to a stylish crowd.

JOHN'S PIZZA **$**

✉ 278 Bleeker Street between 6th and 7th Avenues

☎ 212-243 1680

A great place for brick-oven pizzas.

L-RAY **$$**

✉ 64 West 10th Street between 5th and 6th Avenues

☎ 212-505 7777

🚗 Subway F to 14th Street

A recently opened restaurant that serves up Gulf Rim cuisine from Louisiana, Cuba and Mexico.

TOMOE SUSHI **$$**

✉ 172 Thompson Street between Bleecker and West Houston Streets

☎ 212-777 9346

This place looks pretty grotty outside but has an incredible queue and not without reason. You can get the best sushi in New York here, for about a tenth of the price it would cost you at Nobu.

WEST VILLAGE

CAFÉ DE BRUXELLES **$$**

✉ 118 Greenwich Avenue at West 13th Street

☎ 212-206 1830

🚗 A, C, East to 14th Street

A friendly Belgian bistro.

GARAGE RESTAURANT **$**

✉ 99 7th Avenue South between Barrow and Grove Streets

☎ 212-645 0600

🚗 Subway 1, 2, 3, 9 to Christopher Street

A friendly spot for American food in a great location; it also has live jazz.

GRANGE HALL **$$**

✉ 50 Commerce Street at Barrow Street

☎ 212-924 5246

🚗 Subway 1, 9 to Christopher Street

In one of the Village's prettiest streets, this restaurant serves up American fare with an organic twist. It's inexpensive, unpretentious fun and serves large helpings; 10 per cent discount with NYCard.

A new trend when dining out in New York is to order a selection of starters to eat as a kind of Greek meze and skip the main course altogether.

ITHAKA **$$**

✉ 48 Barrow Street between 7th Avenue South and Bedford Streets

☎ 212-727 8886

A former 1851 row house, which now accommodates a superb Greek restaurant with its own Mediterranean sea mural in the conservatory garden area. Known for large portions, this is a real favourite with the locals.

MARKT **$$**

✉ 401 West 14th Street at 9th Avenue

☎ 212-727 3314

🚗 Subway L to 8th Avenue; A, C, East to 14th Street

A stylish Belgian brasserie with a popular bar.

Save a fortune on buying wine with your meal by taking a bottle with you to Grange Hall. They only charge $10 corkage – incredibly cheap by New York standards.

PHILIP MARIE $$

✉ 569 Hudson Street at West 11th Street

☎ 212-242 6200

🚗 Subway 1, 9 to Christopher St

Hearty American fare. Try the newcomer's parsley salad with country ham, dried tomatoes and Wisconsin cheese.

MEATPACKING DISTRICT

FLORENT $

✉ 69 Gansevoort Street between Greenwich and Washington Streets

☎ 212-989 5779

🚗 Subway A, C, East to 14th Street

Open 24 hours at the weekend, this French restaurant is a popular late-night spot with club crowds.

EAST VILLAGE

BELGO NIEUW YORK $$

✉ 415 Lafayette Street between Astor Place and 4th Street

☎ 212-253 2828.

🚗 Subway 6 to Astor Place

A New York outlet based on London's top Belgian restaurant.

BOP $$

✉ 325 Bowery Street at 2nd Street

☎ 212-254 7887

🚗 Subway 6 to Bleecker Street

Serves excellent Korean dishes to a trendy crowd.

CHEZ ES SAADA $$

✉ 42 East 1st Street between 1st and 2nd Avenues

☎ 212-777 5617

🚗 Subway 6 to Bleecker Street

Moroccan basement restaurant that gets packed with beautiful people. Open late.

Weird but true: some smaller restaurants don't take credit cards. Check in advance.

During Summer Restaurant Week, which runs during the last week of June and often lasts until the end of August, over 150 restaurants offer three-course meals for around $20, excluding tip, tax and drinks. Check out NYC & Co at www.nycvisit.com.

FRANK $

✉ 88 2nd Avenue between 5th and 6th Streets

☎ 212-420 0202

🚗 Subway 6 to Astor Place

A tiny Italian restaurant with a real parlour feel, it serves good Tuscan fare at reasonable prices.

KHYBER PASS $

✉ 34 St Mark's Place between Second and Third Avenues

☎ 212-473 0989

🚗 Subway 6 to Astor Place

For delicious and incredibly cheap fare look no further than this Afghan restaurant with a few Persian dishes thrown in for good measure. Think tangy Indian.

STINGY LULU'S $

✉ 129 St Mark's Place

☎ 212-674 3545

Another great American diner.

YAFFA CAFÉ $

✉ 97 St Mark's Place between 1st and Avenue A

☎ 212-677 9000

A classic American diner with a grungy East Village twist.

CHELSEA

BOTTINO $$

✉ 246 10th Avenue between 24th and 25th Streets

☎ 212-206 6766

This is the place to go if you want to see the chic art dealers in recreational mode.

You can tuck into the delicious Tuscan cuisine in either the minimalist dining room or the back garden. If you don't have time to stop and eat, grab a sarnie to takeaway from the next-door Bottino to Go.

BRIGHT FOOD SHOP $

✉ 216 8th Avenue at 21st Street
☎ 212-243 4433

A classic neighbourhood diner with a twist – it serves south-western and Asian versions of American classics.

CAFETERIA $

✉ 119 7th Avenue at 17th Street
☎ 212-414 1717

Another diner experience, only this time filled with the beautiful people who use the 24-hour joint before and after hitting the local clubs.

THE PARK $$

✉ 118 10th Avenue at 17th Street
☎ 212-352 3313
🚗 Subway C, E to 23rd Street

Once a mechanic's garage, this is one of the 'in' spots for film-industry executives. It's a huge industrial bar-cum-restaurant space with a kind of African safari camp interior serving Mediterranean food.

Bottles of water can cost $10 at some of the pricier restaurants. Save your money! New York has access to the finest and cleanest natural water, direct from the Catskill Mountains upstate.

THE RED CAT $$

✉ 227 10th Avenue between 23rd and 24th Streets
☎ 212-242 1122
🚗 Subway C, E to 23rd Street

One of the earlier arrivals in Chelsea, along with the original galleries, this is a real staple with the art pack. It serves up Mediterranean-influenced American food, but you can just go for a cocktail.

UNION SQUARE

BLUE WATER GRILL $$$

✉ 31 Union Square West between 14th and 15th Street.
☎ 212-675 9500
🚗 Subway L, N, Q, R, W, 4, 5, 6 to Union Square

Not only brilliant for people and celeb-watching, this is a mecca for all those who love their seafood. Dishes include pan-roasted Pacific mahi mahi with lobster mashed potatoes and grilled asparagus and ginger-soy lacquered Chilean sea bass with Chinese broccoli, sticky rice and Wasabi vinaigrette. It also has an oyster bar and a 150-seat jazz club for nightly entertainment and dining. Or you can go on Sundays for the jazz brunch which is served from 10.30am.

CHAT 'N' CHEW $

✉ 10 East 16th Street between 5th Avenue and Union Square West
☎ 212-243 1616
🚗 Subway L, N, R, 4, 5, 6 to Union Square/14th Street

Classic 1950s' American diner with huge servings of meatloaf *et al.*

MESA GRILL $$

✉ 102 5th Avenue between 15th and 16th Streets near Union Square
☎ 212-807 7400
🚗 Subway L, N, R, 4, 5, 6 to Union Square/14th Street

Delicious and inventive south-western cuisine from chef Bobby Flay. A real winner, so give it a try if you are in the area.

REPUBLIC $

✉ 37 Union Square West between 16th and 17th Streets
☎ 212-627 7172
🚗 Subway L, N, R, 4, 5, 6 to Union Square/14th Street

Also in Upper West Side. Specialists in excellent, quick, noodle-based Pan-Asian dishes in a canteen-style environment.

GRAMERCY PARK

ELEVEN MADISON $$$

✉ 11 Madison Avenue at 24th Street
☎ 212-889 0905
🚗 Subway: 6, N, R to 23rd Street

With its soaring ceiling, marble floors and French-influenced dishes, this is one of New York's hottest restaurants. It's expensive but not snooty and the service is attentive, as seen in *Sex and the City*.

GRAMERCY TAVERN $$$

✉ 42 East 20th Street between Broadway and Park Avenue South
☎ 212-477 0777
🚗 Subway N, R to 23rd Street

Another real winner and again always highly ranked by the Zagat survey, this is another excellent American restaurant.

MADISON SQUARE

METRONOME $$

✉ 915 Broadway at 21st Street
☎ 212-505 7400
🚗 Subway N, R to 23rd Street

The cheaper alternative to the Supper Club (see page 125), it serves Mediterranean food in a beautiful candlelit setting and has great jazz from Wednesday to Saturday.

TABLA $$$

✉ 11 Madison Avenue at 25th Street
☎ 212-889 0667
🚗 Subway N, R to 23rd Street

Danny Meyer's bi-level restaurant serving American Indian cuisine is a big hit and attracts a trendy crowd. Downstairs is cheaper, you'll be pleased to know.

MIDTOWN

44 $$

✉ Royalton Hotel, 44 West 44th Street between 5th and 6th Avenues
☎ 212-944 8844
🚗 Subway B, D, F, Q to 42nd Street

A *très* trendy joint in the Philippe Starck-designed Royalton, serving new American cuisine. A favourite with posh magazine editors.

CHINA GRILL $$

✉ CBS Building, 60 West 53rd Street between 5th and 6th Avenues
☎ 212-333 7788
🚗 Subway B, D, F, V to 47th-50th Streets/Rockefeller Center

Classy establishment serving eclectic food in a fairly noisy setting. Has a bar that gets pretty crowded.

DB BISTRO MODERNE $$$

✉ City Club Hotel, 55 West 44th Street between 5th and 6th Avenues
☎ 212-391 2400
🚗 Subway: B, D, F, V, S, 4, 5, 6, 7 to 42nd Street

The latest showcase for one of New York's superstar chefs, Daniel Boulud. It got lots of press for the $29 hamburger, and became an instant scene. Located in the very star-chic City Club Hotel, this is one of the few really good places to eat close to the Theater District.

HARD ROCK CAFÉ $

✉ 221 West 57th Street between Broadway and 7th Avenue
☎ 212-459 9320
🚗 Subway B, D to East 7th Avenue

Classic burger 'cuisine' in a noisy, rock 'n' roll environment.

HARLEY DAVIDSON CAFÉ $

✉ 1370 6th Avenue at 56th Street
☎ 212-245 6000
🚗 Subway B, Q to 57th Street

Home-style American comfort foods like meatloaf and chicken pot pie. The memorabilia includes a huge floor road map of Route 66.

LA CARAVELLE $$$

✉ Shoreham Hotel, 33 West 55th Street between 5th and 6th Avenues
☎ 212-586 4252
🚗 Subway F to 5th Avenue; B, Q to 57th Street

Owned by the welcoming husband-and-wife team of André and Rita Jammet, this landmark paragon of classic French cuisine has an elegant setting. Delicious

THEME RESTAURANTS

All these restaurants serve classic American burger-style dishes in family-friendly environments and all can be found in Midtown Manhattan.

Hard Rock Café: $
Harley Davidson Café: $
Mars 2112: $
Planet Hollywood: $

dishes include truffled pike quenelles in a lobster sauce and crispy duck with cranberries.

MEDI $$–$$$

✉ 45 Rockefeller Center overlooking the Plaza
☎ 212-399 8888
🚗 Subway B, D, F, V to 47th-50th Streets/Rockefeller Center

One of the best locations in the city, quite literally overlooking the famous Rockefeller Center Plaza. The vibrant yellow and blue colour scheme – a tribute to the sand and sea of the Mediterranean from which the restaurant's cuisine draws its inspiration – is a real breath of fresh air among the increasingly monochromatic eateries. Executive Chef Daniel Angerer roams the whole Mediterranean with his menu, presenting food with robust depths of flavour. He includes great sandwich and salad options as well as a good choice of heartier meals.

OPIA $$

✉ 130 East 57th Street at Lexington Avenue
☎ 212-688 3939
🚗 Subway: 4, 5, 6, N, R, W to 59th Street/Lexington Avenue

Antoine Blech, formerly of the neat neighbourhood bistro Orienta, is the very welcoming host at this nifty and trendy hideaway for beautiful people in the Habitat Hotel. The French-inspired cuisine is absolutely delicious.

REMI $$$

✉ 145 West 53rd Street between 6th and 7th Avenues
☎ 212-581 4242
🚗 Subway N, R to 49th Street; B, D, East to 7th Avenue

To New Yorkers, this special restaurant is like a taste of Venice with its enchanting Atrium Garden that offers foreign films and live music to accompany dinner al fresco. It also has rotating art exhibits all year long in the Rialto Room. The food is delicious and you can even get Remi takeaways.

ROCK CENTER CAFÉ $$

✉ 20 West 50th Street between 5th Avenue and Rockefeller Plaza
☎ 212-332 7620
🚗 Subway 47th-50th Streets/ Rockefeller Plaza

A Mecca for tourists, thanks to the scenic setting, though the American dishes are a little disappointing.

RUSSIAN TEA ROOM $$

✉ 150 West 57th Street between 6th and 7th Avenues
☎ 212-974 2111
🚗 Subway B, Q to 57th Street

Originally founded in 1926 by members of the Russian Imperial Ballet, who fled to America following the Revolution, this landmark restaurant served only tea and pastries until the end of Prohibition. Then, during the Second World War, it expanded to full service dining and has remained an icon of New York ever since. A haven for emigrés, it became home to New York City's arts community, attracting a loyal clientèle of impresarios, artists, actors, musicians and dancers from around the world.

When Warner LeRoy bought it in 1995, he spent a staggering $30 million renovating it. Now it occupies seven storeys and includes a two-storey ballroom. The ground floor (the cheap place to eat!) is based on the original Russian Tea Room and is filled with intimate leather banquettes in Russian red, with golden samovars, Christmas-decorated chandeliers and shining green walls. The opulent ensemble is completed by red carpeting with an exquisite Russian motif, a gold leaf ceiling and exotic firebirds on the walls.

The first floor is home to three marvels of LeRoy's – a spectacular tree of Fabergé-inspired Venetian glass eggs, a 4.6m- (15ft-) tall revolving aquarium filled with real fish and one of LeRoy's Tiffany glass ceilings, which had been originally created for Maxwell Plum's restaurant. On the second floor is the two-storey Bear Ballroom, filled with frolicking bears and rabbits, another magnificent stained-glass ceiling and imperial bronze chandeliers. The third floor is almost conservative in comparison with its rich, warm and elegant inlaid woods and beautiful paintings, but is known for its working model of the Kremlin in four seasons. The third and fourth floors are generally only used for private functions, but if they're empty ask to take a peek at them.

Prices for meals at the Russian Tea Room are very good value for money, but it's also possible to get the experience totally on the cheap by enjoying afternoon tea here or going for the Vodka Flights. For around $16 you get three little glasses on a tray for a taste of three different vodkas.

The Tea Room is not only about opulent designs, but also about fabulous food. Starters include salmon aspic with Sevruga caviar; foie gras ballotine with pickled fruit and sauterne jelly; and artichoke salad barigoule. Main courses include Siberian veal and beef dumplings in chicken broth, mustard, dill and sour cream; sautéed squab breast wrapped in filo pistachios, spinach and caramelised onions; and the most amazing beef stroganoff.

Early evening sees the arrival of the famous ice palace sculpture, based on designs by LeRoy. Each castle is 2.7 m (9ft) tall and holds eight bottles of vodka, which are properly chilled by the 318-kg (700-lb) solid block of ice. It's worth taking a look at as it's designed to emulate the look of pure cut crystal – the closest most of us will ever come to it!

SEAGRILL $$$

✉ 19 West 49th Street between 5th Avenue and Rockefeller Plaza

☎ 212-332 7610

🚗 Subway B, D, F, Q to 47th-50th Streets/Rockefeller Center

Surrounded by lush greenery, the outdoor tables, topped with striped umbrellas in summer, offer fine views of the Rockefeller Center. In winter, the outdoor seating is replaced by the famous skating rink. The seafood specialities include Chilean sea bass with wilted spinach, grilled lobster with home-made fettucine and coriander-crusted swordfish. Note that the refurbished restaurant's dresscode has changed to exclude jeans, shorts and trainers.

21 CLUB $–$$$

✉ 21 West 52nd Street between 5th and 6th Avenues

☎ 212-582 7200

🚗 Subway F to 5th Avenue

Despite its name, this landmark restaurant has never been a club, but during Prohibition it was a speakeasy, starting life in Greenwich Village before moving to its Midtown location in 1929. West 52nd Street between 5th and 6th Avenues was known then as the 'wettest block in Manhattan' because there were at least 38 speakeasies. One of the most discreet was the 21 Club, which purposefully remained a tiny, clandestine retreat behind the iron gate of its townhouse façade, to avoid both the gangsters and police raids. Its success depended on an employee, who was assigned to spot gangsters, policemen and revenue agents through the peephole and was so skilful that 21 escaped most raids and troubles except for one in 1930. After that the owners had a new security system designed to create false stairways and walls to hide its 2,000 cases of fine wines. It involved the building of a 2-tonne door to the secret cellar, made out of the original bricks to look like a wall. The cellar is still going strong and now houses $1.5 million of wine, much of which is owned by the celebrities and power brokers who call the 21 Club their own. Liz Taylor and former presidents Nixon and Ford still keep their bottles here.

Once Prohibition ended in 1932, many of the former speakeasies went out of business, but the 21 turned itself into a fine dining establishment that has been attracting celebrities and movers and shakers ever since. They've included Joe DiMaggio, Aristotle Onassis, Franklin D Roosevelt, Humphrey Bogart, Ernest Hemingway and Jackie Gleason. The night before I enjoyed lunch there, Margaret Thatcher had been at a private function and Joan Collins had dined in the main restaurant.

Wine is incredibly expensive in New York. If you buy a glass for $6 you're doing well, and even in mid-range restaurants it can set you back $12. Do as New Yorkers do, have a glass of wine or cocktail before you go out and drink beer with your meal or just stick to the one glass of wine!

The 21 classics include creamy chicken hash, English game pot pie and the 21 burger. Other dishes include mussels marinière, Maine lobster salad, hickory-fired filet mignon with stoneground corn and cepes, or grilled swordfish with white bean purée, cucumbers and spicy paprika sauce. Prix fixe lunch and dinner menus make the restaurant accessible to all and between 2.30 and 5pm there is a special In Between menu with such dishes as Mahi-Mahi wrap with avocado, mango and arugula served with potato soufflés for a mere $17.

MIDTOWN EAST

ASIA DE CUBA $$

✉ Morgan's Hotel, 237 Madison Avenue between 37th and 38th Streets
☎ 212-726 7755
🚗 Subway 6 to 33rd Street; 4, 5, 6, 7 to Grand Central/42nd Street

The Philippe Starck interior guarantees a trendy crowd for the fusion Asian and Cuban food.

CAVIAR RUSSE $$$

✉ 538 Madison Avenue, second floor, between 54th and 55th Streets
☎ 212-980 5908
🚗 Subway F to 5th Avenue

Posh caviar and cigar lounge where you can see how the other half live.

CHIN CHIN $$

✉ 216 East 49th Street between 2nd and 3rd Avenues
☎ 212-888 4555
🚗 Subway 6 to 51st Street

One of New York's finest Chinese restaurants, it frequently plays host to the city's power crowd.

DOCKS OYSTER BAR $

✉ 633 3rd Avenue at 40th Street
☎ 212-986 8080
🚗 Subway 4, 5, 6, 7 to Grand Central/42nd Street

This raw fish and seafood speciality restaurant also has a popular bar.

EUROPA GRILL $$

✉ 599 Lexington Avenue at 53rd Street
☎ 212-755 6622
🚗 Subway E, F to Lexington/3rd Avenue

A welcoming restaurant, which has been designed in natural elements of wood, stone and earth tones to create a soothing and tranquil environment. Lincoln Engstrom, formerly of the River

Café, is the chef and he has created delicious and stylish Mediterranean dishes. They include poussin stuffed with ricotta salata and zucchini, peppers and sage, pomegranate-marinated lamb with crispy panisse and fresh mint, and lemon-cured pork loin served with soft polenta.

FOUR SEASONS **$$$**

✉ 99 East 52nd Street between Lexington and Park Avenues

☎ 212-754 9494

🚗 Subway 6 to 51st Street; E, F to Lexington/3rd Avenue

You have a choice between the Grill Room or the Pool Room at this landmark restaurant, and whichever you opt for will make you feel like one of New York's movers and shakers – this is where they come for their power lunches. The continental dishes are exquisite, the setting elegant and the service impeccable. Pricey? You bet.

ISTANA **$$**

✉ NY Palace Hotel, 455 Madison Avenue at 51st Street

☎ 212-303 6032

🚗 Subway 6 to 51st Street

A little-known but excellent place serving Mediterranean cuisine.

LA GRENOUILLE **$$$**

✉ 3 East 52nd Street between 5th and Madison Avenues

☎ 212-752 1495

🚗 Subway 6 to 51st Street

A sophisticated temple for Francophiles, the exquisite French food is well worth the money. If money's no object, go for dinner, otherwise go for a more economical lunch.

LE CIRQUE 2000 **$$$**

✉ NY Palace Hotel, 455 Madison Avenue between 50th and 51st Streets

☎ 212-303 7788

🚗 Subway 6 to 51st Street

If you seriously want to eat at this landmark restaurant, you'll need to book your table a few months ahead, but you'll be rewarded with the best people-watching in town as this is the place for celebrities and the local élite. Obviously, the haute cuisine matches expectations. Mouth-watering dishes include sea bass in crispy potatoes with red wine sauce, veal with fresh morels and grilled salmon with lemon-grass crust. Divine.

LE PERIGORD **$$$**

✉ 405 East 52nd Street between 1st and 2nd Avenues

☎ 212-755 6244

www.LePerigord.com

🚗 Subway 6 to 51st Street

An institution of the smart Sutton Place district, which is home to ambassadors, millionaires and top business people, yet despite its clientele it remains an unpretentious haven for excellent food and wine. This, of course, has much to do with the Swiss-born proprietor Georges Briguet, who is to the hospitality industry what Muhammad Ali is to boxing – a bit of a legend.

Georges is dedicated to providing the best of everything and in return he is blessed with a faithful following, though he makes no distinction between new and old clients when it comes to using his charm. His recently appointed executive chef, Jacques Qualin, a veteran of New York icons such as Jean-Georges and Le Cirque, has created an impressive menu, which reflects both his rustic French roots and his culinary training. Starters include sautéed frogs' legs savagnin sauce with fresh cranberry bean cake and watercress soup with Sevruga caviar. Main courses include salmon 'filet mignon' with herbs-stuffed cabbage and carbonade sauce, and roasted free-range chicken in vin jaune sauce with Bleu de Gex potatoes gratin and morel mushrooms.

You can either go à la carte or enjoy the three-course prix fixe menus, while there is a very good selection of wines under $50, which, believe me, is rare for restaurants in this price category.

NEW YORK FOODS AND FOOD TERMS

Arugula: The American name for rocket, used in salads.
Bialy: A cousin of the bagel, it originates from Bialystock in Eastern Europe and is kosher Jewish food. The dough is not as chewy as a bagel and there is no hole in the middle, just a depression in which garlic and onions are put. Without any tasty extras such as cream cheese, this is truly boring food.
Bagels: As opposed to bialys, these are the delicious Jewish creations, which are at their very best when filled with smoked salmon and cream cheese (see page 43).
Cannolli: Tubular-shaped cookie bells with fresh cream on the inside, these come from Italy and are truly delicious.
Halva: Sweetened, crushed sesame paste. It originates from all around the Mediterranean, Turkey and Arabia.
Konja: A Chinese dessert, which you can buy in bags – they are individual mouth-size pots of lychee jelly.
Lox: Chopped pieces of smoked salmon, generally sold with a 'schmear' of cream cheese. It tastes the same as a smoked salmon and cream cheese bagel but works out much cheaper.
Morels: Deliciously meaty mushrooms from Oregon.
Pie: Used to refer to an entire pizza. Most are much larger than the ones we eat in the UK, so people tend to buy by the slice or share a whole 'pie'.
Schmear: Spreading of cream cheese on a bagel.

LESPINASSE $$$

✉ St Regis Hotel, 2 East 55th Street between 5th and Madison Avenues
☎ 212-339 6719
🚗 Subway 4, 5, 6 to 59th Street

Fine Asian-French cuisine is served in the plush environs of the St Regis Hotel to the elite of New York. The restaurant has won numerous awards and is open for lunch and dinner.

OYSTER BAR $$

✉ Grand Central Station, lower level, between 42nd Street and Vanderbilt Avenue
☎ 212-490 6650
🚗 Subway 4, 5, 6, 7 to Grand Central/42nd Street

This landmark place was made famous by generations of connoisseurs consuming 1,000 dozen oysters every day at the counters and in the landmark restaurant and atmospheric saloon.

PALM $$

✉ 837 2nd Avenue between 44th and 45th Streets
☎ 212-687 2953
🚗 Subway 4, 5, 6, 7 to Grand Central/42nd Street

The place in New York to get a steak or tuck into a huge lobster. The trademarks of both this establishment and Palm Too across the road (840 2nd Avenue) are the simple décor and the grumpy waiters.

WATER CLUB $$$

✉ 500 East 30th Street at East River
☎ 212-683 3333
🚗 Subway 6 to 28th Street, near Madison Square

Another delightful and special venue from the owner of the River Café, this restaurant also specialises in seafood. Although on the pricey side – though worth it for the fine cuisine – the weekend brunch option at a prix fixe of $20 is an excellent way to sample some delicious dishes while gazing out across the East River.

VONG $$$

✉ 200 East 54th Street at 3rd Avenue
☎ 212-486 9592
🚗 Subway E, F to Lexington/3rd Avenue

Another of Jean-Georges Vongerichten's masterpieces, this Thai-French restaurant has sunken tables and deep booths that keep the trendy crowd happy.

MIDTOWN WEST

BARBETTA RESTAURANT $$$

✉ 321 West 46th Street between 8th and 9th Avenues
☎ 212-246 9171
🚗 Subway A, C, East to 42nd Street

During the summer, the rather special Barbetta garden is one of the city's most sought-after sites for dining, with its century-old trees and the scented blooms of magnolia, wisteria, jasmine and gardenia. Barbetta is the oldest Italian restaurant in New York and features cuisine from Piedmont in the north-west region of Italy.

HUDSON CAFETERIA $$

✉ The Hudson, 356 West 58th Street between 8th and 9th Avenues
☎ 212-554 6500
🚗 Subway A, B, C, D, 1, 2 to 59th Street/Columbus Circle

The restaurant at Ian Schrager's newest hotel is a haven for people and celeb-watching and you'll even enjoy the Asian cuisine!

JEAN GEORGES $$$

✉ Trump International Hotel, 1 Central Park West between 60th and 61st Streets
☎ 212-299 3900
🚗 Subway A, B, C, D, 1, 9 to 59th Street/Columbus Circle

Celebrity chef Jean-Georges Vongerichten's exquisite French dishes are served in an elegant and subtle landmark restaurant designed by Adam Tihany, with superb views of Central Park. It's an unbeatable combination, so plan ahead, book your table and get a rich uncle to take you pronto!

PETROSSIAN $$$

✉ 182 West 58th Street at 7th Avenue
☎ 212-245 2214
🚗 Subway N, R to 57th Street

Take advantage of the $20 prix fixe lunch to tuck into caviar, foie gras and smoked salmon.

SUPPER CLUB $$$

✉ 240 West 47th Street between Broadway and 8th Avenue
☎ 212-921 1940
🚗 Subway 1, 9 to 50th Street

At this special place, you'll find fine dining combined with swing dancing and a cabaret – the show is a mix of Cab Calloway, the Blues Brothers and other swing acts. The food is also delicious, particularly the lobster and steak, and I defy anyone to hate the New York cheesecake – so much lighter than European cheesecake, it just melts in your mouth. Stupendous.

If you want to smoke, eat in the bar area or choose a restaurant with less than 35 seats. Some other restaurants also allow smoking later in the evening.

WORLD YACHT DINING CRUISE $$

✉ Pier 81, West 41st Street at Hudson River
☎ 212-630 8100
🚗 Subway A, C, East to 42nd Street

A beautiful, four-course dining experience with the best views of Midtown and Lower Manhattan plus the Statue of Liberty at this seriously special place. Dishes include Chilean sea bass, rosemary-roasted chicken with scallions, bean purée and sweet garlic jus, red snapper with anchovy paste, topped with sweet and spicy cilantro-chipotte rouille, and herb-roasted rack of lamb served with arugula and couscous, and the chefs are some of the finest around New

York. The prix fixe meal, including a three-hour cruise and live music for dancing, costs $67 from Sun to Thurs, $75 on Fridays and $79 on Saturdays. NYCard holders get a discount.

THEATER DISTRICT

FIREBIRD $$

365 West 46th Street between 8th and 9th Avenues
212-586 0244
Subway A, C, East to 42nd Street

The opulent Russian décor creates a fabulous setting for tucking into the caviar and blinis. There is a prix fixe pre-theatre dinner, which is excellent value at $20.

FRANKIE AND JOHNNIE'S $$

269 West 45th Street between Broadway and 8th Avenue
212-997 9494
Subway A, C, E, N, R to 42nd Street

This is considered to be one of the longest-running shows on Broadway, having first opened as a speakeasy in 1926. Now it still retains its intimate hideaway aura and archetypal New York rep as a classic steakhouse, known for its generous portions.

MARS 2112 $

1633 Broadway at 51st Street
212-582 2112
Subway 1, 9 to 51st Street.

The most recent theme restaurant offering will literally take you out of this world to Mars via the space shuttle. Fortunately, the food is pretty American Earth-bound so you won't be eating little green men. Of course, it comes with the ubiquitous shop where you can buy your very own Martian doll.

PLANET HOLLYWOOD $

1540 Broadway at West 45th Street
212-333 7827
Subway N, Q, R, S, W, 1, 2, 3, 7 to Times Square

Brilliant Hollywood memorabilia with the standard American burger fare.

RENÉ PUJOL $$

321 West 51st Street between 8th and 9th Avenues
212-246 3023
Subway C, East to 50th Street

A great French bistro serving delicious food in a delightful setting.

THEATER DISTRICT

From 6th Avenue in the east to 9th Avenue in the west and from West 40th Street to West 53rd Street, the Theater District is as good a place as any to get a pre-theatre meal. As well as the many theatres, there are hundreds of restaurants and you'd be hard-pressed to go wrong. The main drag for eateries is between 8th and 9th Avenues on West 46th Street and is known as Restaurant Row.

CENTRAL PARK

PARK VIEW AT THE BOATHOUSE $$–$$$

Central Park Lake, Park Drive North at East 72nd Street
212-517 2233
Subway 6 to 68th Street/Hunter College

One of the most wonderful locations in New York. Set right by the lake with its blue rowboats, the restaurant's sparkling lights add to the romance, while the mostly seafood menu is delicious.

TAVERN ON THE GREEN $$$

Central Park at West 67th Street
212-873 3200
www.tavernonthegreen.com
Subway B, C to 72nd Street

Looking at the glitzy razzmatazz that is the Tavern, it's hard to imagine this building started life in 1870 as a house for the sheep that roamed Central Park. By the early 1930s, Parks Commissioner Robert Moses had spotted its potential as a restaurant. He banished the sheep to Brooklyn's Prospect Park and assigned their shepherd to the lion house at the Central Park Zoo. In 1934, he opened what was known as The Restaurant with a coachman in full regalia and the blessing of Mayor Fiorello LaGuardia.

It became an integral part of the city's social life but, by the 1950s, it was showing signs of wear and tear and in 1974 it closed. In stepped Warner LeRoy, who bought it, spent $10 million not only renovating it but also turning it into a spectacle in its own right, creating the Crystal and Terrace Rooms with his lavish use of brass, stained glass, etched mirrors, antique paintings and prints and a cacophony of chandeliers.

The Tavern on the Green was born in 1976 and took the city by storm. Celebrities flocked to it to see and be seen and it became the in place for prestigious charity and political functions. Over the years, additions have been made including state-of-the-art light and sound systems for entertainments, Steinway concert grand pianos, the Park Room and Garden and the Menagerie of Topiaries.

Now the Tavern pulls in out-of-towners, who've all been told by their friends to visit this unique sight, and the restaurant has a staggering turnover of $34 million a year! And what a riot of colours and textures its clients are greeted with. This is possibly the only restaurant in the world where a trio of birthday balloons look right at home floating on the ceiling. But you may have more respect for the myriad different-coloured chandeliers if you know they are made out of genuine Baccarat crystal and the stained glass is genuine Tiffany.

You don't have to eat at the Tavern to enjoy its fabulous garden. From May to October you can enjoy a cocktail in the garden bar.

The food is classic gourmet American with typical main courses including sautéed crabcakes; roast prime rib of beef with Yorkshire pudding, Yukon-gold mashed potatoes and creamy horseradish; and grilled pork porterhouse with peach and apple chutney.

UPPER EAST SIDE

AUREOLE $$$

✉ 34 East 61st Street between Madison and Park Avenues

☎ 212-319 1660

🚗 Subway 4, 5, 6 to 59th Street; N, R to Lexington Avenue

Always among the top 10 restaurants in New York, the courtyard garden is the restaurant's best-kept secret. Tucked behind the brownstone that houses Aureole, away from the hustle and bustle of the street, it's an idyllic spot for outdoor dining and always incredibly romantic when lit by candles at night. Celebrity chef Charlie Palmer's delicious concoctions include wood-grilled lamb mignons with lentil cakes, pan-seared foie gras steak and fricassee of lobster with Provençal artichokes.

BLUE GROTTO $

✉ 1576 3rd Avenue between 88th and 89th Streets.

☎ 212-426 3200

🚗 Subway 4, 5, 6 to 86th Street

This is more York Town than silk-stocking Upper East Side, which is reflected in the reasonable prices. A recent venture, it's already popular with the locals and serves Italian and Mediterranean-style cuisine in a lounge-like space.

CAFÉ SABARSKY $

✉ 1048 5th Avenue at 86th Street

☎ 212-288 0665

🚗 Subway: 4, 5, 6 to 86th Street

This is not just in a fabulous location – all but opposite the Metropolitan Museum, yet quietly tucked away in the new Neue Galerie New York – but is a wonderful pit stop for light breakfasts,

THE AMERICAN DINER

We don't have a real equivalent of in the UK but the closest is probably a cross between a transport café and a Garfunkels – i.e. diners are relatively cheap, have a homey feel to them but are a lot smarter than your average café. They specialise in American comfort food – pancakes, waffles, crispy bacon, eggs, grill foods, meatloaf – the kind of things that we would choose for a brunch. Go to just about any American city or town and you'll find a good smattering of diners. The one exception is Manhattan where they're very thin on the ground. At all costs avoid the touristy Brooklyn Diner on West 57th Street – it's too expensive to give you the real diner experience. Some of the few diners available in New York include:

SoHo

Moondance: 80 6th Avenue between Grand and Canal Streets. Tel 212-226 1191. A cracking spot for a cheap meal, it gets packed at the weekends when it's open 24 hours a day.

NoLiTa

Jones Diner: 371 Lafayette Street at Great Jones Street. Tel 212-673 3577. Pretty dingy-looking from the outside, this is one of the cheapest and best places in the area to get very basic grills and sarnies.

Chelsea

Empire Diner: 210 10th Avenue between West 22nd and West 23rd Streets. Tel 212-243 2736. This is a real New York institution and a great pit-stop for clubbers as it's open 24 hours a day. The interior is fabulous with its art deco style and the people are pretty gorgeous, too.

Garment District

Cheyenne Diner: 411 9th Avenue at 33rd Street. Tel 212-465 8750. In the heart of the Garment District and just around the corner from Penn Street Station, this is a great place to fill up.

Midtown West

Market Diner: 572 11th Avenue at West 43rd Street. Tel 212-695 0415. One of the most famous diners in Manhattan, this is the place where clubbers go to get breakfast or fill up before the evening run.

Midtown East

Comfort Diner: 214 East 45th Street between 2nd and 3rd Avenues. Tel 212-867 4555. A classic retro diner known for its friendliness and also its staples of meatloaf and fried chicken.

Upper East Side

Comfort Diner: 142 East 86th Street at Lexington Avenue. Tel 212-369 8628. The Upper East Side/Yorkville branch of the friendly diner.

Morningside Heights

Tom's Restaurant: 2880 Broadway at 112th Street. Tel 212-864 6137. The exterior was made famous by its use in *Seinfeld.* If you come here you'll be sharing the space with Columbia University students, who enjoy the cheap comfort food.

Harlem

M&G Soul Food Diner: 383 West 125th Street at Morningside Avenue. Tel 212-864 7326. This is the Southern soul food version of a diner and a great venue for a meal in Harlem. You'll also enjoy the background soul music.

lunch and afternoon tea. You'll also love its elegant décor to match the Austrian-German art theme of the museum itself.

CARLYLE **$$$**

✉ Carlyle Hotel, 35 East 76th Street at Madison Avenue
☎ 212-744 1600
🚗 Subway 6 to 77th Street

An old establishment that attracts an older clientele to this landmark restaurant, but if you want to see how the other half lives, try the fine French cuisine for breakfast or brunch. Divine.

CELLO **$$$**

✉ 53 East 77th Street between Madison and Park Avenues
☎ 212-517 1200
🚗 Subway 6 to 77th Street

This is very upmarket and very smart – jackets required – but if you're in the mood for seafood, it is the place to go. Famed chef Laurent Tourondel's creations include marinated Chilean sea bass with honey and parsnip purée.

MARK'S **$$$**

✉ The Mark, 25 East 77th Street at Madison Avenue
☎ 212-879 1864
🚗 Subway 6 to 77th Street

Excellent French-American cuisine. The prix fixe lunch and pre-theatre deals are great value – just make sure you give yourself time to soak up the ambience.

ROSA MEXICANA **$$**

✉ 1063 1st Avenue at 58th Street
☎ 212-753 7407
🚗 Subway 4, 5, 6 to 59th Street

Extremely popular Mexican eaterie that is known as much for its margaritas as for its food.

SERAFINA FABULOUS GRILL **$$**

✉ 29 East 61st Street between Madison and Park Avenues
☎ 212-702 9898
🚗 Subway 4, 5, 6 to 59th Street

Famous for thin-crust pizzas that have been voted the best in the world by gourmets, this is a haunt of both Prince Albert of Monaco and Ivana Trump. Toppings include Al Porcini with porcini mushrooms, fontina cheese and mozzarella and Al Caviale with salmon caviar, potatoes and crème fraîche. The signature focaccias, two layers of stuffed dough with fillings, range from Scottish smoked salmon, asparagus and Italian Robiola cheese to truffle oil and Robiola.

UPPER WEST SIDE

ALOUETTE **$$**

✉ 2588 Broadway between 97th and 98th Streets
☎ 212-222 6808
🚗 Subway 1, 2, 3, 9 to 96th Street

This French bistro attracts the crowds despite having a very simple menu.

CAFÉ DES ARTISTES **$$**

✉ 1 West 67th Street between Columbus Avenue and Central Park West
☎ 212-877 3500
🚗 Subway 1, 9 to 66th Street

A reasonably priced fine dining establishment that serves up wonderful French cuisine in a romantic setting.

OUEST **$$**

✉ 2315 Broadway between 83rd and 84th Streets
☎ 212-580 8700
🚗 Subway 1, 2 to 86th Street

Once you can get your tongue around the title – it's simply called West! – you'll be ready to enjoy the French-American cuisine created by Valenti.

PICHOLINE **$$$**

✉ 35 West 64th Street between Broadway and Central Park West
☎ 212-724 8585
🚗 Subway 1, 9 to 66th Street/Lincoln Center

A beautiful restaurant serving exquisite Mediterranean dishes in a refined and elegant setting. Opt to make it one of your 'special' treats while in the city and you can partake of the amazing cheese trolley – yes trolley, not board. Each day more than 50 different cheeses, out of a total of 70 varieties, are displayed on the trolley and if you have any worries about what to choose, all the waiters have been given lessons in exactly what cheeses go well with what wines and for what kind of palates. Take advantage of their considerable knowledge. A tradition to be savoured.

RUBY FOO'S $$

✉ 2182 Broadway at 77th Street
☎ 212-724 6700
🚗 Subway 1, 9 to 79th Street

Beautiful Asian décor combined with delicious Asian food. Dim sum is a speciality of the house.

SPAZZIA $$

✉ 366 Columbus Avenue at West 77th Street
☎ 212-799 0150
🚗 Subway 1, 9 to 79th Street

This restaurant serves delicious Mediterranean food just a stone's throw away from the American Museum of Natural History.

HARLEM

GEORGE & GINA'S RESTAURANT $$

✉ 169 East 106th Street between Lexington and 3rd Avenues
☎ 212-410 7292
🚗 Subway 6 to 103rd Street

A Puerto Rican restaurant deep in the heart of Spanish Harlem.

If you need a pit stop around 110th Street, drop in for a cuppa and a delicious cake at Make My Cake, 103 West 110th Street at Lenox Avenue/Malcom X Boulevard. Tel 212-932 0833.

MANNA'S RESTAURANT $

✉ 486 Lenox Avenue/Malcolm X Boulevard at 134th Street
☎ 212-234 4488
🚗 Subway 2, 3 to 135th Street

Not so much a restaurant as a great, cheap pit stop used by the locals. There are two huge buffets of hot and cold food plus salads and fruit, which you can buy by the plastic tub and either take away or eat at one of the simple, canteen-style tables. Fresh fruit and salad items cost $3.99 a pound and meats cost $4.99 a pound as opposed to around $8.99 in the Midtown area. The hot buffet includes a tremendous range of chicken, including Southern-style, lamb, beef stews, meatloaf, ribs, vegetables and many different rices. There are also many salads to choose from, including the ubiquitous Caesar's salad, and fruits such as melon, watermelon, orange and papaya. It also has a fresh fruit and vegetable juice bar. Manna's Restaurant is open Monday to Saturday 7am–8pm and Sundays 10am–7pm.

RAO'S $

✉ 455 East 114th Street at Pleasant Avenue
☎ 212-722 6709
🚗 Subway 6 to 116th Street

An institution, you'll only get in if you come across the handful of people who actually have access to this eight-table Italian restaurant! Famous for its sauces, which Sinatra used to have flown to him around the world. Now the jukebox plays all the crooner's favourites.

If you can't get in at Rao's, you can still get a taste of their fabulous sauces, by buying them either direct from the restaurant or from Faicco's Sausage Store in Bleecker Street, Greenwich Village (see page 92).

SYLVIA'S $

✉ 328 Lenox Avenue between 126th and 127th Streets

☎ 212-996 0660

🚗 Subway 2, 3 to 125th Street

Southern home-style cooking – aka soul food. Sylvia's place is a New York institution and famous for its Sunday gospel brunch, but you need to book a few weeks ahead as it gets very busy.

BROOKLYN

GRIMALDI'S $

✉ 19 Old Fulton Street between Front and Water Streets

☎ 718-858 4300

🚗 Subway A, C to High Street/Brooklyn Bridge

Considered the best place in New York to get a delicious pizza at a great price.

RIVER CAFÉ $$$

✉ 1 Water Street under the Brooklyn Bridge

☎ 718-522 5200

🚗 Subway A, C to High Street/Brooklyn Bridge

This is a really special restaurant. For unrivalled views of New York's magnificent Lower Manhattan skyline, this is the place to come and the food matches up to the location. Superb dishes include braised Maine lobster, crisp black sea bass, seared diver sea scallops, grilled, aged prime sirloin of beef and pan-roasted chukar partridge.

CHAPTER 8

Shows, Bars and Nightlife

BROADWAY SHOWS

One of the first things you discover about Broadway is that it is just one tiny stretch of almost the longest thoroughfare on the island of Manhattan. The Theater District (see page 47), as it is known, is actually a congregation of theatres between Broadway and 8th Avenue from about 44th to 52nd Streets (take the N, R, 1, 2, 3, 7, 9, S lines to 42nd Street/Times Square). This is Broadway. You'll also see and hear the terms 'Off Broadway' and 'Off-Off Broadway' (yes, really), which refer to uptown and downtown theatres, particularly in Greenwich Village, East Village and SoHo. Many of the productions in these theatres are well worth a visit for their hilarious, off-the-wall humour, but they do change frequently, so I have only included a sample selection.

Look for discount coupons at neighbourhood information stands and barrows throughout Manhattan.

Of course, Broadway productions also change all the time, but many of the big shows – the ones that most Brits are interested in – do stay around for a little longer. I have included reviews of those shows I believe will be available for the next couple of years, but for a completely up-to-date guide to what's on at the theatre, pick up the *New York Times*, which has comprehensive listings of dance, classical music, opera, Broadway, Off Broadway and Off-Off Broadway every day. Other papers and magazines you can check out include the *New Yorker, Village Voice* and *New York Press.*

BOOKING YOUR TICKETS

You can book tickets in advance in the UK through either your travel agent or Keith Prowse (tel 01232 232425). An alternative is to use the TicketMaster website at **www.ticketmaster.com**.

If booking in New York, try Theatre Direct (tel 800-334 8457, **www.theatredirect.com**); Broadway Line (tel 212-302 4111); Americana Tickets & Travel (tel 212-581 6660); and Premiere Ticket Service (tel 212-643 1274).

For cheaper tickets, go to the Theater Development Fund/TKTS booth in town in the middle of Times Square at 47th Street, which is open Monday, Tuesday, Thursday and Friday 3–8pm, Wednesday and Saturday 10am–2pm and Sunday 11am–7pm. Arrive early for the best selection, then spend the day in Midtown (see Chapter 3, The New York Neighbourhoods). In both cases bear in mind that the booths only accept cash or travellers' cheques. Have plenty of options ready in case there are no tickets for your first show choice.

Watch out for ticket touts – an increasing number of the tickets they sell are fakes.

CURRENT PRODUCTIONS

AIDA

✉ Palace Theatre, 1554 Broadway at 47th Street
☎ 212-307 4747
🕘 Tues to Sat 8pm, matinees Wed and Sat at 2pm, Sun at 3pm

Elton John and Tim Rice teamed up to create the musical score for this new version of the operatic classic. It's a great story of loyalty and betrayal, courage and love as three people are forced to make choices that will change their lives and the course of history.

The Hit Show Club (630 9th Avenue between 44th and 45th Streets, tel 212-581 4211) distributes coupons that can be redeemed at the box office for one-third or more off regular ticket prices. If you don't see them in your hotel, pick them up from the offices.

BEAUTY AND THE BEAST

✉ Lunt-Fontanne Theater, 205 West 46th Street between Broadway and 8th Avenue
☎ 212-307 4747
🕘 Wed to Sat 8pm, Sun 6.30pm, matinees Wed and Sat 2pm, Sun 1pm and 6.30pm

The award-winning Disney version with music by Alan Menken and lyrics by Tim Rice and the late Howard Ashman. It tells the age-old story of how a young woman falls in love with a stubborn but charming beast.

CABARET

✉ Studio 54, 524 West 54th Street between Broadway and 8th Avenue
☎ 212-239 6200
🕘 Tues to Sat 8pm, Sun 7pm, matinees Sat and Sun 2pm

While Berlin prepares for war, inside the cabaret must go on. What makes it so special are the characters, who include Sally Bowles, a tragic British singer desperate for glamour, Fräulein Schneider, the innkeeper and a true survivor, and watching over all the madness, the Master of Ceremonies.

Same-day rear mezzanine tickets for *Cabaret* are available at the box office for $25 Tues to Thurs and Sun and $20 day-of-performance tickets are available for *Chicago* from the box office at 10am.

CHICAGO

✉ Schubert Theater, 225 West 44th Street between Broadway and 8th Avenue
☎ 212-239 6200
🕘 Tues to Fri and Sat 8pm, Sun 7pm, matinees Sat and Sun 2pm

This great musical with wonderful dancing is the winner of six 1997 Tony Awards and has other productions throughout the world, but many still consider this production to be the best. *Chicago* tells the story of a chorus girl who kills her lover and then escapes the noose and prison with the help of a conniving lawyer. If greed, corruption, murder and treachery are your bag, then this is the musical for you!

42ND STREET

✉ Ford Center, 213 West 42nd Street between 7th and 8th Avenues
☎ 212-307 4100
🕘 Mon to Sat 8pm, matinees Wed and Sat 2pm

It's the classic tale of a chorus girl who becomes a star and is based on the 1933 movie famous for its Busby Berkeley production numbers of *The Lullaby of Broadway, We're in the Money, Dames* and, of course, *42nd Street*. And where else to stage this revival than in a theatre in 42nd Street itself? The singing is wonderful and the dancing dynamite.

THE FULL MONTY

✉ Eugene O'Neill Theatre, 230 West 49th Street between Broadway and 8th Avenue
☎ 212-239 6200
🕘 Tues to Sat 8pm, matinees Wed and Sat 2pm, Sun 3pm

Based on the British hit movie, transferred to Buffalo, New York, where six down-on-their-luck steel workers go to great lengths to raise cash for a friend in need. Set to a score by Terrance McNally, with lyrics by David Yazbek.

For fantastic views of Times Square, treat yourself to a drink at the revolving Broadway Lounge on the eighth floor lobby level of the Marriott Marquis Hotel at 1535 Broadway.

THE GRADUATE

✉ Plymouth Theater, 236 West 45th Street between Broadway and 8th Avenue
☎ 212-239 6200
🕘 Tues to Sat 8pm, Sun 7pm, matinees Sat 2pm, Sun 2pm

Based on the original novel and famous movie starring Dustin Hoffman and Anne Bancroft, this tells the story of a college graduate with a very tangled love life.

LES MISERABLES

✉ Imperial Theater, 249 West 54th Street between Broadway and 8th Avenue
☎ 212-239 6200
🕘 Tues to Sat 8pm, matinees Wed and Sat 2pm, Sun 3pm

Musical adaptation of Victor Hugo's classic novel about Jean Valjean. Spectacular sets and heartrending music bring to life the story of thief Jean and his redemption as a result of saving an orphan girl.

THE LION KING

✉ New Amsterdam Theater, 214 West 42nd Street at Broadway
☎ 212-307 4100
🕘 Wed to Sat 8pm, Sun 6.30pm, matinees Wed and Sat 2pm, Sun 1pm

With the original music from Elton John and Tim Rice combined with new music from Hans Zimmer and Lebo M, Disney tells the story of a young lion cub named Simba who struggles to accept the responsibilities of adulthood and his destined role as king. Winner of six Tony Awards in 1998.

MAMMA MIA!

✉ Winter Garden Theater, 1634 Broadway at 50th Street
☎ 212-563 5544
🕘 Mon to Fri 8pm, matinee Sat 2pm

If you haven't had chance to see this fabulously uplifting musical in London, then why not try it in New York? Set on a mythical Greek island, it tells the story of a single mum and her daughter on the eve of her daughter's wedding – and comes with 22 cracking ABBA songs.

THE PHANTOM OF THE OPERA

✉ Majestic Theater, 245 West 44th Street between Broadway and 8th Avenue
☎ 212-239 6200
🕘 Mon to Sat 8pm, matinees Wed and Sat 2pm

Set in 19th-century Paris, this is Andrew Lloyd Webber's famous musical of Gaston Leroux's novel. It tells the timeless story of a mysterious spectre, who haunts the Paris opera house, spooking the owners and falling in love with a beautiful singer.

THE PRODUCERS

✉ St James Theater, 246 West 44th Street between Broadway and 8th Avenue
☎ 212-239 6200
🕘 Tues to Fri 8pm, matinees Wed and Sat 2pm, Sun 3pm

Based on Mel Brooks' zany 1968 movie, this tells the story of a down-on-his-luck theatre producer who hatches a plot to raise cash from a Broadway flop scam.

KIDS' NIGHT ON BROADWAY

The annual Kids' Night on Broadway (KNOB) discount season runs from January to March. KNOB offers each adult who buys a full-price ticket one free ticket for a child aged six to 18. Created by the League of American Theaters and Producers and the Theater Development Fund, the programme includes special 7pm curtain times and restaurant discounts plus a variety of interactive theatre-related activities for children. Call The Broadway Line on 1-888 BROADWAY or 212-302 4111 for information on KNOB and other Broadway and Off-Broadway shows. Tickets for this discount scheme go on sale around the third week in October.

RENT

✉ Nederlander Theater, 208 West 41st Street between 7th and 8th Avenues
☎ 212-307 4100
🕓 Mon to Sat 8pm, Sun 7pm, matinees Wed, Sat and Sun 2pm

The Tony Award- and Pulitzer Prize-winning musical is based on Puccini's opera La Bohème, but is set in New York's East Village. It tells the story of struggling young artists living on the edge in the search for glory.

Queues for the Times Square TKTS booth start long before it opens, so arrive early to get a good choice.

URINETOWN: THE MUSICAL

✉ Henry Miller Theater, 124 West 43rd Street between 6th Avenue and Broadway
☎ 212-239 6200
🕓 Tues to Sat 8pm, matinees Wed and Sat 2pm, Sun 3pm

An hilarious tale of greed, corruption and love based on the premise that the world's water supply has been depleted so severely that the government has put a ban on private toilets.

OFF-BROADWAY

BLUE MAN GROUP: TUBES

✉ Astor Place Theater, 434 Lafayette Street at Astor Place
☎ 212-254 4370
🕓 Tues and Thurs 8pm, Fri and Sat 7pm and 10pm, Sun 1pm, 4pm and 7pm

One of the most successful Off-Broadway shows. Take a trio of post-modern clowns, cover them in blue rubber and allow them to be outrageous with sound and art and you have this wonderful avant-garde extravaganza that is both hilarious and challenging.

CAPITOL STEPS: WHEN BUSH COMES TO SHOVE

✉ John Houseman Theatre, 450 West 42nd Street between 7th and 8th Avenues
☎ 212-674 4573
🕓 Tues to Fri 8pm, Sat 3pm and 7pm, Sun 3pm and 7.30pm

Capitol Steps are a highly acclaimed American comedy troupe and their targets are on the political front line. Obviously filled with American gags that'll go over the heads of most Brits, this is still worth a visit if only to see that not all Americans are gun-toting Republicans with little knowledge of any country beyond their borders.

I LOVE YOU, YOU'RE PERFECT, NOW CHANGE

✉ Westside Theatre, 407 West 43rd Street between 8th and 9th Avenues
☎ 212-391 2434
🕓 Tues to Sat 8pm, Sun 7pm, matinees Sat and Sun 2pm

For a thoroughly modern take on the whole notion of dating and romance, you can't go wrong with this comedy. It's a kind of *Seinfeld* set to music.

MAJOR MUSIC VENUES

APOLLO THEATER
Harlem

✉ 253 West 125th Street between Adam Clayton Powell Jnr and Frederick Douglas Boulevards
☎ 212-749 5838
🚗 Subway A, C, B, D, 2, 3 to 125th Street

This venue started life as a burlesque house for whites only when Harlem was actually a white neighbourhood, but it very quickly changed and became a theatre for blacks with live entertainment. The Amateur Night has been a launching pad for Stevie Wonder and James Brown. When Ella Fitzgerald came here she planned to dance, but at the last moment she decided to sing and, as the saying goes, a star was born. Wednesday's Amateur Night is still going strong and is shown on NBC at 1am on Saturday night/Sunday morning.

CARNEGIE HALL
Midtown West

✉ 154 West 57th Street at 7th Avenue
☎ 212-247 7800
🚗 Subway A, C, B, D, 1, 9 to 59th Street/Columbus Circle

Built in the Beaux Arts style under the patronage of Andrew Carnegie, this is perhaps one of the most famous classical concert venues in New York and a real landmark. Check the listings sections of newspapers or *Time Out* for details of visiting artists or take a guided tour by phoning the number above.

A great way to complete an evening at the Carnegie is to walk a few paces east to the Russian Tea Room where you can get a plate of smoked salmon and caviar for just $15. Sit at the bar to eat and round off your snack with a glass of champagne.

MADISON SQUARE GARDEN
34th Street

✉ 7th Avenue at 32nd Street
☎ 212-465 6741
🚗 Subway A, C, E, 1, 2, 3, 9 to 34th Street/Penn Street Station

New York's biggest and most famous rock venue, which doubles up as a sports stadium. Also the Theater at Madison Square Garden, which is underneath, plays host to big-name stars who want to share some intimacy with their audience.

RADIO CITY MUSIC HALL
Midtown

✉ 1260 6th Avenue at 50th Street
☎ 212-247 4777
🚗 Subway B, D, F, Q to 47th–50th Street/Rockefeller Center

Recently renovated, this home to the Rockettes in its art deco splendour also plays host to some big-name stars. See page 61 for details of the tours.

Pace yourself during the day so you've enough juice left to enjoy one of the many theatre productions.

LINCOLN CENTER
Upper West Side

✉ 65th Street at Columbus Avenue
☎ 212-875 5400
🚗 Subway 1, 9 to 66th Street/Lincoln Center

The major venue for classical music in New York, the Lincoln Center, a collection of buildings that includes the home of the Metropolitan Opera, was built on slums that were featured in the film *West Side Story*. There is the Alice Tully Hall (tel 212-875 5050), which houses the Chamber Music Society of Lincoln Center; the Avery Fisher Hall (tel 212-875 5030), home to the New York Philharmonic; the Metropolitan Opera House (tel 212-362 6000); the New York

CINEMAS

You don't just head to Times Square for theatrical shows, you can see some great blockbuster movies at any of the many sparkling new and renovated cinemas in the area. For complete listings of movies and cinemas near your hotel, check *Time Out*.

AMC Empire 25: 234 West 42nd Street between 7th and 8th Avenues. Tel 212-398 3939.
This boasts 25 screens on five levels and has devoted seven screens on the top floor, known as the Top of the Empire, to repertory classics and independent films. You can catch a pre-show snack in the 42nd Street Food Court, which has everything from pizzas to Chinese and barbecued spare ribs.

Loews 42nd Street E Walk: 243 West 42nd Street between 7th and 8th Avenues. Tel 212-840 7761.
The new Loews E Walk, with 13 screens and all-stadium seating, is billed as a modern-day movie palace. A storey high, hand-painted mural honours the local landmarks of Broadway and Times Square.

Loews Astor Plaza: 44th Street between Broadway and 8th Avenue. Tel 212-505 6395.
Another great Theater District venue for movies.

State Theater (tel 212-870 5570), home to New York City Opera; and the Walter Reade Theater (tel 212-875 5601), home to the Film Society of Lincoln Center.

You can take a behind-the-scenes tour of the Lincoln Center, which is really the only way to see beyond the ornate lobbies of the buildings, unless you're paying big bucks for a performance. The tours are fabulous and give a really good insight into the workings of the various venues. They start at 10.30am, 12.30pm, 2.30pm and 4.30pm each day from the ticket booth in the main part of the Center and cost $9.50. You can also go on a Backstage Tour of the Metropolitan on Monday, Tuesday, Thursday, Friday and Sunday at 3.45pm and 10am on Saturday. The tours are very popular so it's best to book in advance by phoning 212-875 5350.

Pick up a copy of the *Free Time* newspaper for information about free concerts, cinema showings and street fairs.

In addition to the tours, you can enjoy the Lincoln Center environment with a series of free jazz and folk bands that entertain the crowds for free each lunchtime during the summer. Also, there's the Autumn Crafts Fair, which is held in the first week of September.

BARS

Here's a selection of bars to drop into while you are out and about in the city, including some of the hotel bars that stand out from the crowd and lounges that stay open into the early hours.

LOWER EAST SIDE

Good World: 3 Orchard Street between Canal and Hester Streets. Tel 212-925 9975.
A mellow bar with a semi-regular DJ and an attractive young crowd. Stars seen here include Keanu Reeves, Bjork, Courtney Love and Matt Dillon. Best time to go is Sunday to Thursday and order the Scandinavian-style Good World, an elderberry-infused caipirinha.

Idlewild: 145 East Houston Street between Eldridge and Forsyth Streets. Tel 212-477 5005.
Designed to look like an aircraft, it is equipped with aeroplane toilets, reclining seats, bartenders in pilot uniforms and busboys posing as ground traffic controllers. Great fun.

Kush: 183 Orchard Street between Houston and Stanton Streets. Tel 212-677 7328.
Get a taste of paradise by sipping a few cocktails and nibbling on tasty bar snacks like mixed olives and salted almonds in this Moroccan oasis. The décor is fab with wonderful tiling and whitewashed walls lit by candles.

Many of the hip bars get packed out on Friday and Saturday nights with the people who live outside Manhattan. Best nights to go tend to be Sunday to Thursday.

Lansky Lounge: 104 Norfolk Street between Delancey and Rivington Streets. Tel 212-677 9489.
Once the former boardroom of infamous 1920s' gangster Meyer Lansky, the Jewish genius who masterminded many of Bugsy Siegal and Lucky Luciano's biggest moves, the Lansky Lounge has a real speakeasy vibe. Swing, Latin and lounge music nights draw good crowds, and don't forget to sample the superb flavoured martinis – the Diplomat is a favourite. The prices can be a bit steep, though, and in observance of the Jewish Sabbath it is closed on Friday.

Max Fish: 178 Ludlow Street between Houston and Stanton Streets. Tel 212-529 3959.
Part art gallery, part pick-up joint and part downtown party venue, this institution draws a hip but unpretentious crowd of artists, musicians and bohos. You'll get cheap drinks here, and it still has one of the best jukeboxes in town.

Mooza: 191 Orchard Street. Tel 212-982 4770.
Set a few steps down from the street, this bar and bistro has a rich interior of burgundy and gold patterned walls and leopard-print columns. However, it's the paved garden area at the rear that's the real lure. There's a stone fountain, hanging plants, globe lights and marble-covered tables. A popular spot for couples in love and lone writers and readers.

Orchard Bar: 200 Orchard Street between Houston and Stanton Streets. Tel 212-673 5350.
One of the best lounges on the Lower East Side, its décor is very different (think rocks for seats and bamboo shoots hanging from the walls). Cutting-edge DJs, cheapish drinks and a trendy crowd of artists and musicians mean it gets packed at the weekends.

Smithfield: 115 Essex Street between Rivington and Delancey Streets. Tel 212-475 9997.
The closest you'll get to a local in Manhattan. This glass-bricked bar offers everything from pints of Guinness to vodka shots, each served up with a great story by bartender and co-owner Stuart Delves.

SOHO and TRIBECA

Botanica: 47 East Houston Street between Mott and Mulberry Streets. Tel 212-343 7251.
One of the best spots for drinks at decent prices in *très* chic SoHo, this dark basement bar is a favoured watering hole of artists and locals.

Café Noir: 32 Grand Street at Thompson Street. Tel 212-431 7910.
Moroccan comfort food meets Spanish tapas in this little urban oasis. Think tagines, stews and pitchers of sangria. There's also an extensive wine list and occasional live jazz.

Circa Tabac: 32 Watts Street between Broadway and 6th Avenue. Tel 212-941 1781.
Nicotine-addicted New Yorkers rejoiced when Circa flung open its doors and invited them in to light up and enjoy. It has 150 brands of cigarettes on sale, from Silk Cuts to Indian Bidis. Even if you don't like to indulge, it's still worth a visit for the art deco interior alone. You'll feel like you've stepped on to the set of a black-and-white *film noir*.

Merc Bar: 151 Mercer Street between Prince and Houston Streets. Tel 212-966 2727.
A long-time fixture of the SoHo scene, this cool bar attracts an upstate, sophisticated crowd to its luxuriously deep sofas. It's at its best in summer when worn leather chairs get an airing on the sidewalk, which are a great place to sit and people watch. Be warned: the drinks are pricey at $10 plus.

Velvet Restaurant and Lounge: 223 Mulberry Street between Prince and Spring Streets. Tel 212-965 0439.
A truly discreet lounge bar that takes darkness to new depths. The giant sofas and adjoining parlour for chess and backgammon games add to the chilling-out factor.

Void: 16 Mercer Street at Canal Street. Tel 212-941 6492.
Once the preferred watering hole of cybergeeks and short-film-and-video nerds, Void has since matured into a mellow neighbourhood bar. A giant video screen fills one wall and there are film screenings on Wednesdays – think *Blade Runner*. Other nights there's either a DJ or a jazz band.

GREENWICH VILLAGE

Cafe Wha?: 115 MacDougal Street between West 3rd and Bleecker Streets. Tel 212-254 3706.
The city's best-kept secret. There is something fun and exciting on every night of the week here, including live Brazilian dance parties on Mondays, funk on Tuesdays and comedy nights on Saturdays. Best of all, the bill for drinks and snacks won't inhale the entire contents of your wallet. Get there before 10pm if you want to get a table.

Madame X: 94 West Houston Street between Thompson Street and La Guardia Place. Tel 212-539 0808.
There's a real London Soho den-of-iniquity feel to this joint, bathed as it is in red and lit by the glow of lanterns. Known for serving pretty potent cocktails and rare imported beers. In summer, head for the black door at the rear and you'll find the new outdoor alcove, where red lights above the benches bring the boudoir theme outside. Best of all, you'll probably be able to find a free corner.

WEST VILLAGE

Chumley's: 86 Bedford Street between Grove and Barrow Streets. Tel 212-675 4449.
A former literary speakeasy, it's still a great place to drink and have a spot of shepherd's pie while you look over the book jackets that line the wall. Yes, they were all donated by the authors who used to frequent the establishment, like Kerouac and Fitzgerald. You'll find their signatures imprinted in some of the older tables. There's even a roaring fireplace in the winter.

MEATPACKING DISTRICT

APT: 419 West 13th Street at 10th Avenue. Tel 212-414 4245. Subway A, C, E to 14th Street; L to 8th Avenue.
A real hit with trendy New Yorkers since the day it opened, this intimate bar/club makes you feel like you are somewhere extra special. The dark, candlelit first floor is furnished like an apartment, complete with bed, dining table and chairs and sofas, all of which make for comfortable lounging. Charming staff serve up tasty cocktails, like Moscow Mules and Appletinis, for around $10. The wood-walled room downstairs has a more modern vibe, and punters propping up the long bar often end up shaking their

stuff to the DJ's hip tunes. Tip: make reservations in advance for the weekend.

Hogs & Heifers: 859 Washington Street at West 13th Street. Tel 212-229 0930. The Hogs are the motorcyclists and the heifers are the dames, who are known for hanging their bras on the ceiling. There's no more bar dancing here, so there'll be no repeats of Drew Barrymore's performance.

Lotus: 409 West 12th Street between 9th and 10th Avenues. Tel 212-243 4420. Three storeys devoted to nightlife, including a bar, restaurant and club. Jennifer Lopez, Bruce Willis and Britney Spears have been seen here, but the celeb scene has cooled off since it first opened its doors in 2000. It still draws big crowds though, so it's best to go on week nights to avoid the weekend crush. Try the signature tartini – a cosmo with Chambord.

FLATIRON DISTRICT

Tiki Room: 4 West 22nd Street between 5th and 6th Avenues. Tel 646-230 1444. This brand new bar is a homage to Hawaii. There are tropical flowers, a giant rattan lamp shade, images of beaches on the flat screen TVs above the bar and lots of coconut and pineapple-laden fare. A Top 40 sound track provides the sounds.

EAST VILLAGE

Alphabet Lounge: 104 Avenue C at Lafayette Street. Tel 212-780 0202. This pastel-coloured lounge effortlessly attracts a lively crowd of locals, artists and partying members of the music industry to listen to a rotating roster of DJs and live bands.

Angel's Share: 8 Stuyvesant Street between 9th and 3rd Avenues. Tel 212-777 5415.
Dedicated to the art of mixology, this little gem of a bar will rustle up any cocktail you desire. Part of its charm is the fact that it's so hard to find, you'll feel like you've stumbled across a city secret. Take the stairs to the 2nd floor and veer left past the restaurant to the door at the rear. Inside you'll find a the dark, intimate bar where classy city dwellers take their first date.

Beauty Bar: 231 East 14th Street between 2nd and 3rd Avenues. Tel 212-539 1389.
Deb Parker's theme bar is equipped with 1960s-style hairdryers and chairs, great drinks and a heavy dose of the hip and beautiful.

Joe's Pub: 425 Lafayette Street between 4th Street and Astor Place. Tel 212-539 8770.
This promises to continue to be a real hot spot for some time to come. An extension of the Public Theatre, Joe's brings you live music, spoken-word performances and a crowd jam-packed with the trendiest types around. Stars spotted here include Ethan Hawke, Minnie Driver, Janeane Garofalo and Camryn Manheim. The drink to order is the Lady Macbeth – 115ml (4oz) of champagne and 115ml (4oz) of ruby port. Strong stuff!

KGB: 85 East 4th Street between 2nd and 3rd Avenues. Tel 212-505 3360.
As the name suggests, it is decorated with deep-red walls, portraits of Lenin and Brezhnev, propaganda posters and an oak bar preserved from the time when the place was a front for the Communist party. The crowd is a mix of actors, writers and drunks who love the private-parlour feel of the place. Up-and-coming writers and successful authors often do readings for free, so call in advance to see who's on.

Korova Milk Bar: 200 Avenue A between 12th and 13th Streets. Tel 212-254 8838.
The Milk Bar is decorated in a wacky retro-futuristic style that pays homage to Stanley Kubrick's *A Clockwork Orange*. It attracts a sci-fi crowd who love its surreal quality.

CHELSEA

Kanvas: 219 9th Avenue between 23rd and 24th Streets. Tel 212-727 2616.
The latest favourite Chelsea hang-out is owned by two firefighters, who have furnished a couple of giant loft rooms with comfy banquettes, subtle lighting and a chilled line in music. There's also gallery space on both floors so you can snap up some art while you're sipping your sour apple martini, the bar's speciality.

34TH STREET

Fun: 130 Madison Avenue at 34th Street. Tel 212-964 0303.
Halle Berry and Alicia Silverstone have been seen in this techno-futurist playground with avant-garde video installations and cool furnishings.

MIDTOWN

Beekman Bar and Books: 889 First Avenue at 50th Street. Tel 212-980 9314.
A book-lined den tucked away from the throng where you can relax, sip a martini and listen to the subtle music of a jazz trio. Its clubby feel is cosy rather than intimidating.

Russian Vodka Room: 265 West 52nd Street between Broadway and 8th Avenue. Tel 212-307 5835.
A brilliant vodka bar that doesn't require you to take out a second mortgage. There are cheap smoked fish platters, delicious cocktails and marvellous vodka infusions. It tends to attract the publishing crowd.

Russian Tea Room: 150 West 57th Street between 6th and 7th Avenues. Tel 212-974 2111.
A great late-night lounge in the beautiful environs of Warner LeRoy's over-the-top gilded décor, including a 6m- (20ft-) high Tiffany stained glass ceiling and Fabergé-style eggs hanging from trees.

UPPER EAST SIDE

Rooftop at the Met: 5th Avenue and 81st Street. Tel 212-535 7710.
It's a stunning view and you'll get to admire the exhibits at the Metropolitan Museum along the way. Known as a great singles pick-up joint, the best time to go is at sunset. The terrace is open during the summer months.

HOTEL BARS

Hotel bars are currently the hippest place to sip a cocktail in New York. Your only problem will be which one to choose.

FINANCIAL DISTRICT/ BATTERY PARK

Rise at the Ritz Carlton Hotel: 2 West Street between Battery Place and West End. Tel 212-344 0800. Subway 4, 5 to Bowling Green.
A big hit with both visitors and the Wall Street crowd is the 14th floor bar of the newly opened Ritz Carlton Hotel. They go for the comfy, plush chairs with fabulous views of the harbour, Statue of Liberty and amazing sunsets. The bar specialises in a series of colourful martinis served in gorgeous corkscrew-stemmed glassware and 710ml (25oz) margarita, sangria and mojitos, which are a perfect size for sharing. If you fancy a nibble, then either go for the dim sum or signature 'tiers' – platters of food for up to four people. They include the Pacific Union with sesame chicken, cured salmon and seared beef with dipping sauces and The New Yorker, which comes with mini burgers, pastrami sandwiches and shrimp cocktail with home-made potato chips. You can sit inside or outside and, best of all, the service is excellent.

SOHO

The Grand Bar and Salon at the SoHo Grand Hotel: 310 West Broadway between Grand and Canal Streets. Tel 212-965 3000. Subway C, E to Canal Street.
A chic gathering place that has attracted the rich and famous, such as Matt Damon and Venus Williams, since its opening a couple of years ago. It was at the forefront of the lounge-as-living-room trend and is filled with a mix of comfy, retro-chic furnishings that serve

as great perches for drinking and watching the multi-lingual crowd – mostly dressed in classic New York black. Sit back, nibble on the snacks and feel the energetic we're-at-the-centre-of-the-universe buzz.

Thom's Bar at the 60 Thompson Hotel: 60 Thompson Street between Broome and Spring Streets. Tel 212-219 2000. Subway C, E to Spring Street.
A sophisticated décor of dark wood, soft violet seats, brown leather club chairs and white Venetian plaster walls make for pleasant surroundings. The entertainment is provided by the chic crowd who know this latest boutique hotel is the only place to be seen mid-week. Drinks are surprisingly cheap, like flavoured vodka for $7.50.

GREENWICH VILLAGE

C3 Lounge at the Washington Square Hotel: 103 Waverly Place at MacDougal Street. Tel 212-254 1200. Subway A, B, C, D, E, F, Q to West 4th Street/Washington Square.
The small, cosy basement space's classic bar and luxurious, red leather chairs are a reminder of another era, while beautifully stencilled windows offer a glimpse of the current street scene. It attracts a large European crowd, who find it the perfect spot to pore over a map and a Martini, but locals – as well as occasional celebs – can also be found enjoying the laid-back atmosphere.

GRAMERCY PARK

Gramercy Park Hotel Bar: 2 Lexington Avenue, Gramercy Park at 21st Street. Tel 212-475 4320. Subway 6 to 23rd Street.
A home-from-home for media types from around the world. The bar is narrow and maybe a little dark, but friendly and unpretentious. Notable for reasonably priced drinks and the cheese snacks that are served with boundless generosity.

MIDTOWN

Asia de Cuba at the Morgans Hotel: 237 Madison Avenue between 37th and 38th Streets. Tel 212-726 7755. Subway 4, 5, 6, 7 to 42nd Street/Grand Central.
A crowded first floor bar that overlooks the super-trendy restaurant. Heaving with an attitude-heavy Upper East crowd, it's a sleeker, more sophisticated version of the bar that opened in London's St Martin's Lane Hotel. If you like your drinks deliciously expensive and served in punchbowl-size glasses, then you'll love it.

Bar 5757 at the Four Seasons Hotel: 57 East 57th Street between 5th and Park Avenues. Tel 212-758 5700. Subway N, R to 5th Avenue.
The Four Seasons is dynamic early evening when celebs rub shoulders with power-broking businessmen and hip hotel guests, while a pianist provides the background music. Be sure to sample some of the 15 types of martini on offer.

Cellar Bar at the Bryant Park Hotel: 40 West 40th Street between 5th and 6th Avenues. Tel 212-869 0100. Subway B, D, F, Q to 42nd Street/Bryant Park
A must-do for any fashionista, because this new boutique hotel on the block has been adopted by the fashion pack. Expect to see models, designers and magazine editors propping up the bar, but don't even think about dropping in during fashion week – you won't be able to move for the wafer-thin clientele.

Belmont at Central Park Inter-Continental Hotel: 112 Central Park South between 6th and 7th Avenues. Tel 212-757 1900. Subway N, R, B, Q to 57th Street.
Formerly known as The Bar at the Ritz, this is still an institution for wealthy world travellers, who come for the excellent martinis prepared by Norman, bartender extraordinaire.

The Grotto at the Michelangelo Hotel: 152 West 51st Street between 6th and 7th Avenues. Tel 212-765 1900. Subways S, R to 49th Street; B, D, F, Q to 47th–50th Street/Rockefeller Center.
A refined hideaway for sophisticated evenings out in one of the city's more inviting cigar bars. With its tan leather

couches, The Grotto has a more casual atmosphere than the upstairs Limoncello Restaurant but offers the same assortment of gourmet cuisine to those looking for a tasty snack or a full meal.

Skybar at the Best Western Manhattan: 17 West 32nd Street between Broadway and 5th Avenue. Tel 212-736 1600. Subway N, R to 28th Street.
A cross between a backyard deck and a funky beach bar, this partially enclosed rooftop watering hole is packed year-round with international visitors who appreciate the casual atmosphere and towering views of the Empire State Building.

MIDTOWN EAST

Bull & Bear at the Waldorf-Astoria: 301 Park Avenue between 49th and 50th Streets. Tel 212-872 4900. Subways 6 to 51st Street; E, F to Lexington/3rd Avenue.
Filled with bronze images of bulls and bears (funnily enough), this popular wood-panelled spot focuses on the rounded mahogany bar encircling a towering selection of wines and spirits. Specialities include great cigars and port.

Istana at the New York Palace Hotel: 455 Madison Avenue between 50th and 51st Streets. Tel 212-303 7788. Subway E, F to 5th Avenue.
A stylish refuge offering something unique in addition to its extensive wine and cocktail list - a 30-variety olive bar to accompany its huge selection of Spanish sweet and dry sherries. Enjoy!

Oasis at the West New York: 541 Lexington Avenue at 49th Street. Tel 212-755 1200. Subway 6 to 51st Street.
An oasis of tranquillity, things heat up when the fashion, art and music crowd descends for cocktails before dinner at the hotel's Heartbeat restaurant. The ambience is Californian and casual with clever touches that include a waterfall and backgammon tables disguised as tree stumps. Also at the hotel is the Whiskey Blue, overseen by Randy Gerber, otherwise known as Cindy Crawford's husband. The hip clientele enjoy cosy sofas that are great for people-watching and a top-notch sound system that plays until the wee small hours.

Wet Bar at the West Court Hotel: 130 East 39th Street between 5th and Madison Avenues. Tel 212-592 8844. Subway 7 to 5th Avenue.
George Clooney, Whoopi Goldberg and D'Angelo Marc Anthony have all been spotted in this sleek and uncluttered setting, which plays host to professionals and hotel guests. Try their apple martini.

MIDTOWN WEST

Halcyon Lounge at the RIGHA Royal Hotel: 151 West 54th Street between 6th and 7th Avenues. Tel 212-468 8888. Subway N, R to 57th Street.
An elegant setting for pre-theatre cocktails and nightly entertainment.

Hudson Bar at the Hudson Hotel: 356 West 58th Street between 8th and 9th Avenues. Tel 212-554 6000. Subway A, B, C, D, 1, 9 to 59th Street/ Columbus Circle.
This Ian Schrager and Philippe Starck Mecca for the in-crowd provides wonderful theatre. There's a glowing glass floor, flashy DJ and dark and enticing Games Room. In the summer, the after work crowd head to the Private Park - the hotel garden - and sip cocktails next to giant watering cans. Pure, surreal magic.

Jack's Bar at Le Parker Meridien: 118 West 57th Street between 6th and 7th Avenues. Tel 212-245 5000. Subway N, R to 57th Street; B, D, E to 7th Avenue.
With a wall full of black and white photos of famous Jacks, this bar sets a classic tone with martinis served in your own personal shaker. Jack's offers a cosy environment and a refined selection of beers, wines and spirits and the 710ml (25oz) Belgian Duvel beer, which comes capped with a champagne cork. Anyone named Jack (who can prove it) drinks for free 8–10pm.

The Oak Bar at the Plaza Hotel: 5th Avenue at Central Park South. Tel 212-546 5330. Subway N, R to 5th Avenue.
This bar is perhaps most famous for its wall murals by painter Everett Shinn – Cary Grant sat beneath one in a scene from Hitchcock's *North by Northwest.* Today, the bar attracts a mature, business-like crowd, although recent sightings of Kevin Costner and Al Pacino have been reported. Specialities are the views of Central Park, and the world's largest raisins for nibbling with drinks.

The Oak Room at the Algonquin: 59 West 44th Street between 5th and 6th Avenues. Tel 212-840 6800. Subway B, D, F, Q to 42nd Street; 7 to 5th Avenue.
Once world-famous as the New York literary set's salon of choice, this handsome room provides an intimate and civilised setting for some of the country's leading jazz and cabaret artists, who are usually booked for extended runs. The clientele is clubby and patrician, but anyone can buy dinner or drinks.

Hotel Bar at the Royalton: 44 West 44th Street between 5th and 6th Avenues. Tel 212-869 4400. Subway B, D, F, Q to 42nd Street; 7 to 5th Avenue.
The first of the Philippe Starck-designed hotels holds its own against all newcomers and its long, narrow bar is still a place to see and be seen. The loos are wonderful, too.

THEATER DISTRICT

The View at the Marriott Marquis Hotel: 1535 Broadway at Times Square. Tel 212-704 8900. Subway N, R, 1, 2, 3, 7, 9 to 42nd Street/Times Square.

It's incredibly easy to walk past the Royalton, or '44' as it's known – there is no sign outside, just large wooden doors.

As the title suggests, this bar has a magnificent view of the city as seen from Times Square. It is a huge space with ceiling-to-floor windows. The bar itself rotates very slowly to give a 360-degree panorama of the city.

UPPER EAST SIDE

Café Carlyle at the Carlyle Hotel: 35 East 76th Street at Madison and Park Avenues. Tel 212-744 1600. Subway 6 to 77th Street.
A highly glamorous bar and restaurant that specialises in cabaret, and we're not talking dodgy show tune crooners. Woody Allen occasionally drops by to play clarinet on a Monday night and Bobby Short and Eartha Kitt have also wowed the crowds.

Mark's Bar at the Mark Hotel: 25 East 77th Street at Madison Avenue. Tel 212-744 4300. Subway 6 to 77th Street.
This bar has been described as a cosy tea room that feels like a luxury train car. It never gets too noisy and patrons, who perch on forest-green sofas and floral slipper chairs, are treated like guests in an elegant private home. The bar attracts a youngish fashion set, but the crowd can be diverse depending on the evening.

NIGHTCLUBS

This category includes live music venues and late night lounges as well as mainly dance clubs. Hours vary with the event at most clubs, so check out the listings in the *Village Voice, Paper, New York Press* and *New Yorker.* There are also three useful websites to check out the parties at different venues on different nights: **www.papermag.com**, **www.clubnyc.com** and **www.newyork.citysearch.com**.

There are a few rules for making sure you get a good night's clubbing:

➡ On Friday and Saturday nights, clubs get packed with crowds from boroughs outside Manhattan. For a quieter night, try Thursday. Sunday is the big night for Manhattanites, so you'll get the real vibe then, though the joint may be packed!

Above left: Metropolitan Museum of Art

Above right: The Intrepid Sea, Air, Space Museum

Below right: The Frick Collection

Below left: Lower East Side Tenement Museum

Bottom: Brooklyn Museum of Art

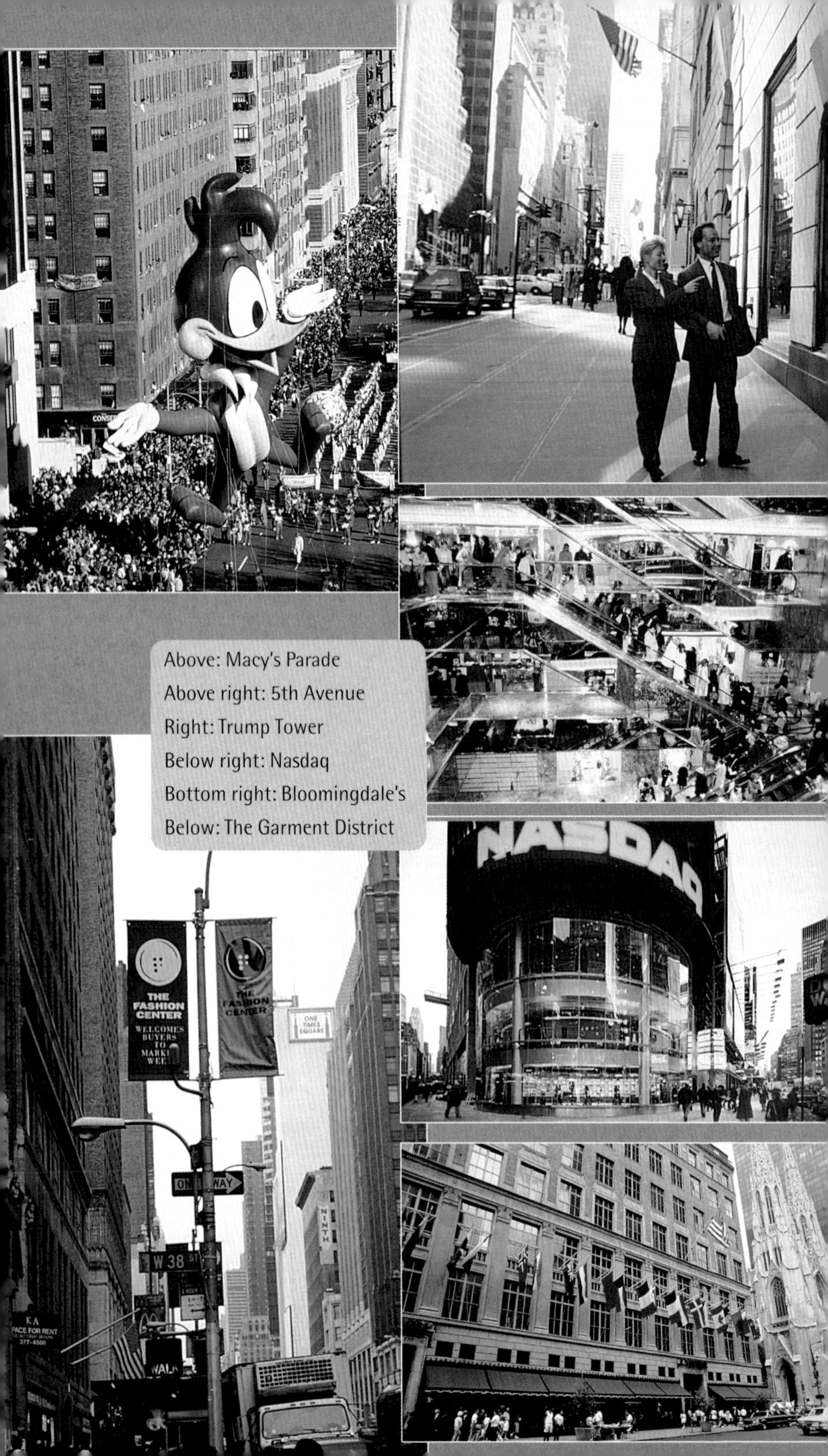

Above: Macy's Parade
Above right: 5th Avenue
Right: Trump Tower
Below right: Nasdaq
Bottom right: Bloomingdale's
Below: The Garment District

Left: The Rockettes

Above: The Lincoln Center

Below: *The Lion King*

Below left: *Rent 2000*

Bottom left: Metropolitan Opera at the Lincoln Center

Above: Russian Tea Room

Below: Europa Grill

Bottom left: Zoe

Left: 21 Club

➡ Call ahead early in the evening to find out if there's a cover charge, when to arrive and how to dress.
➡ The real nightlife doesn't get going until after midnight, so get some zeds in before you go out.
➡ Carry some ID with you just in case – it would be terrible if you couldn't get a drink and you're over 21.
➡ Big groups of men don't stand much chance of getting into straight clubs – you'll have more chance if you're with a woman.

LOWER EAST SIDE

Milk & Honey: 134 Eldridge Street. Tel 212-219 1775. Open selective nights until 4am.
The speakeasy is making a comeback, and this trendy little drinking den is the finest in the city. Hidden behind soundproof doors, its clientele can dance and sip their drinks through aluminium straws until 4am. It was set up last year for New Yorkers looking to escape clubs heavy with attitude and celebrity worshippers, but it's becoming such a hot place to hang out it's starting to attract the crowd it wanted to avoid.

Phone Milk & Honey in advance and leave your name at the door to stand any chance of getting in.

Sapphire Lounge: 249 Eldridge Street between Houston and Stanton Streets. Tel 212-777 5153. Subway F to 2nd Avenue.
Pretension and attitude are left at the door in this tiny dance club that plays a great mix of hip-hop, reggae, acid jazz, R&B and disco classics.

SOHO

Don Hill's: 511 Greenwich Street at Spring Street. Tel 212-219 2850. Open seven days 9pm–4am.
A Mecca for fashion and music celebs, this is a great place to find dance and live music nights. Even the mixed nights have a big gay crowd. The big night is Brit-Pop Tiswas on Saturdays.

Jet Lounge: 286 Spring Street between Varick and Hudson Streets. Tel 212-929 4780. Open Wed to Sat 9.30pm–4am.
The zebra-striped bar is now a legal dancing den thanks to a recently acquired cabaret licence. It's a great space and there is a dance floor, but drinks tend to be pricey.

WEST SOHO

There's a new term for the area that is west of SoHo, north of TriBeCa and south of Greenwich Village – and it's WeVar, which means west of Varick. Whether it will catch on is another matter, but there is a huge congregation of clubs in this area. To get there, take subway 1, 9 to Houston Street.

NV: 289 Spring Street at Hudson Street. Tel 212-929 NVNV. Open Wed to Sun 10pm–4am.
The crowd is trendy and friendly, while the music is a great mix of everything from house to disco to hits from the 1980s. The upstairs has dance-floor energy while the much larger downstairs keeps a mellow lounge atmosphere.

Sway: 305 Spring Street between Hudson and Greenwich Streets. Tel 212-620 5220. Open daily 10pm–4am.
Morocco and martini are the 'two Ms' at the height of fashion in New York, and Sway has both. Its Moroccan-themed interiors are the haunt of models like Kate Moss, who sip cocktails through to the early hours. Sway has a DJ every night and for the most part the music reflects the mood of the crowd, but it can be hard to get into at weekends.

Veruka: 525 Broome Street between Thompson and 6th Avenue. Tel 212-625 1717. Open daily 8pm–4am. Dinner Wed to Sat until 2am.
West SoHo's most elite night spot has been given a facelift since its mid-1990s' heyday when the likes of Mark Wahlberg,

Robert de Niro, Sean Penn, Mariah Carey and Naomi Campbell hung out here. All done out and reopened, MTV celebrated its relaunch with a private party and musos like Nelly Furtado have been spotted there. It's hot again.

TRIBECA

Vinyl: 6 Hubert Street between Greenwich and Hudson Streets. Tel 212-343 1379. Subway A, C, E to Canal Street; 1, 9 to Franklin Street.
A good, mixed crowd and a good mix of music, but not a huge space – and there's no alcohol, either.

GREENWICH VILLAGE

The Wreck Room: 116 MacDougal Street between 3rd and 4th Streets. Tel 212-253 1843. Subway A, C, E, B, D, F, Q to West 4th Street/Washington Square. Open Monday to Sunday 8pm–4am.
Formerly on the site of The Scrap Bar where heavy metal bands played, it's now a cool little club with nightly DJs playing groove, R&B and hip-hop. The welded scrap metal facade has been kept, and inside it's dungeon-like with low ceilings, bare stone walls and candlelight. Thursday is smooth grooves, Friday and Saturday hip-hop, soul and classic and Sunday is new-wave goth.

Do make an effort to get dressed up if you are going clubbing. Don't wear trainers or jeans – you won't get in.

Nell's: 246 West 14th Street between 7th and 8th Avenues. Tel 212-675 1567. Subway A, C, E to 14th Street; L to 8th Avenue.
Attracts a straight crowd who go for the jazz and funky soul upstairs and the reggae and R&B downstairs. Sometimes there are live acts, so call in advance to see who's on.

Roxy: 515 West 18th Street between 10th and 11th Avenues. Tel 212-645 5156. Subway A, C, E to 14th Street; L to 8th Avenue.
A huge venue with plenty of different themes on different nights. Single men beware, though, it's very hard to get in without a female partner!

SOBs: 204 Varick Street at Houston Street. Tel 212-243 4940. Subway 1, 9 to Houston Street.
The name stands for Sounds Of Brazil, which says it all. It's the place to come for the last word in all Latin music from salsa to samba and even reggae.

EAST VILLAGE

Spa: 76 East 13th Street between 4th and Broadway. Tel 212-388 1060. Open Tuesday to Saturday, entrance $20–25.
A plush hip-hop and house venue that opened two years ago and is still top of the clubbing tree. Rap superstar Busta Rhymes loves it, and it's universally recognised as a world-class party venue.

Webster Hall: 125 East 11th Street between 3rd and 4th Avenues. Tel 212-353 1600. Subway L, N, R, 4, 5, 6 to 14th Street/Union Square.
There are lots of different rooms with different sounds, so you're bound to find something you enjoy. The best area is the huge, ornate ballroom, which is the main dance floor. It attracts a fairly straight crowd from the suburbs, but is a fun night out.

CHELSEA

Twirl: 208 West 23rd Street between 7th and 8th Avenues. Tel 212-691 7685. Subway C, E to 23rd Street. Open 10pm–4am.
A very sleek, cavernous space with video screen projections which give it a suitably modern club vibe. The music veers between house, groove and garage, but it is the interior that is the real knock-out. High ceilings, futuristic white decor and curtained alcoves with bed-like seats running along the walls. It attracts a mixed, friendly crowd.

ALL THAT JAZZ

A visit to New York City wouldn't be complete without a visit to one of the various jazz venues, but it can get very expensive, so it's good to know your way around. At all the main venues it'll cost you around $25 to hear one set which only lasts 1–1½ hours. It's worth it if you're happy with the music, but the idea of having to move on after only one set is a bit strange to us Brits, so it's good to be warned!

THE MAIN CLUBS

One of the best jazz clubs is the **Iridium**, under the Empire Hotel opposite the Lincoln Center (44 West 63rd Street at Columbus Avenue, tel 212- 582 2121). It's not too touristy, is smaller than many clubs and has a nice intimate feel. It's pricey, but the $25 entrance fee does include a drink. Then there's the **Village Vanguard** (178 7th Avenue South at Perry Street, tel 212-255 4037), probably the most famous club of all, which always hosts great talent and sets last the full 1½ hours. Another famous Greenwich Village venue is the **Blue Note** (131 West 3rd Street between MacDougal and 6th Avenue, tel 212-475 8592), but this is a lot more touristy, very expensive and has a Las Vegas-style interior. **Swing 46 Jazz and Supper Club** (349 West 46th Street between 8th and 9th Avenues, tel 212-262 9554) offers big bands and small combos to suit hip downtown loungers and traditional uptown swingers – it's rapidly becoming an institution.

Other good venues include **Birdland** (315 West 44th Street between 8th and 9th Avenues, tel 212-581 3080) in Midtown West; the **Jazz Standard** (116 East 27th Street between Park and Lexington Avenues, tel 212-576 2232) near Madison Square; **Sweet Basil** (88 7th Avenue South between Bleecker and Grove Streets, tel 212-242 1785) in the Village; and **Roulette** (228 West Broadway at White Street, tel 212-219 8242) in TriBeCa, which has concerts from March to May and October to December.

CHEAP AND CHEERFUL

One of the best off-the-beaten-track jazz venues is in the heart of Greenwich Village at the **Cornelia Street Café** (29 Cornelia Street, tel 212-989 9319), a haunt of the locals. Prix fixe dinner is $18.50, with reservations at 7pm. The jazz starts at 9pm and costs a mere $5. They don't have big names, but they do have a lot of New York talent. Another good one in the Village is **Smalls** (183 West 10th Street at 7th Avenue, tel 212-929 7565). You bring your own drinks and pay $10 to stay the entire evening, but it does get packed. **Zinc Bar** (90 West Houston Street between Thompson Street and La Guardia Place, tel 212-477 8337), is one of the most intimate places in town to enjoy live jazz, and it's only $5 to get in.

The cheapest jazz clubs to go to tend to be in Harlem, Queens and Brooklyn, but because they can't afford to advertise you really don't hear about them. Furthermore, most don't even have names on the door. Good places to look for venues are the *New York Times* weekend edition and the *Village Voice*. The latter is a lot better and it's free. You can check out their website at **www.villagevoice.com**.

If you're really serious about your jazz and want some more advice try the Ed Lockjaw jazz experience as sold by iMar. He'll explain who's who on the scene and track down a good gig for you (see page 73).

Twilo: 530 West 27th Street between 10th and 11th Avenues. Tel 212-268 1600. Subway C, E to 23rd Street.
It has a huge dance floor, seating around the floor and nice lounges. DJs Sasha and Digweed, who play techno/rave and trance, often drop by to play a set.

MADISON SQUARE

Cheetah: 12 West 21st Street between 5th and 6th Avenues. Tel 212-206 7770. Subway F, N, R to 23rd Street.
An intimate venue with attractive animal-print décor and snuggly booths. Not usually a place for wannabees, just for people chilling with their friends – though stars do sometimes put in an appearance.

MIDTOWN WEST

Copacabana: 617 West 57th Street between 11th and 12th Avenues. Tel 212-582 2672. Subway A, C, B, D, 1, 9 to Columbus Circle/59th Street.
A mostly Latin clientele who go for the live bands playing salsa and merengue. Everyone is fairly well dressed, not casual but not overdone. It's great but it does get packed.

Exit: 610 West 55th Street at 11th Avenue. Tel 212-582 8282. Subway A, B, C, D, 1, 9 to Columbus Circle/59th Street; C, E to 50th Street.
Formerly the Mirage, then Carbon, it has three levels including a massive main dance floor, five lounges and a large roof deck. It has gay, straight and mixed nights.

Float: 240 West 52nd Street between 8th Avenue and Broadway. Tel 212-581 0055. Subway 1, 9 to 50th Street; C, E to 50th Street; B, D, E to 7th Avenue.
Be warned, if you choose this paradise of stockbrokers and models, you will part with wads of cash for a good night out, but the environment is beautiful. There is a main dance floor plus loads of VIP areas for those who think they're important, and plenty of siderooms, small lounges and little cubbyholes to make everyone else feel at home. A night spot for the beautiful people.

Avoid the crowds at Manhattan jazz clubs by going for the late set and avoiding weekends. Also remember that stormy weather puts off New Yorkers from going out, so you could get a great seat if it's raining heavily.

Sound Factory: 618 West 46th Street between 11th and 12th Avenues. Tel 212-643 0728. Subway A, C, E to 50th Street.
One of the better-known venues, it has a reasonable-sized dance floor that can get pretty packed on big party nights. Good for a visit, though, and the crowd is very well mixed. Call 212-489 0001 to get yourself on the guest list and save $5. Leave your name, the number of people in your group and which day's list you want to be put on.

UPPER WEST SIDE

Venue: 505 Columbus Avenue between 84th and 85th Streets. Tel 212-579 9463. Subway 1, 9 to 86th Street. Daily from 7pm–4am.
A good alternative to the large, uptown dance floors, this cute little club has a downstairs lounge covered in fake fur and lit by lava lamps, and an upstairs area where you can really work up a sweat grooving to house and R&B. The toilet attendants even sell cigarettes if you happen to run out!

CHAPTER 9

Gay New York

The West Village was the original home of gays and lesbians in New York, but now that the city is so cosmopolitan and accepting, gay bars, clubs and restaurants have sprung up all over Manhattan. Chelsea, however, has become the new, popular locale for gays.

If you'd like to get to know more about the gay and lesbian culture in New York, Big Onion's tour Before Stonewall – A Gay and Lesbian History Tour – gives a really good insight into the historical side, tracing the development of Greenwich Village as a community Mecca (see Big Onion Walking Tours, page 76). For a tour of the modern-day Gay New York, try iMar's Gay New York insider tour with Patrick, which covers Chelsea, its bars, nightclubs and restaurants (see Insider Tours, page 73).

This chapter is dedicated to those who really do want to get to know the gay scene and has information on everything from accommodation to community centres, restaurants, bars and clubs. It should also be noted that many of the restaurants and bars are open to everyone, whatever their persuasion.

INFORMATION

LESBIAN AND GAY COMMUNITY SERVICES CENTER

✉ 208 West 13th Street between 7th and 8th Avenues

☎ 212-620 7310

www.gaycenter.org

By far the best organisation in New York for getting information, you'll find millions of leaflets and notices about gay life in the city. There are now around 400 groups that meet here and it also houses the National Museum and Archive of Lesbian and Gay History.

PUBLICATIONS

The main gay weeklies are *HX (Homo Xtra)* and *HX for Her*, which tend to be available in gay bars, clubs, hotels and cafés. They include listings of bars, dance clubs, sex clubs, restaurants and cultural events. Check out their website at **www.hx.com** before you go. Good newspapers are the *LGNY* (Lesbian and Gay New York), though it's a lot more serious and covers political issues, and *The Blade*.

ACCOMMODATION

Turn to page 157 for some Hotel Tips and booking info. Prices are per room.

CHELSEA PINES INN

Chelsea

✉ 317 West 14th Street between 8th and 9th Avenues

☎ 212-929 1023

E-mail **cpiny@aol.com**

🚗 Subway A, C, East to 14th Street; L to 8th Avenue

$ Doubles and triples $89–159 including breakfast

In an excellent location in Chelsea on the border with the Village, this is just about the cheapest accommodation you could hope to get in New York, but you need to book at least six to eight weeks in advance. The hotel has recently been given a facelift, and now each room is named after a film star. Yes, there is a Judy Garland. In the morning, guests wake to the aroma of home-made bread and doughnuts. Open to men and women.

COLONIAL HOUSE INN

Chelsea

✉ 318 West 22nd Street between 8th and 9th Avenues

☎ 212-243 9669

www.colonialhouseinn.com

🚗 Subway C, East to 23rd Street

$ Singles $80–140

A beautiful place to stay and also spotlessly clean. The economy rooms are tiny, but all have cable TV, air-con, phone and daily maid service, and smoking is allowed in rooms. The price includes breakfast, which is eaten in the Life Gallery, with works by gay and lesbian artists. Book as early as you can because this place gets packed with groups coming into town for drag conventions and so on. It's especially popular in the summer months because of its roof deck with clothing optional area. Has a 24-hour doorman. Mostly for gay men.

THE EDISON HOTEL

Theater District

✉ 228 West 47th Street between Broadway and 8th Avenue

☎ 212-840 5000

🚗 Subway N, R to 49th Street

$ Doubles $160, suites from $200

One of New York's great hotel bargains. The Edison's 700 rooms have been totally refurbished, and it has a new coffee shop, the Café Edison, considered to be the best place to spot lunching theatre luminaries.

THE HOTEL WALCOTT

Midtown

✉ 4 West 31st Street between 5th Avenue and Broadway

☎ 212-268 2900

www.sales@wolcott.com

🚗 Subway N, R to 28th Street

$ Doubles $120–180

Well, darling, it's location, location, location, for this 300-room hotel. Just three blocks down from 5th Avenue and the Empire State Building, this is a favourite with the serious tourist and budget-minded business traveller. Call in advance to find out the bargain seasonal, weekend and holiday rates.

INCENTRA VILLAGE HOUSE

West Village

✉ 32 8th Avenue between West 12th and Jane Streets

☎ 212-206 0007

🚗 Subway A, C, East to 14th Street; L to 8th Avenue

$ Doubles $99–179

A moderately priced guest house in two red-brick townhouses from the 1840s (old by American standards!). The 12 suites all have kitchens, phones and private bathrooms and some can even accommodate groups of four or five. All the rooms are well decorated with different themes. The Bishop Room is a lovely split-level suite, the Garden Room has a private garden filled with flowers and the Maine Room has a four-poster bed. All rooms are smoker-friendly. There is a 1939 Steinway piano in the parlour and anyone who can is allowed to play.

THE INN AT IRVING PLACE

Gramercy Park

✉ 56 Irving Place between 17th and 18th Streets

☎ 212-533 4600

www.innatirving.com

🚗 Subway L, N, R, 4, 5, 6 to 14th Street/Union Square

$ Rooms $300–480

The building is filled with exquisite antique furniture and elegant décor. All 12 rooms come with private facilities, some even have study areas. There is a 24-hour concierge, plus laptops and fax on request, laundry and dry-cleaning, video rentals, gym within walking distance and 24-hour massage.

THE ROYALTON

Theater District

✉ 44 West 44th Street between 5th and 6th Avenues

☎ 212-869 4400

🚗 Subway 4, 5, 6 to 42nd Street; 7 to 5th Avenue

$ Rooms $235–475

Ian Schrager's beautiful hotel, designed by Philippe Starck, is now considered to be **the** address for gays and lesbians into the power thing. A chic tone is set by the lively fashion and publishing crowd who love the lobby bar and restaurant. The modern rooms all have CD players, VCR, mini bar and two phone lines.

CLUBS AND LOUNGES FOR HIM

CHELSEA

Barracuda: 275 West 22nd Street between 7th and 8th Avenues. Tel 212-645 8613. Subway C, E, 1, 9 to 23rd Street.
Head to the rear lounge which has a better atmosphere than the dingy front bar and a decent pool table. Monday night is the hilarious Star Search, where drag queens battle it out to reign supreme. Open till 4am.

Blu: 161 West 23rd Street at 7th Avenue. Tel 212-633 6113. Subway 1, 9 to 23rd Street.
Faggot Feud hosted by Mona Foot on Wednesdays, is free including a gay game show at 11pm. Gong Show, 12pm on Thursdays, is also free. Hedda Lettuce presides over the cruel but funny 1970s' game show.

Centro-Fly: 45 West 21st Street between 5th and 6th Avenues. Tel 212-627 7770. Subway N, R, F to 23rd Street.
It costs $20–30 just to get in, but boy is it worth it. It's one of the best clubs in the city in terms of music, atmosphere and delicious clientele. GBH on Friday nights is the big one, which has won numerous awards and has been running for three years. Guest DJs have included all the greats including LTJ Bukem and Armand Van Helden.

El Flamingo: 547 West 21st Street between 10th and 11th Avenues. Tel 212-243 2121. Subway C, East to 23rd Street.
If your thang is cross-dressing performers lip-synching along to disco numbers, then The Donkey Show: A Midsummer Night's Disco is for you. It runs from Wednesday to Saturday and costs around $25–30 to get in, but you can also dance your ass off until the wee small hours after the show.

g: 225 West 19th Street between 7th and 8th Avenues. Tel 212-929 1085. Subway 1, 9 to 18th Street.
A super-popular nightly spot for hunks, open 4pm–4am. Its centrepiece is its oval bar, which the sexy clientele prop up when they're not shimmying to house music. It gets packed later on when the queues build up outside. Saturday nights are free.

Heaven: 579 6th Avenue between 16th and 17th Streets. Tel 212-539 3982. Subway F, V to 14th Street.
Decorated with wall-to-wall white paint and mirrors, this three-storey club is a sparkling spectacle that simply must be seen and enjoyed during a trip to NY. Casa Latino on Thursdays has Latin beats pumped out by DJ Super Dave while g-string clad boys strut their stuff. Saturdays at Heaven are pure retro 1980s. Free four nights a week and $5–10 at weekends.

Roxy: 515 West 18th Street between 10th and 11th Avenues. Tel 212-645 5156. Subway A, C, East to 14th Street; L to 8th Avenue.
Saturdays, $20, from 11pm for an evening of gorgeous guys, sexy drag queens and brilliant sounds. This is the award-winning big night out for gay New Yorkers. On Wednesdays, put on your blades and have a blast at the roller disco.

SBNY: 50 West 17th Street between 5th and 6th Avenues. Tel 212-691 0073. Subway L, N, R, 4, 5, 6 to 14th Street/ Union Square.
Formerly known as Splash, this a popular place to hang out any night of the week, and not just because the handsome bartenders are shirtless. Musical Mondays are free. Doors open 5pm for

Happy Hour until 9pm. Dancing after 11pm with DJ Tony L. Tuesdays see a rotating rosta of hot names on the DJ circuit. Wednesday is Hardbar with DJ T-Pro, $5. Virtual Thursdays, free. Dancing after 10pm with DJ Billy Carroll spinning smooth sounds. Full Frontal Fridays, free before 10pm, $7 after, a chance to listen and dance to new DJs on the turntables. Stud Search on Saturdays, 8pm, hosted by drag queen Kenny Dash who runs a contest for hunky punters to win $200. Dancing after 10pm with DJ Max Rodriguez. Extreme Tea on Sundays, free from 9pm till 4am. SBNY also has a happy hour on weekdays from 4–9pm and weekends from 4–8pm.

Tunnel: 220 12th Avenue at 27th Street. Tel 212-695 4682. Subway C, E to 23rd Street.
Kurfew on Fridays, $20, from 11pm when DJs spin the grooves for the college kids.

TRIBECA

Vinyl: 6 Hubert Street between Greenwich and Hudson Streets. Tel 212-343 1379. Subway A, C, East to Canal Street; 1, 9 to Franklin Street.
Be Yourself on Fridays, $20, from 11pm with DJ/producer Danny Tenaglia playing the music. Club Shelter, Saturdays from 11pm, $11, with DJ Timmy Regisford's spirit of the Paradise Garage. An alcohol-free night. Body and Soul, Sundays, $14, from 4pm. DJs Francois K, Danny Krivit and Joe Claussell spin the house classics for a mixed crowd.

WEST VILLAGE

Hell: 59 Gansevoort Street at Washington Street. Tel 212-727 1666. Subway A, C, East to 14th Street.
A cute club that draws an attractive crowd to the Meatpacking District. Hell Tuesday, free, with DJ Dominick spinning loungy house, is a great night.

Lips: 2 Bank Street at Greenwich Avenue. Tel 212-675 7710. Subway 1, 2, 3, 9 to 14th Street.
This buzzy place is the Hard Rock Café of drag, with supper and shows from 5.30–midnight weekdays and until 2am on Friday and Saturday. The Bitchy Bingo Show on Wednesdays, free, open from 8pm, sees Sherry Vine and Yvon Lame preside over the bitchiest bingo game in the world. Tuesdays you can enjoy a spot of drag karaoke.

GREENWICH VILLAGE

The Monster: 80 Grove Street at Sheridan Square. Tel 212-924 3558. Subway 1, 2, 3, 9 Christopher Street/Sheridan Square.
Sabor Latino on Mondays, free. Opens at 4pm, party starts at 10pm with DJ Aurelio Martin and an amateur strip contest. Flashback Tuesdays, free. Opens at 4pm, dancing after 10pm to disco classics. Wednesday is Jesse Volt's Follies, a fabulous drag queen and dazzling go-go boys. Monster Tea on Sundays, free before 8pm, $3 after. DJ Aurelio Martin spins Latin hits until 4am.

EAST VILLAGE

B Bar & Grill: 40 East 4th Street between Lafayette Street and the Bowery. Tel 212-475 2220. Subway B, D, F, Q to Broadway/Lafayette Street; 6 to Bleecker Street.
Beige on Tuesdays, free, from 9pm. This is a super-trendy lounge filled with models and gorgeous people. Madonna has been known to drop in.

The Cock: 188 Avenue A at East 12th Street. Tel 212-777 6254. Subway F to 2nd Avenue, 6 to Bleecker Street.
Cock-A-Two on Wednesdays, free, from 10.30pm with drag divas at midnight. No Wave on Thursdays, $5, from 11pm, with either Scott or Jo Jo on the turntables. Foxy on Saturdays when the audience competes for the title of 'foxiest', $5, opens 10.30pm. Sunday is boys-only night Sperm with DJ Man Parrish.

Lucky Cheng's: 24 1st Avenue between 1st and 2nd Streets. Tel 212-473 0516. Subway F to 2nd Avenue; 6 to Bleecker Street.
The drag lounge and bar beneath the restaurant is past its heyday, but the late-night karaoke is still fun.

Pyramid Club: 101 Avenue A between 6th and 7th Streets. Tel 212-462 9077. Subway F to 2nd Avenue.
One of New York's most famous gay nights is 1984 on Fridays. It's only $5 to get in and you can get all nostalgic to 1980s' dance music until 4am. Locura Saturdays are hip-hop, Latin and house with DJ Cuffy, DJ Houdini and DJ Pipo. There's also open microphone on Sundays and Remission on Thursdays for a goth vibe.

The Hole: 29 2nd Avenue between 1st and 2nd Streets. Tel 212-946 1871. Subway F, V to 2nd Street.
A wild night spot which has gained a cult status largely due to its amusing club night names. Friday is Hole-a-Day Inn, $5, with Larry Tee presenting freak performances and DJ Spencer Product playing electroclash and ghetto tech. Saturday is Body and Hole, $10, with Girlina as DJ and entertainment provided by the Filthy Viagra Go-Go Squad. Sunday is 1979, with DJs Will, Gant Johnson and Lady Bunny playing disco classics.

Wonder Bar: 505 East 6th Street between Avenues A and B. Tel 212-777 9105. Subway F to 2nd Avenue.
A nightly lounge with a packed, mixed crowd enjoying the soul and classic hits. Drinks are very reasonable, around $3.50 for a beer.

FLATIRON DISTRICT

Limelight: 660 6th Avenue at 20th Street. Tel 212-807 7780. Subway F to 23rd Street.
Gay nights on Fridays and Sundays.

MIDTOWN EAST

Red: 305 East 53rd Street between 1st and 2nd Avenues. Tel 212-585 3446. Subway E, V to Lexington Avenue/53rd Street.
The best time to get dolled up and hit this NY hot spot is Thursday night, which is an anything-goes party that has the added bonus of being free. Inside, you'll be exposed to strippers, rub shoulders with porn stars and be dazzled by lap-dancing go-go boys. Great fun.

MIDTOWN WEST

La Nueva Escuelita: 301 West 39th Street at 8th Avenue. Tel 212-631 0588. Subway A, C, East to 42nd Street.
House of Pleasure on Thursdays, $5, $10 after 10pm. DJ Steve 'Chip Chop' Gonzalez plays salsa, merengue and house. Spicy Fridays, $10, from 10pm. Dancing and Latin-style drag show, starring Angel Sheridan and the divas of Escuelita. Azucar Saturdays, $15, from 10pm with house and Latin music. Sunbeam Sundays, $3. Harmonica Sunbeam hosts the tea dance from 5pm.

Xth Avenue Lounge: 642 10th Avenue at 45th Street. Tel 212-245 9088. Subway A, C, East to 42nd Street.
Open daily with a Happy Hour 4–8pm. There is a light menu in the back room. Not exclusively for gays.

UPPER EAST SIDE

Pegasus Bar: 119 East 60th Street between Park and Lexington Avenues. Tel 212-888 4702. Subway 4, 5, 6 to 59th Street; N, R to Lexington Avenue.
Gentlemen's piano bar featuring karaoke and cabaret shows on various rotating nights of the week. Friday and Saturday focus on entertainment for Asian gays. It's also the time of the week when the groovy back room opens up to reveal plastic-wrapped, leopard-print benches and intimate lighting. There are business cards at the bar with space for your name, number and e-mail, in case you get lucky.

HARLEM

Club Chaz: 454 West 128th Street, between Amsterdam Avenue and Convent Avenue. Tel 212-749 8055. Subway 1, 9 at 125th Street.
If you love Latin music then pop in here on a Friday night to have yourself a sizzling time. If you're more of a hip-hop and house guy, drop by Industry on a Tuesday. It's $3 before 12pm and $10 after. Open until 5am.

CLUBS AND LOUNGES FOR HER

FLATIRON

True: 28 East 23rd Street between Madison and Park Avenues. Tel 212-631 1000. Subway 6 to 23rd Street.
A highly charged atmosphere is created by a wild, mixed crowd at this cool club. Check out LoverGirl on a Saturday night. It's a lesbian dance party with DJs May Mac and Chip Chop Gonzalez providing the sounds and sexy go-go girls providing the visuals. $8 to get in before midnight, $10 after 12pm. Wednesday night is Gommorah, a fetish play party. Door charge $5–20, depending on how fabulous your outfit is.

WEST VILLAGE

Crazy Nanny's: 21 7th Avenue South at Leroy Street. Tel 212-366 6312. Subway 1, 9 to Christopher Street/Sheridan Square.
This two-storey bar is popular with locals and out-of-towners. A mix of pool, drag shows, trivia nights and karaoke. Friday and Saturday are DJ nights, $8 cover charge. The bar is open until 4am daily with a Happy Hour 4–7pm.

Flamingo: 219 2nd Avenue between 13th and 14th Streets. Tel 212-533 2860.
An off-beat, trendy club for women. Previously the venue of the **Clit Club**, a famous party night now on the move and looking for a permanent home. It is temporarily being held in B Bar on Friday nights (tel 212-475 2220). Flamingo is best in the summer months when they open up the balcony that overlooks 2nd Avenue.

Henrietta Hudson's: 438 Hudson Street at Morton Street. Tel 212-924 3347. Subway 1, 9 to Christopher Street/Sheridan Square.
A girl bar with great jukebox music. On Tuesdays the party is Out Loud (from 10pm free), then Decadence on Wednesdays, 9pm, free. DJ Merritt mixes up a storm at Bliss on Fridays and DJ Lisa G spins old-skool funk and disco on Saturdays. The bar is open Monday to Friday, 4pm–4am, weekends 1pm–4am, with a Happy Hour weekdays 5–7pm.

EAST VILLAGE

Starlight: 167 Avenue A and 11th Street. Tel 212-475 2172. Subway L to 1st Avenue.
A fabulous bar and lounge that is open Wednesday to Sunday until 3am. Friday is DJ Dave Trumbus, while Sundays are Starlette Night with DJ Jolene playing lush house.

Wonder Bar: 505 East 6th Avenue between Avenues A and B. Tel 212-777 9105. Subway F to 2nd Avenue.
This is a stylish hangout for both men and women, which tends to be fairly mellow during the week, but gets packed out at weekends. Open every day 6pm–4am, the daily happy hour is 6–8pm.

LOWER EAST SIDE

Meow Mix: 269 Houston Street at Suffolk Avenue. Tel 212-254 0688. Subway B, D, F, Q to Broadway/Lafayette Street; 6 to Bleecker Street.
A hip neighbourhood bar that welcomes both women and their men friends. Xena fans unite on the second Tuesday of every month for a full three episodes of the sword-wielding heroine ($3). Other Tuesday nights are We Rise, a chance for artists, singers and performers to take to the stage. Thursdays DJ Nina Skittles plays 1980s' 10–11pm, followed by DJ BK Brewster and then late night, DJ Snatch Nasty takes to the turntables. Frisky Friday is a great dance party with a two-for-one happy hour and a $4–6 cover charge. Gloss takes place on Saturdays ($5). Regulars include Ben Doren and MJ Cole. It's open 5pm–4am. Happy Hour lasts from 5–8pm from Tuesday to Friday and 3–8pm at the weekends.

MIDTOWN EAST

Julie's: 204 East 53rd Street between 2nd and 3rd Avenues. Tel 212-688 1294. Subway E, F to Lexington Avenue; 6 to 51st Street.

A cosy bar for stylish and often professional women, it's packed at the weekends. Monday is R&B night, Tuesday karaoke, Wednesday is salsa and merengue, Thursday is singles' night, Friday is house and reggae, Saturday is Latin night and Sunday is the Tea Dance. Open from 5pm nightly until as late as 4am. Happy hour is 5–7pm daily.

MIDTOWN WEST

La Nueva Escuelita: 301 West 39th Street at 8th Avenue. Tel 212-631 0588. Subway A, C, East to 42nd Street.
Her/She Bar on Friday night is a truly upbeat Latin night. Opens at 10pm, $8 before midnight, $10 after.

RESTAURANTS

CHELSEA

Big Cup: 228 8th Avenue at 22nd Street. Tel 212-206 0059.
A truly gay coffee house that is a great place to hang out on a rainy day. It has a local vibe, and even has the movie times for the local cinema chalked on a blackboard so that you won't miss your film.

Eighteenth and 8th: 159 8th Avenue at 18th Street. Tel 212-242 5000.
The gay restaurant of the gay district of New York, it serves healthy American food. But be prepared for a long wait outside as it's tiny inside.

Empire Diner: 210 10th Avenue at 22nd Street. Tel 212-243 2736.
This humble diner has made appearances in countless commercials and movies. It's very low key and a great pit stop to get a burger at the end of a heavy night. You'll be rubbing shoulders with anyone, from drag queens to artists, in need of a late night snack.

Lola: 30 West 22nd Street between 5th and 6th Avenues. Tel 212-675 6700.
Famous for its American cuisine with Caribbean and Asian influences, it gets packed on Sunday for gospel brunches.

Pad Thai: 114 8th Avenue at 16th Street. Tel 212-691 6226.
Elegant noodle lounge.

Restivo: 209 7th Avenue at 22nd Street. Tel 212-366 4133.
Great Italian cuisine at good prices.

WEST VILLAGE

Benny's Burritos: 113 Greenwich Avenue at Jane Street. Tel 212-727 3560.
The incredibly cheap and huge burritos attract a huge student crowd who don't mind the poor service.

Caffe Dell'Artista: 46 Greenwich Avenue between 6th and 7th Avenues. Tel 212-645 4431.
A European-style café serving simple, light meals and desserts.

Cowgirl: 519 Hudson Street at West 10th Street. Tel 212-633 1133.
Once the Cowgirl Hall of Fame, now just the Cowgirl, this isn't just great for women who feel at home surrounded by cowgirl memorabilia, but is also frequented by families. It serves cheap American food – think fried onion loaf, huge spare ribs and chicken-fried steak – for $21–30 for a main course and is also known for its margaritas. The people-watching outside in summer is a treat. Another bonus? You can now get a 10 per cent discount with your NYCard.

Florent: 69 Gansevoort Street between Greenwich and Washington Streets. Tel 212-989 5779.
Good French food served 24 hours a day at weekends and until 5am weekdays.

Garage Restaurant and Café: 99 7th Avenue South between Barrow and Grove Streets. Tel 212-645 0600.
Serves global cuisine including steaks and a raw bar, with live jazz nightly.

Lips: 2 Bank Street at Greenwich Avenue. Tel 212-675 7710.
Italian menu with dishes named after popular queens, and waitresses in drag.

Nadine's: 99 Bank Street at Greenwich Street. Tel 212-924 3165.
Eclectic and good value food in a funky but glamorous setting.

Rubyfruit Bar and Grill: 531 Hudson Street at Charles Street. Tel 212-929 3343.
Not just for lesbians. Serves good eclectic food both downstairs and in the fun bar upstairs. Live music nightly.

Sacred Cow: 522 Hudson Street at West 10th Street. Tel 212-337 0863.
Healthy vegan food shop and café.

EAST VILLAGE

Astor Restaurant and Lounge: 316 Bowery at Bleecker Street. Tel 212-253 8644.
The Moroccan-style lounge plays host to a gay party on Wednesdays, plus a French/Mediterranean restaurant.

B Bar: 40 East 4th Street between Lafayette Street and Bowery. Tel 212-475 2220.
Home to Beige on a Tuesday night, this gorgeous bistro serves excellent food.

Lucien: 14 1st Avenue at 1st Street. Tel 212-260 6481.
Always packed, this tiny French bistro serves delicious food and is particularly known for its Sunday brunch.

Pangea: 178 2nd Avenue between 11th and 12th Streets. Tel 212-995 0900.
Known for its wonderful home-made pastas and Mediterranean cuisine.

Stingy Lulu's: 129 St Mark's Place between Avenue A and 1st Avenue. Tel 212-674 3545.
A fabulous old-fashioned diner.

SOHO, NOLITA and TRIBECA

Amici Miei: 475 West Broadway at Houston Street. Tel 212-533 1933.
A chic Italian restaurant open for lunch and dinner with outdoor seating.

Basset Café: 123 West Broadway at Duane Street. Tel 212-349 1662.
Tuck into a delicious salad or sandwich, or treat yourself to the home-made cakes at this light and airy haven.

El Teddy's: 219 West Broadway between Franklin and White Streets. Tel 212-941 7070.
A hip hangout with a great bar scene and excellent food.

La Cigale: 231 Mott Street between Prince and Spring Streets. Tel 212-334 4331.
Simple but imaginative continental food and a magical back garden.

THEATER DISTRICT

Coffee Pot: 350 West 49th Street at 9th Avenue. Tel 212-265 3566.
Nice little coffee bar with live music and Tarot card readings.

Mangia East Bevi: 800 9th Avenue at 53rd Street. Tel 212-956 3976.
An excellent, popular Italian in the middle of Midtown's gay district.

Revolution: 611 9th Avenue between 43rd and 44th Streets. Tel 212-489 8451.
A club-like restaurant with great food and music videos. It has a DJ every night, a youngish crowd and American menus.

Vintage: 753 9th Avenue at 51st Street. Tel 212-581 4655.
A hip bar/restaurant that serves dinner till midnight and cocktails till 4am.

MIDTOWN EAST

Comfort Diner: 214 East 45th Street between 2nd and 3rd Avenues. Tel 212-867 4555.
Authentic and delicious American cuisine served in a 1950s-style diner setting.

Regents: 317 East 53rd Street between 1st and 2nd Avenues. Tel 212-593 3091.
Attracts a fairly posh gay crowd for its eclectic cuisine. There is a rotating specials menu and a prix fixe menu at $17.95. Also has an upstairs back terrace and live cabaret nightly, including show tune theme nights and Sinatra specials.

Townhouse Restaurant: 206 East 58th Street between 2nd and 3rd Avenues. Tel 212-826 6241.
This is a real gay haunt – especially among the more mature crowd. It serves delicious food at reasonable prices.

CHAPTER 10

Accommodation

As I explained in Chapter 1, the matter of choosing your hotel should be your last decision, so that you will have the chance first to work out what you want to do while you're in the Big Apple. That way you'll know where you'll be spending most of your time and can decide where best to locate yourself. It may be that if you intend to stay for a week it would work out best to stay at two hotels – one in Lower Manhattan and one in Midtown – so you can save on travelling time and expensive cab fares.

It is worth noting a few of the basic facts about New York hotels, too. For instance, the most expensive hotels tend to be clustered on the East Side from Midtown up to 96th Street. The best deals tend to be around Herald Square and on the Upper West Side, but if you go for these options check you won't be spending too much extra on transport. The average rate for a room that can accommodate two people is $200 a night – so if you get something for less (and there are plenty of ways to do this) you are doing well.

HOTEL TIPS

➡ There are now around 70,000 hotel rooms in New York, yet demand at certain times of the year is such that you will still have a hard time finding a room. Your best bet for both ensuring a bed and getting the best prices is to go in the off-peak times of January to March and also July and August.

➡ Most hotels reduce their rates at weekends – including some of the poshest. If you're staying for more than a weekend, negotiate the best rate you can for the rest of your time or switch to a cheaper hotel.

➡ If noise is a particular problem for you, bear in mind that hotels downtown and uptown tend to be quieter than those in Midtown. Also, addresses on streets tend to be quieter than those on avenues, except those nearer the river.

➡ For longer stays, try to choose a hotel room with a kitchenette, then you won't have to eat out all the time.

➡ Smaller hotels tend not to book large groups, so they often have rooms available even during peak periods.

If you are planning to take in the sights of Lower Manhattan, Chinatown, Lower East Side, SoHo and the Village, choose a hotel in the area. It'll save you loads of time on travel and money on cab fares.

➡ When booking your room, check there isn't going to be a major convention at the same time – if there is, ask to be put on a different floor.

➡ Also ask for a corner room – they are usually bigger, less noisy and have more windows and, therefore, more light than other rooms and don't always cost more.

➡ There is always a lot of renovation work going on in New York hotels, so when reserving a room, ask if any is being done at that particular hotel and, if so, ask for a room as far away as possible from the renovation work.

ALL WIRED UP!

Not only does America have a different style of plug, it also works on a different voltage. Ours is 230 volts, theirs is 115 volts, so you'll need a travel appliance that works on both voltages, or an adaptor plug.

BOOKING IT YOURSELF

Of course, you can use a travel agent to make room reservations, but you can also do it yourself through companies that specialise in offering excellent rates at off-peak and low-peak times or even just guarantee finding you a room during busy periods. They include:

Hotel America Ltd: Tel 01444 410555, **www.hotelanywhere.co.uk**. A British company providing hotel discounts anywhere in the world.

Hotel Conxions: Tel 212-840 8686, fax 212-221 8686, **www.hotelconxions.com** You can find out about availability and price, and book a room on their website.

When making a booking directly with a hotel, make sure they send you confirmation of your reservation (fax is simplest).

Quickbook: Tel 212-779 ROOM, fax 212-779 6120, **www.quikbook.com.** A service providing discounts on hotels all over America. They promise there are no hidden cancellation or change penalties, and pre-payment is not required.

A great Internet discount reservation service can be found at **www.hotres.com** or look for cheaper rates through the hotel discount service on: **www.usacitylink.com/citylink/ny/new-york.**

When discussing room rates with any of these organisations, always check that the prices you are quoted include the

If you're a smoker, make sure you book a smoking room as most hotels now predominantly provide non-smoking rooms.

New York City hotel tax of 13.25 per cent and the $2 per night occupancy tax.

Below I've given a listing of hotels chosen for their location, service, price or the excellent value for money they offer. I have divided them up by price per room, starting with the most expensive, and then arranged them by location.

$	Less than $100
$$	$100-$200
$$$	$200-$300
$$$$	$300-$400
$$$$$	$400 and over

SHEER LUXURY

BATTERY PARK CITY

THE RITZ-CARLTON NEW YORK

$$$$$

✉ 2 West Street between Battery Place and West End

☎ 212-344 0800
Fax 212-344 3804
www.ritzcarlton.com

🚗 Subway 4, 5 to Bowling Green

Not just a new hotel, but a new world-class hotel with art deco-inspired interiors, incredible views of the Hudson River and Statue of Liberty, state-of-the-art business support services and unparalleled service. A 39-storey glass-and-brick edifice in Lower Manhattan, it has 298 sumptuous guest rooms, 113 luxury residences, an outdoor waterfront deck and even the Skyscraper Museum. The rooms come with the very finest Frette linens, feather beds and goose-down pillows, cotton bathrobe, Ritz-Carlton pyjamas, marble bathtubs and separate marble shower stalls, silk curtains, in-room safe, working desk with two chairs, dual-line cordless phones with voice mail and high-speed Internet access. The extensive guest services include a fully equipped health club and spa, massage treatments, limo, complimentary shuttle service in Lower Manhattan and a bath butler! I can assure you, it really is to die for.

MIDTOWN EAST

THE FOUR SEASONS $$$$-$$$$$

✉ 57 East 57th Street between Madison and Park Avenues
☎ 212-758 5700
Fax 212-758 5711
🚗 Subway 4, 5, 6 to 59th Street

Put on your best power suits to rub shoulders with New York's movers and shakers. The art deco-style rooms come with electronically controlled drapes and marble-clad bathrooms.

THE NEW YORK PALACE $$$$-$$$$$

✉ 455 Madison Avenue between 50th and 51st Streets
☎ 212-888 7000
www.newyorkpalace.com
🚗 Subway 6 to 51st Street

The Palace rises 55 floors from its prime spot in Midtown Manhattan and is a favourite stopover for celebs visiting New York. The main hotel is in the Villard Houses, but the adjacent Towers are the more luxurious rooms to stay in. Although it was built in 1882, the furnishings are surprisingly modern, with high-back modern couches and quirky gold lamps in the lobby. It also houses the landmark Le Cirque 2000 restaurant and the Villard Bar and Lounge.

THE PLAZA $$$$-$$$$$

✉ 5th Avenue at 59th Street
☎ 212-759 3000
Fax 212-759 317
🚗 Subway N, R to 5th Avenue

New York's most famous hotel is still as popular today as it was when it first opened in 1907. It's built in the style of a French château and inside is a treasure trove of antique furniture, dazzling chandeliers and elaborate ceilings. Rooms are worn but charming and a good size. Its list of celebrity guest is endless, from Marlene Dietrich to modern day film stars Catherine Zeta Jones and Michael Douglas, who had their wedding reception in the hotel's Grand Ballroom.

THE SHERRY-NETHERLAND $$$$-$$$$$

✉ 781 5th Avenue at East 59th Street
☎ 212-355 2800
Fax 212-319 4306
🚗 Subway 4, 5, 6 to 59th Street
Discount with a NYCard

A true New York secret, this is one of the grand hotels with real charm and is also the permanent home of many a celebrity.

THE WALDORF-ASTORIA $$$-$$$$$

✉ 301 Park Avenue at 50th Street
☎ 212-355 3000
Fax 212-872 7272
www.waldorfastoria.com
🚗 Subway 6 to 51st Street

A colossus of a hotel in more than one sense, it's an art deco marvel with a wonderful history that has been designated a New York City landmark since 1993. It all started in 1893 when millionaire William Waldorf Astor opened the 13-storey Waldorf Hotel at 33rd Street. It was the embodiment of Astor's vision of a grand hotel and came with

DIAMOND DISCOUNTS

There are two ways to cut your room rates through NYTAB. You can take advantage of their tie-up with Express Reservations – visit **www.hotelsinmanhattan.com** or call 303-218 7808. They offer major discounts on over 25 hotels across most price categories. NYTAB has also made arrangements at a few carefully chosen hotels for discounts (see pages 239–40).

two innovations – electricity throughout and private bathrooms in every guest chamber – and immediately became **the** place to go for the upper classes. Four years later The Waldorf was joined by the 17-storey Astoria Hotel, built next door by Waldorf's cousin, John Jacob Astor IV. The corridor between the two became an enduring symbol of the combined Waldorf and Astoria Hotels.

Then in 1929 it closed and on its original site now stands another icon of the New York skyline, the Empire State Building. In the meantime the Waldorf-Astoria was rebuilt in Midtown Manhattan, opening its doors in 1931 and immediately being dubbed New York's first skyscraper hotel. It rose 42 storeys high, stretched from Park Avenue to Lexington Avenue and contained an astonishing 2,200 rooms. It was such an amazing event, opening as it did in the middle of the Depression, that President Herbert Hoover broadcast a message of congratulations. And ever since, the Waldorf-Astoria has had a long association with presidents of countries and corporations.

The art deco aspects of the hotel were brought back into view during a restoration in the 1980s when architects found a huge cache of long-lost treasures, including a magnificent 148,000-piece mosaic, depicting the *Wheel of Life*, by French artist Louis Regal in the Park Avenue lobby, 13 allegorical murals by the same artist and ornate mouldings on the ceilings. The legendary Starlight Roof nightclub, which had epitomised glamour and sophistication in the 1930s and 1940s with its retractable roof, allowing views of the stars, was restored during the same period.

Another $60-million upgrade in 1998 saw the Park Avenue Cocktail Terrace and Sir Harry's Bar being restored to their full art deco glory. Oscar's, named after the Waldorf-Astoria's famous style-setting maître d' Oscar Tschirky, was completely redesigned by Adam Tihany, the hottest restaurant designer in town.

Of course, if you plan to stay here, you'll want to know about the service – excellent – and the standard of the rooms – huge, beautifully decorated and with marble-encased ensuite bathrooms. What more could you ask for?

THE WALDORF TOWERS $$$$$

✉ 301 Park Avenue at 50th Street
☎ 212-355 3100
Fax 212-872 7272
www.waldorf-towers.com
🚗 Subway 6 to 51st Street

A boutique hotel occupying the 28th to the 42nd floors of the Waldorf-Astoria, this is one of the most exclusive addresses in New York, filled as it is with presidents of countries and global corporations. Thanks to the hotel's security arrangements (it has its own private car parking facilities underground), this is the place where treaties and mergers have been negotiated and signed, momentous peace initiatives have begun and unforgettable music has been made.

It has its own dedicated entrance, lobby, concierge desk, reception and private lifts operated by 'white-gloved' attendants. Guests have included the Duke and Duchess of Windsor, who maintained their New York residence here, Jack and Jackie Kennedy, Frank Sinatra and Cole Porter, who wrote many of his most famous compositions here.

The rooms are not so much rooms or suites, but rather more like apartments in their own right. Many come with dining rooms, full kitchens and maids' quarters. Some even have televisions in their bathrooms!

If you hire a car, bear in mind that most hotels charge a parking fee of around $25 a night.

UPPER EAST SIDE

HOTEL CARLYLE $$$$-$$$$$

✉ 35 East 76th Street between Madison and Park Avenues
☎ 212-744 1600
Fax 212-717 4682
🚗 Subway 6 to 77th Street

Famous for its impeccable and discreet service, this is the place where the stars come. The apartment-style rooms are elegant and very plush – some even have grand pianos and all have whirlpools in the bathrooms. By the way, Woody Allen plays jazz here every week.

HOTEL PLAZA-ATHENE $$$$-$$$$$

✉ 37 East 64th Street between Madison and Park Avenues
☎ 212-734 9100
Fax 212 722 0958
🚗 Subway 6 to 68th Street

What its rooms lack in size they make up for in elegant French antique furnishings.

THE MARK $$$$-$$$$$

✉ 25 East 77th Street between 5th and Madison Avenues
☎ 212-744 4300
Fax 212-744 2749
🚗 Subway 6 to 77th Street

In terms of luxury, it vies with the Carlyle – only The Mark has Italian neoclassicism compared with the Carlyle's English gentility. This is a really beautiful up-market boutique hotel with the kind of discreet service its long list of celebrity clients enjoy. Sadly, some of those celebs do get a bit out of hand and Johnny Depp and Kate Moss once had a lover's tiff here, which took its toll on the furniture before Depp was finally arrested at 5am. Fellow celebrity guests George Michael and Ali McGraw were apparently deeply disturbed by Depp's tantrum. On a happier note, such an event is a rarity, which explains why many celebs make The Mark their home-from-home when they're in New York. There's a complimentary car service to Wall Street and the Theater District for all guests, a small health club and a top-notch restaurant.

The posh Mark hotel on the Upper East Side does such good weekend and summer rates that you could afford to stay there and enjoy all that fabulous luxury.

THE STANHOPE $$$$-$$$$$

✉ 995 5th Avenue at 81st Street.
☎ 212-288 5800
Fax 212-517 0088.
🚗 Subway 6 to 77th Street

Well located on Museum Mile, this security-conscious hotel is a hideaway for Hollywood stars and also caters to top business people. Anyone can enjoy its elegance and charm by taking afternoon tea here.

If you're not happy with the quality of your room, change it. Americans wouldn't tolerate anything but the best – so why should you?

A CUT ABOVE

FINANCIAL DISTRICT

MARRIOTT WORLD TRADE CENTER HOTEL $$$$

✉ 3 World Trade Center between Liberty and Vesey Streets
☎ 212-938 9100
Fax 212-444 4094
🚗 Subway C, E to World Trade Center; N, R, 1, 9 to Cortlandt Street

Damaged on September 11, but back in action now, this is geared up to the business person. It offers a complimentary breakfast and use of the rooftop health club, swimming pool, indoor track and saunas.

Hotels in the Financial District can be especially good value for money at weekends when many business people leave the city.

SOHO

THE MERCER $$$$

✉ 147 Mercer Street at Prince Street
☎ 212-966 6060
Fax 212-965 3820
🚗 Subway: N, R to Prince Street

A bijou 72-room boutique hotel slap, bang in the middle of SoHo, it quickly gets packed with the fashionable and young corporate sets. Your room even comes with condoms in the bathroom and video games on the TV.

60 THOMPSON $$$-$$$$$

✉ 60 Thompson Street between Broome and Spring Streets
☎ 212-431 0400
Fax 212-431 0200
www.60thompson.com
🚗 Subway C, E at Spring Street

The latest boutique hotel to open in Manhattan is a real gem. It's a sleek, 12-storey, 100-bedroom hotel that is a great retreat from the bustling streets of SoHo. Rooms are designed for relaxing in, the best are on the top floor which have breathtaking panoramic views of landmarks including the Empire State Building. The front courtyard sheltered by birch trees is a wonderful place to sit and people watch.

SOHO GRAND $$$$

✉ 310 West Broadway between Grand and Canal Streets
☎ 212-965 3000
Fax 212-965 3244
🚗 Subway C, East to Canal Street

Famous for its style, this was the first proper hotel to open in the SoHo area. Cocktails and light meals are served in the Grand Bar, an intimate, wood-panelled club room, as well as the fashionable Salon, a lively lounge that is excellent for people-watching.

TRIBECA

TRIBECA GRAND $$$$-$$$$$

✉ 2 Avenue of the Americas at Church Street.
☎ 212-519 6600
UK freephone 0800-028 9874
Fax 212-519 6700
www.tribecagrand.com
🚗 Subway 1, 9 to Franklin Street

A new sister property to the extremely stylish SoHo Grand, this is the first major hotel to open in the TriBeCa area. In-room amenities include voice mail, data port, complimentary local phone calls and faxes, built-in TV and telephone, personal safes, high-speed Internet access and complimentary web access.

GRAMERCY PARK

INN AT IRVING PLACE $$$$-$$$$$

✉ 56 Irving Place between East 17th and East 18th Streets
☎ 212-533 4600
Fax 212-533 4611
🚗 Subway L, N, R, 4, 5, 6 to 14th Street/Union Square

Delightful, tiny Victorian boutique hotel. Each room comes with a romantic fireplace and four-poster bed.

MIDTOWN

BRYANT PARK $$$$-$$$$$

✉ 40 West 40th Street
☎ 212-869 0100
Fax 212-869 4446
www.bryantparkhotel.com
🚗 Subway 5th Avenue

The new hide-out for the fashion pack overlooks the park that gives the hotel its name. It's just off 5th Avenue, so ideal if you are on a shopping trip and convenient for visiting all of the major sights. Inside, the rooms resemble New York lofts, think white walls, sleek Italian furniture in warm orange and ochre and cool bathrooms with giant porcelain sinks and stainless steel shelves.

THE CHAMBERS $$$-$$$$$

✉ 15 West 56th Street between 5th and 6th Avenues

☎ 212-974 5656
Fax 212-974 5657
www.chambers-hotel.com

🚗 Subway B, Q to 57th Street

A new hotel that has certainly created a buzz. It's owned by the same team behind the Mercer Hotel in SoHo and has already attracted the likes of Jennifer Love Hewitt and Kid Rock to its gorgeous rooms. Its décor is very modern, but also comfortable and luxurious. The bath tubs are deep, there are cashmere throws on the beds and DVD and CD players and flat-screen TVs in every room. Its restaurant, Town, is currently the in place to book for dinner.

LE PARKER MERIDIEN $$$$-$$$$$

✉ 118 West 57th Street between 6th and 7th Avenues

☎ 212-245 5000,
Fax 212-708 7477
www.parkermeridien.com

🚗 Subway B, D, E to 7th Avenue

A classic New York hotel in the design sense yet with a traditional French feel, this hotel is not only in an excellent location just minutes from Central Park and Carnegie Hall, but offers great service and amenities. The rooms, which have all recently been refurbished, have a Zen-like calmness to them thanks to the minimalist and cherry wood décor. Great touches include a revolving unit, which allows you to watch the massive TV screen either in the sitting area or in the bedroom. It also has a useful desk unit, CD and DVD players.

Even if you don't plan to use the pool, do visit the penthouse location to see the fab views of Central Park. Down in the basement is the massive Gravity gymnasium, which covers everything from Cybex training to aerobics, sauna, stretching, massage rooms, spa services and squash and racquetball courts.

Other facilities include the much-raved-about Norma's restaurant in the lobby, which serves creative breakfast dishes throughout the day. The other restaurant is Seppi's, which emulates the intimate atmosphere of the SoHo eatery Raoul's as well as the Raoul family's homeland of Alsace.

Make sure you look upwards when you enter the lifts of Le Parker Meridien – all three have a TV screen offering classic clips of *Abbot and Costello* or *Tom and Jerry*.

PENINSULA NEW YORK $$$$$

✉ 700 5th Avenue at 55th Street

☎ 212-247 2200
Fax 212-903 3943

🚗 Subway F to 53rd Street; 6 to 51st Street

A beautiful hotel which has undergone a $45-million renovation in the public areas, restaurants and all 241 guest rooms.

ROYALTON $$$$-$$$$$

✉ 44 West 44th Street between 5th and 6th Avenues

☎ 212-869 4400
Fax 212-869 8965

🚗 Subway B, D, F, Q to 42nd Street

An 'in' place with the magazine and showbiz crowd, this hotel was designed by Philippe Starck. Each room has a futon, slate fireplace and round bathtub.

MIDTOWN EAST

BOX TREE $$$-$$$$

✉ 250 East 49th Street between 2nd and 3rd Avenues

☎ 212-758 8320
Fax 212-308 3899

🚗 Subway 6 to 51st Street

Despite the skyscrapers, New York still has a few traditional townhouses now turned into 'boutique' – i.e. small – hotels. The romantic Box Tree is one of the best.

ELYSEE **$$$$–$$$$$**

✉ 60 East 54th Street between Park and Madison Avenues

☎ 212-753 1066, Fax 212-980 9278

🚗 Subway 6 to 51st Street

Another boutique offering, dating from the 1930s. Its décor includes antique furnishings and Italian marble bathrooms.

KITANO HOTEL **$$$$–$$$$$**

✉ 66 Park Avenue at East 38th Street

☎ 212-885 7000 Fax 212-885 7100

🚗 Subway S, 4, 5, 6, 7 to Grand Central/ 42nd Street

A first-class, Japanese-run hotel with top-notch service and a deliciously decadent, deep-soaking tub in each room.

MIDTOWN WEST

THE NEW YORK HILTON AND TOWERS **$$$$$**

✉ 1335 6th Avenue at 53rd Street

☎ 212-586 7000, Fax 212-315 1374

🚗 Subway B, D, F, Q to 47th–50th Streets/Rockefeller Center

After a recent $100-million renovation, the city's largest hotel now has a beautiful new façade and entrance lobby, plus two new restaurants and lounges.

UPPER WEST SIDE

INN NEW YORK CITY **$$$$–$$$$$**

✉ 266 West 71st Street between Broadway and West End Avenue

☎ 212-580 1900 Fax 212-580 4437

🚗 Subway 1, 2, 3, 9 to 72nd Street

Confusingly, American hotel lifts use the letter 'L' or the number '1' to indicate the ground floor.

Taking the boutique notion to its limits, this hotel has just four suites, each with a kitchen.

MEDIUM-PRICED GEMS

FINANCIAL DISTRICT

MILLENNIUM HILTON **$$–$$$$$**

✉ 5 Church Street between Fulton and Dey Streets

☎ 212-693 2001 Fax 212-571 2316

🚗 Subway 1, 9, N, R to Cortlandt Street

A black skyscraper geared to business, with fitness centre and a pool. If you want a stunning view of the harbour, ask for a high floor.

WALL STREET INN **$$$**

✉ 9 South William Street opposite 85 Broad Street

☎ 212-747 1500

🚗 Subway 2, 3 to Wall Street; J, M, Z to Broad Street

A boutique hotel in an old office building in the heart of the historic district. Original features include mahogany panels on the walls, and granite floors.

MIDTOWN

CASABLANCA **$$$–$$$$**

✉ 147 West 43rd Street off Times Square

☎ 212-869 1212, Fax 212-391 7585

🚗 Subway 1, 2, 3, 7, 9, N, R, S Times Square/42nd Street

Elegant Moroccan theme includes ceiling fans, palm trees and mosaic tiles. Service is good too!

CITY CLUB HOTEL **$$$–$$$$**

✉ 55 West 44th Street between 5th and 6th Avenues

☎ 212-921 5500 Fax 212-944 5544

🚗 Subway 7 to 5th Avenue; B, D, F, V to 42nd Street

The owner-manager Jeffrey Klein is one of the most socially visible hoteliers in the city and some of his very famous friends cocoon themselves in his hotel. Based in an old gentlemen's club building, it is one of the smartest but least showy boutique hotels in New York. There's no queuing in the lobby as check-in happens in your room, which comes with a big TV hidden in the wall, a day bed and possibly even the latest Jackie Kennedy Onassis biography. For once, the rooms are actually designed to spend time in! Special rate with your NYCard.

MANSFIELD $$$–$$$$$

✉ 12 West 44th Street between 5th and 6th Avenues
☎ 212-944 6050
Fax 212-764 4477
🚗 Subway B, D, F, Q to 47th–50th Street/Rockefeller Center

A beautiful lobby with vaulted ceiling and white marble marks the Mansfield out as an elegant hotel for those also wanting the charm of a boutique hotel.

SHOREHAM $$$–$$$$$

✉ 33 West 55th Street at 5th Avenue
☎ 212-247 6700
Fax 212-765 9741
🚗 Subway F to 5th Avenue

This hotel has recently undergone a renovation and now has a new bar, restaurant, fitness centre and more good-sized rooms.

MIDTOWN EAST

DORAL PARK AVENUE $$$–$$$$

✉ 70 Park Avenue at 38th Street
☎ 212-687 7050,
Fax 212-973 2497
🚗 Subway 4, 5, 6 to 42nd Street

A beautiful, five-star hotel with a bar, restaurant and excellent room facilities.

THE DYLAN $$$–$$$$

✉ 52 East 41st Street between Madison and Park Avenues
☎ 212-338 0500
Fax 212-338 0569
www.dylanhotel.com
🚗 Subway S, 4, 5, 6, 7 to Grand Central/42nd Street

Located in the former Chemist's Club building, this new boutique hotel was developed to preserve the 1903 Beaux Arts structure. Facilities include a mezzanine lounge and bar overlooking the dramatic, high-ceilinged restaurant, RX. In-room amenities include a state-of-the-art digital entertainment system with large cable TV, DVD and CD players that can access a library of thousands of video and CD titles, two-line telephones with voicemail and data port, large safes and complimentary newspaper.

FITZPATRICK $$$–$$$$

✉ 687 Lexington Avenue between East 56th and East 57th Streets
☎ 212-355 0100
Fax 212-355 1371
🚗 Subway 4, 5, 6 to 59th Street

The rooms are equipped with everything from trouser presses to towelling robes, useful after indulging in the whirlpool bath included in many rooms.

FITZPATRICK GRAND CENTRAL $$$

✉ 141 East 44th Street between Lexington and 3rd Avenues
☎ 212-351 6800
Fax 212-355 1371
🚗 Subway S, 4, 5, 6, 7 to Grand Central/42nd Street

The Fitzpatrick Family Group of hotels continues its Irish theme at this hotel just across from Grand Central Station. It includes an Irish pub and you can order a traditional Irish breakfast.

THE ROOSEVELT HOTEL $$–$$$$

✉ East 45th Street at Madison Avenue
☎ 212-661 9600
Fax 212-885 6161
www.therooseveltho tel.com
🚗 Subway S, 4, 5, 6, 7 to Grand Central/42nd Street

Built in 1924, this classy hotel completed a $70-million renovation in 1998 in which the lobby was restored to its original grandeur with crystal chandeliers, columns and lots of marble.

WEST NEW YORK **$$$–$$$$$**

✉ 541 Lexington Avenue between 49th and 50th Streets

☎ 212-755 1200
Fax 212-644 0951

🚗 Subway 6 to 51st Street; E, F to Lexington/3rd Avenue

In 1998, Starwood Lodging joined forces with designer David Rockwell, celebrity restaurateur Drew Nieporent and nightlife impresario Randy Gerber to transform the former Doral Inn into an urban oasis for travellers looking for comfortable, sophisticated accommodation.

MIDTOWN WEST

HUDSON **$$–$$$$$**

✉ 356 West 58th Street between 8th and 9th Avenues

☎ 212-554 6000
Fax 212-554 6001
www.hudsonhotel.com

🚗 Subway A, B, C, D, 1, 9 to 59th Street/Columbus Circle

Built on the site of the former *Sesame Street* studios, this Ian Schrager and Philippe Starck collaboration is heaving with chic guests. It's loud and proud, so don't check in if you are looking for peace and quiet while you're in the city. From the neon entrance escalator to the glowing glass floor of the Hudson Bar, you'll be in the limelight. The rooms are stylish but very small. In a great location for Central Park, the Lincoln Center and Theater District, but definitely on the **west** side of town so keep this in mind depending on your sightseeing plans.

MODERNE **$$$–$$$$**

✉ 243 West 55th Street between Broadway and 8th Avenue

☎ 212-397 6767
Fax 212-397 8787

🚗 Subway C, E, 1, 9 to 50th Street

Opened in 1998, this bijou hotel was converted from a five-storey dance studio.

THEATER DISTRICT

NEW YORK MARRIOTT MARQUIS **$$–$$$$**

✉ 1535 Broadway at 45th Street

☎ 212-398 1900
Fax 212-704 8926

🚗 Subway N, R, S, 1, 2, 3, 7, 9 to Times Square/42nd Street

In 1998, the hotel completed a $25-million upgrade of all its rooms so each one now includes console desks, ergonomic chairs, two phone lines and voicemail. A sushi bar, Katen, is in the atrium lobby.

PARAMOUNT **$$–$$$$$**

✉ 235 West 46th Street between Broadway and 8th Avenue

☎ 212-764 5500
Fax 212-575 4892

🚗 Subway C, E, 1, 9 to 50th Street

A hip hotel with a glorious, sweeping staircase in the lobby.

THE PREMIER **$$$–$$$$**

✉ 45 West 44th Street between 6th Avenue and Broadway

☎ 212-768 4400
Fax 212-768 0847

🚗 Subway N, R, S, 1, 2, 3, 7, 9 to Times Square/42nd Street

The Millennium Broadway in Times Square built this 22-storey tower in 1999 to increase its total room count to 752. The Premier has its own private entrance on 44th Street and elegant, modern guest rooms with large bathrooms, two phone lines, voicemail and a separate modem and fax machine.

TIME HOTEL **$$$**

✉ 224 West 49th Street between 8th Avenue and Broadway

☎ 212-320 2900
Fax 212-245 2305

🚗 Subway C, E, 1, 9 to 50th Street

This boutique hotel in the heart of Times Square features colour-saturated rooms in red, yellow or blue, designed by Adam Tihany, and a restaurant run by celebrity chef Jean-Louis Palladin.

UPPER EAST SIDE

FRANKLIN **$$$**

✉ 164 East 87th Street between 3rd and Lexington Avenues
☎ 212-369 1000
Fax 212-369 8000
🚗 Subway 4, 5, 6 to 86th Street

Known for its good service, this pleasant hotel has lovely touches in its rooms that include canopies over the beds, fresh flowers and cedar closets.

EXCELLENT VALUE

BROOKLYN

NEW YORK MARRIOTT BROOKLYN **$$–$$$**

✉ 333 Adams Street at Tillary Street
☎ 718-246 7000
Fax 718-246 0563
🚗 Subway A, C, F to Jay Street/Borough Hall; N, R to Court Street; 2, 3, 4, 5 to Borough Hall just five minutes' walk away

Opened in 1998, this is Brooklyn's first hotel in 68 years. Over the water from Manhattan, but you get excellent facilities at very good prices.

CHINATOWN/SOHO

HOLIDAY INN DOWNTOWN **$$**

✉ 138 Lafayette Street at Canal Street
☎ 212-966 8898
Fax 212-966 3933
🚗 Subway N, R to Canal Street

Well-equipped, spotless rooms at excellent prices.

FINANCIAL DISTRICT

HOLIDAY INN WALL STREET **$$–$$$$**

✉ 15 Gold Street at Platt Street
☎ 212-232 7700
Fax 212-425 0330
🚗 Subway J, M, Z, 2, 3, 4, 5 to Fulton Street

Opened in 1999, billing itself as the most high-tech hotel in New York, complete with T-1 speed internet connectivity. Discount with your NYCard.

FLATIRON DISTRICT

CARLTON **$$–$$$**

✉ 22 East 29th Street between 5th and Madison Avenues
☎ 212-532 4100
Fax 212-889 8683
🚗 Subway 4, 5, 6 to 28th Street

A tourist-class hotel with a view of the Empire State Building and in an excellent location for 5th Avenue and Garment District shopping. Restaurant, lounge and business services.

GREENWICH VILLAGE

WASHINGTON SQUARE HOTEL **$$**

✉ 103 Waverly Place between 5th and 6th Avenues
☎ 212-777 9515,
Fax 212-979 8373
🚗 Subway A, B, C, D, E, F, Q to West 4th Street/Washington Square

A family-run hotel overlooking Washington Square. The rooms are small but the rates very reasonable and include breakfast.

CHELSEA

CHELSEA HOTEL **$$**

✉ 222 West 23rd Street between 7th and 8th Avenues
☎ 212-243 3700
🚗 Subway A, C, E, 1, 2, 3, 9 to 23rd Street

A true icon of New York city, this hotel has been associated with artistic and literary types since it opened in 1912. Residents have included Dylan Thomas, Jack Kerouac, Mark Twain and Thomas Wolfe and it still pulls in the celebs – Dee Dee Ramone of the Ramones is one of a handful of live-in artistes in the heart of New York's boho community. On the black side, Sex Pistols singer Sid Vicious is alleged to have killed his girlfriend Nancy Spungen here. Besides that, Andy Warhol shot *Chelsea Girls* here, the stairwell has starred in Bon Jovi and Mariah Carey videos, and room 822 was used to shoot

Madonna's *Sex* book. Downstairs in the basement is Serena's, a Moroccan den lounge, which has been attracting a new round of celebs such as Leonardo Di Caprio and Brazilian supermodel Giselle.

MIDTOWN

ALGONQUIN HOTEL $$-$$$

✉ 59 West 44th Street between 5th and 6th Avenues
☎ 212-840 6800
Fax 212-944 1618
🚗 Subway B, D, F, Q to 47th-50th Streets/Rockefeller Center

Famous for the literary meetings held here by Dorothy Parker and her cohorts, the Algonquin has recently undergone a $45-million refurbishment.

METRO $$-$$$

✉ 45 West 35th Street between 5th and 6th Avenues
☎ 212-947 2500
Fax 212-279 1310
🚗 Subway B, D, F, N, Q, R to 34th Street

Well located near the Empire State Building, which can be seen from its roof terrace, this hotel offers good service.

QUALITY HOTEL AND SUITES ROCKEFELLER CENTER $$

✉ 59 West 46th Street between 5th and 6th Avenues
☎ 212-719 2300
Fax 212-790 2760
🚗 Subway B, D, F, Q to 47th–50th Streets/Rockefeller Center

A well-priced hotel with excellent amenities that include a fitness centre, coffee makers and irons in the rooms, free local phone calls and a continental breakfast.

WELLINGTON $$

✉ 871 7th Avenue at 55th Street
☎ 212-247 3900
Fax 212-581 1719
www.wellingtonhotel.com
🚗 Subway N, R to 57th Street

The best thing about this tourist-class hotel is its location – deep in the heart of Midtown within striking distance of Carnegie Hall, 5th Avenue, Rockefeller Center and Times Square. If you can get a corner room with a view of 7th Avenue, you'll understand the big deal about the bright lights associated with the Theater District – they're absolutely stunning viewed from this position. The Wellington may have seen better days, but it is still in pretty good nick and excels as a great value week-day pit stop for travellers. Four people can even stay in certain rooms that cost just $210 to $240 for the night and come with either two bathrooms or one bathroom and a kitchenette. A true bargain.

MIDTOWN EAST

CLARION HOTEL 5TH AVENUE $$-$$$

✉ 3 East 40th Street just off 5th Avenue
☎ 212-447 1500
Fax 212-213 0972
🚗 Subway 7 to 5th Avenue; S, 4, 5, 6, 7 to Grand Central/42nd Street

In an excellent location near Grand Central Station. Rooms have all the latest business equipment.

MIDTOWN WEST

THE AMERITANIA $$

✉ Broadway at 54th Street
☎ 212-247 5000
Fax 212-247 3316
🚗 Subway 1, 9 to 50th Street; B, D, East to 7th Avenue

Located just outside the Theater District and near Restaurant Row. Well appointed with reasonable rooms.

WYNDHAM $$-$$$

✉ 42 West 58th Street between 5th and 6th Avenues
☎ 212-753 3500
Fax 212-754 5638
🚗 Subway B, Q to 57th Street; F to 5th Avenue

Large, basic rooms with walk-in closets. Great location.

THEATER DISTRICT

COURTYARD BY MARRIOTT TIMES SQUARE SOUTH $$-$$$

✉ 114 West 40th Street between 6th Avenue and Broadway
☎ 212-391 0088
Fax 212-391 6023
🚗 Subway B, D, F, Q to 42nd Street

This new hotel, which opened in 1998, is part of the massive redevelopment of Times Square. The spacious rooms all have a sitting area, large work desk, two phones and in-room coffee.

HOLIDAY INN MARTINIQUE ON BROADWAY $$-$$$$$

✉ 49 West 32nd Street at Broadway
☎ 212-736 3800
Fax 212-277 2681
🚗 Subway B, D, F, N, Q, R to 34th Street

Opened in 1998 on the site of the former Hotel Martinique, this hotel is decorated in a French Renaissance style.

UPPER EAST SIDE

BENTLEY $$-$$$

✉ 500 East 62nd Street at York Avenue
☎ 212-644 6000
Fax 212-207 4800
🚗 Subway 4, 5, 6, N, R to Lexington Avenue/59th Street

A recently renovated hotel within walking distance of Bloomingdales. Rates include breakfast.

UPPER WEST SIDE

THE EMPIRE HOTEL $$-$$$

✉ 44 West 63rd Street between Broadway and Columbus Avenues
☎ 212-265 7400
Fax 212-315 0349
www.empirehotel.com
🚗 Subway A, B, C, D, 1, 9 to Columbus Circle/59th Street

In an excellent location just next door to the Lincoln Center, this can be great value for money, but ensure you get the standard of room you've booked – sadly that's not always the case. When the London Symphony Orchestra wanted to stay they were shown recently refurbished rooms but then put in tiny, ugly ones.

HOTEL BEACON $$

✉ 2130 Broadway at 75th Street
☎ 212-787 1100
Fax 212-724 0839
🚗 Subway 1, 2, 3, 9 to 72nd Street

Good-sized rooms with kitchenettes, plus the hotel is well located for the American Museum of Natural History, the Lincoln Center and Central Park.

MAYFLOWER HOTEL ON THE PARK $$

✉ 15 Central Park West between 61st and 62nd Streets
☎ 212-265 0060
Fax 212-265 0227
🚗 Subway A, B, C, D, 1, 9 to Columbus Circle/59th Street

You'll get great views of Central Park without paying through the nose.

BARGAIN GEMS

LOWER EAST SIDE

HOWARD JOHNSON EXPRESS INN $-$$

✉ 135 Houston Street between Forsyth and Eldridge Streets
☎ 212-358 8844
www.hojo.com

The Lower East Side can now celebrate the arrival of its first hotel – the modern, without frills but incredibly well priced Howard Johnson. Right next door is the now renovated Landmark Sunshine Cinema, which was once a showplace for Yiddish vaudeville and films and is now a multiplex for art films.

FLATIRON DISTRICT

GERSHWIN HOTEL $-$$

✉ 7 East 27th Street between 5th and Madison Avenues
☎ 212-545 8000
Fax 212-684 5546
🚗 Subway 6 to 28th Street

A character-crammed budget boutique with some of the best rates in the city. Discount with the NYCard

THE PERFECT APPLE

A major hotel chain, Apple Core, runs five hotels in excellent Midtown locations with extremely reasonable rates – $89–199 a night. They are: Red Roof Inn Manhattan on 32nd Street, west of 5th Avenue; Comfort Inn Midtown on 46th Street west of 6th Avenue; Quality Hotel and Suites Rockefeller Center on 46th Street off 6th Avenue; Best Western Manhattan on 32nd Street west of 5th Avenue and Quality Hotel East Side at 30th Street and Lexington Avenue.

All the hotels offer complimentary continental breakfast, well-equipped fitness centres and business centres. In-room facilities include cable television and pay-per-view movies, telephones with data port and voice mail, coffee makers, irons and ironing boards. The modern bathrooms all come with marble units and hair dryers.

Occupancy rates are above 90 per cent – so book early through Apple Core's central reservations: tel 212-790 2710, fax 212-790 2760, **www.applecorehotels.com.**

HERALD SQUARE HOTEL $

✉ 19 West 31st Street between 5th Avenue and Broadway
☎ 212-279 4017
Fax 212-643 9208
🚗 Subway N, R to 28th Street

Once the headquarters of *Life* magazine, now a small, extremely well-priced hotel near the Empire State Building and Macy's.

THIRTYTHIRTY NEW YORK CITY $–$$

✉ 30 East 30th Street between Park and Madison Avenues
☎ 212-689 1900
Fax 212-689 0023
www.3030nyc.com
🚗 Subway 6 to 29th Street

Formerly the Martha Washington Hotel, this was turned into a modern, sophisticated hotel in 1999.

GRAMERCY PARK

HOTEL 17 $–$$

✉ 225 East 17th Street between 2nd and 3rd Avenues
☎ 212-475 2845
Fax 212-677 8178
🚗 Subway L, N, R, 4, 5, 6 to Union Square/14th Street

A very basic hotel with shared bathrooms.

GREENWICH VILLAGE

LARCHMONT $–$$

✉ 27 West 11th Street between 5th and 6th Avenues
☎ 212-989 9333
Fax 212-989 9496
🚗 Subway F to 14th Street

This is a clean, well-sought-after Village boutique hotel. No private baths in any of the rooms, however.

LOWER EAST SIDE

OFF SOHO SUITES $–$$

✉ 11 Rivington Street between Chrystie Street and the Bowery
☎ 212-353 0860
Fax 212-979 9801
🚗 Subway F to Delancey Street

Good-sized, clean suites with fully equipped kitchens.

MIDTOWN EAST

PICKWICK ARMS HOTEL $

✉ 230 East 51st Street between 2nd and 3rd Avenues
☎ 212-355 0300
Fax 212-755 5029
🚗 Subway 6 to 51st Street

A cheap place to stay in a pricey neighbourhood. The rooms are tiny but the hotel does have a roof garden and cocktail lounge.

BEST-KEPT SECRET

A Hospitality Company has short- to long-term accommodation available throughout Manhattan in everything from studios to three-bedroom apartments.

Everything is available from budget to luxury and each flat comes fully equipped with linen and towels, cable TV, VCR, answerphone, telephone with dataport for Internet access and fully equipped kitchen with cutlery and crockery, microwave, coffee maker, kettle and toaster. They'll even make sure new arrivals have orange juice, muffins, cereal, jam, butter and coffee along with subway and bus maps.

Prices start at just $99 a night for a studio, $125 a night for a one-bedroom flat and $275 a night for a two-bedroom apartment. No minimum stay is required and apartments are available all over Manhattan including the Upper East and Upper West Sides, Midtown, Greenwich Village, Chelsea, SoHo, the Theater District, East Village, Gramercy Park and Murray Hill. You can even check out the apartments in advance by looking at the virtual-reality pictures on their website.

Tel 212-987 1235, **www.hospitalityco.com** and e-mail info@hospitalityco.com.

MIDTOWN WEST

PORTLAND SQUARE HOTEL $

✉ 132 West 47th Street between 6th and 7th Avenues

☎ 212-382 0600
Fax 212-382 0684

🚗 Subway B, D, F, Q to 47th–50th Streets/Rockefeller Center

A family-run hotel (they also run the Herald Square Hotel). The rooms are small but the hotel is very near the Theater District.

OTHER OPTIONS

Abode Ltd: PO Box 20022, New York, NY 10021. Tel 212-472 2000, fax 212-472 8274, **www.abodenyc.com** $-$$$
Unhosted, good-quality studios or apartments all over the city, but you have to book a minimum of four days.

Bed and Breakfast (and Books): 35 West 92nd Street, Apt. 2C, New York, NY 10025. Fax 212-865 8740. $-$$
Hosted and unhosted apartments – and you may end up the guest of a writer.

Bed and Breakfast in Manhattan: PO Box 533, New York, NY 10150. Tel 212-472 2528, fax 212-988 9818. $-$$$
From comfortable to smart and both hosted and unhosted.

Jazz on the Park: 36 West 106th Street at Central Park West. Tel 212-932 1600, **www.jazzhotel.com** $
Clean, comfortable rooms for the budget traveller. Double and 'dormitory' rooms, laundry room, roof-top terrace and garden. Price includes breakfast.

CHAPTER 11

Parks, Gardens and Sports

Visiting New York needn't be all action – you can chill out, too! Obviously Central Park is the main port of call and a beautiful one at that, but there are many other parks dotted throughout the city.

CENTRAL PARK

This is the New Yorkers' playground and meeting place and attracts 15 million visitors every year. Its 341 hectares (843 acres) stretch from Central Park South at 59th Street to Central Park North at 110th Street, with 5th Avenue and Central Park West forming its eastern and western boundaries. It was created over a 20-year period by architect Calvert Vaux and landscaper Frederick Law Olmsted and was completed in the 1860s.

To enter from the south, cross the street from Grand Army Plaza at 59th Street. Immediately in front of you is the Pond, and then the Wollman Memorial Rink, which is open for rollerskating in the summer and ice skating in the winter. Close by is the Visitor Information Center, where you can pick up free maps and schedules of events, including the series of free concerts and dramas performed at the SummerStage (see page 178 for details). Here also are the Gotham Miniature Golf Course (a gift from Donald Trump), the dairy and the antique carousel. Then there is the Children's Zoo and Central Park Wildlife Center, just to the right.

The Sheep Meadow to the north of the carousel is much used by New Yorkers for picnics and sunbathing. To its left is the Tavern on the Green restaurant (see page 126) and to the right is the Mall, a tree-lined walkway. Follow the Mall to the top and you will find the Central Park Bandshell, another concert venue in the park. Furthern north is the Loeb Boathouse, which is home to the Park View at the Boathouse restaurant (see page 126). See also page 175 for details of bike and boat hire there.

You need to plan ahead to see a free concert in Central Park now. Some were attracting crowds of 300,000 to 600,000 so the City has scaled them down because of the toll they are taking on the park.

Continuing north, you will find the Ramble, a heavily wooded area which leads (if you can find the way through) to the Gothic revival Belvedere Castle, housing another information centre. Also here are the Delacorte Theater, home to summer productions by the New York Shakespeare Festival (tel 212-861 7277 for tickets) and the Great Lawn, where the Metropolitan and City Opera (tel 212-362 6000) stage open-air productions during the summer months. See page 178 for details of both of these.

Further north again is the huge reservoir, which is 10 blocks long. The path here is well-trodden by joggers but few people venture beyond this point as the nearby neighbourhoods are considered unsafe. However, in other parts of the park, there is more to see, including the Conservatory Garden, bequeathed by the Vanderbilt family, where there are free tours and concerts in the summer, the Tennis House, the pool and the Lasker Rink.

THE MAIN PARKS

Battery Park: At the southern tip of Manhattan is a beautiful space with fabulous views of the Statue of Liberty (see page 58).

Brooklyn Botanic Garden: Across in the outer borough of Brooklyn. See page 218 for details.

Bryant Park: Thanks to the efforts of the 34th Street Partnership, this park has been cleared of the ne'er do wells and is now a great spot for a picnic lunch. It even puts on free films and concerts. Don't miss the new Beaux Arts-style carousel. It costs $1.50 a ride.

Carl Schurz Park: Up in the Yorkville area of Upper East Side, this park sits right next to Gracie Mansion, the official residence of the mayor of New York.

City Hall Park: A lovely space near the fabulous Woolworth Building and civic buildings.

New York Botanical Garden: A must-see, these wonderful gardens are in the Bronx (see page 218).

Luna Park, Union Square: This is a great space in the middle of what is now one of the hippest new areas of New York. See pages 43–4 for further details.

Washington Square Park: Not so much a park as an area covered in tarmac and filled with a hot-potch of individuals, it's still a great place to snack while you watch New York in action. See page 39.

SPECTATOR SPORTS

Ask any New Yorker and they'll tell you that they read their newspapers from back to front – that's just how important sports are to them. And they have plenty to choose between, from two football teams, to baseball, basketball, hockey, tennis and racing. But it can be really tough to get in to watch some of the games, especially to see the New York Giants and the Mets, but it's worth making the effort just to see another side to New York life! If you can't get tickets directly through the box offices listed, then try TicketMaster on 212-307 7171 – they've got most games covered. An incredibly expensive alternative is to try one of the companies that specialise in selling tickets at exorbitant prices – anything from $100 for a football game to $1,000 for a baseball game. They include Prestige Entertainment on 1-800-2-GET-TIX and Ticket Window on 1-800-SOLD-OUT. A third alternative is to try a ticket tout – they're known as 'scalpers' in New York – outside Madison Square Garden. Your final and probably best bet of all three is to ask the concierge at your hotel – they have an amazing ability to come up with the goods.

MADISON SQUARE GARDEN

This venue on 7th Avenue at 32nd Street (subway A, C, E, 1, 2, 3, 9 to 34th Street/Penn Street) is home to the following:

NBA's New York Knicks basketball team: Season is from November to June. Box office: 212-465 JUMP.

NHL's New York Rangers ice hockey team: Season is from October to April. Box office: 212-308 NYRS.

WNBA New York Liberty women's pro basketball team: From May to August. Call TicketMaster on 212-307 7171.

Women's Tennis Association Tour Championships: November. Call TicketMaster on 212-307 7171.

FOOTBALL

The two teams are the New York Giants and the New York Jets, who both play at the Giants Stadium at Meadowlands, New Jersey (get there on a bus from the Port Authority bus terminal at 42nd Street and 8th Avenue). The box office is 201-935 3900 and you'll have more luck

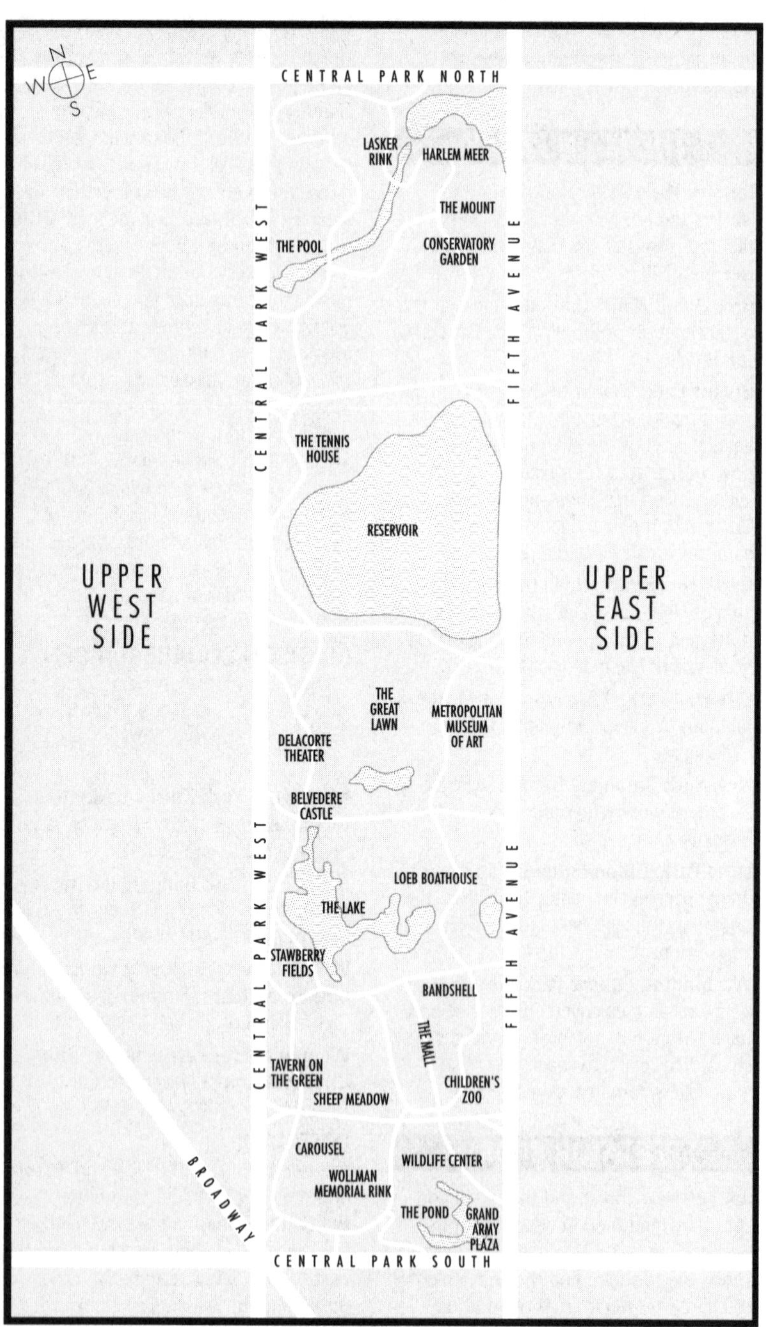

Central Park

getting tickets for the Jets than the Giants. The season runs from September to January.

For a schedule of forthcoming games in all the sports listed, check out the website: www.sportserver.com

BASEBALL

Try the Yankee Stadium (see page 218) in the Bronx at 161st Street (take subways C, D or 4 to 161st Street/Yankee Stadium). The box office number is 718-293 6000.

The New York Mets play at Shea Stadium in Flushing Meadows, Queens (take the 7 line from 42nd Street/Times Square to Willetts Point/Shea Stadium). The box office is 718-507 8499. The season for both is from April to October.

TENNIS

The US Open is held every year at the US Tennis Center in Flushing Meadows, Queens (take subway 7 to Willetts Point/Shea Stadium), from late August to early September. Tele-Charge on 212-239 6250. Tickets for the finals are impossible to get, so go for the earlier rounds.

HORSE RACING

This takes place at Aqueduct Stadium in Queens (take subway A to Aqueduct Racetrack) from mid-October to May, every Wednesday to Saturday. Call 718-641 4700 for information. Also at the Belmont Racetrack (take the Long Island Rail Road's 'Belmont Special' from Pennsylvania Station at 7th Avenue and 34th Street) from May to July.

GET STUCK IN

If you want to take part in some kind of sporting activity while in New York, your best bet is Central Park. Probably the most popular sports here are boating, biking, in-line skating and running.

BIKING

You can rent bikes from the Loeb Boathouse, Central Park, near 5th Avenue and East 74th Street. Tel 212-517 4723. Try tackling the 11-km (7-mile) road loop that is closed to traffic at the weekend. \$20–30 per hour, \$100 deposit.

BOATING

Also from the Loeb Boathouse, you can rent a rowing boat or even a chauffered gondola. \$10 per half hour, \$30 deposit.

IN-LINE SKATING

The Wollman Memorial Rink at the southern end of Central Park is a good place to start, though the more experienced prefer to tackle the 11-km (7-mile) road loop. You can hire skates from Blades at 160 East 86th Street between Lexington and 3rd Avenues (tel 212-996 1644) or 120 West 72nd Street between Broadway and Columbus Avenues (tel 212-787 3911) for \$20 per day plus \$200 deposit without a credit card payment.

RUNNING

Joggers go running in Central Park or Riverside Park on the west side of Manhattan.

A really great way of finding out more about Central Park's history and modern-day uses is by taking the Big Onion walking tour. See page 76 for details.

CHAPTER 12

Festivals and Parades

There are all sorts of special events going on in New York throughout the year, so once you have decided when to go, you'll want to know what's on while you're there so you don't miss out on any of the fun. Happily, New Yorkers like nothing better than a celebration – whether it be for the changing of the seasons, their roots or the arts. They clog up the streets for hours on end but they provide truly spectacular entertainment for the crowds every year. And what's more, apart from the food and drink you choose to imbibe, they're all free!

EVENTS

JANUARY AND FEBRUARY

Winter Antiques Show: 7th Regiment Armory, Park Avenue at 67th Street. Tel 718-292 7392. Mid-January. If you're on a cheapie winter break to New York you'll be rewarded with one of the biggest and best antiques fairs in the world. Here you'll find everything from the very old to art nouveau plus vast collections from all over America.

Chinese New Year Parade: Chinatown at Mott Street. Phone 212-481 1222 for information. Held on the first day of the full moon between January 21 and February 19. Although private fireworks have been banned, there are still plenty of firecrackers and dragons to dazzle onlookers in this stylish Chinese festival. Go to watch, eat, drink and be merry.

Black History Month: See the newspapers and guides for cultural events, concerts and lectures scheduled around the city during the month of February.

AMERICAN HOLIDAYS

New Year's Day: January 1
Martin Luther King Jnr Day: Third Monday in January
Presidents' Day: Third Monday in February
Memorial Day: Last Monday in May
Independence Day: July 4
Labor Day: First Monday in September
Columbus Day: Second Monday in October
Election Day: First Tuesday **after** the first Monday in November
Veterans' Day: November 11
Thanksgiving: Fourth Thursday in November
Christmas Day: December 25

Grammy Awards: The Oscars of the world of TV now take place in Madison Square Garden. You won't get in but if you'd like a gawk at the stars as they arrive in their limos, why not join the crowd? Late February. Call MSG on 212-465 6741 for information.

MARCH AND APRIL

Whitney Biennial: Whitney Museum of American Art (see page 110), 945 Madison Avenue at 75th Street. Tel 212-570 3600. Held every two years (funnily enough!), the Whitney's line-up of what it

Pick up a copy of the *Free Time* newspaper for information about free concerts, cinema showings and street fairs.

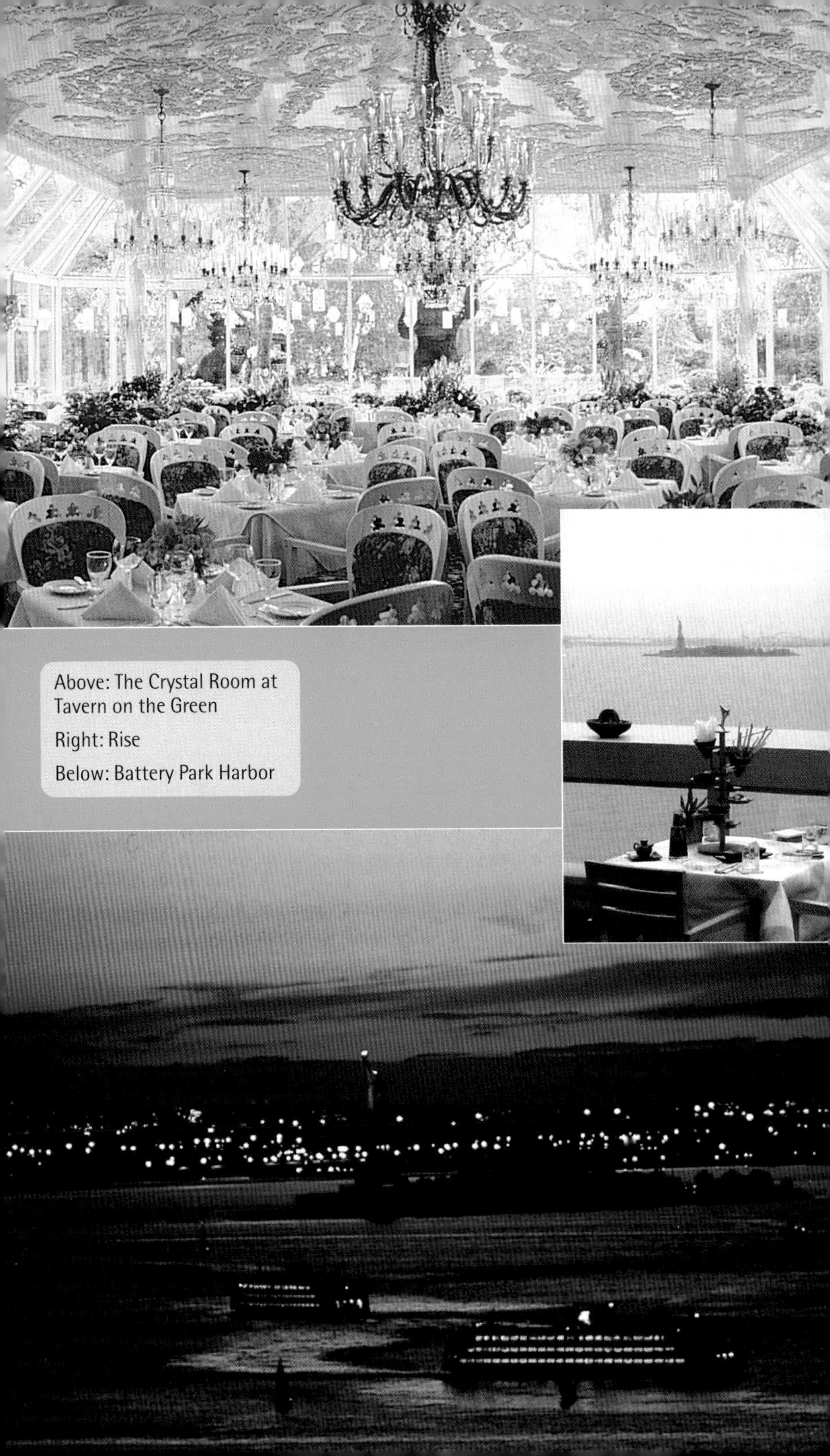

Above: The Crystal Room at Tavern on the Green

Right: Rise

Below: Battery Park Harbor

Above: Niagara Falls
Below: Flushing Town Hall
Bottom left: Madison Square Garden
Left: US Tennis Open

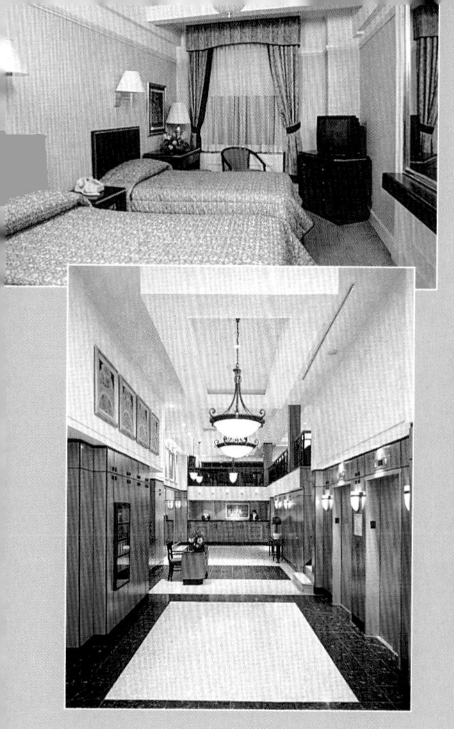

Top left: Wellington Hotel

Top right and above right: SoHo Grand

Below right: Ritz Carlton

Below: Le Parker Meridien

Above left: Apple Core Hotel

Above left: Waldorf Astoria
Above: Carlton Hotel
Above right: Holiday Inn
Left: Best Western Manhattan
Below right: Marriott Marquis

Wrap 9: Lower East Side Tenement Museum (Carol Highsmith), The Frick Collection, Brooklyn Museum of Art. Wrap 10: Nasdaq. Wrap 11: *The Lion King* and *Rent* (Joan Marcus). Wrap 12: Russian Tea Room, Europe Grill (Philippe Dollo), Zoe, 21 Club. Wrap 13: Tavern on the Green, Ritz Carlton. Wrap 14: Niagara Falls Convention and Visitors' Bureau. Wrap 15: Wellington Hotel Hospitality Apartments, SoHo Grand, Le Parker Meridien, Apple Core Hotel (Nancy Friedman PR), Ritz Carlton. Wrap 16: Waldorf-Astoria, Carlton Hotel (Nancy Friedman PR), Holiday Inn, Best Western Manhattan. Other photographs provided by NYC & Co. For further information call 010 7437 8300.

considers to be the most important art around is as controversial as our British equivalent of a sheep suspended in a glass cabinet. The next show is due to be held in late March to June of 2004.

St Patrick's Day Parade: 5th Avenue between 44th and 86th Streets. One of the bigger parades the city has to offer, this takes place on March 17. If you're in town, you won't be able to miss the sea of green that goes with this annual Irish-American day. Starting time is at 11am for the parade up 5th Avenue and the festivities go on late into the night.

Greek Independence Day Parade: Along 5th Avenue from 49th to 59th Streets on March 25. This one's a Zorba-style parade with plenty of Greek food, music and dancing.

Cirque du Soleil: Every other year in spring (more or less), this wonderful Canadian animal-free circus hitches up its tent in Battery Park to the delight of all. The next one is in 2003. Call 800-678 5440 for information.

Easter Parade: 5th Avenue between 44th and 59th Streets. Annually on Easter Sunday. The steps of St Patrick's Cathedral are generally considered to be the most advantageous viewing spot – so they're very popular. Kick-off is at 11am, so arrive early to bag a space.

New York City Ballet Spring Season: New York State Theater, 20 Lincoln Center Plaza, 65th Street at Columbus Avenue. Tel 212-870 5570. Late April to June. I have to admit I'm a ballet nut, and when away from London, I can think of nowhere better than the New York City Ballet to see some of the world's top dancers, who have made a name for themselves as masters of classics by Balanchine and Robbins.

MAY AND JUNE

See also Cirque du Soleil, New York City Ballet and Whitney Biennial (above).

TriBeCa Film Festival: TriBeCa area, second week in May. Tel 212-941 3977, **www.tribecafilm.com**. Founded by Robert de Niro and Jane Rosenthal, this new film festival showcases independent movies, runs workshops and has a children's film programme. During the week, local restaurants offer cut-price meals.

Ninth Avenue International Food Festival: 9th Avenue between 37th and 57th Streets, mid-May. Hungry? Then get on down to 9th where hundreds of stalls line the streets selling every type of food imaginable. Go for lunch and then walk it all off by strolling on down to Chelsea's fabulous art galleries.

Fleet Week: *Intrepid* Sea-Air-Space Museum (see page 100), Pier 86, 46th Street at the Hudson River. Unless you're a boat nut, it's normally not worth visiting the huge armada of US Navy and other ships that visit New York, but if you're here in the last week in May, it'll be hard to miss their presence.

Washington Square Art Exhibition: An old and revered Greenwich Village event which happens on the last two weekends in May and the first two weekends in September. A huge, outdoor art show with easels and food trolleys set up in the streets all around the park.

Lower East Side Festival of Arts: Theater for the New City, 155 1st Avenue at 10th Street. Tel 212-245 1109. Last weekend in May. Deep in the heart of the neighbourhood that helped create the East Coast Beat movement, method acting and pop art, this is an annual arts festival and outdoor carnival.

Puerto Rico Day Parade: 5th Avenue between 44th and 86th Streets. First Sunday in June. You'll get a real flavour of a big New York parade thanks to the floats, colour and noise of this display.

Mermaid Parade: 8th Street between Steeplechase Park and Broadway, Coney Island, Brooklyn. Call 718-372 5159 for information. Catch the B, D or F trains to Stillwell Avenue on the Saturday following the first official day of summer (late June) to sample a taste of real New

York life. It'll be a fishy business, but well worth it!

New York Jazz Festival: Various clubs in early June. Call 212-219 3006 for information. Even those of us who are not true aficionados of jazz can enjoy the festival atmosphere of the 300 acts that take part in this event.

Gay and Lesbian Pride Parade: From Columbus Circle along 5th Avenue to Christopher Street in Greenwich Village. Last Sunday in June. Call 212-807 7433 for information on the week-long events. The Stonewall Riots of 1969, when New York's gay community fought for public acceptance, are now celebrated in an annual street parade that gives way to a full week of events including a packed club schedule and an open-air dance party on the West Side piers.

Thursday Night Concert Series: Main Stage, South Street Seaport, South Street at Fulton Street. Tel 212-732 7678. From the last Monday in May (Memorial Day) to the first Monday in September (Labor Day). Enjoy all types of music – free!

Museum Mile Festival: 5th Avenue between 82nd and 104th Streets. Call 212-606 2296 for information. Museum Mile is neither a museum nor a mile, but a series of museums stretching out along 5th Avenue and Central Park on the Upper East Side. All are worth a visit and on the second Tuesday in June you can get into nine museums, including the fabulous Metropolitan, for free, as part of the open-house festival. An added perk is the fascinating street entertainment.

Central Park SummerStage: Rumsey Playfield, Central Park at 72nd Street, June to August. Tel 212-360 2777. You can experience many kinds of entertainment for free in New York and some of the best are the free weekend afternoon concerts put on by the SummerStage, featuring top international performers. On weekday nights there are also dance and spoken-word events.

Metropolitan Opera Parks Concerts: Various sites in June, phone 212-362 6000 for information. If you can't afford to see the Metropolitan Opera at The Met, take advantage of their free open-air concerts in Central Park and other locations. But, be warned, they're popular events so you'll have to arrive very early.

New York Shakespeare Festival: Delacorte Theater, Central Park at 81st Street. Tel 212-539 8750. Late June to late August. See how top American actors do the Bard – for free. There are two plays each year – one Shakespeare and one American.

Bryant Park Free Summer Season: 6th Avenue at 42nd Street. Tel 212-922 9393. Bryant Park is one of the few green spaces available in the Midtown area, and between June and August things get even better when there is a series of free classical music, jazz, dance and film showings during the day and evening.

Summergarden: Museum of Modern Art, 11 West 53rd Street between 5th and 6th Avenues. Tel 212-708 9400. An added bonus to visiting the little gem that is MoMA is the series of free classical concerts that are presented in the museum's garden between July and August each year.

Celebrate Brooklyn! Performing Arts Festival: Prospect Park Bandshell, 9th Street at Prospect Park West, Park Slope, Brooklyn. Tel 718-855 7882. Here's a very good reason to break out of Manhattan and visit one of the outer boroughs – a series of free music, dance, theatre and film events that lasts a full nine weeks.

If you're going to be out for the day enjoying a festival in the heat of the summer, make sure you have water, sun cream and a hat.

JULY AND AUGUST

See also Thursday Night Concert Series, Central Park SummerStage and New York Shakespeare Festival, Bryant Park Free Summer Season, Summergarden and Celebrate Brooklyn! Performing Arts Festival (all opposite).

Lincoln Center Festival: For the whole of July and August, a veritable feast of dance, drama, ballet, children's shows and multimedia and performance art, involving both repertory companies and special guests at venues inside and outside at the Lincoln Center (see page 136). For information, call 212-875 5400.

Fourth of July: The Americans still insist on celebrating achieving independence from their colonial masters, but at least they do it in style! Throughout New York there are various celebrations going on, but by far the biggest is Macy's Fireworks Display, which is held on the East River between 14th and 51st Streets. A good viewing spot is from the FDR Drive, where you'll see a $1-million firework extravaganza. Another fireworks display is held at South Street Seaport.

Harlem Week: Between West 125th and West 135th Streets. Tel 212-862 8477. Early to mid-August. The largest black and Hispanic festival in the world, its highlight is the street party with R&B, gospel and all that jazz. In addition to the music, there are films, dance, fashion, sports and exhibitions. What a great way to experience Harlem.

Parades are great fun, but they are also peak times for pickpockets, so keep your bags and wallets close to you at all times - and never put your wallet in your back pocket.

SEPTEMBER AND OCTOBER

See also Thursday Night Concert Series (above).

West Indian Day Carnival: Eastern Parkway from Utica Avenue to Grand Army Plaza, Brooklyn. Tel 718-625 1515. First weekend in September. Fabulous festival celebrating Caribbean culture. Brightly costumed marchers put on a special children's parade on the Saturday, with an even bigger event on Labor Day (first Monday in September).

Feast of San Gennaro: Mulberry Street to Worth Street in Little Italy. Tel 212-484 1222. Third week in September. Really the best time to see what is left of the once-bustling Little Italy that is now reduced to one street - Mulberry. There are lots of fairground booths, plenty of food and even more vino.

Columbus Day Parade: 5th Avenue between 44th and 86th Streets. Second Monday in October. The traditional celebration of the first recorded sighting of America by Europeans is now somewhat controversial in some quarters but, despite its lack of political correctness, Columbus Day still gets the big 5th Avenue parade treatment, which is well worth a view.

Culture Fest: Bryant Park. 3rd weekend in October. Tel 212-484 1222 or go to **www.nycvisit.com** and type CultureFest into the search space. A wonderful, completely free exhibition and live performance event which showcases all aspects of New York culture.

Hallowe'en Parade: 6th Avenue between Union Square and Spring Street, Greenwich Village. Tel 212-475 3333, ext 7787. October 31, 7pm. Although a recent addition to its plethora of parades, New York's latest is also one of the best, thanks to the outlandishly over-the-top costumes of many of its participants. The organisers decree a different theme each year and a lot of work goes into the amazing outfits that range from the exotic to the nearly non-existent. It attracts between 60,000 and 100,000 ghouls, ghosts and onlookers.

New York City Marathon: Starts at the Staten Island side of the Verrazano Narrows Bridge as a mad pack of 35,000 men and women run 42km (26.2 miles) around all five boroughs, to finish at the Tavern on the Green in Central Park at West 67th Street. Last Sunday in October/first Sunday in November. If you want to enter the marathon you need to fill out an application form, pay a small fee, and then wait to see if you get picked. Contact the New York Road Runners Club at **www.nycmarathon.msn.com** or by e-mail via **www.nyrrcc.org** or write to New York City Marathon, International Lottery, 9 East 89th Street, New York, NY 10128, or call 212-860 4455.

NOVEMBER AND DECEMBER

See also New York City Marathon (above).

Macy's Thanksgiving Day Parade: From Central Park West at 79th Street to Macy's (see page 81) on Broadway at 34th Street. Tel 212-494 4495. Thanksgiving Day at 9am. Definitely one for the family, this is the Big Mama of all New York's parades, with enormous inflated cartoon characters, fabulous floats and the gift-giving Santa Claus himself. It is even televised for the rest of America. If you miss the parade, you can go to see Santa at Santaland in Macy's until Christmas.

Christmas Tree Lighting Ceremony: 5th Avenue between 49th and 50th Streets. Tel 212-484 1222. Early December. The Rockefeller Center (see page 61) in front of the towering RCA building provides the magical setting for the switching-on of nearly 8km (5 miles) of lights on the huge tree.

New Year's Eve Fireworks: 5th Avenue and 90th Street or Bethsheda Fountain (Central Park at 72nd Street) are the best viewing spots. The hot apple cider and spirit of camaraderie begin at 11.30pm.

New Year's Eve Ball Drop: Times Square (see pages 47–9). This event is a real New York classic, though you may prefer to watch safely on TV rather than be packed in with the freezing masses. Remember, Times Square is a misnomer – it's a junction, so there isn't really that much room and all the side streets get packed too. If you do manage to get a good spot, though, you'll see the giant glitterball of 180 bulbs and 12,000 rhinestones being dropped to bring in the New Year.

CHAPTER 13

Walking Tours of Manhattan

Everybody in New York walks. This is particularly true in Manhattan. Even if you had a car, it would probably be clamped, ticketed or towed, and anyway you wouldn't get to see nearly as much. As *A Brit's Guide* reader, you don't just want to join those aimlessly milling around Midtown when the whole of Manhattan is packed with shopping, culture, dining and sightseeing. So, put on some comfortable shoes and follow us.

We at NYTAB, the New York Travel Advisory Bureau, are expert at preparing itineraries for top journalists who have not a minute to waste. We've designed the following tours especially for you. They cover different areas and interests, from hip shopping on the Lower East Side to off-the-beaten-track sightseeing. They include the really important must-sees and some true insider secrets. Each itinerary helps you get to know a manageable chunk of the city and should take three to four hours to complete. To really get the most out of the tours, read Chapter 3, The New York Neighbourhoods, first. And bear in mind that detailed information about the following sights, museums, shops and attractions are given in the relevant chapters.

You'll notice the first two tours concentrate on downtown New York, the historic and financial centre of the city. In spite of the events of September 11, 2001, this area is again a place to visit. We in no way wish to minimise the tragedy that occurred that day, but we urge you not to ignore this part of town. Instead, take advantage of its beautiful parks, good shopping, interesting museums, great restaurants and world-class hotels. Workers and residents alike will welcome you.

1 HISTORICAL DOWNTOWN

New York has always been America's principal gateway for new arrivals. For much of the city's history Downtown was New York. This is where Washington was sworn in as the first president, where Congress first sat and where new states were carved out to add to the 13 born of the original 13 colonies

At the foot of the island was the finest port on the Atlantic, and into it flowed the goods and people that fuelled the expansion of the city. The rush of trading and dealing that built New York has since been masked by smooth skyscrapers. But there are still tall ships and cobblestones, gaslights and ancient churches, side by side with the great banks and financial institutions that now affect commerce around the world. This tour offers glimpses of the way things were, glimpses of the way things are, and glimpses into the human condition: stunning vistas, memorable museums, historical landmarks.

If you're in the mood for a detour, find Coenties Slip and wander up pretty cobbled Stone Street for a sense of old New York charm.

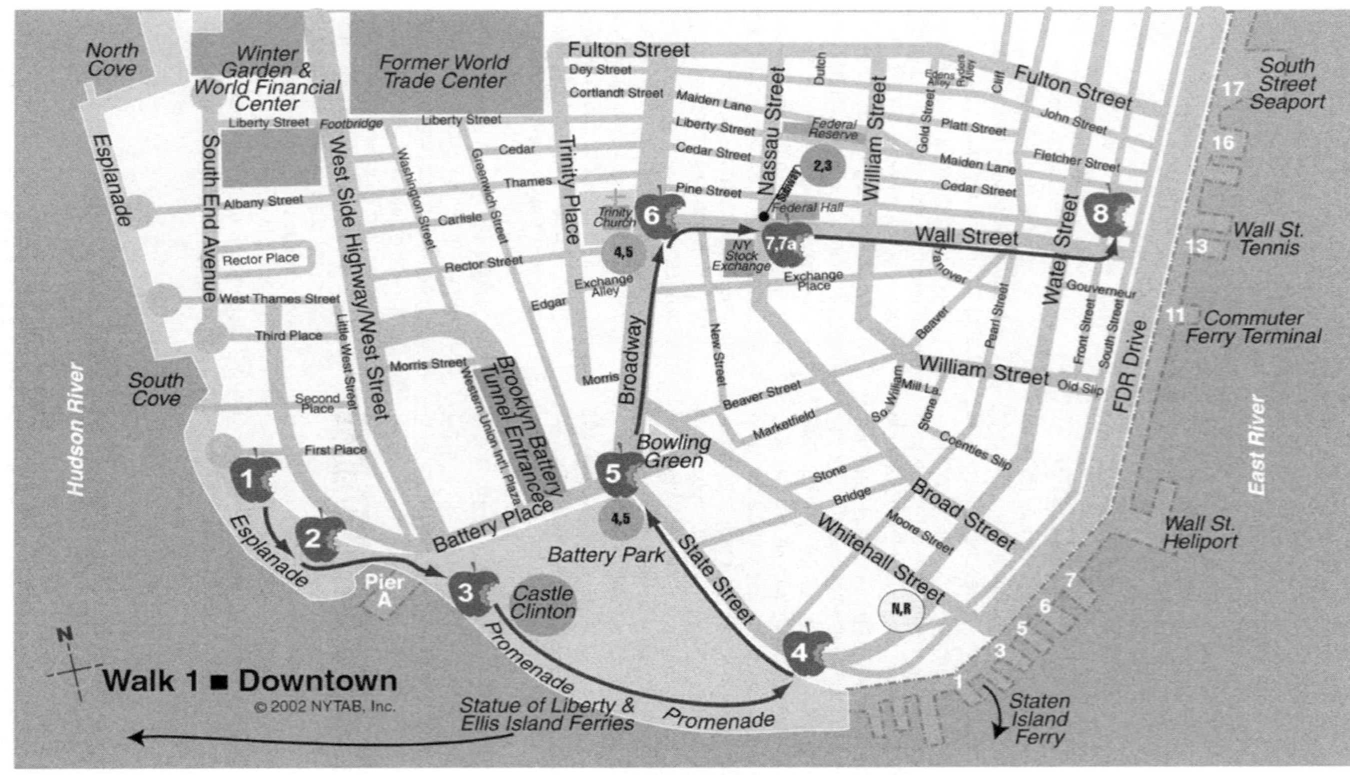

Walk 1 ■ Downtown
© 2002 NYTAB, Inc.
Hudson River
East River
North Cove
South Cove
Esplanade
South End Avenue
Winter Garden & World Financial Center
Former World Trade Center
West Side Highway/West Street
Liberty Street
Footbridge
Rector Place
Albany Street
West Thames Street
Third Place
Second Place
First Place
Little West Street
Pier A
Battery Place
Brooklyn Battery Tunnel Entrance
Western Union Intl. Plaza
Morris Street
Washington Street
Carlisle
Rector Street
Greenwich Street
Thames
Cedar
Edgar
Trinity Place
Exchange Alley
Trinity Church
Morris
Castle Clinton
Battery Park
Promenade
Statue of Liberty & Ellis Island Ferries
Bowling Green
Broadway
State Street
Fulton Street
Dey Street
Cortlandt Street
Maiden Lane
Liberty Street
Cedar Street
Pine Street
New Street
Beaver Street
Marketfield
NY Stock Exchange
Nassau Street
Subway
Federal Hall
Federal Reserve
Dutch
Exchange Place
William Street
Gold Street
Edens Alley
Ryders Alley
Platt Street
John Street
Maiden Lane
Fletcher Street
Cedar Street
Cliff
Wall Street
Whitehall Street
Broad Street
Moore Street
Bridge
Stone
So. William
Mill La.
Stone
Coenties Slip
Hanover
Beaver
William Street
Pearl Street
Water Street
Front Street
South Street
Old Slip
Gouverneur
Fulton Street
FDR Drive
Staten Island Ferry
Wall St. Heliport
Commuter Ferry Terminal
Wall St. Tennis
South Street Seaport

1 MUSEUM OF JEWISH HERITAGE

18 First Place at Battery Place. Tel 212-968 1800. Discount with your Nycard. This hexagonal building (think Star of David) with a tiered roof is one of New York's newest and perhaps most worthwhile cultural attractions. The museum shows a darker shade of the human condition (spot the snakes and ladders-like children's board game called 'Jews Out!') but, as you reach the top floor and a stunning panoramic view of the Statue of Liberty, the message goes beyond regret and sect to hope and the possibility of renewal (see page 100).

2 GIGINO AT WAGNER PARK

20 Battery Place at Hudson River. Tel 212-528 2228. (see page 111)
When leaving the museum, walk into the park towards the river. Just a little further south is a sculptural viewing platform. Beneath it is this small Italian restaurant, complete with a takeaway concession. So whatever the weather, grab a steaming coffee or an iced drink and linger awhile. While you absorb the wonderful view of the harbour, the Statue of Liberty and the broad expanse of the Hudson over to the Jersey shore, children will have great fun clambering all over the cleverly designed platform.

3 BATTERY PARK PROMENADE

Continue down the esplanade, past the old firehouse at Pier A and into Battery Park. You are now at the very tip of Manhattan. As you stroll along the promenade with the harbour to your right, you'll pass the red sandstone Castle Clinton on your left which, before landfill, was 91m (100yd) offshore. Though it never saw military action, it found use as an entertainment hall, then as an immigration centre (before Ellis Island) and later became the New York Aquarium. As you face south across the water, Governor's Island is to your left, directly ahead is Staten Island (you'll almost certainly see the famous yellow Staten Island ferry coming or going). Further to your right is the Statue of Liberty, just west of that is Ellis Island, and to your hard right is New Jersey (see page 31).

The queues for the Statue of Liberty and the Ellis Island Immigration Museum can be enormous (see page 58). All harbour cruises stop for photo ops at the foot of the large green lady – and the Lower East Side Tenement Museum (see Lower East Side: Walk 3) offers an excellent look at the immigration story.

4 NUMBERS 7 AND 17 STATE STREET

What a contrast! The sleek, curved blue-mirrored skyscraper at 17 State Street towers over the last of New York's first wave of mansions. No 7 State Street, the Watson House, is now known as the Rectory of the Shrine of St Elizabeth Ann Bayley Seton, the first American saint. The columns along the house's bowed front are said to have been carved from the masts of ships.

5 NATIONAL MUSEUM OF THE AMERICAN INDIAN

Smithsonian Institution, 1 Bowling Green. Tel 212-668 6624. Free admission (see page 107).
Before you, came the immigrants; before the immigrants, came the traders; before the traders, were the Indians. Find out about them here. The museum is located in the former Customs House, one of New York's grandest Beaux-Arts buildings. The statues on the outside depicting Asia, America, Europe and still-sleeping Africa, are by sculptor Daniel Chester French, whose mammoth statue of President Lincoln in Washington, DC you've seen a thousand times.

The handkerchief-size Bowling Green in front of the Museum of the American Indian is the oldest public park in Manhattan. Blink and you'll miss it!

6 TRINITY CHURCH

Broadway and Rector Street. Tel: 212-602 0872.

The ghost of Alexander Hamilton, America's first Secretary of the Treasury, shot in a duel by political rival Aaron Burr, is said to haunt the grounds of this 1681 churchyard. There's a tiny 'museum' inside and benches for summer musings. Sitting at the top of Wall Street, this is very much the Financial District's church. You'll even see it from the East River if you take a sightseeing cruise (see Walk 2).

7 FEDERAL HALL

26 Wall Street at Nassau Street. Entrance on Pine Street. Tel: 212-825 6888.

One block north of Federal Hall on Liberty Street is the Federal Reserve Bank of New York, definitely a banker's bank. It has more gold than Fort Knox – the reserves of approximately 80 foreign countries, stored five floors below ground.

7A NEW YORK STOCK EXCHANGE

20 Broad Street at Wall Street.
Tel: 212-656 3000.

If you're heading uptown now, there are express stops on subway 4, 5 (green line) right by Trinity Church which will take you to Grand Central Station in about 10 minutes. But first, take a few steps down Wall Street to see the Greek Revival solidity of Federal Hall (1842) opposite the stock exchange. This site has always served the city or the nation. George Washington was inaugurated as the first President in an earlier building on the same spot. At the time of writing the public is not allowed inside the stock exchange, but you still simply have to stroll by this home of bulls and bears, crashes, slumps and instant fortunes (see page 66).

8 KOODO SUSHI

129 Front Street between Pine and Wall Streets, lower level of Seaport Suites Hotel. Tel 212-425 2890. 10 per cent off dinner with your NYCard.

This is a pretty plain establishment, but local office workers have quickly discovered that the chef, Lok (known as Lucky), is a master of design and taste combination. Eat in or take away a selection of sushi down to the pier a block away to enjoy by the water. Because of its position near Wall Street, this restaurant is relatively unhurried at night. Lucky and Michelle, the maitre d', will not only spend time introducing you to all sorts of delicacies in the evening, they'll also take 10 per cent off your dinner bill. If you're a sushi lover, Lucky and Koodo Sushi are the places to go and a great deal less expensive than SoHo or Midtown Japanese (see page 112).

Make your trips to Downtown on a weekday. The world's most powerful financial centre has an extra hum about it during the working week.

2 DOWNTOWN SHOPPING AND SIGHTSEEING

This walk offers some of the best views to be had in New York, from the water's edge and from the harbour itself. You'll see some of the city's most impressive historic architecture, be able to shop at two of the city's best discount stores and you'll even find out how to get married.

1 CIRCLE LINE – THE BEAST SPEEDBOAT TOUR

Pier 16 at South Street Seaport. Tel 212-563 3200, May to October. Discount with your NYCard.

Start on Front Street and turn right on Fulton Street to Pier 16. The ticket office for Circle Line Cruises is directly in front of you. The best way of admiring the Manhattan skyline is from the water. You can always take the free Staten Island Ferry, but *The Beast* is less time-consuming (just 30 minutes) and zips you around the harbour at high, jet-lag-defeating speeds – great fun. New York harbour, by the way, is very clean (see page 71). Seahorses and even whales have been spotted here.

2 SOUTH STREET SEAPORT

Fulton and Front Streets. Tel 212-732 7678 for programme of free events.
South Street Seaport Museum
207 Front Street. Tel 212-748 8600.

Back on land there's some browsing to be done. There are shops, of course, and a clutch of bars and restaurants. You may find some of the shops a bit average, but others, like Ann Taylor for quality but well-priced women's clothing, and Brookstone's for high-tech gadgets, are well worth checking out. Both are located in the pretty former counting houses lining lower Fulton Street across from the pier. If you wander off the pier and the main Fulton Street pedestrian way, you'll find treasures on the cobbled side streets most tourists miss, like Pepper Jones on Beekman Street (café and gifts), and a few doors up, the authentic Carmine's restaurant (known for its lobster).

The museum has a good children's programme and interesting collections of artefacts in several locations around the seaport. And you can enjoy great views of the Brooklyn Bridge and downtown skyline through the rigging of one of the best collections of tall-masted historic ships anywhere (see page 110).

The new location for the TKTS kiosk is in the Pier 17 complex at the South Street Seaport. This is where you can get same-day half-price tickets for Broadway shows, as well as next-day tickets for matinees.

Stroll up Fulton Street past a branch of the famous Strand Bookstore which has a huge selection, often half price, including a good travel section. Further up, you'll cross Nassau Street. This is a pedestrian area during the day, and contains a mix of discount and speciality stores frequented by local office workers. When you reach Broadway, turn left, then right on Cortlandt Street. There's always a number of special events – free concerts, for example, or food tastings by local restaurants – and seasonal markets in the Downtown area. To find out what's on when, call South Street Seaport on 212-SEAPORT or World Financial Center on 212-945 0505.

3 CENTURY 21

22 Cortlandt Street between Broadway and Church Street. Tel 212-227 9092.

If discounts are your thing, you'll love one of New York's most famous discount department stores, with everything from designer fashions to household goods, so take time to explore all four floors.

Leave by the Dey Street entrance and turn right. Immediately to your left as you exit, is the 6.5-hectare (16-acre) recovery and construction site of the former World Trade Center (see page 58). Depending upon the works progress, where you're standing may be a good vantage point. So far, that progress has been astounding. Both Century 21 and St Paul's Chapel where you're going next, were remarkably undamaged though covered in a thick layer of dust.

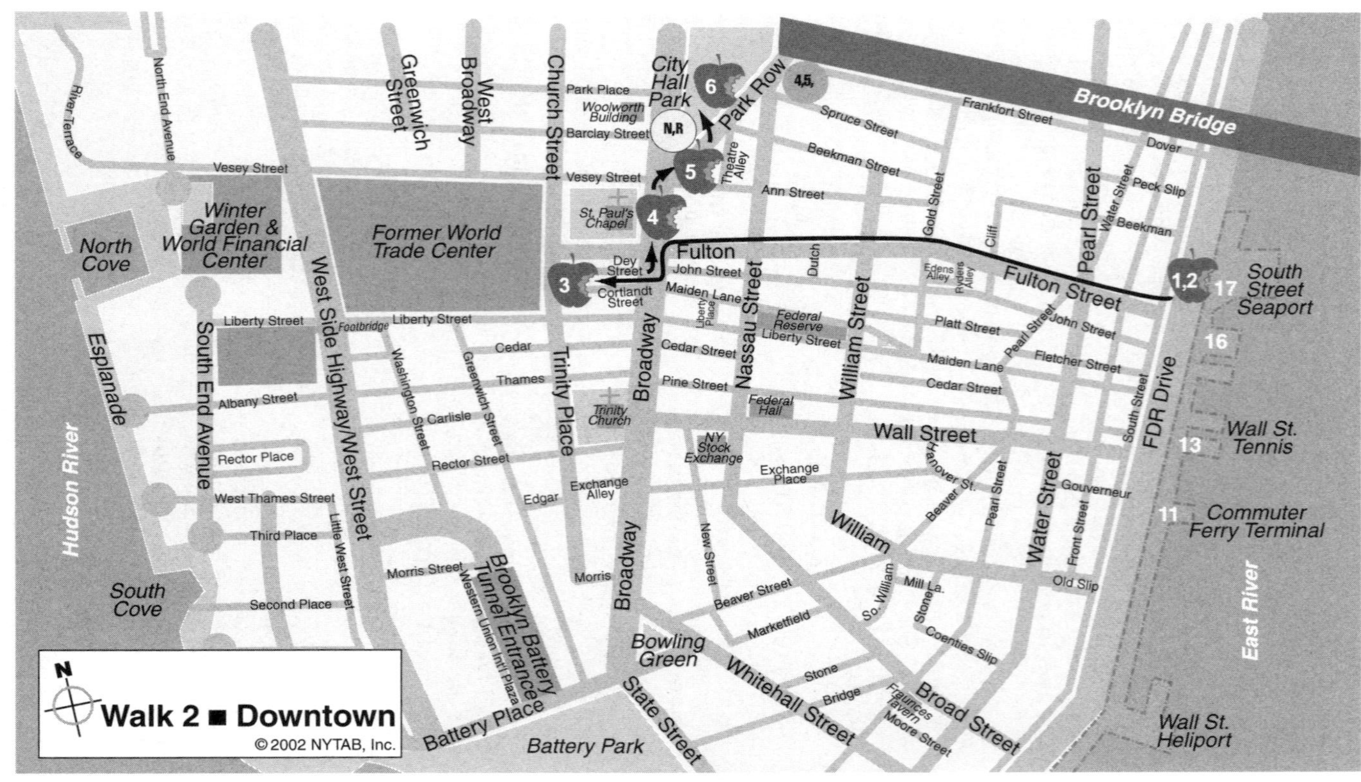
Walk 2 ■ Downtown
© 2002 NYTAB, Inc.
N
River Terrace
North End Avenue
Vesey Street
Winter Garden & World Financial Center
North Cove
Former World Trade Center
Greenwich Street
West Broadway
Church Street
Park Place
Woolworth Building
Barclay Street
Vesey Street
City Hall Park
N,R
Park Row
4,5,
Spruce Street
Frankfort Street
Brooklyn Bridge
Dover
Beekman Street
Theatre Alley
Ann Street
Gold Street
Cliff
Pearl Street
Water Street
Peck Slip
Beekman
St. Paul's Chapel
Fulton
Dey Street
John Street
Cortlandt Street
Maiden Lane
Dutch
Edens Alley
Ryders Alley
Fulton Street
South Street Seaport
1,2
17
16
Esplanade
South End Avenue
Liberty Street
Footbridge
Liberty Street
West Side Highway/West Street
Cedar
Thames
Trinity Place
Broadway
Liberty Place
Federal Reserve
Liberty Street
Nassau Street
William Street
Platt Street
Pearl Street
John Street
Cedar Street
Maiden Lane
Fletcher Street
Albany Street
Washington Street
Greenwich Street
Carlisle
Pine Street
Federal Hall
Cedar Street
Trinity Church
Wall Street
South Street
FDR Drive
Wall St. Tennis
13
Rector Place
Rector Street
NY Stock Exchange
Hanover St.
Exchange Place
Gouverneur
Hudson River
West Thames Street
Edgar
Exchange Alley
Beaver St.
Pearl Street
Water Street
Front Street
11
Commuter Ferry Terminal
Third Place
Little West Street
William
Morris Street
Brooklyn Battery Tunnel Entrance
Western Union Int'l Plaza
Morris
New Street
Broadway
Old Slip
South Cove
Second Place
Beaver Street
So. William
Mill La.
Stone
Marketfield
Coenties Slip
East River
Bowling Green
Stone
Whitehall Street
Bridge
Fraunces Tavern
Broad Street
Moore Street
Battery Place
Battery Park
State Street
Wall St. Heliport
3
4
5
6

4 ST PAUL'S CHAPEL

Broadway and Fulton Streets. Tel 212-602 0874.

Seem familiar? Possibly, as one of Manhattan's oldest buildings was modelled on St Martin-in-the-Fields in Trafalgar Square. Notice the presidential seal, the first ever, underneath which is George Washington's pew. He and all of Congress prayed here after the first presidential inauguration. Washington continued to attend services for the two years New York was the capital.

Spot the crown on the pulpit of St Paul's Chapel – very rare in a country that rejected monarchs.

5 J & R COMPUTER, MUSIC AND ELECTRONICS

Park Row between Ann and Beekman Streets. Tel 212-238 9100.

This is actually a series of stores, strung along Park Row in no particular order. It may take several tries until you find the right entrance for what you're looking for, but persevere. This is one of the city's best sources for software, manuals, electronic gizmos and what-nots. A pretty good music selection, too.

Men can stop for a haircut at Antonella Barbershop, 8 Beekman Street (between Park Row and Nassau Street), tel 212-233 1830. Antonella and her crew have trimmed many a mayoral mop, including Mayor Guiliani.

6 CITY HALL PARK

City Hall may appear smaller than it was in your imagination, but the park it sits in is pretty, whatever the season: the meticulously laid out flower beds and the startling dogwood trees in spring, the gushing fountain on a hot summer's day, and the pathways' gaslights on a winter evening. To the west, look up at FW Woolworth's 'cathedral of commerce', New York's tallest skyscraper once, and paid for in cash. Behind City Hall is the very grand Tweed Courthouse. Built in 1878 under the corrupt mayor 'Boss' Tweed, it took $14 million to get the job done with only about $4 million going towards the construction; the rest found its way into the pockets of greedy politicians and their cohorts. To the right is the huge wedding cake-topped Municipal Building – city offices. And talking of weddings, if you want to get married in New York, this is the place to come for a licence and then return 24 hours later for the civil ceremony.

3 LOWER EAST SIDE

Shoppers interested in cutting edge fashion, unique finds and great bargains will love this tour as much as those who want to explore the roots of America's immigration story.

Millions – from Italy, Ireland, Russia and points beyond – started their new lives in America on the Lower East Side in narrow, ill-lit, overcrowded tenement houses. Even today, some people wear their family's connection to the area like a badge, one that marks them out as having honourably arrived. This melting pot still simmers. Today, young, cutting edge fashion designers, artists and even restaurateurs are migrating here, bringing an edgy style to the mix of Jewish fabric and leather sellers, Asian luggage salesman and Hispanic bodega owners.

1 LOWER EAST SIDE TENEMENT MUSEUM

90 Orchard Street at Broome Street. Tel 212-431-0233. Discount with your NYCard.

This is a must-see for an understanding not only of this neighbourhood, which continues to function as a launching pad

The best days to visit the Lower East Side are Tuesday, Wednesday and Thursday. These are the days when everything in the area is open and at its bustle-y best.

for fresh generations of artists and retailers, but also for the 'American success story' (see page 98).

The houses are visited by guided tour only. Depending on the day, tours start between noon and 1pm, departing approximately every 30 to 40 minutes. They last about an hour. Reserve your place early in the day (starting at 11am) for the 3.20 or 4pm tour later in the day.

The rest of this itinerary (depending on how fast a shopper you are, what nose you have for your own discoveries and how long you linger over lunch) should take about two to three hours.

2 FORWARD

72 Orchard Street between Broome and Grand Streets. Tel 646-264 3233.
The Lower East Side is crammed with young designers. This narrow, brick-walled space shows off the works of a selection of brand new talent. Designers are shown for six months, before a new group is brought in. This is your chance to acquire something unique, to stock up now on the offerings of what might be tomorrow's big fashion name.

PLANNING TIP

Only 15 people at a time are able to go on the Tenement tour recommended in the Brit Tip. So begin this itinerary at about 11am when they begin accepting reservations in person for tours later the same day. Ask for one of the later times – you'll need at least a couple of hours for shopping and perhaps an hour for lunch in our lovely little restaurant suggestion on page 190.

3 BRIDGE 1

98 Orchard Street between Broome and Delancey Streets. Tel 212-979 9777.
The leather industry has been big business in this part of New York since 1680. Bridge 1 is the nicest of the many leather clothing stores that dot the neighbourhood.

If you're travelling with children, then choose a Saturday or Sunday to take the Tenement Museum's Confino Family tour. You'll be treated as newly arrived immigrants and allowed to try on period clothing.

4 ECONOMY CANDY

108 Rivington Street between Essex and Ludlow Streets. Tel 212-254 1531.
This shop will remind you of your childhood – or your dentist. A huge selection of sweets from many countries at low prices. This has been here since before the Second World War.

5 ALIFE RIVINGTON CLUB

158 Rivington Street between Clinton and Suffolk Streets. Tel 212-375 8128.
The athletic shoe as art? Then this is the gallery. The Alife Rivington has three doors. Choose the glass one to the right as you face the building and buzz to be let in. Don't be put off by the 'Members Only' doormat. Just admire the 50 or so examples of footware exotica, individually lit and displayed. Many limited edition designs are available in just a couple of locations in the whole world. If you have a 'trainer nerd' or a 'trainer freak' friend, this is how to make him truly green with envy. Prices start from a surprisingly affordable $55 and gallop on up to $800.

6 INTENSITY HEADQUARTERS

157 Rivington Street between Clinton and Suffolk Streets. Tel 212-995 2089.
The women's clothing here won't ever be

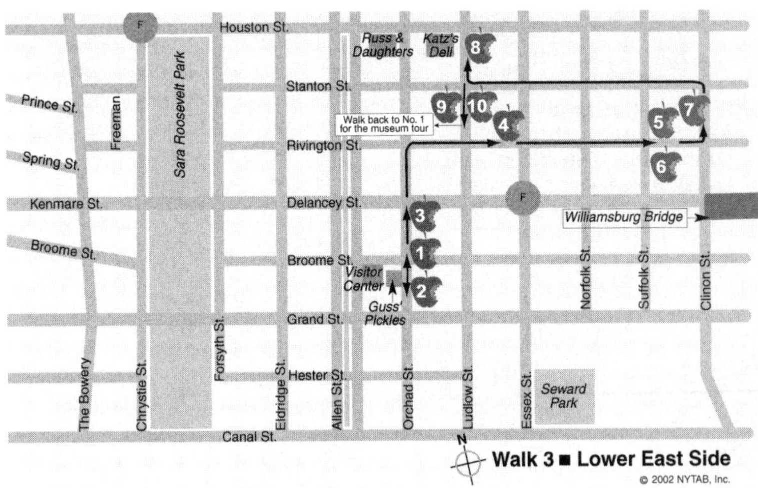

stuck in a single decade, thanks to the classic-with-a-twist approach of designer Intensity (yup, that's her name). You'll find interesting detailing and lots of organic materials like cotton, linen, and canvas in a collection that's cool enough to covet but not outrageous.

The Lower East Side Visitor Center has more leaflets than you can shake a stick at, and could be useful if you're trying to track down something we haven't mentioned: 261 Broome Street (between Orchard and Allen Streets). Tel 212-226 9010. Open 10am–4pm, closed Saturdays.

7 aKa

49 Clinton Street between Stanton and Rivington Streets. Tel 212-979 6096.
10 per cent discount with your NYCard.
You've been looking at things in windows all over town – now here's your chance to be the window display yourself. This one-time dress shop is now a very fashionable (but friendly) restaurant. Chef Scott Ehrlich mixes ingredients (many of them, like pickles and bialy rolls, from local suppliers) in ways that sound adventurous but always taste great (see page 113).

8 TG-170

170 Ludlow Street between Houston and Stanton Streets. Tel 212-995 8660.
This shop collects new designers. It was an early arrival to this area's women's fashion scene, and over the years, it's developed a nose for the hip.

9 KNOTS NYC

143 Ludlow Street between Stanton and Rivington Streets. Tel 212-673 2630.
This shop is doing very well. A bus will pull up outside and a crowd of Japanese will cram themselves into the small space and everyone will buy 10 of everything. Why? Because the labels, 68 & Brothers and Material, have not only achieved cult status in Japan, but sell there for 30 per cent more. It is the only one in America, so if you like what you see (T-shirts and jackets and more for men and women), join them here.

10 MARY ADAMS

138 Ludlow Street between Stanton and Rivington Streets. Tel 212-473-0237.
Closed Monday and Tuesday.
Dozens of regimented ribbons, corset-like bodices, gold-embroidered vests, bustles

If you want to create a picnic for your hotel room, then don't miss the delicious smoked salmon, caviar and whitefish salads available at Ross & Daughters at 179 Houston Street (tel 212-475 4880).

and flowing silks. All of Mary Adams' designs are dramatic and hint at a variety of romantic periods in history, from the Renaissance to the court of Louis XVI. All the pieces are fun to look at and wearable on the street or in the Rise Bar at the Ritz-Carlton Hotel.

1 LOWER EAST SIDE TENEMENT MUSEUM

Now, it's back here for the tour you reserved.

4 CHINATOWN and LITTLE ITALY

There are only a couple of streets left to give a flavour of what was once a huge Italian community. Perhaps the true Little Italy, certainly in terms of food, has moved to Arthur Avenue, between the New York Botanical Garden and the Zoo in the Bronx. Still, thousands of Italian Americans come here to point out to children the way things were. And there's still the street feast of San Gennaro offering Italian colour and nourishment in the third week of September.

As for Chinatown, it has grown immensely over the years and as it has grown it has diversified. Most original inhabitants were from Guangdong Province in China proper, however, many more recent arrivals have come from Chinese communities in Malaysia, Vietnam and elsewhere. The area is a riot of sensation. This is where you come for those truly fake gen-u-wyne brand-name luxury pens and watches, for some of the tastiest and cheapest food, for silk-slipper bargains and world-class tat, for karaoke bars with laser disc screens, for street hawkers and art shops, plumbing goods stores and all manner of mysterious Eastern goods!

1 PEARL RIVER MART

277 Canal Street at Broadway, 2nd and 3rd Floors. Tel 212-431 4770.

Start at the corner of Broadway and Canal. All of the hustle and bustle of the streets makes this intersection one of Manhattan's busiest. Everybody is buying and selling, delivering and collecting. Join in with a short climb upstairs to this, Chinatown's version of the department store.

2 KAM MAN

200 Canal Street (between Mulberry and Mott Streets). Tel 212- 571 0300.

Walk east along Canal Street, but take your time. There are so many things to seduce your attention, from 'Gucci' watches and wind-up toys to porcelain and luggage. Both kids and adults will find the sights, sounds and smells fascinating.

Kam Man is one of the most comprehensive of Chinatown's umpteen million grocery stores. They speak very little English here, so you'll have a hard time identifying a good portion of what you see. And you'll see a lot, all crazily juxtaposed, from Ovaltine to ginger jars.

2003 is the Year of the Goat. Head for Chinatown on February 1 and join in the New Year celebrations.

3 AJI ICHIBAN

37 Mott Street at Pell Street. Tel 212-233 7650.

A sweet shop, oriental style. Hugely colourful and what a choice – sugar-coated crab anyone?

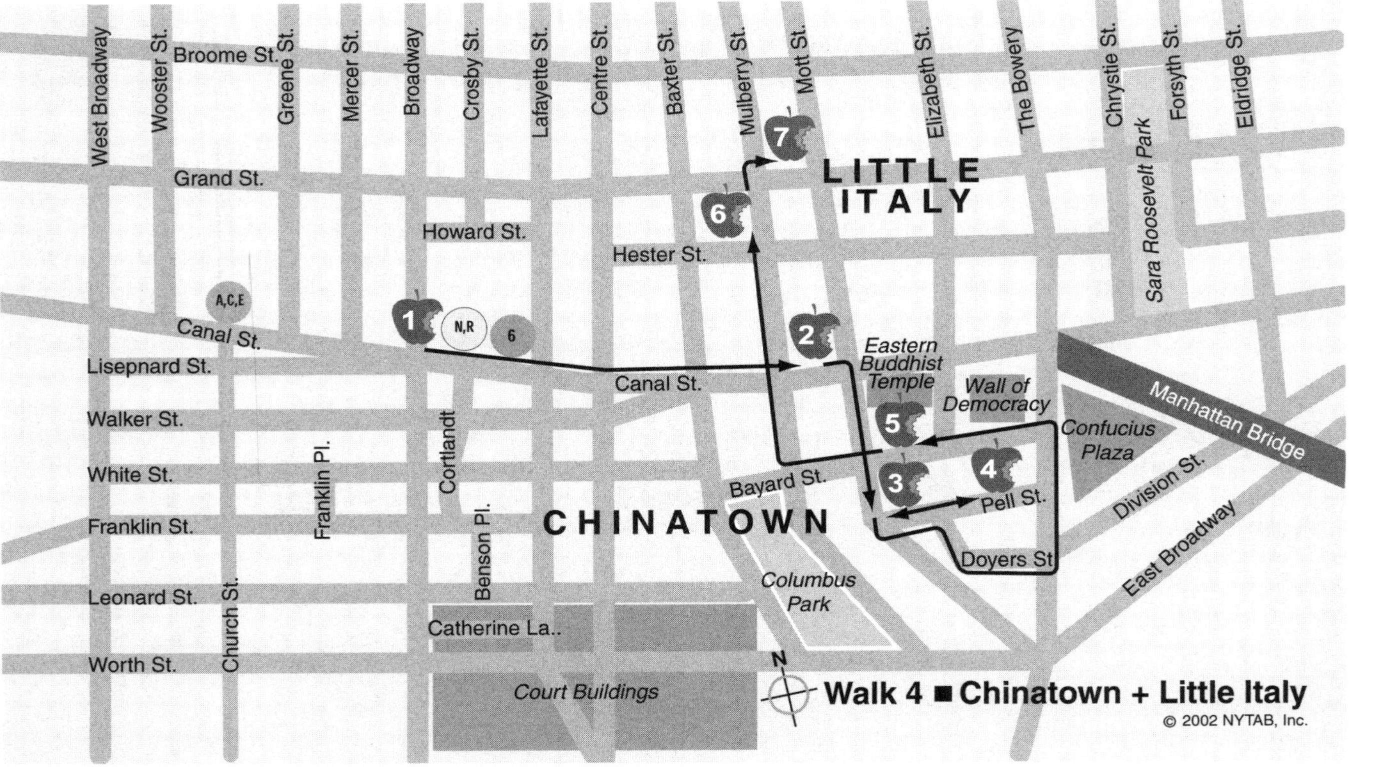
Walk 4 ■ Chinatown + Little Italy
© 2002 NYTAB, Inc.
West Broadway
Wooster St.
Broome St.
Greene St.
Mercer St.
Broadway
Crosby St.
Lafayette St.
Centre St.
Baxter St.
Mulberry St.
Mott St.
Elizabeth St.
The Bowery
Chrystie St.
Forsyth St.
Eldridge St.
Sara Roosevelt Park
Grand St.
LITTLE ITALY
Howard St.
Hester St.
A,C,E
Canal St.
N,R
6
Lisepnard St.
Canal St.
Eastern Buddhist Temple
Wall of Democracy
Manhattan Bridge
Walker St.
Confucius Plaza
White St.
Franklin Pl.
Cortlandt
Bayard St.
Pell St.
Division St.
Franklin St.
Benson Pl.
CHINATOWN
East Broadway
Doyers St
Leonard St.
Columbus Park
Catherine La..
Church St.
Worth St.
N
Court Buildings
1
2
3
4
5
6
7

4 JOE'S SHANGHAI

9 Pell Street (between Doyers Street and Bowery). Tel 212-233 8888.
It's impossible to walk through Chinatown without feeling hungry. We're not the only ones who think the dumplings here are delicious, so it's a good idea to come at off-peak times to avoid the queues. Just be careful, the dumplings are very hot inside (see page 113).

Backtrack along Pell Street and turn left on to Doyers Street. These two streets mark the boundaries of the original Chinatown. They are today among the most picturesque streets in the area and as you look around it's easy to feel you've been transported to an entirely different cultural planet.

Walk all the way along Doyers Street, then turn left on to the Bowery, passing Confucius Plaza (spot his statue). Turn left on to Bayard Street past the Wall of Democracy where you can theoretically keep up with the latest developments in, or criticisms of, Beijing – if you can read Chinese!

5 CHINATOWN ICE CREAM FACTORY

65 Bayard Street between Mott and Elizabeth Streets. Tel 212-608 4170.
Pop your head in and check out the flavours. It may look a little shabby, but this place supplies most of the city's Japanese restaurants with green tea ice cream and other exotic flavours.

Follow Bayard Street to Mulberry Street and turn right. As you head north, China magically transforms into Italy.

6 FORZANO ITALIAN IMPORTS

128 Mulberry Street at Hester Street. Tel 212-925 2525.
Maybe you didn't come to New York for a picture of the Pope or an espresso machine – or maybe you did!

7 FERRARA PASTRIES & CAFÉ

195 Grand Street between Mulberry and Mott Streets. Tel 212-226 6150.
Little Italy is a bit of an artefact, and is now contained in just a few blocks around Mulberry Street. This pastry shop is one of the oldest in the country. It's a great place to rest at the end of your walk. There are handy loos upstairs and you'll enjoy trying their world-famous nougat and biscotti, which they send all over the world.

5 SOHO

The following two walks take you through arguably the most stylish area in Manhattan. You can do the two walks as one, or treat them as separate mini-tours.

SoHo stands for South of Houston Street. Its huge cast-iron lofts were earmarked for demolition in the 1960s. They were saved by the protests of artists who had discovered the buildings' big spaces and low rents. The use of cast iron (first developed in Britain) for buildings was a huge innovation, allowing classic styles to be mass produced, sold by catalogue and assembled on site. The result is an architecture that has inspired not just artists, but successive waves of galleries, interior and fashion design firms and multimedia start-ups. The area has moved from cutting-edge to chic, and the inevitably rising rents have forced out many of the original pioneers. Today, SoHo is more design than art. It has a sleek style visible in people's dress, in shop displays, even in restaurant menus.

If you've decided to split your day between the neighbouring districts of SoHo and the Financial District, try being chauffeured by pedal power rather than taking a taxi. In a Ponycabs' bicycle rickshaw, you'll really feel a part of it all. Lovely when the weather is fine, and cosy under a blanket in winter. Discount with your NYCard. (See page 70.)

1 BALTHAZAR

80 Spring Street between Broadway and Crosby Street. Tel 212-965 1414.
One of the city's hottest restaurants, this is a celebrity – and a celebrity-spotter – favourite. Great for breakfast or brunch (see page 114).

You'll find masses of shops and galleries in SoHo, and it's a lot of fun just following your own nose. The next two are very well known, and should focus your browse along Broadway.

2 CANAL JEANS

504 Broadway between Spring and Broome Streets. Tel 212-226 1130.
Those whose mission is to shop will find seemingly infinite racks of basics at basic prices – jeans, T-shirts, etc. – and quite a selection of vintage gear (see page 87).

3 AVIREX

595 Broadway (between Prince and Houston Streets). Tel 212-925 5455.
Just south of Houston Street you'll find this well-known source for aviator and varsity jackets.

As you walk back to Prince Street, you'll pass what has become known as Museum Row. Many of the artists that once made SoHo a hotbed of creativity have been priced out, but the museums this talent attracted remain.

4 PRADA NEW YORK EPICENTER

575 Broadway at Prince Street. Tel: 212-334 8888.
A cylindrical glass lift glides down, a striped zebrawood floor swoops from ground floor to basement, opposite amphitheatrical steps that can seat up to 200. What is this place? It's half shop, half theatre – it's the new Prada store. Designed by superstar architect Rem Koolhaas (what a great name for an architect), the space is so SoHo and an absolute must-visit. Even if you have no intention of buying any of the men's or women's blow-out-fabulous-darling fashion, try something on in the changing rooms, with their sci-fi 360 degree mirrors that, through time-lapse imagery, show you your back even after you've turned around. Flick a switch and the changing room door turns transparent to give your companion a quick peek. Real performance shopping (see page 88).

5 KATE'S PAPERIE

561 Broadway at Prince Street. Tel 212-941 9816.
If you want to report your New York discoveries on hand-made paper, this is the spot to find it. Note the building the shop is in, the Little Singer Building, with its pretty cast-iron balconies decorated with porcelain.

6 DEAN AND DELUCA

560 Broadway at Prince Street. Tel 212-226 6800.
If you cross the street, you'll find this very swish grocery store, a good reflection of SoHo's particular style: food as art – an astonishing display!

SoHo is calm in the mornings, and undergoes a slow, almost Continental, wake-up. We suggest breakfast, or better still, Saturday brunch, here.

6 CONTINUING THE SOHO EXPERIENCE

1 FANELLI'S

94 Prince Street at Mercer Street. Tel 212-431 5744.
Here's where to take a break at the end Walk 5, or kick off Walk 6. The pub-like bar is easily the oldest in SoHo. If you're ready for a bite to eat, their burgers are delicious and the atmosphere is completely unpretentious and real. This isn't a tourist joint (see page 114).

MERCER AND GREENE STREETS

Although Broadway is a major thoroughfare and West Broadway has

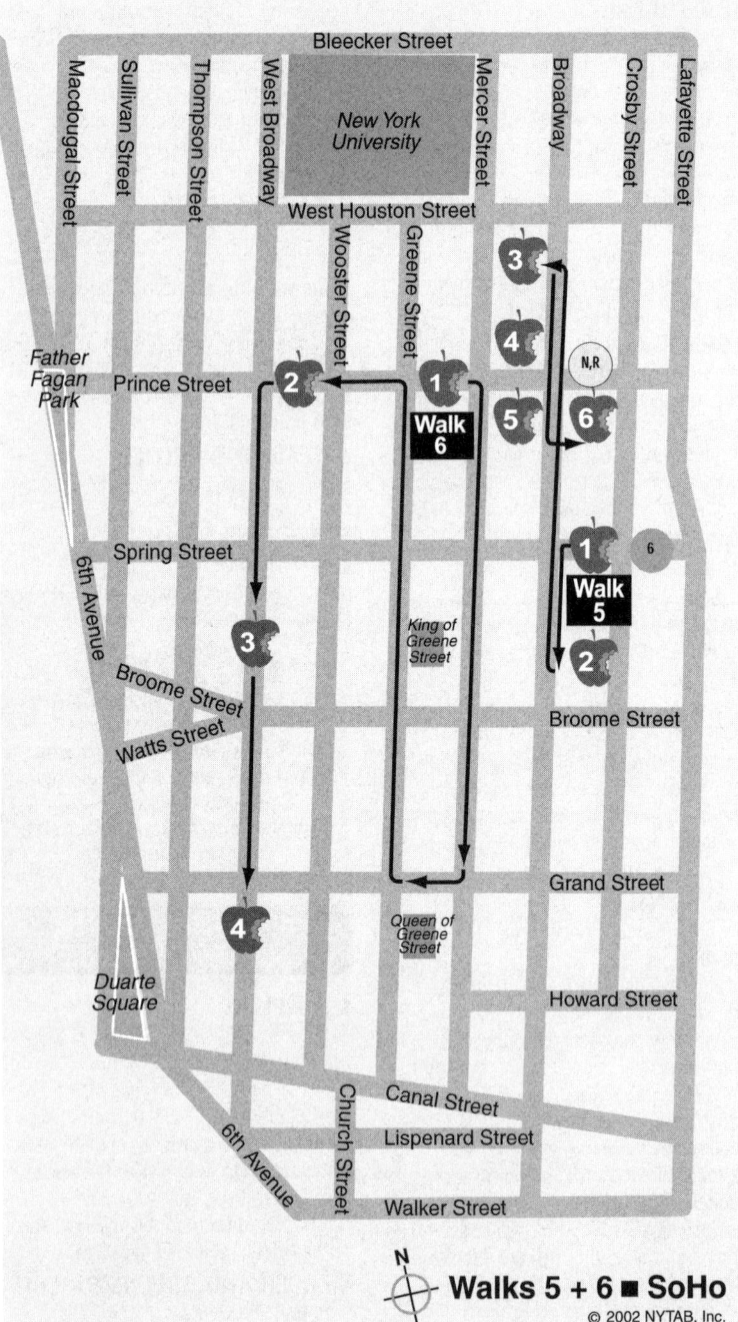

Bleecker Street
Macdougal Street
Sullivan Street
Thompson Street
West Broadway
New York University
Mercer Street
Broadway
Crosby Street
Lafayette Street
West Houston Street
Wooster Street
Greene Street
N,R
Father Fagan Park
Prince Street
Walk 6
Spring Street
6th Avenue
Walk 5
King of Greene Street
Broome Street
Watts Street
Broome Street
Grand Street
Queen of Greene Street
Duarte Square
Howard Street
Canal Street
Church Street
Lispenard Street
6th Avenue
Walker Street
N
Walks 5 + 6 ■ SoHo
© 2002 NYTAB, Inc.

the best shopping, it's the cobbled streets between them that hold the most charm. Take the time to stroll down Mercer and up Greene. (Note how New Yorkers leave off the word 'avenue' or 'street' when giving addresses or directions, e.g. 'I live on Park'.) Greene Street is rich in the cast-iron façades the area is so famous for. No 72, with its many columns and pedimented entrance, is known as 'the King of Greene Street'. The 'Queen', by the way, is the one at No 30 with the Second Empire façade.

Had enough shopping? Take a 15-minute stroll west to 278 Spring Street (between Hudson and Varick Streets). The tiny NYC Fire Museum is full of polished nostalgia.

2 PHAT FARM

129 Prince Street between Wooster Street and West Broadway. Tel 212-533 7428.
Hip-hop fashion was invented in New York. Richard Simmons' shop is one of the original sources of those drop-crotched pants, now installed in high-rent glory. It's an amazing contrast to its street-corner vendor beginnings (see page 88).

3 ROBERT LEE MORRIS

400 West Broadway between Spring and Broome Streets. Tel 212-431 9405.
West Broadway (not to be confused with Broadway) has great shops. Take your time! This store belongs to one of the very few American jewellery designers who have an international reputation.

4 SOHO GRAND HOTEL

310 West Broadway between Grand and Canal Streets. Tel 212-965 3000.
If you've followed both SoHo tours in one day, you're going to enjoy – and you certainly deserve – a cocktail in the Grand Bar, up the iron staircase of this converted industrial space. Both it and its clientele are very stylish, very SoHo (see page 162).

Directory inquiry operators in New York are helpful for more than telephone numbers. If you're trying to find a particular shop or restaurant, simply dial 411 on any pay phone and ask for the street address. It won't cost you a penny.

7 GREENWICH VILLAGE

In the higgledy-piggledy maze of streets that makes up the delightful confusion of Greenwich Village, it is the solidity of Washington Square's triumphal arch that marks the district in people's minds. The arch commemorates George Washington's inauguration as the first president, and the country's freedom from colonial rule.

The area has long represented one form of freedom or another. First, it was a countryside haven north of the city that offered a retreat from cholera and yellow fever epidemics. Later, it was freedom from conformity that attracted avant-garde artists, the Beat movement, Off-off Broadway and a myriad of alternative lifestyles. The results have sometimes had worldwide repercussions, like the Stonewall Riot on Christopher Street in 1969, which is credited with having launched the gay rights movement. The Village today has an air of settled prosperity, but it still offers freedom from the city's famous towering heights and frantic pace. Its shops and its inhabitants range from the outright weird to the charmingly old-fashioned.

The Village is one of the few parts of Manhattan in which it's possible to get lost. Don't worry if you do, you'll soon find your way out. If you stick to the itinerary below, you'll spend a leisurely two to three hours walking through some of the most picturesque streets and popping into a few of our many

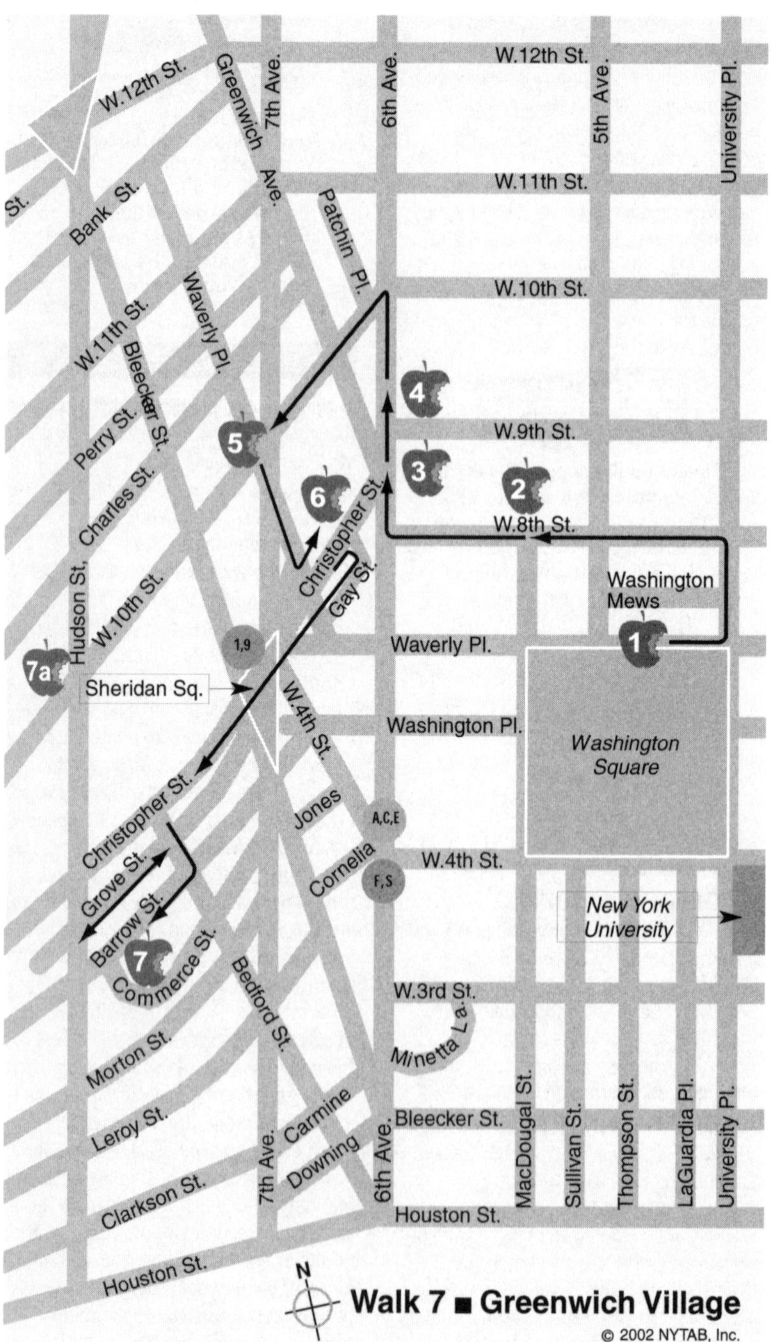
W.12th St.
Greenwich Ave.
7th Ave.
6th Ave.
5th Ave.
University Pl.
W.12th St.
St.
Bank St.
W.11th St.
Patchin Pl.
W.10th St.
Waverly Pl.
W.11th St.
Bleecker St.
Perry St.
W.9th St.
Charles St.
Christopher St.
W.8th St.
Hudson St.
W.10th St.
Gay St.
Washington Mews
1,9
Waverly Pl.
Sheridan Sq.
W.4th St.
Washington Pl.
Washington Square
Christopher St.
Jones
A,C,E
Cornelia
W.4th St.
F,S
Grove St.
Barrow St.
New York University
Commerce St.
Bedford St.
W.3rd St.
Minetta La.
Morton St.
Leroy St.
Carmine
Bleecker St.
7th Ave.
Downing
6th Ave.
MacDougal St.
Sullivan St.
Thompson St.
LaGuardia Pl.
University Pl.
Clarkson St.
Houston St.
Houston St.
N
Walk 7 ■ Greenwich Village
© 2002 NYTAB, Inc.

favourite shops. If you start out in the morning at about 10, you'll end in perfect time for lunch. If you begin at about 4pm (light permitting), you might be ready for an early dinner before taking in some of the many jazz offerings in the neighbourhood (see page 147).

1 WASHINGTON SQUARE PARK

Washington Square functions as a village playground: chess players, skateboarders, performance artists, there's always something to see. Both the original 1889 wooden arch and the current marble replacement were designed by Stanford White, one of the city's most famous architects and a native of the Village. Note the elm tree in the north-east corner. It is possibly the oldest tree in Manhattan (well over 300 years), and the local executioner found its branches ideal for hangings between 1797 and 1819.

WASHINGTON MEWS

Glance along here on your way north up University Place. The buildings you can see were the stables for the pretty Greek Revival houses situated along the north side of the park.

2 UNTITLED

26 West 8th Street between 5th and 6th Avenues. Tel 212-505 9725.

8th Street is home to a large number of edgy shoe and fashion shops. This shop may not be 'very you', but it is very Village and a major source for club kids. You'll find some pretty outrageous late-night garb here. The range includes some top international names as well as local favourites.

3 C O BIGELOW CHEMISTS

414 6th Avenue between West 8th and West 9th Streets. Tel 212-533 2700.

You don't have to have jet lag or stomach upset to come here (though the staff would be helpful if you did). The shop is full of charm and they have their own highly praised cosmetics, which make ideal, unique gifts to take home for family and friends.

4 BALDUCCI'S

424 6th Avenue at West 9th Street. Tel 212-673 2600.

Despite the crowds and the crush, this is an institution you definitely do want to be locked up in. One of the city's best food shops and a riot of smells, colours and, of course, tastes.

PATCHIN PLACE

Cross 6th Avenue at West 10th Street and follow it towards the south. Glance up tiny Patchin Place on your right – No 4 was home to poet e e cummings for 40 years.

5 THREE LIVES BOOKSTORE

154 West 10th Street at Waverly Place. Tel 212-741 2069.

Everything a bookshop should be: a great selection, knowledgeable staff and an atmosphere that encourages you to browse. You could look for a novel set in the neighbourhood.

6 AEDES DE VENUSTAS

The basement at 15 Christopher Street between 6th and 7th Avenues. Tel 212-206 8674.

You've travelled thousands of miles to be in New York. The least you can do is allow the folks here help you choose a scent that is truly you, a statement of your individuality – tomato leaf, perhaps? Very Village!

Take a tiny detour through Gay Street, New York's second shortest street (after nearby Weehawken Street). As you exit on to Waverly Place turn right and look at the street sign. You're at the cross streets of Waverly Place and Waverly Place – what a tangle!

ST LUKE-IN-THE-FIELDS

Head along Christopher Street's bustle to quiet Bedford Street. Note the wood-frame house on the corner of Grove Street, perhaps the best preserved in Manhattan. Take a step down Grove Street towards Hudson Street and you'll see St Luke-in-the-Fields (1822) whose first warden, Clement Clarke Moore, wrote a poem for his children: 'Twas the night before Christmas and all through the house...'

75½ BEDFORD STREET

Stepping back into Bedford Street you will find the city's narrowest house, just 3m (9½ft) wide. Some say its neighbour, at No 77, is the oldest Greenwich Village house still standing.

COMMERCE STREET AND THE CHERRY LANE THEATER

38 Commerce Street. Tel 212-727 3673. This backwater, where Barrow meets Commerce Street, is one of the most nostalgic parts of the Village, summer or winter. There's even a gaslight burning at the street's elbow. The Cherry Lane Theater just beyond the bend has hosted many a star. One actor who did not perform there but lived in a bachelor pad above it in the 1920s was Archie Leach – he later became much better known as Cary Grant.

7 GRANGE HALL

50 Commerce Street at Barrow Street. Tel 212-924 5246. 10 per cent discount with your NYCard.

A New York favourite with a delightful bistro atmosphere. In homesteader days a grange hall was the communal building used for get-togethers in sparsely populated farm country. Families would ride many miles in their best clothes in the wagon with their plumpest lamb or chicken. So, here, expect cooking from the heartland of America – chops, spare ribs, potatoes. All the restaurant's produce comes fresh from the farmers' market in Union Square. Reasonable prices (see page 116).

7A COWGIRL

519 Hudson Street at West 10th Street. Tel 212-633 1133. 10 per cent discount with your NYCard.

As reasonable as Grange Hall's prices are, there's an even less expensive choice just up the road. This restaurant is another local favourite with a bit more of a scene, a bit more noise and a bit more spice. The food hails from cowboy country, which means you can lasso yourself some salsa, corn fritters, even an excellent burger. (See also page 155.)

8 MIDTOWN: 34TH STREET

If you're in town for almost no time at all and need to work your way down a serious shopping list, this walk is for you. You'll find most things in the four stores listed, and still have time for a major attraction, a civilised museum and a wonderful secret lunch spot.

1 MACY'S

34th Street at Broadway. Tel 212-695 4400.

'The Largest Store in the World' they shout to everyone – and they're right. You can get just about anything here. By the way, in this megashopolis, we think The Cellar kitchenware department is well worth a visit (see page 81).

The 34th Street area has really come up in the world and is filled with great shops. In addition to those mentioned in this walk, there are also Old Navy and Banana Republic – so wallets at the ready!

2 DAFFY'S

1311 Broadway at West 34th Street. Tel 212-736 4477.

Let's face it, you're unlikely to come out of Macy's where you expected to – it's just too huge. But find your way back to the corner of Broadway and 34th Street, and you'll see Daffy's opposite, with its clever slogan 'Clothing Bargains for Millionaires'. There are several branches in town, all stocking clothing and accessories for men, women and children. Hunt through the racks for bargains galore, from top-name designers and everyday necessities to one-off samples.

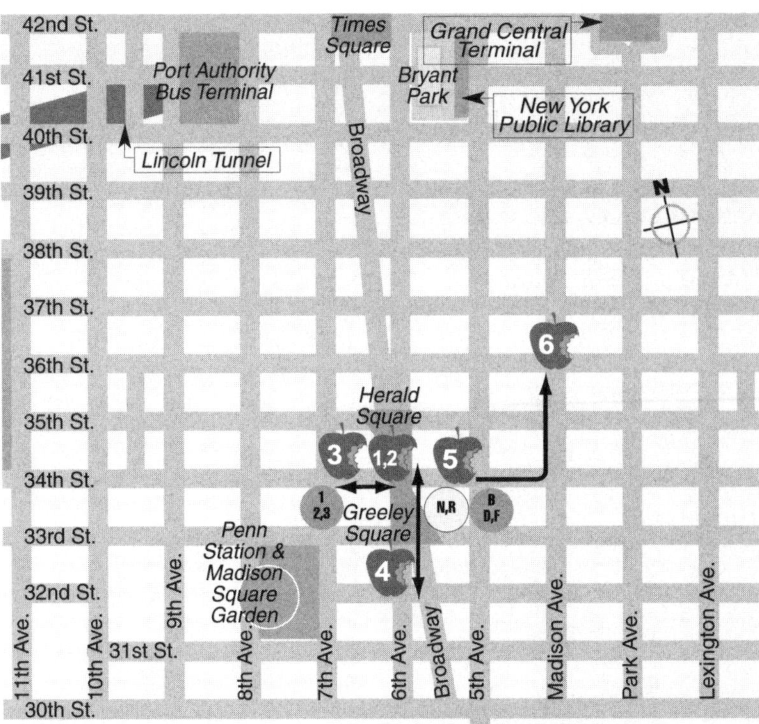

3 SEPHORA

130 West 34th Street between Broadway and 7th Avenue. Tel 212-629 9135.

If you've got the dollars, this is where you get your scents – and polish and powder and glitter and concealer. This shop has a huge selection of major-brand make-up. Just as impressive is their funky selection of lesser-known designer brands (see page 92).

4 MANHATTAN MALL

6th Avenue between West 32nd and West 33rd Streets. Tel 212-465 0500.

Malls are rare in Manhattan, though very popular in the rest of America. This 11-storey block is worth exploring for the sheer diversity of products offered.

5 EMPIRE STATE BUILDING OBSERVATORY

350 5th Avenue at 34th Street. Tel 212-736 3100.

Without a shadow of a doubt, the Empire State Building is the most famous skyscraper in the world: a hang-out for King Kong, 102 storeys of sheer New York exuberance – it was built in the face of the Great Depression.

6 THE MORGAN LIBRARY

29 East 36th Street at Madison Avenue. Tel 212-685 0610. Discount with your NYCard.

You end this tour at a true insider's secret. Your NYCard gives you membership for a day, which means free admission plus a discount in the shop. Use it like a member. Wander around the human-scale museum (it was a house, after all). Have lunch in the peaceful, courtyard café. It's glazed in and wonderful all the year round. J Pierpont Morgan collected like a Renaissance prince, and you'll see Michelangelo,

Dürer, not one but three Gütenberg Bibles, and the original manuscript of Charles Dickens' *A Christmas Carol.*

The Morgan Library is scheduled to close in April 2003 for expansion and refurbishment (see page 105).

9 HUDSON RIVER

To see one of the world's most stunning skylines and to get a feel for how important the harbour is to this city, you need to get out on to the water. Winter or summer, the views are phenomenal.

To reach the piers, catch the M42 bus at any of the many bus stops along 42nd Street. Going the other way (east) will get you to the UN building.

Two companies offer a selection of cruises – lower harbour, sunset, dinner, music. We suggest you take a cruise around the entire island of Manhattan. You'll not only see the famous landmarks, but the winding upper reaches of the East and Harlem Rivers (see pages 70–1).

1A CIRCLE LINE CRUISES

Pier 83, W. 42nd Street and 12th Avenue. Tel 212-563 3200. Year round. Discount with your NYCard.

This is the more leisurely option. Circle Line has been showing the city to visitors and locals alike since 1945. Many of the boats are fully restored landing craft and tender ships used in the Second World War. The Full Island Cruise takes three hours.

1 NY WATERWAY CRUISES

Pier 78, W 38th Street and 12th Avenue. Tel 800-533 3779. May to November. Discount with your NYCard.

This high-speed catamaran will whisk you around the whole of Manhattan in just two hours.

2 MARKET DINER

572 11th Avenue at West 43rd Street. Tel 212-695 0415.

You'll find diners all over America, but not many authentic ones in New York. This one is a classic – a nondescript building, truck drivers and an endless menu (including our favourite: pancakes, bacon and syrup). Open 24 hours a day.

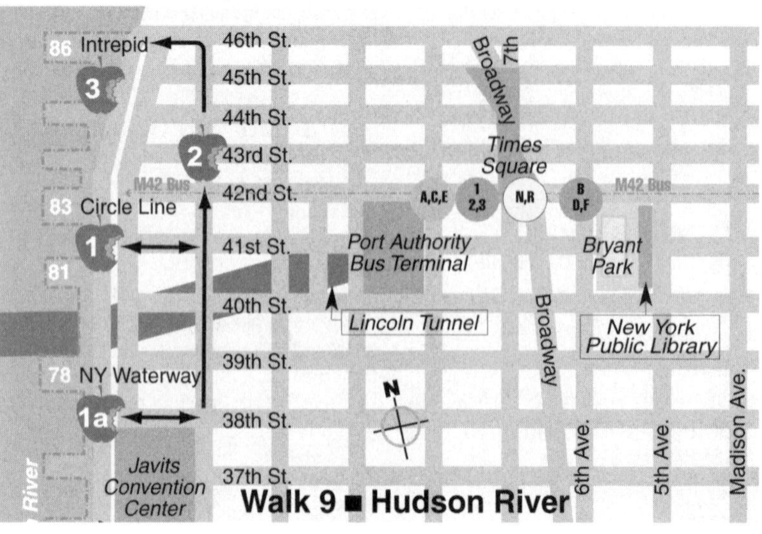

3 INTREPID SEA-AIR-SPACE MUSEUM

Pier 86, West 46th Street and 12th Avenue. Tel 212-245 2533. Discount with your NYCard.
After lunch, return to the water across the West Side Highway. Moored just a few blocks up is one of the city's most popular attractions. And when you see the serious hardware you're allowed to clamber over and generally play with, you'll understand why. This museum is a Second World War aircraft carrier and the deck is crammed with fighters (see page 100). Berthed next to it is a nuclear submarine - head there first for a tour before the crowds build.

Don't miss the flight simulator inside the *Intrepid* Sea-Air-Space Museum! You do pay extra, but it's thrilling to see action through the eyes of a fighter pilot.

10 MIDTOWN: TIMES SQUARE

Even New Yorkers passing through Times Square tend to tilt back and gawk. This walk gives you time to take in the razzle-dazzle, do a spot of shopping, and get behind one of those famous neon façades. Later, you'll stroll along famous 42nd Street to one of the most spectacular train stations in the world for a well-deserved drink off the tourist track, or even a very American steak dinner.

Though the Midtown walks can be done in any order, this is the one we think you should start at dusk or early evening, when the energy and neon of Times Square are at their brightest.

1 TIMES SQUARE VISITOR CENTER

1560 Broadway between West 46th and West 47th Streets. Until 8pm.
Situated in the old and very pretty Embassy Theatre, this is the place to meet friends out of the heat, the cold or the crowds. And if you have to wait a few minutes, you could send a few free e-cards home.

TIMES SQUARE

Broadway slices through the Theater District with so many lit hoardings that it became known as the Great White Way. Stroll southwards and get the full neon feel, enough souvenir mugs to fill a black hole, enough tourist traffic to populate a nation! It's loud, it's brash, it's a must-see.

New Yorkers are used to running into the famous and powerful in the local chemists, restaurants, or on the street. You can get a quick course on the faces to look out for at Madame Tussaud's new Times Square museum. See page 61.

2 VIRGIN MEGASTORES

1540 Broadway between West 45th and West 46th Streets. Tel 212-921 1020. Open until 1am.
Richard Branson's emporium shouts at you from the east side of the street. He realised a few years ago that it was cheaper to open a store than rent the advertising space in this most famous of 'squares'. A *big* selection, and although the prices of CDs are not as keen as they once were, you'll still find a bargain.

3 NASDAQ MARKETSITE

4 Times Square (Broadway and West 42nd Street. Tel 1-877-627 3271, Mon to Thurs, Sun until 8pm; Fri to Sat until 10pm. Discount with your NYCard.
You can't miss Nasdaq's cylindrical digital billboard, the world's largest LED screen, soaring seven storeys over Broadway. The guided tours will give you a quick lesson on investing. See how many millions you can make - or lose - in the interactive

investment game, which throws you and your stock portfolio into a real market. Your personal portfolio screen displays the rises and falls as they actually happened at some point in the past. You're up against the clock and it's up to you and the steeliness of your nerves how much you buy, what you hold and when to sell.

Since September 11, the folks at Nasdaq have temporarily stopped individual members of the public from entering, so if this is your prime reason for coming to Times Square, call first (see page 62).

BRYANT PARK

42nd Street between 5th and 6th Avenues.

Once a hang-out for bums and home to seedy peep-shows, the whole area is now wonderfully sanitised and even has its own carousel.

Bryant Park's Summer Festival of free films on Monday evenings is a great picnic opportunity, and very New York. Films start at sunset but you need to go early to get a good spot. To find out what's showing, call 212-512 5700.

4 THE NEW YORK PUBLIC LIBRARY

5th Avenue between 40th and 42nd Streets. Tel 212-930 0830. Mon to Thurs, Fri until 6pm; Tues, Wed until 7.30pm.

The public library is housed in some 80–90 buildings, but it's this one, guarded by the lions Patience and Fortitude, that everyone thinks of as the real library. Why should you go in? For the main reading room, where up to 700 can sit in splendid study, and for the exhibitions, which are usually very good and free (see page 66).

5 GRAND CENTRAL STATION

42nd Street between Lexington and Vanderbilt Avenues. Until 1am.

This public palace is an example of New York's love affair with the Beaux Arts style. The main hall is truly spectacular. It's 114m (375ft) long, 38m (125ft) high; glass, marble, brass, and the vast starry night of the painted ceiling. The entire station recently underwent a complete cleaning and renovation. Only one small rectangle at the edge of the ceiling was left uncleaned: can you spot it? (See page 64.)

MICHAEL JORDAN'S STEAKHOUSE

Gallery Level, Grand Central Station. Tel 212-655 2300. Until 12.30am.

Have dinner or drinks here. The famous basketball player's restaurant overlooks the main floor of the station and is known for its immense, and perfect, porterhouse steaks.

Take to the water for a spectacular dinner and dancing cruise on World Yacht. Board at 6.30pm at Pier 81 (West 41st Street and Hudson River). The boat leaves at 7pm and returns at 10pm. Reservations: 212-630 8100. Jackets required. Discount with your NYCard.

CAMPBELL APARTMENT BAR

Gallery Level, Grand Central Station. Tel 212-953 0409. Until 1am.

Up the narrow stairs on the other side of the gallery from Jordan's, this apartment used to be the office/salon of the 1920s' tycoon John W Campbell. The beamed ceiling, huge leaded-glass window and the massive stone fireplace make a unique, almost castle-like space. But the dark wood, couches and club armchairs make it a cosy place for a drink.

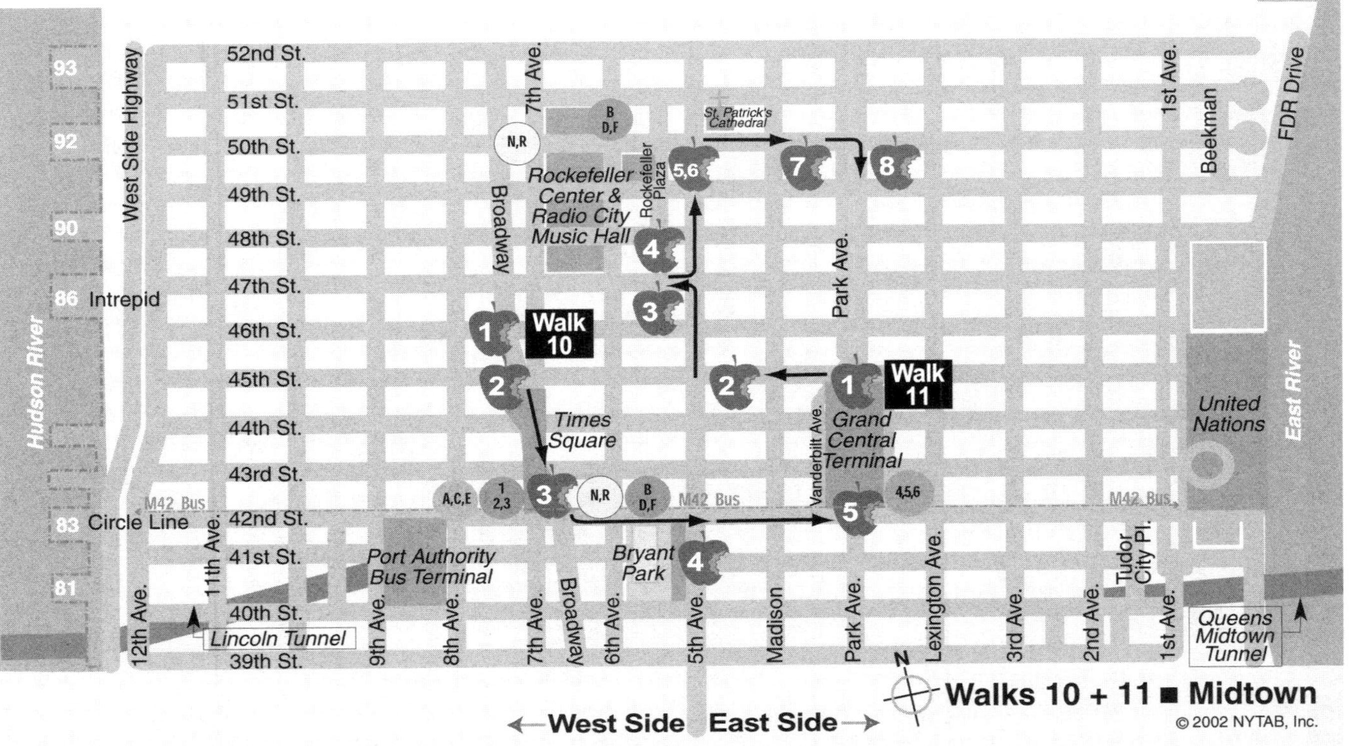
Walks 10 + 11 ■ Midtown
© 2002 NYTAB, Inc.
West Side
East Side
N
Walk 10
Walk 11
Hudson River
West Side Highway
93
92
90
86
Intrepid
83
Circle Line
81
M42 Bus
52nd St.
51st St.
50th St.
49th St.
48th St.
47th St.
46th St.
45th St.
44th St.
43rd St.
42nd St.
41st St.
40th St.
39th St.
12th Ave.
11th Ave.
9th Ave.
8th Ave.
7th Ave.
Broadway
6th Ave.
5th Ave.
Madison
Park Ave.
Vanderbilt Ave.
Lexington Ave.
3rd Ave.
2nd Ave.
1st Ave.
Beekman
FDR Drive
Lincoln Tunnel
Port Authority Bus Terminal
Times Square
Bryant Park
Rockefeller Center & Radio City Music Hall
Rockefeller Plaza
St. Patrick's Cathedral
Grand Central Terminal
Tudor City Pl.
United Nations
East River
Queens Midtown Tunnel
N,R
B D,F
A,C,E
1 2,3
4,5,6

11 MIDTOWN: SHOPPING

Midtown is so big and so exhilarating that it's easy to miss some of the greatest bits. This walk organises things for you. You'll pass some major American clothing stores for both kids and adults, and some major New York landmarks like Rockefeller Center and St Patrick's Cathedral. And there's a civilised break at the end in one of the city's oldest and most famous hotels.

1 GRAND CENTRAL STATION

42nd Street between Lexington and Vanderbilt Avenues.

There are many food options in this temple to travel, from the famous Oyster Bar to fast food franchises, and even a high-quality food hall. If you begin this itinerary in the afternoon, treat yourself to a frozen custard dessert at Custard Beach, tucked into the northern side of the station's lower level.

Once you've explored the station, head up the main stairs towards the gallery level and exit on to Vanderbilt Street (past Michael Jordan's restaurant).

The shops surrounding Brooks Brothers on Madison have traditionally dressed the American professional male. Keep an eye out for Johnston and Murphy at Madison and West 44th (shoes) to Paul Stuart at Madison and West 45th Street (just about everything else including custom-made shirts).

2 BROOKS BROTHERS

346 Madison Avenue at East 44th Street. Tel 212-682 8800.

For 'button-down' read: East Coast Establishment. The phrase refers to button-collared shirts and denotes smartness, steadiness and conservatism. Once upon a time, if you had any aspirations to any of those qualities, your shirts (and much more besides) probably came from this iconic men's clothier. Today, believe it or not, its parent company is Marks and Sparks and it has a full-scale women's department. Nevertheless, it's still a window on the American soul.

3 DIAMOND ROW

47th Street between 5th and 6th Avenues.

As you walk north on 5th Avenue, sneak a look into this, one of the world's most important diamond trading centres. Of all the diamonds in the United States, 80 per cent are cut, set, sold or prepared for sale here. Except for a couple of large retail stores, all the action takes place in small stores and workshops, and the business is dominated by Orthodox Jews. You can feel the atmosphere of 'the deal' in the streets.

4 OSH KOSH B'GOSH

586 5th Avenue between 47th and 4th Streets. Tel 212-827 0098.

Having loaded up on men's clobber, here's the place for boys and girls. Famous for its denim overalls, this iconic American brand is cheaper here than at home (when you can find it).

5 SAKS 5TH AVENUE

611 5th Avenue between 49th and 50th Streets. Tel 212-753 4000.

One of the world's most famous department stores, and still one of 5th Avenue's busiest. If you're here at Christmas you may be in time to catch the magnificent window displays. By the way, a possibly critical piece of information is that the lavatories for men are on the sixth floor and for women on the fourth floor. Standing outside this store gives you a near perfect view of Rock Center across the street.

6 ROCKEFELLER CENTER

West 47th to West 51st Streets between 5th and 6th Avenues. Tel 212-632 3975. (See page 61.)

The 8th-floor restaurant of Saks 5th Avenue, The Café, has great views of St Patrick's Cathedral and the Rockefeller Center ice rink. It's open for breakfast and lunch.

A total of 19 buildings make up this phenomenal city within a city. Building began in 1929 and – remarkably – continued throughout the Great Depression.

Turn into the garden walkway, known as the Channel Gardens, directly opposite. At the end is the golden statue of Prometheus who holds his torch over winter's ice-skating couples and summer's lunching lovers. Behind him, at Christmas, 8km (5 miles) of lights are strung on New York's favourite (and massive) tree.

RADIO CITY MUSIC HALL

1260 6th Avenue at West 50th Street. Tel 212-247 4777 for show tickets and tours.
Also part of the centre, the Radio City Music Hall is famous for its Christmas Spectacular and the Rockettes.

ST PATRICK'S CATHEDRAL

5th Avenue between 50th and 51st Streets. Tel 212-753 2261.
This is America's largest Catholic church. Surrounded by skyscrapers, you need to go inside to realise its true scale – it seats a congregation of 2,400 (see page 68).

7 THE VILLARD HOUSES

457 Madison Avenue between East 49th and East 50th Streets. Tel 212-935 3960 for Municipal Art Society. Tel 212-935 3595 for Urban Center Books.
You'll easily spot this wonderful courtyard with trees dressed in fairylights. The left wing of brownstone houses contains the Municipal Art Society, which offers some of the best architectural walking tours of the city, and a bookshop dedicated to architecture. In this city, that certainly isn't boring.

Immediately behind the Villard Houses is the soaring New York Palace Hotel. Its super-stylish Villard Bar is set on two floors and in four rooms with different opulent themes. So, you could decide to end your walk here. Alternatively, walk one block further east to the Waldorf-Astoria Hotel.

8 THE COCKTAIL TERRACE OR SIR HARRY'S OR THE BULL AND BEAR

Waldorf-Astoria Hotel, 301 Park Avenue between East 49th and East 50th Streets. Tel 212-355 3000.
The Waldorf-Astoria is the perfect place for that well-deserved cocktail. You have several choices within this one building. The Cocktail Terrace overlooks the main lobby, has a piano, and is great for people-watching. Another possibility is Sir Harry's bar (a useful tip for night-owls is that it's open until 2.30am). The Bull and Bear is pub-like, pours a decent drink and serves a decent steak.

12 UPPER WEST SIDE

The Upper West Side has two obvious mega-attractions: the American Museum of Natural History and the Lincoln Center for the Performing Arts. But there's also an atmosphere to absorb – the bars, the cafés, the slightly Continental boulevard feel – and the following walk gives you an experience of both.

The Upper West Side has the biggest concentration of cinemas anywhere in New York. There are four major complexes clustered along Broadway between 62nd and 68th Streets, including the Lincoln Center's Walter Reade Theater and the immense Sony multiplex with an IMAX screen.

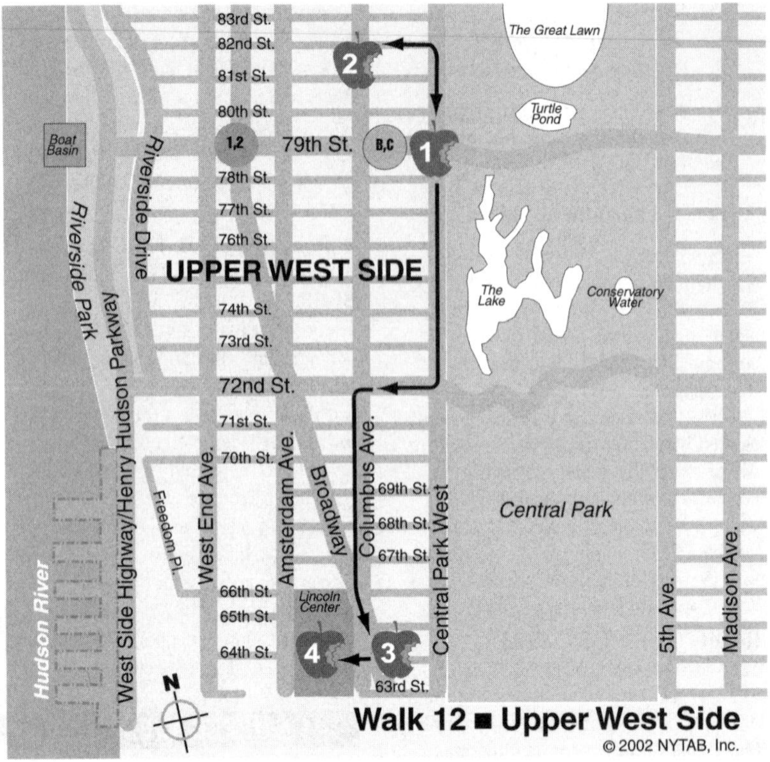

Walk 12 ■ Upper West Side

1 AMERICAN MUSEUM OF NATURAL HISTORY

West 79th Street and Central Park West. Tel 212-769 5100.

This is the real thing – the kind of place that sends researchers through swamps, up mountains and across deserts to discover such things as 80-million-year-old dinosaur eggs. It's the largest natural history museum in the world, with some 35 million objects and specimens and an IMAX theatre, all crammed into 22 buildings sprawled over three city blocks. The recently finished Rose Center Hayden Planetarium is a multimedia spectacular, and one of the finest examples of the American trick of converting learning into entertainment (see page 96).

There can be long ticket queues for Hayden Planetarium. You can order tickets in advance for the Space Show at the planetarium, or for a specific IMAX film, lecture or event, call 212-769 5200.

2 MAXILLA AND MANDIBLE

451 Columbus Avenue between West 81st and West 82nd Streets. Tel 212-724 6173.

You can buy a real fossil here – a bone of your own. A most unusual shop, worth the small detour for that hard-to-please someone on your gift list.

CENTRAL PARK WEST

The next formal stop on this walk, Picholine restaurant, is 15 blocks south. Walk down Central Park West or take a taxi.

Just below the Natural History Museum (at West 77th Street and Central Park West) is the neoclassical building of the **New York Historical Society** which, apart from being the city's oldest museum, has two collections of note: 150 Tiffany lamps and 432 original Audubon watercolours from *Birds of America* (see page 52).

At the corner of West 72nd Street and Central Park West is the **Dakota,** one of the first and certainly one of the most famous, apartment buildings in the city. One resident, John Lennon of The Beatles, was shot in front of the building in December 1980 by a deranged fan. Just opposite in Central Park is the garden his widow Yoko Ono created as a memorial, Strawberry Fields. It is shaped like a tear. Sadly, the original 25,000 strawberry plants were quickly eaten by birds. But 161 different varieties of plants and trees (representing the number of countries in the world at the time) remain (see page 51).

COLUMBUS AVENUE

Turn right from Central Park West and continue down Columbus Avenue. Along with Broadway and Amsterdam, this street is one of the neighbourhood's main boulevards, lined with shops, bars, cafés and other local haunts to discover.

3 PICHOLINE

35 West 64th Street between Broadway and Central Park West. Tel 212-724 8585.
This is one of the finest restaurants in the city, worth every penny in every way. At lunch, your pennies go very far indeed with the $24 prix fixe menu, so treat yourself. By the way, the chef, Terrance Brennan, is famous for his love of cheeses (see page 129), and the cheese selection is consequently huge. Dress: smart casual.

You don't have to 'shell out the big bucks' to experience the marvel that is the Metropolitan Opera. Family Circle tickets sell for just $25, and though you practically need binoculars from that height, many say the sound quality is the best in the house.

4 LINCOLN CENTER

Broadway between West 62nd and West 66th Streets. Tel 212-769 7020 for Visitor Services guided tours. Tel 212-769 7406 for Juilliard School of Music.
This is the largest performing arts complex in the country (see page 136) and houses some of the best talent in the world, from opera to orchestral, from ballet to jazz. Even if you have no plans to attend a performance, take a tour. There are sculptures by Rodin and Henry Moore, paintings by Chagall, and the NY State Theater was designed by the 95-year-old architectural aristocrat, Philip Johnson.

You can buy a ticket to one of the New York Philharmonic's midweek rehearsals for just $12.

If you are skipping lunch, the Julliard School offers a free, calorie-free, alternative: one-hour chamber music concerts on Wednesdays in term time at 1pm in Alice Tully Hall.

13 UPPER EAST SIDE

Madison Avenue may mean advertising to some, but on the Upper East Side, it's pure shopping. High quality, high style, and often (but not always) high prices. You'll find the very tip top international and American designers, and this tour walks you down Madison's prime stretch. The time you take poking in and out of the stores depends on your own stamina and interest, but whatever your timing preference, do try to make the time to take the detour to the Frick Collection, one of the most enjoyable museums in the city.

1 RALPH LAUREN

867 Madison Avenue at East 72nd Street. Tel 212-606 2100.
Ralph Lauren based many of his designs on old English themes. Over the years, they've become very much his own. The same is true of this shop, his flagship. Once a private house, it's now a display case for his men's and women's clothing lines, mixed in with silver snuff boxes, walking canes and linens, all draped on and around fireplaces, old leather armchairs and deep-pile rugs.

2 FRICK COLLECTION

1 East 70th Street at 5th Avenue. Tel 212-288 0700. Note that children under 10 are not allowed (see page 101).
Henry Clay Frick may have made his millions in coal, but he's remembered for the oils he left behind, a world-class collection of Fragonard, Turner, Rembrandt and more. The joy of the Frick Collection is that it is still housed in the mansion he had built for himself when he moved to the city in 1900. Along with the paintings, there's exquisite furniture, porcelain and sculpture. Altogether, this not only gives you a sense of the scale on which Frick lived, but also makes the collections more accessible, more personal. For a break, sit for a while near the peaceful indoor reflecting pool.

Even though its address is on 3rd Avenue, Bloomingdale's is a full block wide, so you can enter on both 3rd and Lexington Avenues.

3 BLOOMINGDALE'S

1000 3rd Avenue between East 59th and East 60th Streets. Tel 212-705 2000.
Bloomingdale's has been a part of city life since April 1872. Just about every New Yorker finds a need to visit here at one time or another, and many on the Upper East Side treat it as their all-purpose general store, for everything from tea kettles to evening gowns. If you haven't yet found that perfectly off-beat gift for your nieces, you'll find knickers here with 'Bloomie's' printed across the front.

On the mezzanine just above the Lexington Avenue entrance is the Visitors' Services Desk. Show your NYCard for a free gift with any purchase.

4 BILLY MARTIN'S WESTERN WEAR

220 East 60th Street between 2nd and 3rd Avenues. Tel 212-861 3100.
If anyone can upmarket the cowboy, it's New York's Upper East Side. A great place for getting in touch with your inner Wild West soul.

The Roosevelt Island Arial Tramway gives wonderful views of the East Side's skyscrapers for the price of a standard subway or bus fare ($1.50). It departs every 15 minutes from 2nd Avenue at 60th Street. Tel 212-832 4543.

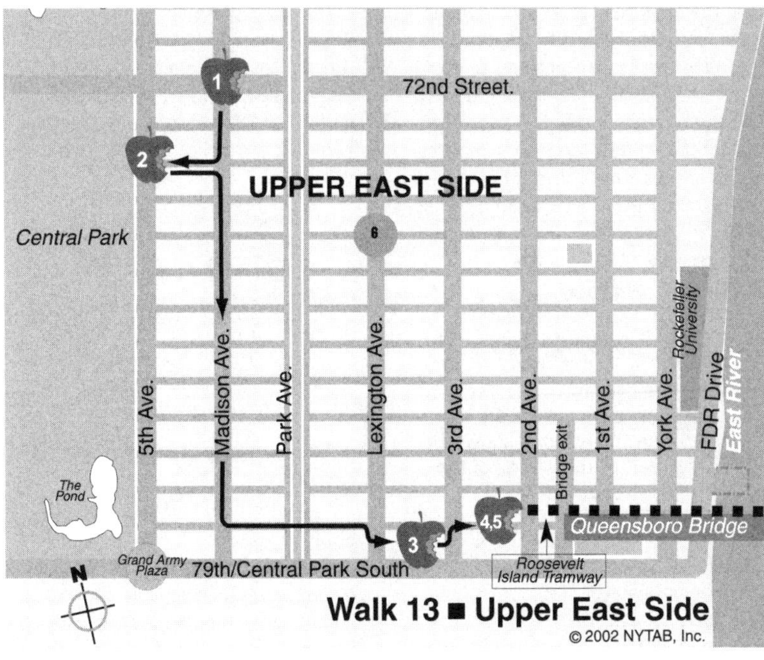

5 SERENDIPITY 3

225 East 60th Street between 2nd and 3rd Avenues. Tel 212-838 3531.

Don't be fooled. Make your way straight through the toy shop (you'll have time for it later) to one of the round tables at the back. Order a caviar omelette, a foot-long hot dog, or maybe a Forbidden Broadway sundae (Blackout Cake, hot fudge, and much more). You might even spot Mariah Carey or some other Upper East Side celebrity, brought here as a child and unable to break the habit.

14 UPPER EAST SIDE: THE METROPOLITAN

This tour takes in one of the most important museums in the world, the Metropolitan; a distinctly non-touristy pizza house for lunch; and a trip back to childhood (and an excuse to see New York in a delightfully different way).

1 METROPOLITAN MUSEUM OF ART

5th Avenue and East 82nd Street. Tel 212-879 5500 (see page 96).

Millions of objects covering 5,000 years of history spread over 139,500sq m (1.5 million sq ft) – you do not 'do' this museum, you'd die trying.

We have set out one suggested plan of attack, but the trick is to know what you want to see, and find out how to get there. Pick up a museum map at the entrance and formulate your plan.

A must is the Temple of Dendur on the ground floor. The Egyptian section is renowned and this temple, given by the Egyptian government and rebuilt here stone by stone, is truly superb.

You could then pick out some single (magnificent) object, like the Harp Player which dates from the third century BC in the Greek and Roman Antiquities section, also on the ground floor.

The delightful Costume Institute on the lower level, with its 45,000 costumes, and the American Wing on the ground floor, are both reached through the Egyptian section. American art is often given short shrift in European museums, but here it really shines. Our two favourites are the reconstruction of the living room of Frank Lloyd Wright's Little House, and the bucolic paintings of the Hudson River School. There are Sargents here too, notably *Madame X*.

There are concerts on Friday and Saturday evenings, and a bar 4–8pm on the balcony above the Great Hall at the Metropolitan Museum of Art.

In the comprehensive European art section, choose just one or two pictures from one or two countries. How about Vermeer's *Woman With A Jug* or Cézanne's *Cardplayers on* the first floor?

The museum has examples of everything, so head straight for things that interest you: musical instruments (first floor), medieval art (first floor), African, American Indian and Oceanic art (ground floor), Asian art (first floor), Oriental antiquities (first floor) – it's all here, and will still be here the next time you visit.

If you'd like to picnic in Central Park, go to Grace's Marketplace, 1237 3rd Avenue at East 71st Street, for a gourmet spread.

2 SERAFINA FABULOUS PIZZA

1022 Madison Avenue at East 79th Street. Tel 212-734 2676.
Stroll across to the corner of Madison Avenue and 79th Street. This is super-quality pizza. There are beautiful people and the glazed-in roof terrace (walk up one more floor) is the place to head for. Try the Margherita Pizza and its ultra-thin crust. You may find another

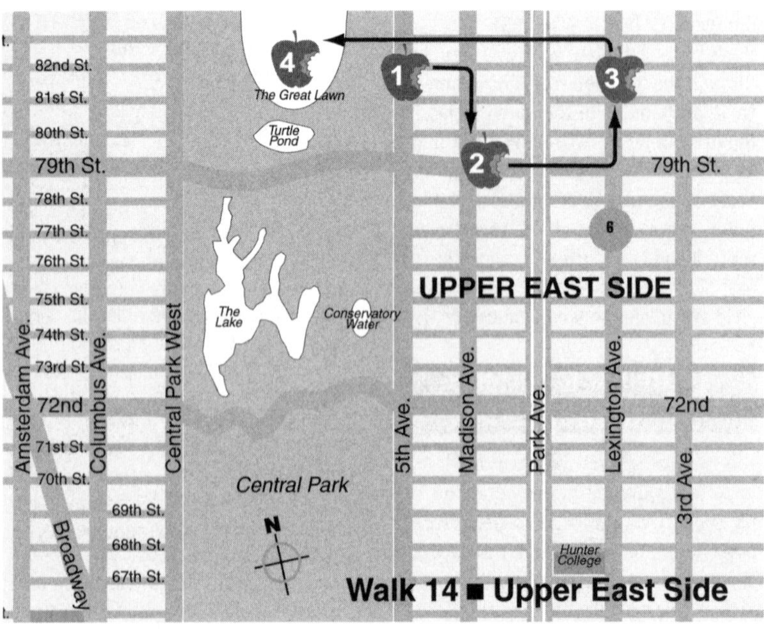

international traveller, but you won't find a tourist in this chic spot.

3 BIG CITY KITE

1210 Lexington Avenue at East 82nd Street. Tel 212-472 2623.
Now, you have a mission – and you don't need children to fulfil it. Go and fly a kite! Big City Kite is a treasure trove of designs. Finding one that suits you and flying it in one of the world's great urban open spaces will be a treasured New York memory. And, as a souvenir, it isn't hard to pack!

4 GREAT LAWN

This is where you fly your kite, in the centre of over 800 acres of green.

As you head south out of the park, spend a few minutes to find one oddity that most people never discover but which has been known to startle the occasional jogger: the bronze cat that lurks without pedestal or warning in the high foliage above the East Drive at about East 76th Street. It was sculpted in 1881 by Edward Kemeys who worked for the Parks Department. He loved native animals, especially felines. This sculpture (called *Still Hunt*) represents an American mountain lion.

15 UPPER EAST SIDE: NORTH CENTRAL PARK

Many of the city's museums stand on 5th Avenue. Most face Central Park, although the mighty Metropolitan (see Walk 14) is in it. This itinerary helps you walk off a delicious soul food lunch, takes you into two of the most famous museums on Museum Mile, and helps you discover some very pretty corners of New York's great green 'lung', Central Park.

1 EMILY'S

1325 5th Avenue between 111th and 112th Streets. Tel 212-996 1212.
If you haven't taken a bus yet during your stay, you'll find this a bargain sightseeing tour. Catch the M2, M3 or M4 anywhere along glittering Madison Avenue and do some drive-by window shopping. Get off just as the bus turns left on to Central Park North (110th Street), and walk one block north to Emily's.

Locals know that Emily's has perhaps the best Southern-fried chicken in town. Oh, and the ribs! Good at any time of year, but if you're travelling in winter, lunch here will stoke up the furnace nicely for the walk ahead.

When planning museum visits and walks, remember that many museums are busy at weekends and many are closed on Mondays.

2 MUSEUM OF THE CITY OF NEW YORK

1220 5th Avenue at East 103rd Street. Tel 212-534 1672. Discount with your NYCard. (See page 106.)
If New York and its history is beginning to intrigue or even fascinate you, then this museum is one not to miss. The constant battle with fire, great toy, Broadway and silver collections, thousands of photographs – it's the detail that creates the big picture. You can get two-for-one admission with your NYCard, and groups can take advantage of their family entrance price of $9. They interpret 'family' very loosely and any obviously friendly group of under six people qualifies.

CONSERVATORY GARDEN

5th Avenue at 105th Street.
Cross 55th Avenue and enter Central Park through the Vanderbilt Gate at 105th Street. This is one of the few formally laid out areas of the park. It's beautiful enough to attract newly-weds for their formal portraits.

Stroll southwards towards the reservoir. A little-known fact is that the lamp posts all have a plate with a four-digit number on them. The first two digits indicate the approximate cross

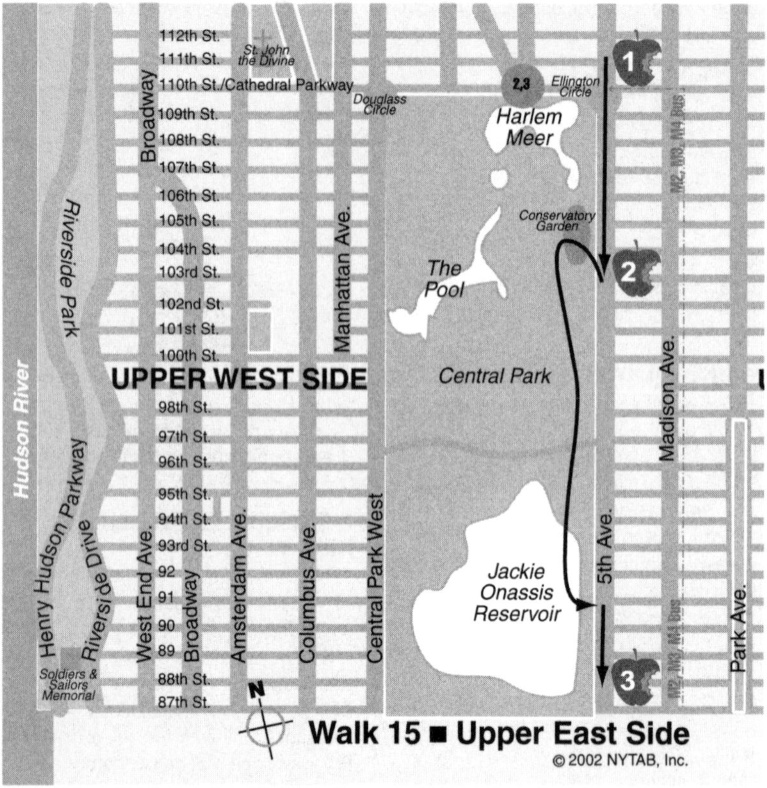

WALKING TOURS OF MANHATTAN

Walk 15 ■ Upper East Side

street, so 9712 would mean you have reached the level of 97th Street near the top end of the Reservoir. If you prefer not to walk, catch a cab or bus the 15 or so blocks to the Guggenheim Museum.

Members of the New York Road Runner's Club often use the path around the Reservoir as a jogging track. The club has an all-season schedule and welcomes visiting joggers. Tel 212 860 4455.

THE RESERVOIR

Between 86th and 96th Streets.
Central Park consists of 340 hectares (843 acres) of pastoral scenery in the English romantic tradition. Around 20,000 workers blasted, dug and planted what has become Manhattan's lung. It opened in 1859 and, today, it would only qualify as pastoral if you're used to the countryside being full of roller-bladers, skateboarders, bicyclists, joggers, the sports-inclined, the tai chi-inclined and the simply reclined. And yet, with all the activity, the place is still a restful retreat.

The reservoir stopped being a part of the city's water supply in 1993. The 43-hectare (106-acre) expanse of water – 4.5 billion litres (1 billion gallons), 12m (40ft) deep – is a favourite backdrop for joggers.

3 GUGGENHEIM MUSEUM

1071 5th Avenue at East 89th Street. Tel 212-423 3500. Discount with your NYCard. (See page 101).

Leave the park via Engineers Gate at 90th Street and head for one of the most famous gallery buildings in the world.

Designed by Frank Lloyd Wright, the Guggenheim's remarkable spiral has important permanent collections of modern art (including more than 200 Kandinskys). But it's the shows dedicated to such quasi-art objects as motorbikes and Armani's couture collection that make this gallery exciting, contemporary and different.

Unlike most museums, the Guggenheim is closed on Thursdays, so plan accordingly.

16 MORNINGSIDE HEIGHTS

This walk takes in a pretty, but often ignored park, a president's tomb, one of the nation's most famous universities, two important churches and a treat for the tummy at the end.

1 RIVERSIDE CHURCH

Riverside Drive between West 120th and West 122nd Streets. Tel 212-222 5974.
This church almost shoots skyward using skyscraper, steel-frame technology. It's noted for its stone carving, stained glass, and 74-bell carillon – the largest in the world. But it's actually the church's lofty position in Riverside Park by the Hudson River that makes this a really worthwhile destination. The observation platform, 108m (355ft) up with stunning views, is a bit of a secret.

2 GRANT'S TOMB

Riverside Park at West 122nd Street.
The rather grand, tiered affair you may spot just north of Riverside Church was, until the First World War, one of New York City's most important attractions. Although Ulysses S Grant was elected president in 1868, it was his performance as a soldier and strategist in the Civil War that ensured his place in the memory of the nation. He's the only president to be buried in New York City.

3 COLUMBIA UNIVERSITY

Broadway and West 116th Street. Tel 212-854 1754.
This is the surprisingly peaceful campus of one of America's elite, 'Ivy League' universities. There's a pretty main quadrangle and a very grand library building.

4 ST JOHN THE DIVINE

1047 Amsterdam Avenue at West 112th Street. Tel 212-316 7540.
The largest church in the US is still growing. The first stone was laid in 1891, but it will probably be another 20 years before the final piece of masonry is dressed! The main vault is 38m (124ft) high and 183m (601ft) long – impressive.

5 MAKE MY CAKE

103 West 110th Street at Lenox Avenue. Tel 212-932 0833.
Stroll along the northern edge of Central Park or catch the M4 bus to end this walk.

New York has some famous cheesecake bakers, but the owners of this shop, the Baylor family, have put their own delicious stamp on the classic. Their speciality is sweet potato cheesecake and it's a must-try.

17 HARLEM

This is a brief introduction to Harlem. Former President Clinton has set up office here on 125th Street. On and above this main cross-town street, easily accessible by subway and bus, are some sights and tastes you may want to sample.

1 APOLLO THEATRE

253 West 125th Street between Adam Clayton Powell and Frederick Douglas Boulevards. Tel 212-531 5300 for tour information and show tickets.
It's now a television studio, but still holds the famous Amateur Nights on Wednesdays. For decades after it began putting on live shows in the 1930s, the Apollo could justly be called the world's

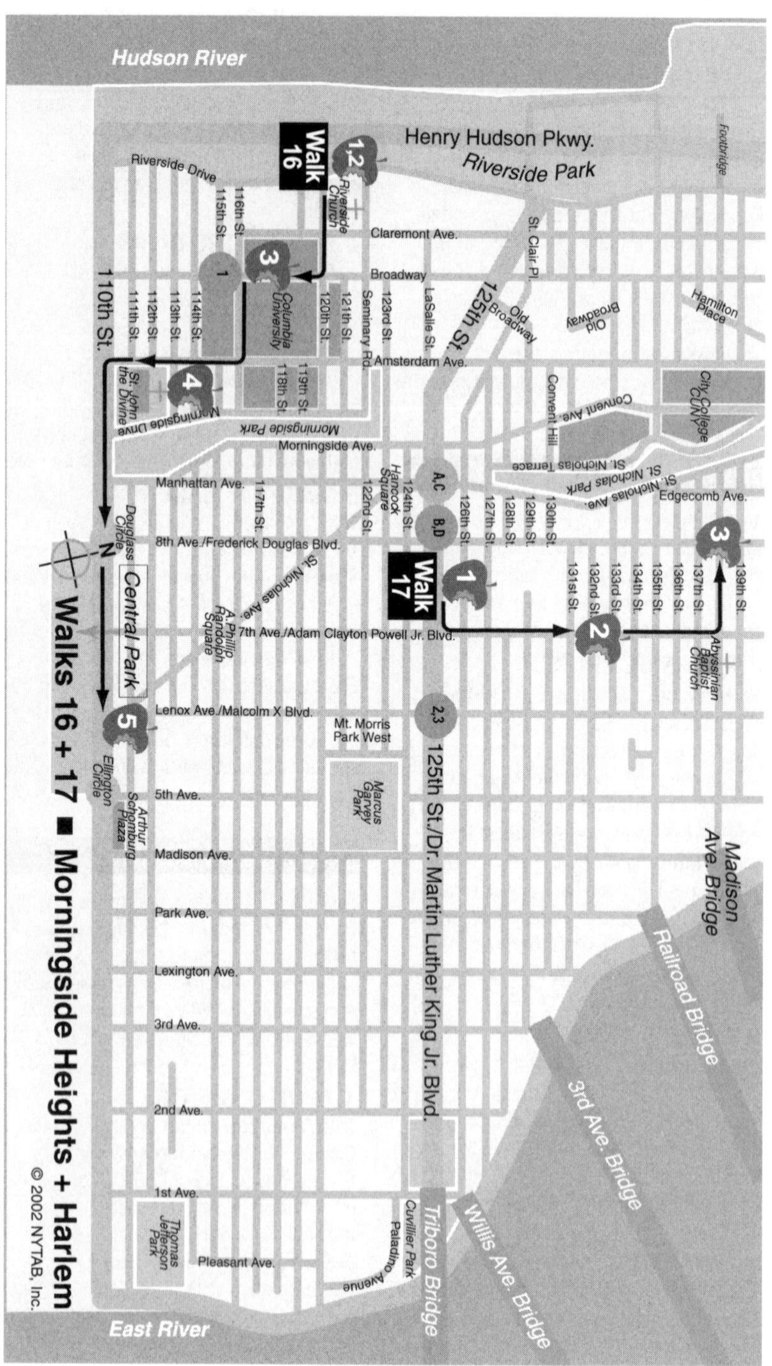
Walks 16 + 17 ■ Morningside Heights + Harlem
© 2002 NYTAB, Inc.
Hudson River
East River
Henry Hudson Pkwy.
Riverside Park
Riverside Drive
Walk 16
Walk 17
Riverside Church
Columbia University
St. John the Divine
Morningside Park
Morningside Drive
Morningside Ave.
Claremont Ave.
Broadway
Amsterdam Ave.
Manhattan Ave.
8th Ave./Frederick Douglas Blvd.
7th Ave./Adam Clayton Powell Jr. Blvd.
Lenox Ave./Malcolm X Blvd.
5th Ave.
Madison Ave.
Park Ave.
Lexington Ave.
3rd Ave.
2nd Ave.
1st Ave.
Pleasant Ave.
110th St.
111th St.
112th St.
113th St.
114th St.
115th St.
116th St.
117th St.
118th St.
119th St.
120th St.
121th St.
122nd St.
123rd St.
124th St.
125th St.
126th St.
127th St.
128th St.
129th St.
130th St.
131st St.
132nd St.
133rd St.
134th St.
135th St.
136th St.
137th St.
138th St.
Seminary Rd.
LaSalle St.
St. Clair Pl.
Old Broadway
Hamilton Place
Convent Hill
Convent Ave.
City College CUNY
St. Nicholas Terrace
St. Nicholas Park
St. Nicholas Ave.
Edgecomb Ave.
Abyssinian Baptist Church
Hancock Square
A. Phillip Randolph Square
Douglass Circle
Central Park
Ellington Circle
Arthur Schomburg Plaza
Mt. Morris Park West
Marcus Garvey Park
125th St./Dr. Martin Luther King Jr. Blvd.
Thomas Jefferson Park
Paladino Avenue
Cuvillier Park
Triboro Bridge
Willis Ave. Bridge
3rd Ave. Bridge
Railroad Bridge
Madison Ave. Bridge
Footbridge
A,C
B,D
2,3
N

showcase for black musical talent. Lena Horne, Sarah Vaughan and James Brown, among an astonishing list of greats, got their start here. Even today, if 125th Street is Harlem's high road, then the Apollo is the Town Hall. Tours of the landmark are very entertaining.

2 WELL'S

2247 Adam Clayton Powell Boulevard between West 132nd and West 133rd Streets. Tel 212-234 0700.
Famous for Mrs Well's crispy-fried-chicken-and-waffles-with-strawberry-butter dish, this place also has a popular Sunday gospel brunch.

3 STRIVER'S ROW

West 138th and West 139th Streets between Adam Clayton Powell and Frederick Douglas Boulevards.
After your stick-to-the-ribs fare, take a short stroll up to 138th Street. Note the Abyssinian Baptist Church to your right, where the well-known Reverend Calvin Butts preaches to congregations up to 2,000-strong.

Turn left on 138th Street and you'll come to Striver's Row named, aptly enough, for those who had strived successfully for middle-class status. The block is one of the prettiest in Harlem.

MORRIS JUMEL MANSION

65 Jumel Terrace between 160th Street and Edgecombe Avenue. Tel 212-928 8008. Discount with your NYCard.
It's not close to either of our northern Manhattan walks, but the Morris Jumel Mansion is worth a visit. It's the oldest house in Manhattan (1765), and was briefly the headquarters of George Washington during the Americans' fight against the British.

The big white clapboard house is just north of Sugar Hill, which extends from about 145th to 155th Streets, and which became the very comfortable neighbourhood of the black middle class. Duke Ellington, Count Basie, Cab Calloway and the boxer Sugar Ray Robinson all lived here, enjoying the 'sweet life'.

The best way to get there is to catch the M101 bus anywhere on 3rd Avenue (on this bus you come back downtown on Lexington Avenue). Sit near the front and ask the driver to let you off near the mansion.

CHAPTER 14

A Taste of the Outer Boroughs

For those with limited time in New York, you may not be able to get as far as the outer boroughs of the Bronx, Queens, Brooklyn and Staten Island. But they have a lot to offer in terms of museums, parks, restaurants, zoos, tours and atmosphere. If you do get a chance, the following chapter will give you a few ideas.

A TASTE OF BROOKLYN

Brooklyn was once a city in its own right, until it became part of New York City in 1898. Some still refer to the event as its annexation and the borough certainly has its own unique style and language. Famous Brooklynites include Woody Allen, Barbra Streisand and Mel Brooks and there is still such a thing as Brooklynese, which is most obvious in the pronunciation of words such as absoid (absurd), doity (dirty), noive (nerve) and toin (turn).

Nowadays, many of the different parts of Brooklyn have their own unique cultures, but by far the two most important 'sightseeing' areas are Brooklyn Heights and Prospect Park.

BROOKLYN HEIGHTS

Whether you've had lunch or dinner, a walk across the stunning **Brooklyn Bridge** will certainly help the digestive system. It's the most famous bridge in New York and was the world's largest suspension bridge when it was completed in 1883. The views are fantastic and strolling along the wooden walkway gives an insight into why it took 16 years to build. If you've walked to Brooklyn from Manhattan via the bridge, you'll find yourself in the heart of Brooklyn Heights. Down by the water's edge is the **River Café** (1 Water Street at Cadman Plaza West, tel 718-522 5200), a refined and elegant setting to soak up fantastic views of the Manhattan skyline. Night time is best – the twinkling lights in the skyscrapers look just like a picture postcard. Have a drink at the bar to enjoy the best views before tucking into a sumptuous supper. It is expensive and you will have to book in advance, but it's an experience you'll never forget. Jackets are essential after 5pm.

The **Heights** themselves are home to some of the most beautiful and sought-after brownstone townhouses in New York. These were built in the early 18th century when bankers and financiers chose to escape Manhattan, yet still be close enough to keep an eye on their money. Once again, Brooklyn Heights is much in demand as an area of tranquillity close to the madness and mayhem of Manhattan. If you walk along the Esplanade, then down below you are the former docks that were the setting for Marlon Brando's movie *On The Waterfront.*

New York City Transit Museum: Schermerhorn Street at Boerum Place. Tel 718-243 3060. Subway M, N, R to Court Street, G to Hoyt/Schermerhorn Streets. Open Tues, Thurs, Fri 10am–4pm, Wed 10am–6pm, Sat and Sun noon–5pm. Entrance $4 adults, $2 under 12s.

This is a great museum for children and transportation buffs of all ages, located in an old subway station in Brooklyn Heights. There is a display of old subway cars that you can get on and you can even hang on to one of the original leather straps, that created the nickname of 'straphangers' for people who use the subway. They've now been replaced by metal poles and bars. There is also a film about the building of the subway, old turnstiles, maps and a gift shop.

PROSPECT PARK AND PARK SLOPE

This part of Brooklyn is one of its most beautiful areas and home to both Prospect Park and Grand Army Plaza. Laid out by Olmsted and Vaux after they'd completed Central Park, many feel their Plaza and Prospect Park creations were even better than their more famous Central Park one. You get here by taking subway 1 or 2 to Grand Army Plaza.

Big Onion does a walking tour of the landmark district of Park Slope, known as Brooklyn's Gold Coast because of its fine residential architecture and history. See page 76 for details.

BROOKLYN MUSEUM OF ART

✉ 200 Eastern Parkway at Washington Avenue
☎ 718-638 5000
🚗 Subway 1, 2 to Eastern Parkway
🕒 Sun 11am–6pm, Wed to Fri 10am–5pm. First Sat of month 11am–11pm, all other Sats 11am–6pm
$ Suggested donation $6 adults, $3 students, seniors and over 12s, members and under 12s free

The saddest thing about this huge museum, which is housed in a beautiful 19th-century Beaux Arts building, is that not many people bother to come out to Brooklyn to see it. However, that means all the more space for you to admire one of the best collections of Egyptian art in the world. Since it opened in this building in 1897, it has become known for its collection of African art and was the first-ever museum to display what were once considered to be anthropological objects as fine art. It has a long tradition of collecting non-Western art and, since 1934, it has concentrated on fine art. The collections are divided into six different departments that comprise Egyptian, Classical and Ancient Middle Eastern Art; Painting and Sculpture; Arts of Africa, the Pacific and the Americas; Asian Art; Decorative Arts; and Prints, Drawings and Photography.

The Brooklyn Museum of Art is known for its ground-breaking exhibitions and has a cinema theatre in which it screens movies and documentaries that coincide with the exhibitions. It also has an Education Division which organises gallery talks, films, concerts, tours and performances for children and adults. On the first Saturday of each month is an event known as First Saturday, offering a free programme of events including a look at art, a film, activities for all the family and a live band to dance to.

It's useful to know that the museum, which has its own subway stop at Eastern Parkway, is just one stop down from Brooklyn's Grand Army Plaza. This stands in a complex of 19th-century parks and gardens that includes Prospect Park, the Brooklyn Botanic Garden and the Wildlife Center. It takes about 30 minutes to get to the museum from Midtown Manhattan. As you enter, the cloakroom (signposted Coat Check) is on your immediate right, the men's WC is on the immediate left and the women's WC is at the back on the right. If you want a drink, go to the sunny Mummy's Café.

If you want a delicious cup of cappuccino or latte, then it costs exactly the same as a cup of filter coffee at the Brooklyn Museum of Art, though the sarnies and rolls cost around $8.

BROOKLYN CHILDREN'S MUSEUM

- ✉ 145 Brooklyn Avenue at St Mark's Avenue
- ☎ 718-735 4400 **www.brooklynkids.org**
- 🚗 Subway 1 to Kingston Avenue
- 🕘 Mon to Fri 9am–5pm, Wed to Fri 2–5pm to the public, Sat and Sun 10am–5pm
- $ Suggested donation $4

A fabulous place for children, this was once part of the Brooklyn Museum of Art until it set up on its own in 1899. Now children can have a ball here playing with synthesisers, walking on the large-key piano or taking part in the workshops.

BROOKLYN BOTANIC GARDEN

- ✉ 900 Washington Avenue between Eastern Parkway and Empire Boulevard
- ☎ 718-623 7200
- 🚗 Subway 1, 2 to Eastern Parkway
- 🕘 Tues to Fri 8am–6pm, Sat, Sun 10am–6pm
- $ Entrance $3 adults, $1.50 students and seniors, under 16s free

Right next door to Prospect Park and the Brooklyn Museum of Art, it has a Rose Garden, Japanese Garden, a Shakespeare Garden and the Celebrity Path, which commemorates some of Brooklyn's more famous children. It is most famous, though, for its Japanese cherry trees and its huge collection of beautiful bonsai.

A TASTE OF THE BRONX

The Bronx has a scary reputation, but parts of it are very safe and have attractions that make a visit to the area well worthwhile. The Bronx history dates back to 1609 when Henry Hudson took refuge from a storm here. It is the northernmost borough of New York and the only one on the mainland. In 1639 Jonas Bronck, a Swedish captain from the Netherlands, settled here with his wife and servants. The story goes that when people left Manhattan to visit the family, they would say they were going to the Bronck's and the name stuck.

The horrible part is the south Bronx, but even here things are improving. The more northern reaches are home to the beautiful Botanical Garden that includes a huge chunk of the original forests that once covered all of New York, and the Bronx Zoo, one of the world's leading wildlife conservation parks.

YANKEE STADIUM

- ✉ River Avenue at 161st Street
- ☎ 718-293 4300
- 🚗 Subway 4, C, D
- 🕘 Tours start at noon daily Mon to Sat. No reservations needed
- $ Tickets $8 adults, $4 under 15s

Sporting aficionados will be delighted to see the tribute to past players, the field, dugout, clubhouse, locker room and press box. Babe Ruth hit the first home run in the first game played here in 1923.

NEW YORK BOTANICAL GARDEN

- ✉ 200th Street and Southern Boulevard
- ☎ 718-817 8700
- 🚗 Subway 2, 5 to Bronx Park East. If going there direct, take the C, D or 4 subway to Bedford Park and then the BX36 bus
- 🕘 Tues to Sun and Mon holidays 10am–6pm April to Oct, 10am–4pm Nov to March
- $ Entrance $3 adults, $1 under 12s, under 3s free; winter $1.50

Originally supported by magnates Cornelius Vanderbilt, Andrew Carnegie and JP Morgan, society folk still support it today. The iron and glass conservatory, which was modelled on the one at Kew Gardens, has been refurbished to perfection. The grounds include the stunning Bronx River Gorge where the meandering waterway tumbles over rocky outcrop formed by the retreat of the Wisconsin Ice Sheet. For thousands of years, New York was covered by a hemlock forest and a 16-hectare (40-acre) fragment remains in the gardens. Look for the rock carving of a turtle drawn by the Weckquasgeek Indians.

The Botanical Gardens are just a road away from the Bronx Zoo – sadly that is an eight-lane highway and the entrances are a mile apart. In the absence of a pedestrian link, take a short taxi ride. Call Miles Taxi Co, 718-884 8888.

LITTLE ITALY

Technically, this area is known as either Belmont or simply Arthur Avenue, but it is tagged the Little Italy of the Bronx. Take the D train to Tremont Avenue and walk east to Arthur Avenue. Treat yourself to lunch at one of the many restaurants where you can eat fresh pasta, nibble pastries and sip cappuccino. The old-world Belmont District is a charming area filled with shops, selling every Italian delicacy, plus the Enrico Fermi Cultural Center in the Belmont Library (610 East 186th Street, tel 718-933 6410) and the old Belmont Italian American Theater (2385 Arthur Avenue, tel 718-364 4700), which still shows films. Afterwards, walk north on Arthur, then east on Fordham Road past Fordham University to the Bronx Park.

TAKE THE BUS

If the thought of heading off into the great unknown of the Bronx is daunting, take advantage of the bus tours conducted by New York Visions. The simple Bronx Tour, which starts at 9am and finishes at 1pm takes in South Bronx, Yankee Stadium, the art deco architecture of the Grand Concourse, affluent Riverdale and Arthur Avenue. The day-long Triboro Tour (9am–6pm) includes all the highlights of the Bronx, Brooklyn and Manhattan's Lower East Side. A further tour of the outer boroughs, called Downtown and Brooklyn Tour, starts at 2pm and finishes at 6pm. **New York Visions:** 690 8th Avenue between West 43rd and West 44th. Tel 212-391 0900. Subway A, C, E to 42nd Street. Area: Midtown.

BRONX ZOO AND WILDLIFE CONSERVATION SOCIETY

⊠ Bronx River Parkway and Fordham Road

☎ 718-367 1010

www.wcs.org

Subway 2, 5 to Bronx Park East

Mon to Fri 10am–5pm, weekends and holidays until 5.30pm, Nov to March 10am–4.30pm daily

$ Entrance $11 adults, $7 seniors, $6 2–12s, under 2s free. Wednesdays free. Children under the age of 17 must be accompanied by an adult. Cheaper rates Jan to March

The Bronx Zoo is respected worldwide for its tradition of conservation and ecological awareness, and the naturalistic habitats it provides, such as its African Plains where antelope roam. It is the largest urban zoo in America and houses 4,000 animals – 560 species. The latest exhibit to open is the Congo Gorilla Forest, a $43-million, 2.5-hectare (6-acre) rainforest, inhabited by two troops of gorillas. Disney-style rides include a guided monorail tour through Wild Asia, an aerial safari, camel rides and a zoo shuttle. There is also a children's zoo. Some of the exhibits and rides are only open between April and October.

For a tour by Friends of Wildlife Conservation, call 718-220 5141.

BRONX MUSEUM OF THE ARTS

⊠ 1040 Grand Concourse

☎ 718-681 6000

$ Entrance $3 adults, under 12s free

Housed in an attractive glass building, the museum's collection consists of more than 700 contemporary works of art in all media by African, Asian and Latin American artists.

A TASTE OF QUEENS

The largest of all the New York boroughs, Queens has the highest percentage of first-generation immigrants. There are many distinct areas, though the most important in terms of attractions are Astoria, Jackson Heights, Jamaica, Flushing and Corona.

Given the borough's suburban look, it is hard to imagine it as the densely forested area it was four centuries ago. Then it was inhabited by the Algonquin Indian tribes, who fished in its freshwater streams and creeks, hunted game and gathered shellfish from its bays. It is also difficult to picture 17th-century Queens and its early Dutch and English farmers, along with Quakers, fighting for religious freedom.

Yet there remain places where such scenes can be easily reconstructed, such as at the Jamaica Bay Wildlife Refuge (tel 718-318 4340) with its open marshlands, once the territory of Jameco Indians and now home to many species of birds, and the Queens County Farm House Museum (73-50 Little Neck Parkway, Floral Park, tel 718-347 FARM). This has the largest tract of farmland left in New York and its colonial farmhouse is thought to date back to 1772.

Today Queens is as much about the ethnic diversity of the borough, though, and in each of the places mentioned in this section, you will find many examples of the cultures of people from Asia, the West Indies, Latin America and Greece.

LITTLE INDIA

Take the International Express – subway 7 – from Times Square to the 74th Street/Broadway station and, at 74th Street between Roosevelt and 37th Avenues at Jamaica Heights, you will find this Indian haven. Stroll through the cumin-infused streets looking at the intricately embellished gold and silk on display. Two stops you should include are the Menka Beauty Salon (37 74th Street, tel 718-424 6851) where traditional henna designs are drawn on the skin, and the Butala Emporium (37 74th Street, tel 718-899 5590), which sells everything from Southern Asian art and children's books in Punjabi to Ayurvedic medicine and religious items.

Lunch: Travel one stop to 82nd Street in Elmhurst for an Argentinian lunch at La Fusta (80 Baxter Avenue, tel 718-429 8222) or two stops to the 90th Street station for Peruvian fare at Inti Raymi (86 37th Avenue, tel 718-424 1938).

QUEENS MUSEUM OF ART

✉ New York City Building, Flushing Meadows/Corona Park

☎ 718-592 9700

🚗 Subway 7 to Willets Point/Shea Stadium

$ Entrance $3

The most famous exhibit here is the miniature scale model of the entire city of New York, complete with miniature lights, which turn dark every 15 minutes, and aeroplanes flying into the airports. You can rent binoculars to check out where you're staying. The museum is on the site of the 1964 World Fair and has had a recent $15-million renovation.

SHEA STADIUM

☎ 718-507 6387

Stroll through Corona Park to the home of the Mets baseball team. On the way you will see huge remnants of both the 1939 and the 1964 World Fairs, plus a series of weird buildings such as the New York Hall of Science. The park also has barbecue pits and boating on the lake. This is where Flushing Meadows plays host to the US Open tennis championship.

THE NEW YORK HALL OF SCIENCE

✉ 4701 111th Street, Flushing Meadows/Corona Park at 48th Avenue

☎ 718-699 0005

www.nyscience.org

🚗 Subway 7 to 111th Street

🕘 Mon to Wed 9.30am–2pm, Thurs to Sun 9.30am–5pm

$ Entrance $7.50 adults, $5 seniors and children

The bubble-shaped building features memorable daily science demonstrations and 175 interactive exhibits explaining the mysteries of digital technology, quantum theory, microbes and light and also offers seesaws, slides, whirligigs, space nets and a giant teeter-totter.

BOWNE HOUSE

✉ 37-01 Bowne Street, Flushing

☎ 718-359 0528

$ Entrance adults $2, children $1

You can walk to this NYC landmark from the park. Built in 1661 by John Bowne, it is a rare example of Dutch-English architecture with an unusual collection of decorative arts, painting and furniture, all of which belong to nine generations of the Bowne family. Bowne was a pivotal figure in the fight for religious freedom in the New World.

QUEENS BOTANICAL GARDEN

✉ 43 Main Street, Flushing

☎ 718-886 3800

$ Entrance free

Walk back to the north-east corner of Corona Park to see the 16 hectares (39 acres) that were created for the 1939 World Fair.

AMERICAN MUSEUM OF THE MOVING IMAGE

✉ 35th Avenue at 36th Street, Astoria

☎ 718-784 0077
www.ammi.org

🚗 Subway G, R to Steinway Street

🕘 Tues to Fri noon–5pm, Sat and Sun 11am–6pm

$ Entrance $8 adults, $5.50 seniors and students, $4.50 5–18s

If you're into the making of films, then you will want to take the 15-minute train ride out to Queens to see this museum. Set in the historic Astoria Studios, which are still used today, it is home to screening rooms, rebuilt sets, costumes, props, posters and other

ALL THAT JAZZ

The Queens Jazz Trail shows you the homes of the jazz greats, their haunts and culture. Call Flushing Town Hall for information on 718-463 7700. It's a great tour even if you aren't a real jazz buff, as it gives an insight into the lifestyles of another era. The tour includes a visit to the newly opened home of Louis Armstrong, the Louis Armstrong archives at Queen's University (fantastic views of Manhattan's skyline) and the Addisleigh Park area, home to celebrated sports stars and top jazz and pop entertainers, including Ella Fitzgerald, Lena Horne, Count Basie, Billie Holliday, Milt Hinton and Thomas 'Fats' Waller. Other famous musicians who lived in different parts of Queens include Dizzy Gillespie, Bix Beiderbecke, Glenn Miller and Tony Bennett. The tour includes a delicious traditional soul-food lunch or dinner and a jazz concert at the newly renovated concert hall at Flushing Town Hall.

If jazz really is your thing, then avoid the tourist-trap venues on Manhattan and head out to Queens for a cheap jazz night out. Underground clubs include Carmichael's Diner, 117 Guy Brewer Boulevard, Jamaica. Tel 718-224 1360. Entrance $10. Open 8-10.30pm on Wednesday nights. The action takes place in the basement. Be warned: there are no signs, but it definitely happens! Also contact Flushing Town Hall (137 Northern Boulevard, Flushing, tel 718-463 7700) for details of forthcoming jazz concerts and the Cultural Collaborative Jamaica (Jamaica Avenue and 153rd Street, Jamaica, tel 718-526 3217). Not only is it cheaper to get into venues in Queens, but you can also usually stay for both sets rather than being forced to leave after just one.

memorabilia. The museum is full of interactive delights, such as the perennially popular diner set from *Seinfeld* and a life-sized dummy of Linda Blair from *The Exorcist*, complete with rotating head. Who knows, when they've finished filming *Friends*, a set or two could end up here! Then there's the interactive Behind the Scenes exhibit, where you can see how it's all done and even make your own short film.

Astoria is the heart of New York's Greek community and filled with delis and restaurants. After you've been to the Museum of the Moving Image, head to 31st Street and Broadway for a spot of lunch.

MUSEUM OF MODERN ART

Until early 2005, MoMA exhibitions will be mounted at a temporary space at 45 33rd Street near Queens Boulevard. To get there take subway 7 to 33rd Street and follow the signs to the museum – just a short walk away.

ISAMU NOGUCHI GARDEN MUSEUM

⊠ 36th Street and 43rd Avenue Sunnyside Queens
☎ 718-204 7088 or 718-721 2308
🚗 Subway 7 to 33rd Street
🕘 April to Oct only, Wed to Fri 10am–5pm, Sat and Sun 11am–6pm
$ Suggested donation $5 adults, $2.50 students and seniors

If you love your ballet and *Balanchine* in particular, you'll love seeing some of the sets created by this Japanese artist, who strove to bring art and nature into the urban environment. These were Noguchi's studios where there are now more than 300 of his works on display. A fascinating spot for art and ballet buffs.

SOCRATES SCULPTURE PARK

⊠ Broadway at the East River, Long Island City
☎ 718-956 1819
🚗 Subway N to Broadway/Long Island City
🕘 10am–sunset daily
$ Free

A great place to take children as they can climb, romp and run around these massive sculptures that have been laid out in the park.

LITTLE ASIA

Roosevelt Avenue and Main Street. The nearby jumble of Chinese, Korean, Thai and Vietnamese markets and restaurants offer everything from soft-shell turtles, bentwood bows, kimchi and wire baskets. At 45 Bowne Street is the beautiful Hindu Temple Society of North America building, which is adorned with carvings of Hindu gods.

The Queens Council on the Arts produces an annual Cultural Guide, which is filled with information about the borough. Order from their website at www.queenscouncilarts.org

Dinner: Choopan Kabab House, 42 Main Street. Tel 718-539 3180. A great place to try out Afghan fare. Alternatively, you could sample Korean food at Kum Kang San, 138 Northern Boulevard. Tel 718-461 0909.

Nightclubs: Try Chibcha, 79 Roosevelt Avenue, tel 718-429 9033, subway 7 to 82nd Street, a Columbian nightclub and restaurant. Or, if you prefer, Sunday night is Irish music night at Taylor Hall, 45 Queens Boulevard, subway 7 to 46th Street. For something more exotic, there are operettas, flamenco and tango shows at the Thalia Spanish Theater, 41 Greenpoint Avenue. Tel 718-729 3880.

Subway 7 to 40th Street. For more information contact the Queens Council on the Arts on 718-647 3377 or visit **www.queenscouncilarts.org**

A TASTE OF STATEN ISLAND

With its picturesque scenery, Staten Island deserves its Indian name 'Monacnong', which means 'enchanted woods'. This borough offers a relaxed contrast to the hustle and bustle of the city, and it's easy to reach by ferry or bus.

If you only have a few days in New York, you may not be able to squeeze in a visit, although you should try to fit in a trip on the Staten Island Ferry, which leaves Manhattan Island from Battery Park (see page 183) and offers brilliant views of Downtown and the Statue of Liberty.

ST MARK'S PLACE, ST GEORGE

If you take the Staten Island Ferry (see page 63) and decide to get off, then you have two places of interest to visit – St Mark's Place and Historic Richmond Town. The former is on the hill above the St George Ferry terminal and is the only landmarked historical district on Staten Island. Here New York's fabulous skyline forms a dramatic backdrop to a wonderful collection of residential buildings in Queen Ann, Greek revival and Italianate styles. Look on the web for a self-guided walking tour at **www.preserve.org/stgeorge**

HISTORIC RICHMOND TOWN

✉ 441 Clarke Ave, Richmondtown, Staten Island

☎ 718-351 1611

🚗 Take the S74 bus from the ferry to Richmond Road and St Patrick's Place

A magnificent 40.5-hectare (100-acre) village that features buildings from 300 years of life on the island including the oldest schoolhouse still standing, which was built in 1695 (that's really old by American standards!). In the summer season, costumed interpreters and craftspeople demonstrate the chores, gardening, crafts and trade of daily life in this rural hamlet.

CHAPTER 15

Niagara Falls

America is blessed with an abundance of natural wonders but the jewel in the crown of New York State is Niagara Falls. Just a 45-minute flight from New York, it's no wonder so many people like to combine a visit with their New York trip.

There are actually two falls: the American Falls – 58m (190ft) high and 320m (1,060ft) wide – and the Horseshoe or Canadian Falls – 56m (185ft) and 675m (2,200ft) wide. The average water flow over the Horseshoe Falls is an amazing 12,800–27.400m^3 (42,000–90,000ft^3) per second.

The Great Lakes were formed during the last Ice Age and the Falls were created 12,000 years ago as huge torrents of water, released by the melting ice, poured over the edge of the Niagara Escarpment at what is now the pretty village of Lewiston. Since then, the Falls have carved their way more than 11km (7 miles) upstream, creating the Niagara Gorge.

Such is the impact of the water on the region that Niagara has its own ecosystem. The moisture that evaporates from the lakes inhibits cloud formation in summer and moderates air temperature in winter, creating a temperate climate, warmer than the surrounding areas in winter, with more days of sunshine per year than many cities in what America calls the 'sun belt'.

Little is known of early inhabitants, but the Niagara River became an important link in the French water transport systems of the 17th century and, in 1679, they built a log fort at the mouth of the river where it joins Lake Ontario. Other more solid structures followed, culminating in a heavily fortified stone chateau, now known as the French Castle. During the 1750s, the French were so busy fighting the Native Americans, that the British were able to gain control of the fort and Niagara region in 1759. It remained in British hands until 1796 when the US government took control after the American Revolution.

In 1815, settlements sprang up, making the most of the fertile land and temperate climate. People soon began to see the potential of Niagara Falls as an attraction and when the Erie Canal opened in 1825, connecting the Hudson River from New York with Lake Erie, it quickly became part of a heavily travelled water route between the Atlantic and America's Midwest. In 1855, a suspension bridge was built for cars and trains over the gorge, further linking the east coast with Detroit and Chicago.

British, German and Italian settlers established Niagara village in 1848 and, by 1892, it had become a city. In 1885, New York State created the Niagara Reservation parks system to preserve the beauty of the Falls and guarantee that the public would always have free access to them. Ten years later, the Edward Dean Adams hydroelectric generating station opened, which for the first time enabled widespread use of electricity.

Today, the Niagara Reservation gets nearly 10 million visitors a year. The Visitors' Center has exhibits and a wide-screen cinema show, which gives a thrilling introduction to the Falls. In front of the centre are the Great Lakes Gardens, which include large-scale models of the Great Lakes system created from living plants.

GETTING TO NIAGARA

There is a range of internal flights from New York to Buffalo (flying time about 45 minutes), then it's a 30-minute drive to Niagara. The flat taxi fare is $40 (plus tip and toll), but there are regular scheduled buses from the airport to the Niagara hotels and some hotels have courtesy buses.

VIEWING THE FALLS

NIAGARA RESERVATION STATE PARK

⊠ PO Box 1132, Niagara Falls, NY 14308-0132

☎ 716-278 1766

The New York State park surrounding the American Falls is the oldest state park in America. It includes the official information centre, Cave of the Winds, Prospect Point and Observation Tower.

Buy a Niagara Reservation Masterpass from any park attraction for discounts on the Viewmobile, Cave of the Winds, Festival Theater, *Maid of the Mist*, Observation, Aquarium and other attractions. $23 adults, $16 for 6–12s.

OBSERVATION TOWER AT PROSPECT POINT

Next to the falls is the New York State Observation Tower, which stands 60m (200ft) above the base of the Niagara Gorge and has spectacular views. From here you can also get access to the Crow's Nest by a series of stairs to the edge of the American Falls where you can feel the spray wash over you (50-cent charge). From the observation deck, glass-walled lifts (50-cent charge) carry you down to the base for access to the *Maid of the Mist* Boat Tour.

NIAGARA FALLS STATE PARK VISITORS' CENTER

⊠ Prospect Park

☎ 716-278 1796

www.niagarafallsstatepark.com

An introduction to the Falls and surrounding parks with exhibits, tourist information, a café and WCs. The Festival Theater has a giant screen History Channel film called *Niagara, A History of the Falls*, plus there's a virtual-reality helicopter simulator ride. Entrance to the cinema show is $2 adults, $1 for 6–12s. It's shown on the hour every hour 10am–8pm.

Get your bearings at the visitors' center, then use the State Park Viewmobile trams (716-278 1730) to get around the park. All-day tickets are $4.50 adults, $3.50 for 6–12s.

MAID OF THE MIST

⊠ 151 Buffalo Avenue, Niagara Falls

☎ 716-284 5446

www.maidofthemist.com

$ $8.50 adults, $4.80 for 6–12s, under 6s free.

Without doubt, this is the top-of-the-pile way to view the Falls – and one of the wettest, though the entrance fee includes a souvenir raincoat! You will be taken as close as is safely possible to the different falls and the spray – hence the name. The gorge has to be completely free of ice before boats can run, so check ahead if you're travelling in April, when the service starts; it continues to around the third week in October. Opening times are about 9.45am–5pm, and 9am–7pm from the end of June to the end of August but do check in advance. There are two boats on the American side and two on the Canadian side. Each holds 400 people and there are departures every 15–20 minutes so queues are rarely too long.

CAVE OF THE WINDS TRIP

✉ Goat Island
☎ 716-278 1730
🕘 From May to Oct
$ $6 adults, $5.50 for 6–12s. Children must be at least 106cm (42in) tall.

An incredible chance to soak up the Falls experience, this trip takes you closer to the waters than you thought possible. Clad in a yellow raincoat and wearing the special footwear provided, you follow a tour guide over wooden walkways to the Hurricane Deck, where the railing is a mere 6m (20ft) from the billowing torrents of Bridal Veil Falls. The rushing waters loom above you, dousing you with a generous spray, as you face the thundering Falls head-on. Rainbows are usually visible day or night.

Admission is free for under 6s to all attractions in the Niagara Falls State Park, including the Observation Deck, Viewmobile, Cave of the Winds and Festival Theater.

THE GREAT BALLOON RIDE

✉ 310 Rainbow Boulevard South
☎ 716-278 0824
www.flightofangels.com
🕘 Open 10am–10pm April, May and Oct; 8am–12pm June to Sep
$ $18 adults, $9 under 12s, under 3s free. Special rate for the Firework Spectacular evening on summer Friday nights is $25 adults, $13 under 12s

The newest attraction in Niagara, this is a soft adventure 15-minute ride to 120m (400ft) above Niagara in a stationary balloon giving unequalled views of the Falls. The weather is the major variable, though the balloon can withstand winds of up to 25 knots.

If you're taking a balloon ride, bear in mind that the wind tends to pick up late morning to mid-afternoon.

WHIRLPOOL JET

✉ At the Riverside Inn, Lewiston
☎ 1-905 468 4800
www.whirlpooljet.com
$ $38 adults, $32 under 14s

This is a white-water rapids ride from Lewiston up through the Devil's Hole Rapids to the Niagara Whirlpool. You can opt for the Wet Jet tour, which comes with a full-length splash suit, wet boots and lifejacket, or the jet Dome tour, which gives you the white water excitement without getting wet!

HELICOPTER RIDES

✉ Rainbow Air Inc, 454 Main Street
☎ 716-284 2800
www.rainbowairinc.com
🕘 Open daily 9am–dusk.

A fabulous 10-minute overview of the Niagara Falls and gorge.

BIKES AND HIKES

✉ 526 Niagara Street
☎ 716-278 0047
www.bikesandhikes.com
$ $10 and hour or $22 per day

Choice of bikes including mountain and comfort cruisers. The bike path starts across the road from this shop and it is less than half a mile to the Niagara Reservation State Park and the Falls.

THE SCHOELLKOPF GEOLOGICAL MUSEUM

✉ New York State Office of Parks, Recreation and Historic Preservation, off the Robert Moses Parkway near Main Street, Niagara Falls
☎ 716-278 1780
🕘 Open daily April to Oct. Closed Nov to March

Get an insider view of the history and

geological background of the Falls at the museum, located within the park, just a few hundred metres north of the American Falls. Reach it by car, on foot or via the Viewmobile.

OTHER ATTRACTIONS

OLD FORT NIAGARA

✉ PO Box 169, Youngstown
☎ 716-745 7611
www.oldfortniagara.org
🕒 Open daily 9am–dusk (4.30–7.30pm) year round.
$ $7 adults, $4 for 6–12s, under 6s free

One of the best non-Falls attractions is about 15 minutes from Niagara by car or bus. You can explore the Old Fort buildings, preserved as they were in the 1700s, see the old uniforms and watch musket demonstrations and other living-history displays. Then follow signs to the historic and picturesque village of Youngstown to browse around the shops and eateries at one of the first settlements to grow outside Fort Niagara in the late 1700s.

GRAND LADY CRUISES

✉ 100 Whitehaven Road, Grand Haven
☎ 716-744 8594
www.grandlady.com
$ Prices from $14 for cruise only to $43 for dinner cruise

Luxury lunch, brunch and dinner cruises on the Niagara River above the Falls. Tours last around two hours and run May 1 to October 31.

AQUARIUM OF NIAGARA

✉ 701 Whirlpool Street
☎ 716-285 3575
🕒 Open daily, except Thanksgiving and Christmas Day, 9am–5pm Sept to May and 9am–7pm June to Aug
$ $6.75 adults, $4.75 for 4–12s, under 4s free

A great rainy-day activity, the aquarium is home to 1,500 aquatic animals including sharks, Californian sea lions, eels and even a colony of endangered Peruvian penguins. Sea-lion feeding times every 90 minutes; plus regular penguin- and shark-feeding.

The Aquarium's first-floor observation deck has wonderful views of the gorge.

NIAGARA AEROSPACE MUSEUM

✉ 345 Third Street
☎ 716-297 4148
www.niagaramuseum.org
🕒 Open Mon to Sat 11am–9pm, Sun 11am–5pm

One for buffs of anything that flies, this museum has an extensive range of artefacts and displays on the local contribution to the Apollo Lunar Landing and Agena Rocket Engines, classic aircraft engines, aircraft restoration facilities and the Aviation Hall of Fame.

NIAGARA'S WAX MUSEUM OF HISTORY

✉ 302 Prospect Street opposite New York State Parking Lot
☎ 716-285 127
🕒 Open 9am–10pm in summer, otherwise 10am–5pm

Life-size wax figures of explorers, statesmen and others prominent in the history of the Frontier, plus a replica Native American village, old-time street and store scenes and the barrels used for going over the Falls and through the rapids.

ARTPARK

✉ 450 South 4th Street, Lewiston
☎ 716-754 4375
www.artpark.net
🕒 Open for matinee and evening performances every day except Mon from April to Dec

This is an 81-hectare (200-acre) park that has its own musical theatre season, as well as presenting live theatre shows, concerts and musicals. It also has art workshops for children and adults. It is in the pretty and historic village of Lewiston, which has retained much of its character (unlike Niagara city) and is well worth a visit. Just 10 minutes from the Falls, it is also home to the Lewiston Historic Museum (469 Plain Street, tel 716-754 4214). Further details from the Visitor Information Center at the Gateway to Greater Lewiston, 732 Center Street, Lewiston. Tel 716-754 9500, **www.niagara-lewiston.org**.

WHERE TO STAY

ELIZABETH HOUSE BED & BREAKFAST

✉ 327 Buffalo Avenue
☎ 716-285 1109
In a Georgian-style house within walking distance from the Falls and with an outdoor pool.

HOLIDAY INN SELECT

✉ 300 Third Street
☎ 716-278 2622
Fax 716-285 3900
The biggest hotel in town is convenient for all attractions and the convention centre. The rooms are comfortable and spacious and the hotel has a sky-lit indoor swimming pool, whirlpool, saunas and exercise equipment, plus a wedding chapel service.

RAMADA INN AT THE FALLS

✉ 240 Rainbow Boulevard
☎ 716-282 1212
Fax: 716-282 0051
A full-service hotel conveniently located near all the major attractions.

RED COACH INN

✉ 2 Buffalo Avenue
☎ 716-282 1459
Fax 716-282 2650
www.redcoach.com
Essentially just an inn, this has a lot of appeal because of its quaintness and the fact it overlooks the rapids as they approach the Falls. It has only 14 suites/apartments so book well in advance.

WHERE TO EAT

COMO RESTAURANT

✉ 2220 Pine Avenue
☎ 716-285 9341
Classic American family dining, serving delicious Italian and American food at reasonable prices.

GOOSE'S ROOST

✉ 343 4th Street at the corner of Niagara Street
☎ 716-282 6255
An unpretentious American diner serving breakfast, lunch and dinner. You can also order takeaways.

HARD ROCK CAFÉ

✉ 333 Prospect Street
☎ 716-282 0007. Open daily from 11am
1950s-style outdoor/indoor diner owned by local Tommy Ryan, so the boast is it's better than the chain.

LA HACIENDA

✉ 3019 Pine Avenue
☎ 716-285 2536
In the heart of Niagara's Italian district, this classic Italian restaurant has been run by the Aldo Evangelista family for decades. Delicious food, well priced and busy, so book in advance if you plan to give it a try.

RED COACH INN RESTAURANT

✉ 2 Buffalo Avenue
☎ 716-282 1459.
This is as posh as it gets in Niagara Falls and at lunchtime it's usually filled with local business people as well as tourists. A quaint building, good service and delicious gourmet American cuisine. Booking is advisable.

TOP OF THE FALLS RESTAURANT

✉ Falls end of Goat Island
☎ 716-285 3311
www.niagarafallsstatepark.com
A fabulous spot, open seasonally, overlooking the Horseshoe Falls.

WHERE TO SHOP

PRIME OUTLETS

✉ 1900 Military Road, Niagara Falls
☎ 716-297 0933
www.primeoutlets.com

Little do we Brits know, but Niagara is popular for something other than the Falls: its factory outlet shopping mall, with more than 150 shops. Open daily 9am–9pm, there is a free, regular trolley service between the mall and Niagara hotels. Shops include Liz Claiborne, Off Fifth, Reebok, Guess, GAP, Van Heuson, Brooks Brothers, Tommy Hilfiger, Burberry's, Levis, Donna Karan plus toys and shoes. Nearby is the Red Lobster restaurant, famous for its steaks and seafood.

It's worth looking at the Prime Outlets website before your visit to Niagara to check out any offers.

GETTING MARRIED

Niagara is the undisputed honeymoon capital of America with an estimated 50,000 couples starting their lives together here. Locals put it down to the negative ions generated by the falling water, said to be an aphrodisiac, but it may just be its affordability! Many couples are now also getting married here.

All you need do is get a marriage licence from Niagara Falls City Hall, 745 Main Street, tel 716-286 4396. There is a 24-hour waiting period after the application has been filed and divorcees will need certified copies of their most recent divorce. No blood test needed; current fee is $25.

NIAGARA WEDDING CHAPEL

✉ Inside the Holiday Inn Select, 300 Third Street
☎ 716-278 2622
www.traveltoniagara.com

Chris Shiah has been running his own wedding chapel service for more than a decade and conducts up to 1,500 ceremonies a year. You can wed in the chapel or at other spots including Goat Island, Terrapin Point and Luna Island, next to Bridleview Falls. Most people marry between May and October, though October is the busiest month because of Americans coming to see the autumn colours. Chris gets a lot of Brits contacting him and can organise just about everything via e-mail. He has his own romantic two-roomed Chapel Inn with fireplace and maid service for honeymooners, which costs $99–399 a night depending on the time of year.

CHAPTER 16

Safety First

TRAVEL INSURANCE

The one thing you should not forget when travelling anywhere around America is insurance - medical cover is very expensive and if you are involved in any kind of an accident you could be sued, which would be very costly indeed. If you do want to make savings in this area, don't avoid getting insurance cover, but do avoid buying it from tour operators as they are notoriously expensive. I took a random selection of premiums offered by tour operators specialising in North America and found that two weeks' worth of cover for one person varied in price from £39 to a staggering £82.25. If you're travelling for up to four weeks, the premiums go up to nearly £100 per person.

The alternative, particularly if you plan to make more than one trip in any given year, is to go for an annual worldwide policy direct from the insurers. These can start at around £55 and go up to £112, and will normally cover all trips taken throughout the year up to a maximum of 31 days per trip. These world-wide annual policies make even more sense if you're travelling as a family. For instance, cover for four people bought from your tour operator could easily cost you £160 for a two-week trip, which is little different from an annual world-wide family policy premium.

Companies offering annual world-wide insurance policies include AA (0191-235 6513), Barclays (0345 573114), Bradford & Bingley (0800 435642), Columbus (020 7375 0011), Direct Travel (01903 812345), General Accident Direct (0800 121007), Our Way (020 8313 3900), Post Office (0800 169 9999), Premier Direct (0990 133218) and Travel Insurance Direct (0990 168113). Many of these companies also offer straightforward holiday cover for a given period, such as two weeks or three weeks, which again will be cheaper than insurance offered by tour operators.

CHECK YOUR COVER

Policies vary not only in price, but in the cover they provide. In all cases, you need to ensure that the one you choose gives you the following:

➡ Medical cover of at least £2 million in America.

➡ Personal liability cover of at least £2 million in America.

➡ Cancellation and curtailment cover of around £3,000 in case you are forced to call off your holiday.

➡ Cover for lost baggage and belongings of around £1,500. Most premiums only offer cover for individual items worth up to around £250, so you will need additional cover for expensive cameras or camcorders.

➡ Cover for cash (usually around £200) and documents, including your air tickets, passport and currency.

➡ A 24-hour helpline to make it easy for you to get advice and instructions on what to do, if necessary.

THINGS TO WATCH OUT FOR

Sharp practices: In some cases your tour operator may imply that you need to buy their travel insurance policy. This is never the case: you can always arrange your own. Alternatively, they may send you an invoice for your tickets that includes travel insurance unless you tick a certain box - so watch out.

Read the policy: Always ask for a copy of the policy document before you go and if you are not happy with the cover offered, cancel and demand your premium back – in some cases you will only have seven days in which to do this, so look sharp!

Don't double up on cover: If you have an 'all risks' policy on your home contents, this will cover your belongings outside the home and may even cover lost money and credit cards. Check if this covers you abroad – and covers your belongings when in transit – before buying personal possessions cover.

NYCARD DISCOUNTS

If you are a UK or EU resident, your NYCard gives you access to an excellent 12-month, multi-trip, world travel insurance policy. There are also good prices for families. For full details, contact ExtraSure, one of the longest-established Lloyd's underwritten specialists in the UK. Tel 202 7480 6871. Quote the code SS00027 on your NYCard to get the unique NYTAB rates. As with all policies, check it to make sure it covers what you want.

MORE THINGS TO CHECK

Gold card cover: Some bank gold cards provide you with insurance cover if you buy your air ticket with the gold card, but, in fact, only the Nat West Gold MasterCard provides sufficient cover for travel in America.

Dangerous sports cover: In almost all cases, mountaineering, racing and hazardous pursuits such as bungee jumping, skydiving, horse riding, windsurfing, trekking and even cycling are not included in normal policies. There are so many opportunities to do all of these activities and more – and they are so popular as holiday extras – that you really should ensure you are covered before you go.

Make sure you qualify for full cover: If you have been treated in hospital during the six months prior to travelling or are waiting for hospital treatment, you may need medical evidence that you are fit to travel. If your doctor gives you the all-clear (the report may cost £25) and the insurance company still says your condition is not covered, shop around to find the right cover.

HEALTH HINTS

Don't allow your dream trip to New York to be spoilt by not taking the right kind of precautions – be they for personal safety or of a medical nature.

MEDICATION

If you are on regular medication, make sure you take sufficient for the duration of your trip. Always carry it in your handbaggage, in case your luggage goes astray, and make sure it is clearly labelled. If you should need more for any reason, remember that many drugs have a different name in the US, so check with your GP before you go.

Always carry plenty of water even in the depths of winter. Air con and heating are incredibly dehydrating and you'll find yourself wanting to keel over very quickly without a good lubricant. It is also best to avoid alcohol during the day.

IN THE SUN

Although the biggest season for New York is winter, many Brits still travel to America at the hottest time of the year – the summer – and most are unprepared for the sheer intensity of the sun. Before you even think about going out for the day, apply a high-factor sun block, as it is very easy to get sunburnt when you are walking around sightseeing or shopping. It is also a good idea to wear a hat or scarf to protect your head from the sun, especially at the hottest times of the day from 11am–3pm, to prevent you from getting sunstroke. If it is windy you may be lulled into thinking that it's not so hot.

SECURITY

AT YOUR HOTEL

In America, your hotel room number is your main source of security. It is often your passport to eating and collecting messages so keep the number safe and secure. When checking in, make sure none of the hotel staff mentions your room number out loud. If they do, give them back the key and ask them to give you a new room and to write down the new room number instead of announcing it (most hotels follow this practice in any case). When you need to give someone your room number – for instance when charging a dinner or any other bill to your room – write it down or show them your room card rather than calling it out. When in your hotel room, always put on the deadlocks and security chains and use the door peephole before opening the door to strangers. If someone knocks on the door and you don't know who it is, or they don't have any identification, phone down to the hotel reception desk. When you go out, make sure you lock the windows and door properly and even if you just leave your room to go to the ice machine, still lock the door.

CASH AND VALUABLES

Most hotels have safe deposit boxes so use these to store important documents such as airline tickets and passports. Keep a separate record of your travellers' cheque numbers. When you go out, do not take all your cash and credit cards with you – always leave at least one credit card in the safe as an emergency back-up and only take enough cash with you for the day. Using a money belt is also a good idea and if your room does not come with its own safe, leave your valuables in the main hotel safe. Also, be warned: American banknotes are all exactly the same green colour and size so familiarise yourself with the different bills in the safety of your hotel room before you go out. Keep large denominations separate from small bills.

SAFETY IN CARS

Unless you have a driver, a car in New York is not a good idea. If you do hire a car, however, be sensible. Never leave your car unlocked and never leave any valuable items on the car seats or anywhere else where they can be seen.

EMERGENCIES

For the police, fire department or ambulance, dial **911** (9-911 from a hotel room).

If it's a medical emergency, call the front desk of your hotel as many have arrangements with doctors for house calls. If they don't, they may tell you to go to the nearest casualty (emergency) department, but that's really not a good idea (I mean, have you seen *ER*?). Instead, you have three choices: contact New York Hotel Urgent Medical Services on 212-737 1212, Dial-a-Doctor on 212-737 2333 or walk in or make an appointment at a DOCS Medical Center. There are three in Manhattan: 55 East 34th Street, (tel 212-252 6001), 1555 3rd Avenue (tel 212-828 2300) and 202 West 23rd Street (tel 212-352 2600).

There are several 24-hour pharmacies, mostly run by the Duane Reade chain. The most centrally located 24-hour pharmacy is at Broadway and 57th Street (tel 212-541 9208) near Columbus Circle.
For a dentist, you can call 212-679 3966 or 212-371 0500. If you need help after hours, try the 24-hour Emergency Dental Associates on 1-800 439 9299.

Put maps and brochures in the glove compartment as these will be obvious signs that your car belongs to a tourist.

NEW YORK STREET SAVVY

The city is nowhere near as dangerous as it used to be, but it is still a large city and there are always people on the lookout for an easy opportunity. To reduce your chances of becoming a victim, there are some simple things you can do and important advice to follow:

➡ Always be aware of what is going on around you and keep one arm free – criminals tend to target people who are preoccupied or have both arms laden down with packages or briefcases.

➡ Stick to well-populated, well-lit areas and, if possible, don't go out alone.

➡ Don't engage any suspicious people, such as street beggars, though you can tip buskers if you wish.

➡ Visible jewellery can attract the wrong kind of attention. If you are a woman wearing rings, turn them round so that the stone or setting side is palm-in.

➡ If you're wearing a coat, put it on over the strap of your shoulder bag.

➡ Men should keep wallets in their front trouser or inside coat pockets or in a shoulder strap.

➡ Pickpockets work in teams, often involving children, who create a diversion.

➡ Watch out for pickpockets and scam artists especially in busy areas, as you would in any big city.

➡ Do not carry your wallet or valuables in a bumbag. Thieves can easily cut the belt and disappear into the crowds before you've worked out what has happened.

➡ A useful trick is to have two wallets – one a cheap one carried in your hip pocket or bag containing about $20 in cash and some out-of-date credit cards and another hidden somewhere on your body, or in a money belt containing the bulk of your cash and credit cards. If you are approached by someone who demands money from you, your best bet is to get away as quickly as possible. Do this by throwing your fake wallet or purse in one direction, while you run, shouting for help, in another direction. The chances are that the mugger will just collect the wallet rather than chasing after you.

If you hand over your wallet and just stand still, the mugger is more likely to demand your watch and jewellery, too. This advice is even more important for women who are more vulnerable to personal attack or rape if they hang around.

It cannot be stressed enough that you should only ever walk about with as little cash as possible and never, EVER count your money in public.

Index

Major references are shown in **bold**

How to Use Your NYCard

Your free NYCard offers discounts at all of the city's must-sees and must-dos: attractions, hotels, dining, transport and even travel insurance. Just ask for the NYCard rates when booking or buying tickets. Quote the code on the card when ordering travel insurance, show your NYCard when checking in or paying for a meal. That's all there is to it – you automatically receive the discount.

New NYCard discounts are constantly being added, so keep up to date by visiting NYTAB's web site at **www.nytab.com**.

If your card is missing or you're travelling in a large group, you can obtain another card, and NYTAB's complete official visitor kit, by sending £1.95 per kit to: NYTAB, PO Box 42101, London SW8 3YQ. Within the UK, you can also call 0906 11 22 668. Calls cost about £4 but there's no further charge for delivery – even Global Priority Mail which takes just five days – from New York to your door. You can order online at **www.nytab.com**. Allow 28 days for general delivery. And always let NYTAB know your departure date, so they can do their best to make sure you get your kit.

Need another NYCard? When ordering the NYTAB visitor kits by phone, say the magic words 'I'm a *Brit's Guide* reader' and you can get up to three kits for no further charge.

TRAVEL INSURANCE

You can pay an awful lot for insurance. NYCard holders can obtain 12-month, multi-trip insurance for less than some policies charge for a single trip, plus there are equally good rates for families, longer stays and EC residents — even car insurance. For details, call Extrasure in the UK on 020 7480 6871 and quote the special code SS00027 for NYTAB rates.

AIRPORT TRANSPORTATION

With the NYCard, door-to-door service, to and from any airport and any hotel in Manhattan is $14. Between any airport and a private residence in Manhattan, it's $18, with other passengers in the same group or family travelling for only $9 each. All prices include tolls, and credit cards are accepted. Rates are subject to change.

When you land, call SuperShuttle on 212-209 7011 from the courtesy phones at the Ground Transportation Desk near baggage claim (all airports, all terminals) to arrange for a pick-up. Reserve a seat for your return to the airport 48 hours before your departure.

HOTELS AND RESERVATIONS

Save hundreds of dollars – up to 50 per cent off – at the following hotels. Simply contact the hotel directly, ask for the NYTAB rate and present your NYCard at check in. Rates can vary by season.

The Sherry-Netherland: 781 5th Avenue at Central Park South. Tel 212-355 2800. Fax 212-319 4306. The best address in New York. Starts at an incredible year-round rate of $265 per room.

City Club Hotel: 55 West 44th Street between 5th and 6th Avenues. Tel 212-921 5500. Fax 212-944 5544. The city's smartest boutique hotel at the astounding NYCard rate of $225 per room.

The Holiday Inn Wall Street: 15 Gold Street at Platt Street. Tel 212-232 7700. Fax 212-425 0330. Low NYCard rates Thursday to Sunday at this high-tech hotel in historic Downtown. $129 per room with occasional black-outs.

Gershwin Hotel: 7 East 27th Street off 5th Avenue. Tel 212-545 8000. Fax 212-684 5546. Rates at the very hip, arty Gershwin start at under $110 per room.

You can also save on some 40 other hotels around Manhattan through NYTAB's partner, **Express Reservations**. They help you choose the right hotel for you, make and confirm the reservation. You simply pay the hotel as usual, at check out. There are no fees and no pre-payment requirements. Call 303-218 7808 or visit **www.hotelsinmanhattan.com**.

TOP SIGHTSEEING

Empire State Building Observatory: A spectacular and romantic overview of the entire city. 10 per cent off with your NYCard.

New York Visions & Harlem Spirituals Tours: The best bus tours of the city with the best guides (see page 71). $5 off all tickets purchased at the main 8th Avenue office with your NYCard.

Ponycabs of New York: The ride is part of the adventure in these bike-powered cabs (see page 70). $5 off the 30-minute SoHo-to-South Street Seaport Tour.

TOP CRUISES

New York is surrounded by water and has one of the greatest natural harbours in the world, fed by the mighty Hudson River and linked to Long Island Sound by the East River.

Full Island Three-hour Cruise: Circle Line, Pier 83 at West 42nd Street and 12th Avenue (take the westbound M42 bus anywhere on 42nd Street to the Hudson River). Tel 212-563 3200. Sail all the way around the entire island of Manhattan on this three-hour cruise and take in three rivers, seven major bridges, five boroughs, a host of famous landmarks and a dramatic close-up of the Statue of Liberty. $3 off with your NYCard.

Full Manhattan Two-hour Cruise: NY Waterway, Pier 17 at South Street Seaport or Pier 78 at West 38th Street and 12th Avenue (catch their own NY Waterway buses around Midtown). Tel 800-533 3779. Circumnavigate the island in their high speed twin-hulled ferry. 15 per cent off with your NYCard.

Semi-Circle Two-hour Cruise: Circle Line, Pier 83 (see above). This cruise covers all the major sights of mid- and Lower Manhattan. $3 off with your NYCard.

Harbour Lights Two-hour Cruise: Circle Line, Pier 83 (see above). This is an irresistible combination of the downtown skyline at sunset with cocktails. $3 off with your NYCard.

Seaport Liberty One-hour Cruise: Pier 16, South Street Seaport Tel 212-563 3200. A quick nip out on to the water, with close up views of the Statue of Liberty and Ellis Island. $3 off with your NYCard.

Seaport Music Cruises: Pier 16, South Street Seaport Tel 212-630 8888. Cruise to live blues, jazz or rock and soul. Phone ahead for summer months' line-up. On Fridays and Saturdays, there's a floating dance party with top New York City DJs. $3 off with your NYCard.

The Beast Speedboat Ride: Circle Line Pier 16, South Street Seaport or Pier 83 (see above). A 30-minute jet-lag-defeating thrill ride. $3 off with your NYCard.

World Yacht Dinner Cruise: Pier 81 at West 41st Street and 12th Avenue. Reservations: Tel 212-630 8100. Spectacular three-hour cruise that combines dinner and dancing with a tour of the city's harbour. Go mid-week, when reservations are easier to get and the prices are more gentle. Jackets required. 10 per cent discount with your NYCard.

TOP MUSEUMS

Solomon R Guggenheim Museum: The most famous museum building in the world gives you art from Armani to Kandinsky. The Guggenheim is the first museum to open (at 9am), so if you're jet-lagged and up early, take advantage of the calm. $2 off with your NYCard.

Intrepid Sea-Air-Space Museum: The world's largest naval museum on a Second World War aircraft carrier (see page 100). $2 off with your NYCard.

Lower East Side Tenement Museum: How millions of immigrants began their American dream is preserved here, in this incredibly moving, child-friendly museum (see page 98). 25 per cent off with your NYCard.

Museum of the City of NY: The museum that makes New York's history come alive (see page 106). Two-for-one admission with your NYCard.

Museum of Jewish Heritage: A moving experience and a stupendous location (see page 100). Two-for-one admission with your NYCard.

TOP INSIDER TIPS

Morgan Library: Beautiful and a great place for lunch (see page 105). Free admission for two plus 10 per cent gift shop discount with your NYCard.

Morris Jumel Mansion: The oldest house in Manhattan (see page 66). Two-for-one admission with your NYCard.

Nasdaq MarketSite: The famous electronic stock exchange (see page 62) $2 off with your NYCard.

Bloomingdale's: Take the receipt from any Bloomingdale's purchase and your NYCard to their visitor centre on the mezzanine and receive a free gift.

TOP RESTAURANTS

We have chosen our NYCard restaurants very carefully. Only World Yacht is known by tourists as well as New Yorkers – for the breathtaking views and the sheer fun of sailing, dancing and drinking against such a backdrop. Only the lucky out-of-towner would stumble across the others listed below without an invitation from a local. Have fun!

aKa Café: An inexpensive secret (see page 113).
Alias: Classy, Lower East Side (see page 113)
Cowgirl: A great night out (see page 155).
Grange Hall: Great food, great atmosphere (see page 116).
Koodo Sushi: The insider's choice (see page 112).
World Yacht Dinner Cruise: (see page 71 and Top Cruises above).
10 per cent off dinner at Koodo Sushi, and 10 per cent discount at all other listed restaurants with your NYCard.